Visions of Poverty

D1564683

RHETORIC AND PUBLIC AFFAIRS SERIES

Visions of Poverty

Welfare Policy and Political Imagination

ROBERT ASEN

Michigan State University Press

East Lansing

Michigan State University Press
East Lansing, Michigan 48823–5202

Printed and bound in the United States of America.

08 07 06 05 04 03 02   1 2 3 4 5 6 7 8 9 10

LIBRARY OF CONGRESS CATALOGING-IN-PUBLICATION DATA

Asen, Robert, 1968–
Visions of poverty: welfare policy and political imagination / Robert Asen.
   p. cm.— (Rhetoric and public affairs series)
Includes bibliographical references and index.
   ISBN 0-87013-600-3 (Cloth : alk. paper)— ISBN 0-87013-606-2 (Paper: alk. paper)
1. Public welfare— United States. 2. Poverty— United States. I. Title. II. Series.
HV95 .A848 2002
361.6'5'0973— DC21   2001005115

Cover design by Heather Truelove
Book design by Valerie Brewster, Scribe Typography

Visit Michigan State University Press on the World Wide Web at:
www.msupress.msu.edu

To Rochelle,
whose keen mind, kind heart,
and generous spirit have been
sources of inspiration.

Contents

Visions of Poverty

Acknowledgments

The writing and publication of this book demonstrate what welfare reformers sometimes have attempted to deny: individual accomplishments depend crucially on the support of numerous others. The encouragement, counsel, and sponsorship I have received from colleagues, friends, and family evidence the significance of community, which I advance as an alternative framework for deliberating welfare policy against the market model that guided retrenchment-era welfare policy debates.

This book grew out of a doctoral dissertation completed at Northwestern University. The members of my dissertation committee— G. Thomas Goodnight, David Zarefsky, and Dilip Gaonkar—provided trenchant advice on conceptualizing primary research questions, analyzing important bodies of discourse, and situating my analysis within relevant sociopolitical histories. Moreover, they offered thorough suggestions for developing a dissertation into a book manuscript. Tom, David, and Dilip have been trustworthy mentors and colleagues.

John M. Murphy, David Henry, and Martin Carcasson reviewed the book manuscript for Michigan State University Press. Their comments were comprehensive, specific, and encouraging, which enabled me to construct a clear plan for revisions. Their efforts certainly bolstered this project. Martin J. Medhurst, editor of the Rhetoric and Public Affairs Series, was an exemplar of professionalism throughout the publication process. From initial submission to final manuscript preparation, he answered my questions promptly and clearly, and he suggested important revisions to the book manuscript.

My analysis of welfare policy debates benefited from discussions with many people, and I want to acknowledge explicitly the contributions of a few regular interlocutors. As a colleague and a collaborator on various research projects, Dan Brouwer has been an irreplaceable intellectual and motivational resource. Dan offered insightful critiques of portions of this manuscript. Jean Goodwin and I held innumerable engaging discussions on the conceptual and topical issues addressed in this work. I have greatly appreciated Jean's distinctive combination of intellectual acumen and social conscience. Cara Finnegan and I have shared, among other scholarly pursuits, an interest in the history of the U.S. welfare state. Our discussions elucidated my understanding of this topic. Susan Zaeske and Kevin Porter provided helpful feedback on chapter one.

My wife Rochelle Klaskin, to whom this book is dedicated, supported this project since its inception. She has been a true pillar of the community.

CHAPTER 1

Imagining Others in Public Policy Debate

The 1962 publication of Michael Harrington's *The Other America* helped focus the gaze of the nation on a problem it had overlooked as many Americans experienced unprecedented affluence amidst a post–World War II economic boom—the impoverished condition of many of its citizens. In the 1950s and early 1960s, between forty and fifty million people lived in an other America that maimed body and spirit. They lived with hunger and without adequate housing, education, and medical care. Harrington sought to open the eyes of his readers. He worried that "American society is creating a new kind of blindness about poverty. The poor are increasingly slipping out of the very experience and consciousness of the nation."[1] Harrington's book signaled a modern paradox of seeing the poor. From the end of the Great Depression to the beginnings of a War on Poverty in the mid-1960s, large numbers of poor people lived in relative invisibility at the margins of public debate. Harrington's book contributed to a rediscovery of poverty that brought poor people into view where they have obtained, at times, an almost hyper-visibility. Yet this visibility has not been entirely uplifting. Visibility may have enabled the undoing of programs originally implemented to combat poverty. As poor people have become objects of intense public scrutiny, visibility has called attention to their supposedly baneful attitudes and behaviors. Our current vision has constricted along these lines as policymakers have dismantled federal structures and rescinded past promises in a decisive reorientation of social policy since the 1960s.

Seeing is more than the perception of objects with the eyes. Sometimes it does not involve this kind of sensory perception at all. Seeing engages the imagination. It proceeds in this manner through the construction of mental images and impressions. This mode of seeing invokes the polysemous quality of seeing as understanding, cognizance, acceptance, knowledge, experience, and heedfulness. Expressions such as "I see your point" and questions like "Why can't you see what's happening here?" denote these meanings. Harrington recognized these qualities in this mode of seeing. Referring to the increasing invisibility of the millions of poor people in the United States, he exhorted that "[h]ere is a great mass of people, yet it takes an effort of the intellect and will even to see them."[2] Not sense perception alone, but the coordinated faculties of the intellect and will bring the poor into view.

However difficult, seeing others in this way is especially important for social and political action. As Elaine Scarry explains, "the way we act toward 'others' is shaped by the way we imagine them."[3] Imagining entails individual and collective effort, as Scarry's use of the plural pronoun implies. Collective imagining is intrinsic to social orders; it bears directly on a society's self-understanding. Benedict Anderson has traced how imagining lies at the heart of the idea of nationhood. He explains that the nation "is *imagined* because the members of even the smallest nation will never know most of their fellow-members, meet them, or even hear of them, yet in the minds of each lives the image of their communion."[4] Imagining one's relationship to others also occurs in face-to-face interactions among members of a political community: the physical presence of another does not displace images. Moreover, just as members of a political community may imagine their shared belonging with one another, they may imagine others in their midst as internal exiles — people who have abdicated conditions of membership. Citizens and their elected representatives often imagine this relationship when they consider the residents of the other America.

The collectivity invoked in collective imagining and its connection to social understanding indicate that collective imagining does not principally or even necessarily address visual artifacts. Rather, collective imagining signals an activation of the capacity of *discourse* to envision others. Collective imagining may not be discerned by aggregating the products of individuals' imagination. It emerges instead through social dialogue as people in their everyday lives encounter others in contexts of varying structure, scope, and formality. And the role of discourse in these encounters is not limited to the transmission of information. Discourse is productive; it constructs our images of others.

Processes of discursive construction may be most active in public debates and controversy. At these times the collective imagination, which often serves as a diffused background of shared assumptions, values, perceptions, and beliefs for matters identified explicitly as topics of discussion, becomes unsettled. Public debates often prompt collective reflection about previously held commitments and affiliations. In such moments, advocates often call upon their auditors to rethink relations to one another. Hoping to inspire such rethinking, Harrington highlighted the intimate connection between public debate and seeing the poor. Concession and compromise among elected officials could not envision an inclusive national community. He held out no hope for the abolition of poverty without "a new period of political creativity." He explained that "[w]hat is needed if poverty is to be abolished is a return of political debate, a restructuring of the party system so that there can be clear choices, a new mood of social idealism."[5] Harrington believed that debate was crucial for the formation of a collective will necessary to enact a creative vision. He asserted that only collective will — and not individual acts of altruism alone — would alleviate poverty in the United States. Of course, enacting any vision is not an uncomplicated process. Contestation accompanies processes of discursive construction. Advocates have to sustain their visions against competing versions as they engage interlocutors. Through public debate and controversy, collective imagining itself is continually refashioned.

This book examines collective imagining about poverty and the poor in the institutional forums of public policy debate. Members of a political community come together through public policy debate to formalize agreed-upon rights, responsibilities, and obligations; debate also presents an opportunity for new understandings of these areas to emerge. In public policy and other forums, the modern paradox of seeing the poor has been evident. The vision of debate participants has narrowed considerably. In the mid-1960s, participants declared unconditional war on poverty, recognizing poverty as a multifarious phenomenon affecting diverse types of people. In the 1980s and 1990s, participants renounced federal interventions, viewing poverty as "dependence" on government public assistance — "welfare" — programs by a black, urban "underclass." A policy trajectory that ended in the repeal of the principal government public assistance program providing monetary assistance to poor families, Aid to Families with Dependent Children (AFDC), developed contemporaneously with this narrowed vision. This repeal trajectory began in the early-1980s with budget reductions in AFDC and other programs. It proceeded in the mid-1980s with a reorientation of AFDC that placed new demands on adult recipients. This trajectory culminated in the 1990s with legislation that repealed the AFDC program. Together, this narrowed vision and repeal trajectory constituted a retrenchment era in welfare policy discourse.

Retrenchment was one of four eras that make up the larger history of AFDC. The program developed successively through periods of enactment, early operation, expansion, and retrenchment. Title IV of the 1935 Social Security Act (SSA)—the Aid to Dependent Children (ADC) program, which was renamed Aid to Families with Dependent Children in 1962— in effect federalized mothers' pension laws that had been enacted by forty-five states. The Committee on Economic Security (CES), President Roosevelt, and the Children's Bureau all viewed ADC as a noncontroversial component of the SSA. In its report to the president, the CES recommended that ADC families "should be differentiated from the permanent dependents and unemployables."[6] Suspicious of "relief," FDR did not regard ADC mothers as relief recipients because he did not view them as part of the potential paid labor force. The program avoided controversy in its early operation between 1936 and 1960 because local administrators decided to exclude from the rolls potentially eligible cases that may have drawn the ire of local constituencies. Writing in 1939, Jane Hoey, director of the Bureau of Public Assistance, complained that many of the local administrators applied rigid character tests for granting aid "on a basis of 'promoting' the 'nice' families." She reported that only 2 percent of children receiving ADC lived with an unmarried mother.[7] Racial discrimination also limited distribution of aid. In the South, ADC coverage by county decreased as the percentage of black residents increased. Nationwide, the average payment per child by county decreased as the percentage of black residents increased.[8] Yet events during this era presaged future conflict as amendments to the SSA in the 1940s and 1950s altered the composition of the ADC caseload by making greater numbers of "worthy widows" eligible for social insurance programs.

Between the mid-1960s and mid-1970s, AFDC expanded dramatically and public hostility toward the program emerged. Governmental, community, and judiciary forces combined to prompt a large increase in the percentage of families that applied for public assistance through the 1960s. The most telling statistic of the decade concerned the sharp rise in the number of eligible families who actually were assisted. In the early 1960s, *33 percent* of eligible families participated in AFDC; in 1971, *90 percent* participated.[9] At the same time, AFDC came under increasing scrutiny as a flawed program. State and local governments engaged in highly publicized efforts throughout the 1960s to reduce AFDC caseloads. In 1969

President Nixon proposed a Family Assistance Plan (FAP) that embodied these divergent tendencies. His speech introducing the FAP rebuked AFDC as a program corrupted by the increased power of the federal government. Yet his solution in effect would have established a national minimum income guarantee. Though benefit levels dropped by 30 percent in inflation-adjusted figures through the 1970s, retrenchment commenced in earnest in 1981 as Ronald Reagan and his supporters sought to reduce federal spending by removing reputedly non-needy recipients from the AFDC rolls. In the following chapters, I present an overview of the eras preceding retrenchment and trace the policy debates of the retrenchment era and the images of the poor that circulated therein. In so doing, I tell the story of how the least controversial component of the 1935 Social Security Act became the only component to be repealed.

Imagining, Controversy, and Tensions of Representation

The repeal of AFDC transpired in the imagining of policymakers as much as in the votes legislators cast on the House and Senate floors. Affirmative votes in these two chambers would not have been recorded without significant shifts in processes of collective imagining. In light of its import, imagining in its multiple meanings as mental faculty, social force, and representational process merits closer scrutiny. In a quotidian and fundamental meaning, imagining denotes forming mental images and impressions or conceiving or pondering matters, as in a faculty of the mind.[10] Although conceiving or pondering often operate jointly with perception, imagining as a mental faculty also focuses on things not present to the senses. On this functional understanding, imagining appears as the method by which most Americans come to know their poorer compatriots. Americans increasingly live and work in economically segregated settings. The daily lives of middle- and upper-class Americans place them less frequently in any significant contact with the poor. Importantly, imagining, as a method of coming to know others, is not an idle, inconsequential activity. Its consequence emerges in other meanings of the word. Imagining engages a creative energy. If imagining can conceive of things that are not present to one's senses but perhaps existing elsewhere, then it also invokes actions or events not yet in existence. Imagining looks beyond the bounds of the existing and the limits of the established order to create and consider that which is not yet. Moreover, the energy of imagining engenders an expectation: that which is created in one's imagination is anticipated, viewed as likely to come into existence.

These additional meanings reveal that imagining and the imagination may act as a social force. In this way, imagining is a productive act with consequences for imaginers and others subjected to their imagination. Some commentators, such as anthropologist Arjun Appadurai, see the manifest force of the imagination as a positive, recent development. He maintains that "there is a peculiar new force to the imagination in social life today."[11] Appadurai attributes its newfound power to the exposure of more and more of the world's population to global media channels. He believes that as a result people who live even the most dreary of everyday lives may regard their present circumstances not as an inevitability, but as a compromise between imaginative play and existing opportunity. That is, such individuals may live their lives significantly in the imaginative space that emerges between circulating media images of glamorous lifestyles of pleasurable consumption and the constraints imposed on them by their subordinate socioeconomic status. Retrenchment-era welfare policy debates suggest an ominous alternative role for the imagination: imaginative "play" may disempower some people by representing them through disabling images. Imagining may be a means by which established interests sustain and perhaps even strengthen their positions of privilege.

This ideological use of the imagination has functioned crucially in constructing and maintaining dividing lines over social justice in the U.S. welfare state. The 1935 Social Security Act bifurcated social welfare into public assistance and social insurance programs. Public assistance programs occupy an inferior position in the U.S. welfare state in comparison to social insurance programs. Public assistance programs are federal-state programs administered almost completely by state governments. They disperse meager grants that vary in each state and some localities, do not keep pace with inflation, and require satisfaction of corollary conditions. Social insurance programs are administered by the federal government and distribute generous grants that maintain uniformity across geography, index to inflation, and require no further actions from recipients. Recipients of social insurance—"social security"—have been portrayed as independent citizen-workers rightfully claiming money earned. In contrast, public assistance recipients have been depicted as clients benefiting from public charity.[12] Performing their ideological function, these contrasting images occlude the similarities between social insurance and public assistance. The practice of social insurance belies its honorific contributory status.[13] Retirees receive benefits out of proportion to their contributions. Money paid by current workers is not held in millions of separate accounts but used as general revenues. Moreover, whole classes of workers have been excluded from social security since its inception.

Imagining as a social force indicates that its creative energy is not coextensive with our social world generally, with what some theorists have referred to as the "social construction of reality."[14] Imagining may participate in constructing our shared social world, but it is not the only participant. In this way, Charles Taylor situates the collective imagination as a mediator between the realm of social habit and that of explicitly articulated ideas, doctrines, and ideologies.[15] To advance this distinction, however, is not to insist that imagining cannot order our shared social world. This is precisely the role ascribed to the imagination by political philosopher Cornelius Castoriadis.[16] He holds that some imagined notions—he references such concepts as the "citizen," "justice," "money," and others—serve a central role in structuring societies. Collective understandings of these intertwined central notions order relationships among the people and objects through which they are represented. People and objects, in turn, make these notions tangible. The controversial history of welfare reform suggests that "welfare" often functions in this manner. Our collective understanding of welfare informs relations among potential recipients, proposed programs, prospective administrative agencies, and, often in the guise of the financier, the general public. These people and objects, in turn, represent welfare as a material practice. However, these valuable formulations of the imagination as a structuring force risk circumscribing a passive, background role for imagining: imagining in this mode exists in the background of public debate at a level below that of explicit argumentation. Imagining as a social force, though it often establishes an implicit context for topics identified as "public issues," may operate actively, especially in those historical moments when imaginings shift.

The controversial history of welfare reform has countenanced significant shifts in collective imaginings of appropriate public assistance recipients. These shifts have occurred within and without the retrenchment era. From the enactment of AFDC to its repeal, images of the adult female recipient highlighted variously her often competing roles as family caregiver and paid worker. In important respects, the controversial nature of welfare reform has contributed to shifts in collective imagining. As a quality of some public arguments, controversy raises the stakes of engagement for debate participants and those affected by debate outcomes.[17] Controversial issues often are highly visible issues that rally widespread support and opposition and stir strong feelings. This import of controversy belies traditional scholarly understandings that treat controversy as something to be avoided because it putatively departs from or perverts formal rules of disputation or reason. Against this orientation, G. Thomas Goodnight advances a view of controversy that acknowledges its significance for explicit issues under debate and beyond.[18] Goodnight explains that controversy may call into question unspoken rules and procedures that inform public argument as well as contexts of understanding drawn through public argument: controversy may make explicit and potentially alter previously taken-for-granted relationships between communication and reasoning, and controversy may reveal and potentially reconfigure contexts through which people understand issues. These functions operate significantly in welfare policy debates as, for example, some advocates regard certain types of evidence, such as social scientific program evaluation data, as inherently superior to other types. Also, advocates holding different views of the appropriate role of government action draw contexts placing differing emphasis on matters regarding the family, the workplace, and the public good. These qualities of controversy suggest that it engenders moments especially amenable to shifts in imagining. Controversy unsettles collective imagining as a background understanding and engages imagining as an active social force.

The active role of imagining in moments of controversy betrays another meaning of the term, one that has informed my discussion thus far but has not been addressed directly, namely, imagining as a process of representing people, objects, or ideas. This process is by no means innocent. Increased critical scrutiny of representation has drawn attention to a "politics" of representation.[19] To assert that representation enacts a politics is to assert that all representation is tendentious. We do not represent people, objects, or ideas to ourselves and others in a transparent, value-neutral fashion. No one-to-one correspondence exists between the representation and the person, object, or idea represented. Representing entails contest and struggle as participants in public debates and controversies seek to sustain, modify, or supplant representations that circulate through public discourse. Representing engages the creative and consequential force—the powerful force—of the imagination, and yet representations exhibit qualities that occlude this character. As Frank

Lentricchia explains, the authority of any representation lies in its assertion of an inherent, ontological claim, "used like a hammer, that some
part of the whole *really does* stand in for the whole." Representations insist that they depict people, objects, or ideas as they truly are. Representing thus becomes a "cover-up" in concealing itself as "an agency of specific political power" and in obscuring "social and cultural difference and
conflict."[20] This political dimension informs the images of the poor that
circulate in welfare policy debates. Such images purport to be natural, essential, and universal renderings of the people they imagine.

The political nature of representation is obscured further by a fundamental tension in representation between absence and presence, between
standing for something and embodying that something. In his *Keywords*,
Raymond Williams notes that representation historically has meant, and
not without considerable overlap in meaning, "standing for something
that is not present" and "making something present to the mind."[21] Representation as presence emerges, for instance, in aesthetic theories that
judge paintings and other artworks by their ability to portray in a lifelike
manner the elements of our physical world. Representation as absence
informs certain theories of democracy whereby elected officials in par-
liamentary or legislative bodies speak on behalf of their constituents. Yet
neither invocation dispenses with the other.[22] The representation is and
is not the person, object, or idea represented. In retrenchment-era welfare policy debates, recipients of public assistance suffered doubly from
this tension in representation: representation as "standing for" kept
many recipients out of the debates and representation as "making present" brought recipients into the debates through disabling images. For
the most part, those claiming to speak for the poor, not the poor who
were likely affected by changes in public assistance programs, participated in welfare policy debates. But the poor were by no means absent
from the debates: vivid images of current and potential public assistance
recipients elicited intense scrutiny from most participants.

Tensions of representation also arise in discussions in the "public
sphere," a term that signifies the social space generated when members of
a political community come together to discuss issues of common concern. The social space they generate is a discursively constituted space.
As Jürgen Habermas explains, "[t]his space stands open, in principle [if
not always in practice], for potential dialogue partners who are present
as bystanders or could come on the scene and join those present."[23]
In important respects, the public sphere is an imagined space, for its

manifestation does not require participants to occupy the same physical location nor does its appearance mandate that discussions proceed contemporaneously. The newspaper reader perusing a letter-to-the-editor, for example, brings a public sphere into being when this person imagines oneself as part of a larger audience and in this manner engages the views expressed by the letter writer. Motivated significantly by a concern for who may secure representation and how one may be represented, scholars in a wide range of disciplines have sought to conceptualize the public sphere more inclusively. Their efforts bear upon the institutional forums of public policy debate, since lines between the public sphere and governing institutions often blur, especially in settings such as congressional committee hearings, where citizens interact communicatively with state officials.

Scholarly efforts toward conceiving greater inclusiveness have envisioned public debate as multiform and fluid. From this perspective, observers see public debate as an activity that occurs across multiple constellations of partly overlapping public spheres rather than in a singular sphere, enables the thematization of differences among participants as a resource rather than as an obstacle to meaningful social dialogue, and constitutes and clarifies notions of the public good in processes of debate rather than as a priori stipulations.[24] These various prescriptions for greater inclusiveness support Harrington's view that engaged political debate may offer the best hope for producing new periods of political creativity — in this case to alleviate the debilitating consequences of representation.

Deliberation holds the promise of perspective-taking, which may engender among more powerful political actors recognition of the struggles and aspirations of poor people without resorting to disabling representations.[25] This potential for perspective-taking arises in the ways that deliberation may unsettle and make available for examination individual desires and suggest their possible transformation. Deliberation asks participants to judge critically their own claims and the claims of others. This critically reflective dimension has been illuminated by Seyla Benhabib, who advances three reasons to support the claim that deliberation may generate democratic legitimacy.[26] First, deliberative processes impart information. No single person can articulate all the perspectives through which social and political issues may be perceived by different people nor possess all the information relevant to a decision affecting many people. Second, deliberation does not proceed from a methodological fiction of an individual with an ordered set of coherent preferences. Deliberative processes enable participants to discover, clarify, and/or alter their views and preferences through communicative interaction with others. Third, the very act of articulating a view in public imposes a certain reflexivity on individual preferences and opinions. The publicity of deliberation prompts participants to support their positions with good reasons or risk the dismissal of their views as unsupported assertions. An embrace of non-deliberative alternatives for policymaking such as bargaining processes and patronage rewards relies on the very resources that the poor lack — money, access, and power.[27]

Without attending to the circulation and functioning of images of poor people in welfare policy debates, efforts to reconfigure a deliberative public sphere more inclusively may not be enough to counter the doubly disabling tendencies of representation. That is, images may disable even if more citizens participate in public policy debate and even if deliberation is open to various topics and different ways of speaking. Images of the poor link up with the arguments of participants in welfare policy debates to bolster or weaken policy initiatives and to advantage or disadvantage participants. Images may help sustain particular configurations of power, but the creative energy of imagining suggests that any one configuration, for better or worse, will not persist indefinitely. Especially in moments of controversy, imagining may unsettle established evaluations of policy initiatives and positions of advantage and disadvantage. The anticipatory quality of imagining signals further that the outcomes of debates in these controversial moments may be crucial for setting in motion a particular policy trajectory. The retrenchment era of welfare policy debate appeared as one such instance of unsettling and anticipating — and its key episodes set in motion a repeal trajectory.

Seeing the Poor from Rediscovery through Retrenchment

The general contours of retrenchment-era debates are familiar even to the casual observer: the federal government cannot act effectively to ameliorate social problems; public assistance programs erode the work ethic and dissolve family bonds; most welfare recipients are members of an undeserving, black, urban underclass; social workers and other social service providers are power-hungry bureaucrats; and, for all these reasons, AFDC is a conspicuous waste of taxpayers' money. If one recalls that many policymakers of various backgrounds had voiced these complaints and chipped away at the foundations of public assistance for twenty years, AFDC's repeal in 1996 might have appeared as an inevitability. Yet as the power of the imagination intimates, repeal was not predestined; events could have been otherwise. Indeed, an expansionist era in welfare policy immediately preceded retrenchment. In this expansionist era, the total number of recipients and total government spending on public assistance increased dramatically. Moreover, decidedly different qualities characterized the tenor of welfare policy debates. Those who rediscovered poverty in the 1960s viewed AFDC receipt as an unfortunate circumstance, but they understood AFDC receipt as a consequence of inefficient economic performance that excluded some citizens from widespread national prosperity. They did not regard welfare receipt as a cause of economic inefficiency, as some retrenchment-era advocates argued. These rediscoverers of poverty expressed concern with dependency, but they committed themselves to rehabilitating recipients. They maintained that increased spending on AFDC constituted an investment that would produce future returns. They saw recipients and social workers as capable agents, and they discerned rural as well as urban backgrounds in welfare recipients. Before embarking on an examination of the larger historical context of retrenchment and the debates themselves, I consider briefly an expansionist-era welfare policy episode to illustrate the magnitude of the policy reversals carried out in the retrenchment era.

In 1962, the same year in which Michael Harrington introduced many Americans to an other America, President Kennedy and the Congress passed legislation reforming public assistance. The Public Welfare Amendments (PWA) of 1962 were the first attempt to rethink the aims and expectations of the ADC program, which was renamed AFDC through the legislation. The PWA attempted to move the ADC program away from strict cash assistance to a service-based approach that reformers hoped would reduce the need for cash assistance through job training and support services. In important respects, the legislation anticipated programs of the War on Poverty. Robert Levine, who served in varying capacities at the Office of Economic Opportunity, writes that the job training component of the PWA served as the basis for the Work Experience provision of the Economic Opportunity Act, the legislative front in the War on Poverty. James Sundquist, who participated in the task force that authored the Economic Opportunity Act, holds that this rehabilitative turn in public welfare converged with other forces to constitute the programs that gave substance to the War on Poverty.[28]

Observing the changed face of poverty in America, President Kennedy justified the need for welfare reform in a February 1962 message to Congress. Despite widespread national economic growth since the dark days of the Great Depression, poverty today, Kennedy observed, "persists in the midst of abundance."[29] He maintained that the contemporary poor should not be treated suspiciously, for many people received welfare grants because of conditions beyond their control. Yet neither should recipients receive unqualified monetary aid. He argued instead that public welfare programs increasingly must be directed toward prevention and rehabilitation and called for welfare agencies to "mount a concerted attack on the problems of dependency." He framed this effort as helping, not punishing, recipients. In this vein, Kennedy suggested that some women on assistance should be encouraged to work. But he cautioned that earning one's welfare payment "must be an opportunity for the individual on welfare, not a penalty."[30] Kennedy concluded his message to Congress by gainsaying decisions in some local communities to address dependency through the imposition of "ruthless and arbitrary cutbacks" in ADC rolls. He explained that such cuts produced temporary, chimerical savings — root problems and their economic and social costs remained. The president urged communities to pursue a "rehabilitative road." More costly when first enacted, reforms nevertheless promised to restore human dignity and save money in the long run. In communities pursuing rehabilitation, "families have been restored to self-reliance, and relief rolls have been reduced."[31]

Welfare "success stories" circulated throughout the policy debates. In testimony regarding the PWA before the House Ways and Means Committee, Health, Education, and Welfare secretary Abraham Ribicoff reiterated the contextual frame developed by President Kennedy in his message to Congress on welfare reform. Ribicoff highlighted the differences between poverty in the 1930s and in 1962. He described the contemporary poor as "devoid of hope in the midst of a society providing abundantly and well for most of us."[32] Expressing the views of other witnesses who appeared before the committee, Ribicoff explained that the contemporary poor suffered the negative consequences of geographic mobility and automation. People increasingly moved about the country at a rapid rate, uprooting themselves from the bonds of family and community that sustained individuals through difficult economic circumstances. Many of these same people also fell victim to the very technological advancements that increased the wealth of other citizens. Automation phased out jobs that had offered livelihoods to previous generations of Americans. Ribicoff held that welfare programs needed to be updated in order to address these social and economic transformations. Echoing the president and other committee witnesses, he characterized the administration's support of skilled, professional services as an investment in rehabilitation that would pay future dividends.

Illustrating the important role that services could play in helping recipients overcome dependency, Ribicoff shared several case studies with the committee. One case told of the tribulations of a mother of six children abandoned by her husband. The stresses of an unhappy marriage and eventual abandonment had been so traumatic that by the time she came into contact with the ADC program "there was a strong possibility that she would need treatment in a mental institution."[33] The woman had been trained as a nurse before her marriage, but the daily demands of raising six children prevented her from seeking paid employment. The family received a $240 monthly check to meet its immediate needs. A welfare worker assigned to this case began to assist the mother in preparing a long-term solution. As the first person to take a cordial and genuine interest in the family's problems, she became an advisor and friend. She encouraged the mother to shop for bulk foods. She worked with the mother to determine a monthly budget to pay bills on time. After discovering that the oldest son in the family had been truant from school, the welfare worker spoke with the boy's teacher and learned that his absences began when the boy received a small part in a class play but stopped attending school because he felt shame about his ragged clothes. The welfare worker guided the mother in purchasing used clothes and located a sewing machine so that the clothes could be tailored to fit. In these ways, the welfare worker helped the mother turn her life around. Ribicoff testified that the mother had sought appropriate arrangements for the care of her children and planned to resume nursing work part-time. He concluded that "[t]here is no question that she will become self-supporting, the children will have been kept with their mother, the taxpayers eventually will be 240 dollars a month richer, and society will benefit from her services as a trained nurse."[34]

A focus on this mother's "rehabilitation" brings to light some complexities of welfare policy discourse. From one perspective, her transformation manifested surveillance of the poor. The abandoned mother succeeded only after the welfare worker scrutinized every aspect of her daily life. Yet from the perspective of the retrenchment era, this example is important in that it imagined an effective program involving capable clients and workers. Ribicoff characterized ADC not as money wasted or abused, but as tax dollars well spent. Ribicoff portrayed the social worker as a person concerned with the well-being of this family, not someone interested in lining her pockets or increasing her bureaucratic authority. He depicted the adult ADC recipient as a capable and willing individual who did not require coercion to change her situation. He described her as a person who participated in instruction gladly and engaged in proactive measures to return to nursing. Though a few witnesses identified fraud and waste in ADC as serious problems that demanded congressional attention, most agreed with Ribicoff's representation.

Reformers did not view welfare receipt as an exclusively urban phenomenon; they maintained that want and deprivation also existed in rural areas and that a rural background contributed to welfare receipt in urban areas. Explaining the latter, Ribicoff noted that increased geographic mobility often brought movement from rural to urban areas, and many rural people arrived unprepared for city life.[35] Other witnesses stressed this dimension of dependency to the Ways and Means Committee. Fern Colborn, social education and action secretary for the National Federation of Settlements and Neighborhood Centers, explained that movement from rural to urban areas disconnected poor people from family and community. She held that "[o]ften these families beget big trouble that began with little troubles, but the friendly hand has been absent to help them through these little troubles. In their home communities, a relative may have given this support; in the urban areas these relatives are not present." [36]

The very complexity of urban life confounded rural migrants and compounded their isolation. This image of transplanted ruralites extended significantly to other programs aimed at poor people. President Kennedy, for example, invoked this image in an October 1963 statement announcing a federal grant for a youth training demonstration project in New Haven, Connecticut. The project was one of a few important precursors of the community action programs of the War on Poverty. The president observed that thousands of families moved each year from rural areas to urban slums. He characterized their situation as foreboding, for they "find themselves in strange, alien surroundings. Many have the added problem of racial discrimination." The children in these families entered overcrowded schools only to become disillusioned with formal education and drop out. "Finding no work and little hope," Kennedy warned, "too many of them turn to juvenile crime to obtain the material goods they think society has denied them. Others turn to drink and narcotics addiction. And soon the cycle repeats itself."[37]

Reformers in the 1960s believed that the problems of welfare and poverty could be overcome by increasing abundance and that the federal government could play an important role in this effort. The most outspoken proponent of this view was Lyndon Baines Johnson. In his 1964 State of the Union address, in which he declared "unconditional war on poverty in America," the president expressed confidence that national prosperity could be enriched. The War on Poverty aimed to "help more Americans, especially young Americans, escape from squalor and misery and unemployment."[38] Record numbers of jobs had been created in the past year, and the economy promised to provide even more. In his March 1964 message to Congress outlining his battle plan for the War on Poverty, Johnson asserted that aiding the poor would benefit all citizens. He maintained that "helping some will increase the prosperity of all." Investing in the skills of poor people "will return its cost many fold to our entire economy." Johnson cited history as proof. He asserted that "[o]ur history has proved that each time we broaden the base of abundance, giving more people the chance to produce and consume, we create new industry, higher production, increased earnings and better income for all."[39]

Johnson also championed the view shared by reformers that the government could act as a positive force in society. In a June 1964 speech at Swarthmore College, he objected to the position held by some that "the federal government has become a major menace to individual liberty."[40] Through a series of questions, Johnson enumerated positive results brought about through such federal action as social insurance benefits, rural electrification, savings deposit insurance, anti-pollution measures, public health initiatives, and civil rights legislation. He contended that government at its best liberated individuals from the enslaving forces of their environment. Yet government was not an external force that acted upon its people. The phrase "government," the president explained, did not "mean just the politicians, technicians, and the experts in Washington. I do not mean only the agencies that make up the federal system, or the departments and bureaus of your state government or your local municipality. I include you. I include every citizen." He maintained that this inclusion could not be dismissed or devalued, for the government derived its power from the consent of the governed. The government represented the people acting in concert; the "government is the sum total of the people it serves."[41]

As this brief recounting of themes and images from 1960s' rediscovery debates suggests, the 1996 repeal of AFDC did not constitute a historical inevitability. The federal government need not have been disdained as a usurping force. Social workers need not have been disparaged as its inept agents. Poor people need not have been denounced as members of a dangerous underclass. Increased funding for social welfare programs need not have been dismissed as money wasted. To be sure, 1960s' reformers did not celebrate AFDC or tolerate the program quietly. This expansionist era countenanced countervailing forces, competing opinions, and opposing policy preferences. But these constituents had to be engaged and brought into productive relations, and alternative visions had to be imagined. Repeal would not have occurred if welfare policy debates had continued to exhibit influentially the discursive qualities of the 1960s. From rediscovery to retrenchment, the politics of visibility held its intensely scrutinized subjects precariously in view. Visibility that once spurred efforts to ameliorate the lives of the poor turned reformers against programs for the poor. In the succeeding chapters, I consider this paradoxical consequence of poverty's rediscovery.

Three Significant Policy Episodes in the Retrenchment Era

The development of retrenchment-era debates through moments of reduction, reorientation, and repeal evolved from three significant policy episodes focused on reform legislation: the 1981 Omnibus Budget Reconciliation Act (OBRA), the 1988 Family Support Act (FSA), and the 1996 Personal Responsibility and Work Opportunity Reconciliation Act (PRWORA). These three episodes ground my analysis of collective imagining in welfare policy debate. My analysis seeks to develop a context within which initial images of poverty emerged in the public sphere and to examine how participants revisited, expanded, recombined, or transformed these images over time. Retrenchment-era debates forwarded a set of demeaning representations of poor people as delinquents, contract workers, and wards that drew upon past characters and addressed

economic conditions as a moral drama. These images gradually undermined social welfare provision until in the mid-1990s, those who had
long been at the core of anti-poverty efforts — mothers and children in
need — became unwitting protagonists in a drama performed in the name
of "reform."

Chapter two provides a historical framework for my analysis by explicating in detail key moments in the historical discourses of poverty. A
series of oppositions has shaped fundamental contradictions in these discourses. Sustenance and deterrence have been articulated as the cross-
purposes of public assistance. Deserving and undeserving have been
evoked as indexes to determine the eligibility of recipients. Rights and
non-rights claims have been advanced as the basis of recipients' eligibility. Intersections of the cross-purposes of sustenance and deterrence and
indexes of deservingness and undeservingness have been the crucial
points of departure. Public assistance has been designed at the same time
to force the "able-bodied" poor into the low-wage labor market and to
provide relief for the deserving poor.

My analysis of retrenchment-era welfare policy debates begins in
chapter three with an examination of deliberations regarding the 1981
Omnibus Budget Reconciliation Act. President Reagan engaged valuational clusters highlighting the virtues of the marketplace to create a
discursive context favorable to government retrenchment. In this way,
Reagan and his supporters reversed prevailing political language and returned to moralistic, individualistic interpretations of a person's socioeconomic status. Reagan established frames of reference for the budget debates in two speeches he delivered in the weeks after his inauguration.
The president allied the American people, the individual worker, the
business operator, American industry, and himself against non-needy recipients, politicians, and bureaucrats. The budget debates were in large
measure about demographic proportions and contrasting images of the
typical AFDC recipient. Supporters defended proposed cuts by asserting
that large numbers of cheats, shirkers, and double-dippers populated the
rolls. Those opposed countered by stressing that the caseload consisted of
struggling recipients and voiceless children. Images of non-needy recipients operated in conjunction with argumentative nexus. These images
reinvented the power of the poor so that this power overtook a sense of
duty to the voiceless. Reagan and his supporters invented a Gospel of
Wealth for the 1980s, gesturing to the New Deal in their recollection and
reconfiguration of historical images. The contesting demographies of the

AFDC population implied distinct relations between the federal government and the citizenry; the budget-cutters successfully articulated a new social vision.

I consider the debates concerning the 1988 Family Support Act in chapter four. By the mid-1980s, need became a necessary but not sufficient condition for receipt of aid. A consensus emphasizing mutual obligation emerged. This consensus manifested itself in the idea of a contract. Most participants agreed that women no longer could be exempted in policy from private employment but private employment required public support of some mothers.[42] Yet this consensus was precarious: agreement on broad sociocultural terms did not indicate clear policy initiatives. Participants preserved consensus at the expense of deliberation by suppressing divergent interests as explicit topics of debate. Their consensus needed a vehicle to make tangible its broad contours in an image that could gain the assent of various participants. Toward this end, participants invoked the notion of a contract and identified the teenage welfare mother, who embodied the long-term recipient, as the appropriate contract signee. Participants demanded parental support from absent fathers. For people "inside" the consensus—participants who indicated an association with the consensus at some point in the deliberations—the reform consensus functioned to obscure their differences in policy directions and interests in reform. For those "outside" the consensus, it functioned as a disciplinary force that situated their views beyond the bounds of reasonable reform. The consensus delimited the vision of those who advanced it, recasting poverty as dependency and truncating human motivation as economically driven.

In chapter five, I examine the debates surrounding the 1996 Personal Responsibility and Work Opportunity Reconciliation Act, which ended the retrenchment era. Repeal of AFDC was by no means certain as the 1990s reform debates began. In his first speech on welfare reform as president, Bill Clinton pledged his commitment to the FSA. Two discursive factors, however, precipitated AFDC's demise. First, debates in 1993 and 1994 brought about a shift in representations of the AFDC mother: a youth in need of strict, didactic, and constant supervision supplanted the contract signee. This shift allowed for weakened commitments to recipients because the bargaining position of the wayward youth was considerably weaker than the position of the contract signee, whose claims could not be accommodated through the uncertainty of the block grants that surfaced as an alternative to AFDC. Second, the legislators who assumed control of Congress after the 1994 national elections advanced an all-out attack on the welfare bureaucracy as part of a confident discernment of a brave new world of information capital. Reformers argued that the system had wrought an array of social ills: teen pregnancy, out-of-wedlock births, unemployment, welfare dependency, and poverty. Their remedy was to recover volunteerism and to free the states. If the repeal of AFDC reflected participants' confidence in a changed world of increasingly mobile capital, then the figure of the immigrant, who emerged in the mid-1990s debates without antecedents in prior episodes, represented their anxieties in the face of globalizing economic and social forces. The 1990s debates also witnessed the return of an ensemble of recipients cast as non-needy as participants' calls for retrenchment spread to Supplemental Security Income, the Earned Income Tax Credit, and other programs. On the periphery of the debates stood the image of the citizen-worker as a positive representation of AFDC recipients.

These three policy episodes manifested the crucial role of collective imagining in public policy debate. Any future policy agenda that seeks to ameliorate the lives of the poor must first come to terms with the doubly disabling tendencies of representation that structured retrenchment-era debates. Participants may counteract these tendencies by including in future debates a more diverse range of perspectives and by imagining poor people anew. This second step calls for participants to go beyond debunking disabling images to invent and circulate affirming images. Debate participants may envision affirmative images by promoting an inclusive political community as an alternative to the market ideal that framed retrenchment-era debates. Welfare policy debate then may proceed as an effort to bring about the minimum conditions necessary for all members to participate fully in community life. By confronting the doubly disabling tendencies of representation, participants still may bring about a "new period of political creativity" that Michael Harrington foresaw in 1962.

Cross-Purposes and Divided Populations: The Historical Contradictions of Poverty Discourse

The welfare reform debates of the retrenchment era did not represent the emergence of a unique late-twentieth–century social crisis. The debates reengaged and enacted historical discourses on poverty, which became manifest in deliberations over a federal public assistance program and an associated set of policies directed at poor single parents and their children. For example, Charles Murray's influential 1984 thesis that federal social welfare programs actually injured the people they were designed to help recalled a sentiment expressed by Alexis de Tocqueville 150 years earlier. In a lecture delivered to the Royal Academic Society of Cherbourg, he stated: "I am deeply convinced that any permanent, regular, administrative system whose aim will be to provide for the needs of the poor, will breed more miseries than it can cure, will deprave the population that it wants to help and comfort."[1] Historical parallels included representations of citizen-types. Defending a federal budget that reduced social spending sharply for fiscal year 1982, cosponsor Representative Delbert Latta pledged his allegiance to the person whom he thought paid for social programs, "that poor individual back in my district who goes to work everyday, making $4, $5, $6 an hour."[2] Latta's constituent summoned William Graham Sumner's similarly situated late-nineteenth–century "forgotten man": "the simple, honest laborer, ready to earn his living by productive work."[3] These invoked histories implicated critical social values regarding worthiness and independence.

Reappearing at different historical moments, significant appeals have been subjected to alternative inflections, recombinations, and reversals as advocates have deployed the discourses of poverty in a shifting and conflicted terrain. This uncertain ground intimates fundamental contradictions in the discourses of poverty themselves, which have taken shape through a series of oppositions: sustenance and deterrence, deserving and

undeserving, non-rights and rights. These oppositions have appeared in
the statements of policymakers and other advocates and have structured
their attempts to articulate respectively the *purposes* of public assistance,
the *eligible persons* who may receive it, and the *basis* of their eligibility.
The purposes of public assistance have been understood as providing
sustenance to some and deterrence to others. Measures of deserving and
undeserving have been employed to warrant eligibility. For those deemed
deserving, non-rights (need, duty, sympathy) and rights claims have
legitimated receipt of aid. Further, gaps between the justification and
practice of public assistance have appeared across these oppositions.

Such oppositions have produced a history of welfare discourse rife
with conflict and ambiguity. The cross-purposes of sustenance and deterrence and their intersections with indexes of deservingness and undeservingness have been the crucial points of departure. Public assistance
has been designed at the same time to force the "able-bodied" poor into
the paid labor market and to provide relief for the deserving poor. These
competing aims have produced meager grants, exclusions of whole
groups of people from the relief rolls, and strict rules for those who receive assistance. They also have produced tensions even in those cases
where advocates have agreed upon categories of eligibility, as the basis of
this eligibility has been advanced alternatively by claims of sympathy,
need, duty, and right. Most often, eligibility has been supported through
some combination of the first three non-rights claims. At times, right has
emerged as a legitimate issue. Some Progressive Era and War on Poverty
reformers intimated transcendence of the ambiguities in welfare policy
through their use of rights claims. These moments have been fleeting,
however, and rights claims have been frustrated by the failure of practice
to comport with justification.

This chapter explicates in detail key moments in the discourses of
poverty. The significance of this historical survey lies in the persistence
of the past in present-day debates. To understand the retrenchment era of
AFDC, one has to consider the historical conflicts that give rise to contemporary reversals. This survey begins with poverty discourses in Stuart-
Tudor England, which reveal the historical persistence of categories of
deservingness. I then turn to eighteenth- and nineteenth-century American social and cultural practices and theory, focusing on the "Gospel of
Wealth." The preachers of the Gospel of Wealth spoke eloquently of the
benevolence of wealth and the ease of upward social mobility for the virtuous individual. The relief practices of the era told a different tale: public

frustration with the failures of poorhouses and orphanages contributed to the twentieth-century movement for mothers' pensions. I situate mothers' pensions within the Progressive Era context. Progressive reformers remained committed to self-reliance and individual virtue as they exposed corruption, vice, and exploitation with the assistance of "muckrakers."

Progressive reformers' defense of the work of motherhood propelled subsequent passage of Title IV of the 1935 Social Security Act, the Aid to Dependent Children (ADC) program. The initial "deservingness" of the ADC population began to erode, however, as a series of shifts in the composition of the caseload and popular attitudes began shortly after passage and accelerated rapidly in the 1960s. This conflicted decade culminated in Nixon's simultaneous rebuke and proposed expansion of federal social welfare programs, manifesting again the cross-purposes of welfare.

From the Early English Poor Laws through the Gospel of Wealth

Poor relief in Stuart-Tudor England reveals the entrenched history of practices and social hierarchies that orient present-day debates. The transformation of a feudal economy into early modern capitalism brought on social dislocations that prompted reactions to poverty and the poor. England's population grew considerably at this time, especially from the 1560s to the 1640s. The population of London grew even more dramatically as a result of internal migration. Changing patterns of land use and ownership forced peasants off the countryside and into cities and developing industrial areas. As the English wool industry emerged, raising sheep became more profitable. Some landowners converted their tillage to pastures, displacing many tenant farmers and agricultural workers. "Bills of Enclosure" contemporaneously auctioned common land to large farming interests. By 1850 more than six million acres of formerly common land—one-quarter of the total arable acreage—had been made private.[4] In 1572 Parliament approved the Elizabethan Poor Laws, which established a local tax known as the "poor rate" for financing poor relief and assigned justices of the peace to supervise its administration.

A distinction between "sturdy" beggars and rogues and the truly "impotent" was the standard Tudor division of the poor.[5] For the genuinely poor, diseased, and destitute, public opinion held that Christian charity prescribed the giving of relief as a duty. The public imagination both despised and feared sturdy beggars and rogues and yet romanticized them as well. Public figures represented the poor paradoxically even in their malevolent depictions. On the one hand, they described beggars and rogues as disordered, chaotic, and without self-discipline. On the other, public figures ascribed to them the power to make plans, form conspiracies, and organize themselves hierarchically. The notion of the "beggar's holiday" stood as a counterpoint to these demonic portrayals. In this view, the beggar's wandering signaled his freedom from social restrictions. The story went that though his body begged, the beggar's soul was king.

Attempts to frustrate the schemes of beggars and rogues engendered a kind of "penal semiotics."[6] Relief administrators reviled sturdy beggars and rogues for their powers of disguise and deception. They claimed that some vagabonds had mastered the codes of civil society, infiltrating the very society from which they purportedly chose to dissociate themselves. Authorities devised several methods, all of which ultimately proved ineffective, to distinguish the sturdy from the impotent. They marked the truly poor or diseased with conspicuous signs to certify officially their status as approved beggars. But others prepared fraudulent badges, and marking did little to reduce the number of people seeking relief. Authorities then attempted to mark the bodies of unlicensed beggars through branding and whipping. This meant that the punishment for vagrancy became an outward physical sign that the beggar could not escape. The mark thus preserved the condition it sought to control and suppress. In Stuart-Tudor England as in subsequent historical periods, the cross-purposes of relief and the categorization of the poor produced conflicting representations and self-defeating practices.[7]

To a considerable degree, English attitudes and practices made their way across the Atlantic to the North American colonies. Four principles guided early American poor relief. First, the public, in the person of an overseer of the poor, assumed responsibility for relief. Second, each locality financed and organized its own system of relief. Third, officials denied relief to people with kin who could take poor relatives into their homes. Fourth, overseers required able-bodied poor to work for local farmers and artisans.[8] Communities applied these principles through four practices: auctions sold the poor to the lowest bidder, who agreed to maintain them with public funds; contracts placed the poor in private homes at public expense; outdoor relief offered small grants or relief-in-kind to those outside the walls of institutions; and poorhouses confined people in institutions owned by towns.[9]

In the late-eighteenth and early-nineteenth centuries, the poorhouse rose in prominence as a relief practice. It was one of a set of institutions that responded to changing social conditions in the young republic. The use of poorhouses and other institutions, such as those for the mentally ill or the blind and/or deaf, rested on optimistic assumptions about the possibilities of reform, rehabilitation, and education. As a means of socialization, "[t]he new institutions were heavy artillery in an assault on popular culture that accompanied the diffusion of wage labor as a template for human relations."[10] The poorhouse instructed its wards in the necessity of a "work ethic." It aided the transformation of casual, episodic, and flexible work patterns into steady, punctual, and predictable labor. It also represented a move away from rewards based on kinship, friendship, or patronage and toward the universal exchange standards of wage labor.

The rise of the poorhouse also stemmed from public perception of an alarming rise of pauperism as evidenced by increases in the poor rate. Many observers located the cause for these higher taxes in poor relief practice itself, which they believed eroded the work ethic and destroyed character. From this vantage point, the poorhouse foregrounded a principle of deterrence. Though American practice did not expressly forbid outdoor relief, it followed the dictates of England's Royal Poor Law Commission Report of 1834. The report described the deterrence principle in no uncertain terms: "Into such a house none will enter voluntarily; work, confinement, and discipline will deter the indolent and vicious; and nothing but extreme necessity will induce any to accept the comfort which must be obtained by the surrender of their free agency, and the sacrifice of their accustomed habits and gratifications."[11] The report expressed cogently the contradictions of poverty discourse. It endorsed divisions among the poor, acknowledging the "extreme necessity" of some people. At the same time, fear of pauperizing the "able-bodied" reduced this necessity to bare survival. Though supporters of poorhouses identified their task as balancing the purposes of deterrence and sustenance, the operation of poorhouses more closely resembled the description set forth in the commission report.

The inculcation of work habits and discouragement of relief-taking also occurred in the cultural sphere, most famously in the tales of Horatio Alger. Though schoolboys may no longer read his stories, Alger remains

an "apostle of the self-made man," a "saint of the American cult of success."[12] One hundred and thirty novels have been attributed to him and
claims occasionally surface regarding the discovery of heretofore-un-
known manuscripts. Estimates of the total number of Alger novels sold
range between 200 and 400 million volumes.[13] In the turbulent milieu of
the Gilded Age, Alger's principal themes appealed to readers of various
ages. As interesting locales and fantastic plots attracted children, an expressed desire for social peace in the aftermath of the political upheaval
of the Civil War addressed the anxieties of readers across generations.
Alger reassuringly asserted a model of economic activity that no longer
held sway in late-nineteenth–century America: a multiplicity of small
businesses or partnerships.[14] As the twentieth century approached, economic control shifted from local merchants to large manufacturers and
financiers.[15]

Alger's stories participate in a tradition of didactic novels of self-
improvement. His hero, a young boy, aims for middle-class respectability. Modest and smart — but not too smart — the hero also demonstrates
those traits that "might be called the employee virtues: fidelity, punctu-
ality, and courteous deference."[16] The benevolent businessman, the central
adult figure in Alger's stories, exhibits honesty and practices ethical commerce. Once poor, he has worked hard to attain his present success. The
hero's mother usually is depicted as a dependent and admiring observer.
Alger's plots almost invariably follow the same structure: through a series
of adventures and coincidences, the hero escapes traps laid by his enemies
and attains the patronage of the businessman. His novels affirm the values
of the middle-class reader — thrift, frugality, piety — and reveal the often
critical role of luck in one's life experiences, which partly belie his exhortations to work hard. Equally important, they suggest that outer appearances, especially the donning of a new suit, manifest inner attainments.

While Alger's stories shunned the conditions of his time, nostalgically
reviving the past, the proponents of the Gospel of Wealth confronted and
celebrated the economic conditions of the Gilded Age. Drawn from a title subsequently appended to an essay by Andrew Carnegie, the Gospel of
Wealth represented the social theory of the Gilded Age. Its proponents
saw the unequal distribution of wealth as an ineluctable phenomenon
with both natural and divine sources. Natural justifications drew upon
popular ideas of Social Darwinism developed by British philosopher Herbert Spencer. In his titular essay, Carnegie asserted that civilization depended on the sacredness of property. Though the unequal distribution

of wealth sometimes was hard on the individual, it was best for the race because it ensured the survival of the fittest. And society rightly rewarded those possessing the skills that advanced the cause of humanity. Carnegie insisted that "this talent for organization and management is rare among men … it invariably secures for its possessor enormous rewards."[17] Like the Alger hero's new suit, the outward displays of the wealthy capitalist signaled his inner virtue. Carnegie's evaluation of the social dislocations of his time oscillated between praise and inevitability: these developments were welcome and yet, for good or ill, beyond our power to change. In his 1902 essay on the same subject, William Graham Sumner, a professor of political and social science at Yale University whose activities and reputation reached beyond the academy, attributed the concentration of wealth to a grand process of social evolution. In a bald expression of Social Darwinism, he wrote that "millionaires are a product of natural selection."[18] Besides, no man was able to acquire a million dollars without helping a million other men increase their fortunes. Both Carnegie and Sumner suggested that if the rich man exhibited a natural superiority, then poverty arose as a consequence of individual character flaws.

The Right Reverend William Lawrence, Episcopal bishop of Massachusetts, elucidated the divine source of economic inequities in a 1901 essay. Lawrence explained that for every biblical passage denouncing riches, one could cite another passage celebrating wealth. This proved for Lawrence that Jesus did not concern himself with material conditions. History, however, demonstrated that "Godliness is in league with riches."[19] Only moral men became wealthy, which signaled their naturally strong and vigorous character. The rich man possessed a self-mastery never known by the pauper. Moreover, the millionaire spent only a fraction of his income on pleasure and luxury. He reinvested the rest to make wages for others. Lawrence admitted the occasional presence of crass materialism among successful men, but he retorted that "the vulgarest [materialism] of all is not the diamond-studded operator, but the horde of mothers crushing each other around the bargain counter in their endeavor to get something, and that so small, for nothing."[20] This image of the poor mother invoked earlier paradoxical representations. She did not know self-mastery yet she schemed and swindled virtuous others.

The preachers of the gospel argued for the benevolence of wealth and the men who controlled it. Though his remarks implied a disdain for the poor, Lawrence advocated a stewardship of wealth. Carnegie made the case most cogently, arguing that the rich ought to administer their wealth during their lives. He promised that "in this we have the true antidote for the temporary unequal distribution of wealth, the reconciliation of the rich and the poor—a reign of harmony."[21] He insisted that the rich could manage the financial affairs of the poor better than the poor themselves. For money management required wisdom. In fact, $950 of every $1,000 spent on charity for the poor was spent unwisely. Carnegie offered his readers a vision of benevolent bliss: the "millionaire will be but a trustee for the poor; intrusted for a season with a great part of the increased wealth of the community, but administering it for the community far better than it could or would have done for itself."[22]

Carnegie and his associates believed that the meritorious poor would rise above their ranks. In an 1885 address to the students of Curry Commercial College in Pittsburgh, Carnegie warned his listeners to watch out for the boy who began by sweeping floors, for one day he would be a partner. On the road to business success, he told the audience, one should avoid liquor, endorsing, and speculation. Of this last prohibition, Carnegie observed that the man of business knew that "only by years of patient, unremitting attention to affairs can he earn his reward."[23] One needed to concentrate on a particular business venture and to live frugally. Carnegie congratulated the boy born poor and expressed sympathy for rich youths, the majority of whom "sink to unworthy lives."[24] In his famous "Acres of Diamonds" speech, which he delivered more than 6,000 times, Russell Conwell shared this view. He stated: "I am sorry for the rich men's sons unless their fathers be wise enough to bring them up like poor children."[25] He, too, lauded hard work. His popular acres of diamonds tale suggested that success entailed working hard at one's vocation, not embarking on wild excursions or half-baked plots. In fact, "[a]ny man may be great, but the best place to be great is at home."[26]

The philosophy of government of the Gospel of Wealth rested on noninterference in the economy, save the protection of property. One prominent spokesperson for this view was Yale University president Noah Porter. He advocated the view that "[g]overnments exist very largely—in the view of many, they exist solely—for the purpose of rendering this service [of defending rights in property]."[27] This position represented an explicit embrace of previously de facto economic conditions. In his history of American democratic thought, Ralph Henry Gabriel notes that in "pre-Sumter decades, when the small entrepreneur was the typical American Industrialist, *laissez faire* was more a condition than a theory."[28] Promoters of the Gospel of Wealth spoke of the ruinous consequences of economic reform for individuals, especially the "forgotten man." Sumner described the forgotten man as the victim of the reformer, the social speculator, and the philanthropist. In a society based on free contract, men interacted as free and independent persons bound by mutual advantage and agreement. The social bond was without sentiment; altering this bond only introduced sentiment and "always produces mischief." When a reformer gave money to a poor man, one took it from another. According to Sumner, "this other man who would have got it but for the charitable sentiment which bestowed it on a worthless member of society is the Forgotten Man."[29] Not only did government interference harm industrious individuals, Lawrence added, but it also abetted those leaders of the newly arrived, ignorant masses who were ever alert to strike at riches.[30]

Although the commitment of the Gospel of Wealth preachers to a discoverable, causal relation between character and wealth signaled the deservingness of one's economic situation, their advocacy of a stewardship of wealth admitted, however reluctantly, the necessity of relief. Moreover, their celebration of the social mobility of the virtuous belied their deterministic understandings of class position. The preachers of the gospel did not promise to resolve nor did they even acknowledge these contradictions, but they trusted that the wealthy person could discern the deserving poor—those for whom poverty was only a way station—from the undeserving just like the benevolent benefactor in the Horatio Alger tale. Government, seen as a usurper of freedom, could not make such discriminating judgments. Yet even as the Gospel of Wealth's spokespersons sought to place relief into the hands of the wealthy, conflicts arose. A stewardship of wealth suggested compassion and sympathy as a basis for aid. But Sumner and others saw a social bond without sentiment. From this vantage point, necessity arose as a legitimization—a need to maintain social order against the threat of the recently arrived masses. In this way, the Gospel of Wealth signaled a growing concern with immigration that continued in the Progressive Era as reformers sought to Americanize the poor whom they aided.

The poor relief practices of the Gilded Age reflected its legitimating discourses. In the 1870s, leading voluntarists began to articulate a new approach termed "scientific charity" in an effort to abolish outdoor relief and to make assistance primarily private. Its advocates advanced scientific charity in part as a response to the social upheavals of the decade—the depression that began in 1873 and the great railroad strike of 1877.[31] They proposed to bridge the widening gap between classes through human contact. S. Humpreys Gurteen, one of the prominent adherents of scientific charity, explained that the "chief need" of the poor was "not alms-giving, but the *moral support of true friendship*."[32] Paid agents visited poor families as both investigators and friends. They regarded displays of deference as signs of improvement.

The practice of family breakup was most prominent in the 1870s and 1880s. Its widespread use stemmed partially from increasing concerns about the hereditary nature of poverty. The most infamous articulation of this view may have been Richard L. Dugdale's study of a poor family he called the "Jukes." Dugdale identified two kinds of pauperism: hereditary and induced. He held that "[p]auperism in adult age ... indicates a hereditary tendency which may or may not be modified by the environment." He noted more optimistically that the "pauperism of childhood is an accident of life rather than a hereditary characteristic."[33] Dugdale's study suggested an approach that focused on children already born, and it appeared to justify the attempts of others to bar the "feeble-minded" from marriage and even force sterilization.[34] In a more common approach, various organizations formed to rescue children from their baneful environments. The Society for the Prevention of Cruelty to Children and the Children's Aid Society (CAS) used family breakup as a primary method. Calling hereditary pauperism the greatest evil he ever encountered, Charles Loring Brace, founder of the New York CAS, rebuked his detractors for promoting a false sense of charity.[35] In an article published in 1900 in the *Charity Organization Review*, J. J. Kelso, a Canadian reformer who argued that his country adopt the CAS treatment method, wrote that "unfortunately there is a class who, from inherent laziness, will not work or make any effort to improve the condition of themselves or their children."[36]

The Federalization of Mothers' Pensions in the Social Security Act and Beyond

After the turn of the century, a diverse coalition of reformers called for the adoption of mothers' pensions. This widespread support was unique in an era when public opinion opposed new spending measures that might replicate the corruption of Civil War pensions.[37] Objections to the regimentation of institutions, the inability to dispense individual care, and unprepared graduates elicited a public outcry against orphanages. Support for pensions also relied heavily on a celebration of women's domesticity. Private charities almost singularly opposed mothers' pensions. They defended institutional placement and private administration. Charity workers countered that governments would be subject to corruption and political influence, would not attract competently trained administrators, and would not provide adequate supervision. Charity workers objected to the rights claims implicit in pensions, which they believed would repress self-help, self-respect, and independence.[38]

By the time of the 1909 White House Conference on the Care of Dependent Children, which demonstrated the burgeoning national prominence of the movement for mothers' pensions, progressive journalists already had written many articles detailing corruption and vice in many aspects of public life and demanding new approaches to old social problems. These "muckrakers"—so named in a 1906 speech by Theodore Roosevelt—uncovered wrongdoing in politics, business, and religion.[39] Their political exposés told stories of big-city bosses who lived lavishly on illegal bribes, campaign contributions, and extortion. In a 1909 article for *Collier's,* Will Irwin detailed an annual ball hosted by Chicago aldermen "Bathhouse John" Coughlin and "Hinky-Dink" Kenna. The two men "dominated the [first] ward for nearly half a century. They ran it to suit their own needs and every year they threw a huge ball. An invitation was tantamount to a large contribution."[40] Irwin narrated a glamorous event attended by well-heeled guests whose revelry continued into the early-morning hours. Wine dealers supplied party-goers with free champagne. Aspiring socialites and ogling locals in their best attire witnessed the proceedings.

Business exposés told of less-alluring, though equally disturbing, misdeeds. In a series of articles for *McClure's,* Ida Tarbell disclosed the predatory business tactics of Standard Oil and John D. Rockefeller. In her first installment, Tarbell depicted Rockefeller as a man of great imagination and will, but someone who substituted fastidious observation of religious ceremony and conspicuous acts of charity for "notions of justice and regard for the rights of others."[41] Perhaps their readers expected depravity in politics and business, but the muckrakers exposed evil in putative spheres of goodness. In a shocking article for *Everybody's Magazine,* Charles Edward Russell described the bleak conditions of the Lower West Side of New York City: "All about you to the south blink the frowsy, scaly, slatternly, bleary, decayed and crumbling old houses, leering from dirty windows like old drunkards through blood-shot eyes; the broken shutters awry like deformities, the door agape like old, toothless mouths." He asked who owned such gruesome places and the answer came back — Trinity Church. Russell observed that "[w]herever you walk in this dreadful region, you find something that Trinity owns, and, as a rule, it is something that you know she ought not to own."[42] As these examples suggest, the muckrakers uncovered corruption and vice in its many forms.

These writers also told the stories of those who suffered from unchecked greed and vice. In the context of the movement for mothers' pensions, recurring articles detailing the ills of child labor were especially important. Their stories revealed the consequences of social policies that forced poor mothers to choose between family breakup and bare, brutal survival. Edwin Markham's essay on the children of the cotton mills portrayed lives void of nurturing familial bonds and interaction and full of hopeless repetition:

> Children rise at half-past four, commanded by the ogre scream of the factory whistle; they hurry, ill fed, unkempt, unwashed, half dressed, to the walls which shut out the day and which confine them amid the din and dust and merciless maze of machines.... A scant half hour at noon breaks the twelve-hour vigil, for it is nightfall when the long hours end and the children may return to the barracks they call "home," often too tired to wait for the cheerless meal which the mother, also working in the factory, must cook, after her factory day is over.... Frequently they snatch only a bite and curl up undressed on the bed, to gather strength for the same dull round tomorrow, and tomorrow, and tomorrow.[43]

Markham's essay broached a theme that would be highlighted by the attendees of the 1909 White House Conference: desperate economic conditions forced single mothers to neglect their traditional and rightful domestic obligations. Other authors exposed the exploitation of children in alternative settings. William Hard recounted the nocturnal lives of Chicago newspaper and messenger boys, who eked out a meager existence in the streets of the cities while businessmen and professionals retired to their comfortable homes.[44]

Progressive reformers remained committed to the idea of the virtuous individual and the fundamental justness of American society. Corruption and exploitation, however, had impeded opportunity and contravened fair play. As Richard Hofstadter explains, reformers saw reality as "a series of unspeakable plots, personal iniquities, moral failures, which, in their totality, had come to govern American society only because the citizen had relaxed his moral vigilance."[45] The reformer's first task was to arouse the apathetic citizen so that this individual would reclaim authority previously abdicated. The Progressive reformer believed in the remedial capacity of the law. Once citizens resumed their active public roles, they would be in a position to pass needed new laws and to enforce existing ones. Moreover, reinvigorated citizens would choose highly moral people as their leaders. Progressives believed that "[w]hen they [citizens] had regained control of affairs, moral rigor would not flag again."[46] In an editorial in the magazine bearing his name, muckraking publisher S. S. McClure bemoaned widespread law-breaking in many areas of public life. He argued that neither lawyers, nor judges, nor churches, nor colleges could be trusted to restore justice. The problem and its solution lay in the people. He insisted that "[t]here is none left; none but all of us.… We all are doing our worst and making the public pay. The public is the people. We forget that we all are the people; that while each of us in his group can shove off on the rest the bill of today, the debt is only postponed; the rest are passing it on back to us."[47] In the same issue, Lincoln Steffens recounted the heroics of Hovey C. Clarke, a grand jury foreman who vanquished corruption from Minneapolis city government through the application of everyday know-how and "simple business methods."[48]

Within this reformist milieu, the 1909 White House Conference called for a noninstitutional strategy centered on home life. Pres. Theodore Roosevelt convened the conference upon receipt of a letter from activists in the child-saving movement.[49] In his opening address, Roosevelt emphasized the significance of the conference theme. Urging the attendees to adopt a progressive stance, he argued for reforms enabling single mothers to care for their children in cases "where the father has died, where the breadwinner has gone." Roosevelt stressed that "[s]urely in such a case the goal toward which we should strive is to help that mother, so that she can keep her own home and keep the child in it; that is the best thing possible to be done for that child."[50]

Despite the presence of a vocal minority of institutional supporters, attendees voted unanimously for a series of resolutions aimed at preserving maternal relations. The first resolution dealt with home care.

> Home life is the highest and finest product of civilization. It is the great molding force of mind and of character. Children should not be deprived of it except for urgent and compelling reasons. Children of

parents of worthy character, suffering from temporary misfortune and children of reasonably efficient and deserving mothers who are without the support of the normal breadwinner, should, as a rule, be kept with their parents, such aid being given as may be necessary to maintain suitable homes for the rearing of the children. This aid should be given by such methods and from such sources as may be determined by the general relief of each community, preferably in the form of private charity, rather than of public relief. Except in unusual circumstances, the home should not be broken up for reasons of poverty, but only for considerations of inefficiency or immorality.[51]

This resolution, quoted here in its entirety, revealed the constitutive qualities of the deserving mother whose image circulated in the Progressive and New Deal eras. Mothers had to be "moral" women who maintained suitable homes. They had to suffer temporary misfortune brought on by the loss of a breadwinner through death or desertion. The resolution also affirmed local autonomy and, as a possible concession to private charity representatives, the superiority of private relief. In his subsequent report to Congress, Roosevelt identified the first and third sentences of this statement as the keynote of the conference.

In the ensuing years, a variety of groups joined the movement for mothers' pensions. Reformist judges engineered the first mothers' pensions. Judge E. E. Porterfield of Kansas City, Missouri, persuaded his state legislature to pass a bill that applied to his jurisdiction. Judge Merritt Pinckey of Cook County, Illinois, lobbied quietly for the passage of a statewide bill, which was subsequently restricted to widows. Both men attributed hooliganism to motherly neglect and wished to keep children in school and out of the labor force. Prominent social settlement women— including Lillian Wald, Jane Addams, Florence Kelley, and Edith and Grace Abbott—broke ranks with their charity peers and endorsed mothers' pensions. The American Federation of Labor pledged its support at its thirty-first annual convention in November 1911. Members adopted resolution 172, which stated that public policy should "take the mothers out of the economic struggle and put them where they properly belong, in the home."[52] These and other supporters saw mothers' pensions as payments for valuable services rendered rather than outdoor relief.

As the muckraking magazines faded in prominence, women's magazines and major newspapers advocated for mothers' pensions directly. The *Delineator,* once edited by 1909 conference attendee and well-known author Theodore Dreiser, may have been the most influential. Its advocacy hit full stride under William Hard's editorship. In 1912 the magazine published a Christmas wish for women: "Set the children free! Let them go back to their mothers! And let the mothers earn their living from the State by doing the most useful thing they could possibly do—bring up their children!"[53] Other magazines with larger circulations—such as *Good Housekeeping,* with a circulation of 375,000, and *Collier's,* with a circulation of more than 2 million—ran positive essays and columns. The Scripps-McRae and Hearst newspaper chains announced editorial support. In December 1912, the *New York Times* published its first annual "Hundred Neediest Cases." One vignette told the story of Mrs. C, a widow with two children. Almost totally blind, she worked in a brush factory to try to "keep up her little family." Yet Mrs. C and her children "dread the day of her blindness with a kind of stupefied terror."[54] This case and others reiterated the values of deservingness and faultlessness expressed in the 1909 conference resolution.

The most important advocacy role may have been played by two women's groups: the General Federation of Women's Clubs and the National Congress of Mothers.[55] Their members invoked positive symbols and feelings about motherhood in support of the pensions and brought to bear impressive organizational resources. The two groups comprised a coalition of elite and middle-class women. The General Federation of Women's Clubs endorsed reforms at the national level at its 1912 Biennial. Its state federations became key promoters as pension plans surfaced across the country. From its inception, the National Congress of Mothers celebrated the special importance of mother-love. Its members viewed this quality as irreplaceable; the absence of mother-love produced social ill.

A speech by Mrs. G. Harris Robertson, president of the Tennessee Congress of Mothers, at the 1911 Second International Congress on Child Welfare assured the commitment of the national organization. The speech was remarkable for its adamant assertion of rights claims. Noting the deplorable home conditions of many single mothers, Robertson insisted that "we cannot afford to let a mother, one who has divided her body by creating other lives for the good of the state, one who has contributed to citizenship, be classed as a pauper, a dependent. She must be given value received by her nation, and stand as one honored." Robertson described mothers' pensions as payments owed. She exhorted: "To-day let us honor the *mother* wherever found—if she has given a citizen to the nation, then the nation owes something to her."[56] Robertson refused to distinguish between public and private assistance and widows and others. After hearing her speak, a moved audience voted unanimously to recommend that state branches make mothers' pensions their work for the upcoming year.[57] Subsequent articles in the organization's publication, *Child-Welfare Magazine,* reinforced the themes of the speech. Titles such as "Putting Motherhood on the State Payroll" depicted mothers and pensions as different from paupers and relief.

Robertson's appeal was exceptional, for most reformers did not advance rights claims or agree with the universal assistance such claims implied. They viewed assistance as one part of a larger project of moral education. As Linda Gordon writes, "middle-class women reformers indulged in rescue fantasies, imagining themselves raising downtrodden women up to the norms of respectability they deemed essential to proper family and polity."[58] Proponents of mothers' pensions wanted the new laws to symbolize community support for what they believed were universal family norms. Though many needy mothers came from multigenerational citizen families, reformers viewed single motherhood primarily as an immigrant problem.[59] This stemmed in part from their charity work in large cities, where the majority of recent immigrants settled. As with previous eras, their desire to help arose from feelings of compassion and perceived threats to the "American" family. Although he did not link his remarks to mothers' pensions, Theodore Roosevelt marked the acute national consciousness of immigration as a threat in a 1915 speech. He admonished his audience that the nation had "no room" for "hyphenated Americans." The former president demanded that citizens express a "pure" allegiance to the United States, likening ethnic loyalties to treason. He charged that "[f]or an American citizen to vote as a German-American, an Irish-American, or an English-American, is to be a traitor to American institutions; and those hyphenated Americans who terrorize American politicians by threats of the foreign vote are engaged in treason to the American Republic."[60] Reformers hoped to Americanize recent immigrants. They used pensions as rewards for women who submitted to instruction in such things as dietary habits. They instructed some immigrants, for example, to avoid garlic.

Despite their calls for new approaches to social problems, Progressive reformers continued to subscribe to the cross-purposes of welfare. Judge E. E. Porterfield invoked sustenance and deterrence in an essay that explained the operation of mothers' pensions in Kansas City. He asserted that since its passage, the law had been a tremendous success. He boasted that "[t]here is no other law that touches the home so directly, and by building it up, fortifying and preserving the home it contributes to good citizenship."[61] Yet the law granted aid that only partially supported the family. "It would be unwise, if not a vicious law," Porterfield contended, "that would provide fully for the family for it would impoverish them and tend to impoverish the community. We take great care to prevent such a result." Rearing children may have been an important job, but community residents also expected the single mother to engage in paid labor. Porterfield explained that "[w]e expect and require the mother to earn all she can at home by washing, sewing, baking bread for her neighbors, sometimes teaching music and getting odd jobs from the mercantile houses to be done at home." He also noted the presence of morals tests: "the mother must, in the judgment of the Juvenile Court, be a proper person, physically, mentally, and morally, for the bringing up of her children."[62] The law required mothers to submit to regular visits to ensure that they kept a proper home. In most settings, conflicts between justification and practice arose as reform efforts intersected with state socioeconomic conditions. Theda Skocpol writes that "states with relatively high proportions of females over age ten engaged in wage labor, and states with relatively high proportions of child laborers in manufacturing, were likely to enact mothers' pensions late or not at all."[63]

Reports by the Children's Bureau showed operating pension programs to be small in size and restricted to "deserving" families. In a 1926 study for the Children's Bureau, Emma Lundberg noted that less than one-third of eligible persons actually received pensions.[64] A comprehensive 1931 Children's Bureau report found that widowed families comprised 82 percent of the total mothers' pension caseload. Deserted women comprised another 5 percent. In only 55 out of 60,119 cases—less than one-tenth of 1 percent—did the family consist of an unwed mother. The report also disclosed that black families made up only 3 percent of the caseload. Monthly grants ranged from a high of $69.31 in Massachusetts to a low of $4.33 in Arkansas. Though the cost of living in these two states differed, the bureau alluded to alternative reasons that may have explained the variations: "The small average grant in some States would seem to indicate that in some local administrative units mothers' aid was considered as a pittance to keep the family alive rather than as a means of maintaining family life."[65] Consensus regarding the critical importance of motherly care spurred the adoption of state mothers' pensions, but concern with sustenance, deterrence, and deserving recipients informed their implementation. Operating state mothers' pensions, in turn, served as references for designers of federal legislation.

In an important implicit endorsement of prevailing practices and their legitimating discourses, Title IV of the 1935 Social Security Act (SSA) inscribed the model of state mothers' pensions into federal law. In his 1935 State of the Union address, Franklin Delano Roosevelt asserted his commitment to established relief practices. He noted the necessity of benefits to secure mothers and children against the hazards of life. Yet these groups and others outside of the labor force "must be cared for as they were before." FDR announced his intention to return control to localities. He stated that "common sense tells us that the wealth necessary for this task existed and still exists in the local community."[66] In its report to the president, the Committee on Economic Security (CES), the chief architectural body of the SSA, supported the continuance and expansion of mothers' pensions. In its opening sections, the report held that families best met children's security needs. Many dependent children "need only financial aid which will make it possible for their mothers to continue to give them normal family care."[67] The report explained that forty-five states permitted mothers' pensions, but insufficient funds prevented their implementation. Staff studies developed this position in greater detail. A summary statement observed that "recommendations regarding security for children do not set up any new or untried methods of procedure, but build upon experience that has been well-established in this country."[68] The summary noted differences in participation, coverage, and benefit levels among states and recommended supplementary federal funding.

As the statements of FDR and the CES suggest, the Aid to Dependent Children (ADC) program was a noncontroversial component of the Social Security Act. Its noncontroversial status signaled the continued saliency of the images and assumptions of the 1909 White House Conference and the beliefs articulated in Porterfield's description of operating pensions. Gordon writes that the executive director of the CES, Edwin Witte, "accepted as given, from the moment he first heard the Children's Bureau plan, that there should be federal contributions to the state and local mothers' aid programs and left the design to the bureau."[69] Grace Abbott, Katharine Lenroot, and Martha Eliot quickly drafted the ADC proposal. Their speed reflected a lack of controversy and the low priority of ADC. Even the Children's Bureau considered the program to be of secondary importance to a child and maternal health services plan. The bureau regarded the health services plan as new and innovative in contrast to ADC, which it saw as assisting already established programs. These programs sought to return "deviant" single-mother families to prior states of "normalcy" by acting as the breadwinner in his absence. Upon receipt of aid, the single mother could resume unfettered, if only in ADC's legitimating discourses, her proper role as nurturing caregiver. Though it did not proscribe benefits to unmarried mothers, the SSA defined "dependent child" as one who has been "deprived of parental support or care by reason of the death, continued absence from the home, or physical or mental incapacity of a parent."[70] These three references to deprivation intimated once-nuclear families.

Public figures sought to distinguish ADC from relief programs. In its report to FDR as well as in staff reports, the CES called for this differentiation: "We are strongly of the opinion that these families should be differentiated from the permanent dependents and unemployables."[71] ADC families did not incur the censure leveled at the latter because the absence of an officially regarded breadwinner characterized these fatherless families. In his 1935 State of the Union address, FDR denounced relief as counterproductive and contrary to American values. He asserted unequivocally that the "federal government must and shall quit this business of relief." In a statement often repeated by present-day critics of social welfare programs, the president maintained that the "lessons of history, confirmed by the evidence immediately before me, show conclusively that continued dependence upon relief induces a spiritual and moral disintegration fundamentally destructive to the national fibre. To dole out relief in this way is to administer a narcotic, a subtle destroyer of the human spirit."[72] As this passage intimates, FDR elevated job creation programs over relief. Yet he did not doubt the capabilities of the federal government to administer such programs. In a "Fireside Chat" given later that year, FDR admitted the possibility of mismanagement or fraud but cautioned against generalizing from isolated cases. He reflected that "long experience in government has taught me that the exceptional instances of wrong-doing in government are probably less numerous than in almost any other line of endeavor."[73] FDR chided cynics who doubted the likelihood of "honest and efficient" democracy.

FDR's privileging of public policies simulating private-market labor conditions found parallels in popular culture, notably in John Steinbeck's *The Grapes of Wrath*. The novel articulated the left-leaning sympathies of the era, which clearly angered some.[74] In California, the Associated

Farmers orchestrated a statewide propaganda campaign to depict the conditions of migrant field workers as rosy. This included the publication of Marshall Hartranft's *The Grapes of Gladness.* Reactions to Steinbeck's book prompted FDR to comment in support that "500,000 Americans ... live in the covers of that book."[75] As FDR's numbers implied, the story of the Joads told the stories of an entire generation. Forced from their land by natural and economic disasters, the Joads headed West in search of a better life picking fruit in the Edenic fields of California.

Left-labor themes pervade the narrative. Reification figures prominently as bankers and others deny their culpability in creating social misery. When confronted by an angry farmer who reminds him that the bank is made only of men, a representative retorts: "No, you're wrong there—quite wrong there. The bank is something else than men. It happens that every man in a bank hates what the bank does, and yet the bank does it."[76] The novel also interrogates religion as a mystification of social conditions. A major figure in the narrative is Jim Casy, an ex-clergyman who, bothered by contradictions between his sermons and actions, quit preaching the Gospel. He enters the plot having just completed a period of self-imposed isolation. His solitary wandering in the wilderness has led him to the belief that "maybe that's the Holy Sperit—the human sperit—the whole shebang. Maybe all men got one big soul ever'body's a part of.' Now I sat there thinkin' it, an' all of a suddent—I knew it. I knew it so deep down that it was true, and I still know it."[77] Finally, class solidarity looms large. Toward the end of the novel, contemplating Casy's death from the blow of an ax handle wielded by a deputy sheriff, the protagonist Tom Joad wonders why an experience at a government-sponsored migrant worker camp could not structure society generally: "I been thinkin' how it was in that gov'ment camp, how our folks took care a theirselves, an' if they was a fight they fixed it theirself; an' they wasn't no cops wagglin' their guns, but they was better order than them cops ever give. I been a-wonderin' why we can't do that all over. Throw out the cops that ain't our people. All work together for our own thing—all farm our own lan.'"[78]

Even in this ostensibly friendly environment for rights claims, the Joads' people share FDR's view of charity as dishonorable. When a resident of the government camp states her reluctance to purchase groceries on credit at the camp store, even after admitting that her family is starving, a member of the women's committee rebukes her sternly: "'This ain't charity, an' you know it,' Jessie raged. 'We had all that out. They ain't no charity in this here camp. We won't have no charity." Jessie's outburst prompts another woman to share her experiences with Ma Joad. The experiences left a lasting memory: "If a body's ever took charity, it makes a burn that don't come out." Recalling an encounter at the Salvation Army, the woman continues: "I hate 'em.... I ain't never seen my man beat before, but them—them Salvation Army done it to 'im."[79] In literary and political spheres, participants regarded social policy as a means of buttressing threatened domestic and social relations.

By incorporating mothers' pensions and their contradictions uncritically, Title IV of the Social Security Act prefigured the inferior position of ADC in comparison to other components of the expanding U.S. welfare state. Though its designers envisioned ADC's placement in the Children's Bureau, a congressional conference committee eventually sent ADC to the newly created Social Security Bureau (SSB) under a new Bureau of Public Assistance. At the SSB, ADC became the weak sister of Old Age Insurance (OAI). The SSB actively championed its social insurance program at the expense of public assistance programs such as ADC. It launched a public relations campaign to promote OAI as "an honored citizenship entitlement," portraying "public assistance as charity and OAI as getting back something of one's own."[80] In important respects, however, officials at the SSB were enforcing divisions inscribed in the SSA itself. The SSA constructed OAI as a completely federal program that did not require recipients to undergo means-testing. Moreover, the SSA prescribed for OAI uniform grant amounts and eligibility conditions that did not vary from state to state. Affected by the stigma of assistance programs, ADC occupied an inferior position in relation to trumpeted insurance programs at the SSB. Ever since, this bifurcation of federal social welfare policy into public assistance and social insurance programs has positioned the recipients of "assistance" as clients while reserving the honorific title of citizen for recipients of "insurance" payments.

In its adopted form, Title IV significantly weakened proposed federal standards. The definition of a dependent child narrowed from one who had no adult other than a caretaker to provide for him or her to one whose family had been affected by death, desertion, or mental or physical incapacity. The bill called for grants to maintain children in "decency and health"; the SSA set maximum grant levels of eighteen dollars for the first child and twelve dollars for each additional child. The bill provided for rules and regulations "necessary to effectuate the purposes of this title"; the SSA prohibited federal rules pertaining to the selection, tenure, and compensation of local administrative personnel. A desire to protect employers' access to the black and Latino agricultural and domestic labor forces of the South and Southwest and a desire to retain control over patronage jobs in local public assistance programs motivated this attack on federal standards.[81]

Some reformers hoped to overcome the ills of mothers' pensions, such as low monthly grants and parochial eligibility guidelines, through federal administrative and financial participation, but local officials continued to enforce unwritten regulations in the years after the passage of the SSA. Jane Hoey, director of the Bureau of Public Assistance from 1936–53 and a former member of the Advisory Committee on Child Welfare to the CES, called attention to these practices in a co-authored article for the 1939 *Social Work Yearbook*. Though the SSA assisted 600,000 children, between one and two million children were in need. Hoey held that "opinion" and "attitude" blocked further expansion of ADC. Administrators adhered to rigid character standards. They faulted parents failing to fit a particular preconceived mold, using grants to promote "nice families." Hoey reported that "[p]arents whose behavior is not considered acceptable are sometimes given to understand, in effect, that unless they mend their ways the allowance will not be continued." She noted that only 2 percent of children accepted for aid lived with unmarried mothers. Still, she did not propose that ADC mirror OAI and dispense unrestricted grants as a right. Citing needs for services in housing, health, and social adjustment, Hoey maintained that an adequate ADC program "extends far beyond determination of eligibility and the granting of a cash allowance."[82]

The rise of social work as an approach to social welfare programs and the increasing prominence of social insurance affected the structure and composition of ADC in the years between 1940 and 1960, adumbrating the turn against ADC in the 1960s as a program that served the undeserving poor. Despite her criticisms of administrative biases toward "nice families," Hoey committed the Bureau of Public Assistance to a social-work approach that focused on the particular family rather than the universalized citizen claimant. In a 1938 radio address, she observed approvingly that "more and more, States are coming to realize that public welfare is on a par with, let us say, public health and public education.... [I]ts administration requires persons equipped with special training and experience."[83] In contradistinction to Federal Emergency Relief Administration leaders such as Harry Hopkins, she saw financial aid as one tool in treatment, not the answer to a problem diagnosed as exclusively economic.

Within the social-work community itself, rehabilitative approaches became increasingly popular in the wake of post-World War II applications of psychoanalytic theory. Social workers welcomed the new emphasis on psychology as one that highlighted their professional skills. In her history of twentieth-century professional discourses on single mothers, Lisa Brush identifies psychotherapeutic diagnosis and treatment as the dominant model of the era. For instance, the authors of an article in the *American Journal of Orthopsychiatry* offered this interpretation of unmarried women who chose not to give up their children for adoption: "Since it is only aggressive women who are able to retain these children, it is quite obvious that they are treated much as penis embodiments rather than human beings."[84] The rehabilitative approach implied a natural division of labor. Social insurance administrators simply issued checks; social workers sought involvement in discretionary social welfare.

Significant amendments expanding eligibility and increasing benefit levels of the social insurance programs also affected the composition of ADC recipients. A set of 1939 amendments moved up the starting date for OAI payments to beneficiaries from the original inaugural date of 1 January 1942 to 1 January 1940, enabled elderly wives of beneficiaries to receive OAI, and prescribed a new method of benefit calculation to increase monthly payments. Most important for ADC, the amendments authorized survivor benefits for widows over sixty-five and for all widows with dependent children: OAI became Old Age and Survivors' Insurance (OASI). Further amendments in 1950 expanded eligibility to include some groups of agricultural workers and self-employed people. Potential OASI eligibility extended to 75 percent of the labor force. The 1950 amendments also increased benefits 80 percent to align OASI monthly payments, which averaged $25.30 in 1949, with the more generous Old Age Assistance (OAA) monthly grants, which averaged $44.75 in 1949. ADC amendments signaled some dissatisfaction with the program. One required notification of appropriate law enforcement officials when desertion prompted receipt of ADC. Another, known as the Jenner Amendment, allowed ADC rolls to be made public.

The extension of eligibility for OAI and OASI in 1939 and 1950 meant that fewer widows received ADC but at the same time ADC became the most populous federal assistance program as some OAA recipients shifted

to social insurance.[85] In 1931 the Children's Bureau reported that 82 percent of mothers' pensions involved the death of the father. By 1950 the
figure dropped to 17 percent. By 1960 it fell further to 10 percent. During
the same period, the number of people receiving ADC rose. In 1950,
2.2 million people received ADC, 2.8 million received OAA, and 3.5 million
received OASI. In 1957, more people received ADC than any other public
assistance program—2.497 million to OAA's 2.48 million. By this time,
the number receiving OASI had climbed to 10.95 million. As the 1960s began, just over 3 million people received ADC while the number receiving
OAA fell slightly to 2.3 million. The number of OASI recipients had climbed
higher still, totaling 14.1 million. Meanwhile, the costs of ADC had
nearly doubled, rising from $556 million in 1950 to $1.056 billion in 1960.

These changes occurred despite legislators' and administrators' beliefs
that expansion of social insurance would engender the "withering
away" of public assistance. In a 1949 Ways and Means Committee hearing, SSB chairperson Arthur Altmeyer testified, and the committee report
later concurred, that "in time the residual load of public assistance would
become so small in this country that the States and the localities could
reasonably be expected to assume that load without Federal financial participation."[86] His bold prediction invoked the maternal image prominent
in the resolution of the 1909 White House Conference: the "deserving"
woman suffering temporary misfortune.

From the War on Poverty to the War on Welfare

In the 1960s, attention shifted from poverty to "dependency" as the contradictions of poverty discourses exploded onto the national political
scene. Forces that had been developing since 1935 accelerated rapidly during the decade—rising costs, altered caseloads—so that what started in
the beginning of the 1960s as an attempt to address the ills of poverty became an attempt to address the ills of the welfare system. Though incidents early in the decade signaled the increasing unpopularity of ADC, the
War on Poverty deflected for some time what might have been more sustained criticism. The travails of the Office of Economic Opportunity
(OEO), the explosive growth of ADC, the reconnection of race and
poverty, changing women's roles, and a shift from a casework to an economic approach all contributed to Richard Nixon's 1969 declaration that
"the present welfare system has to be judged a colossal failure."[87]

Many Americans rediscovered poverty in the 1960s. Early in the decade, a new generation of "muckraking" books about poverty appeared. One of the reasons for this trend was an influential 1962 book by Michael Harrington entitled *The Other America*. James Patterson writes that the book "catalyzed" poverty's rediscovery.[88] A detailed *New Yorker* review by Dwight MacDonald enhanced its circulation. MacDonald wrote that "in the last year we seem to have suddenly awakened, rubbing our eyes like Rip van Winkle, to the fact that mass poverty persists." After discussing the major themes of Harrington's book and exhorting that the existence of an other America should make one uncomfortable, he called for concerted action. That the government had an obligation to provide a minimum living standard for "all who need it should be taken as much for granted as free public schools have always been in our history."[89] Commentators have noted that the book and its review played a significant role in Kennedy's introduction of anti-poverty measures.[90]

The Other America reads less like an ethnography and more like a travelogue as Harrington guides his readers through the hidden locales of its residents. Like the muckrakers before him, Harrington illuminates social forces through personal scenes of despair. He identifies his goal as an attempt to "describe the faces behind the statistics, to tell a little of the 'thickness' of personal life in the other America."[91] Harrington composes vivid, compelling, and melancholy vignettes of the lives of the urban poor, the once-prosperous poor, the rural poor, the elderly poor, the Bowery poor, and the Bohemian poor. Harrington pays special attention to the plight of the black poor. Though they can be found in each of these categories, they must also fight the viciousness of racial discrimination.

The other Americans live in relative invisibility. Harrington observes that "[p]overty is off the beaten track." Rural poor live in desolate company towns in such places as the valleys of Pennsylvania and in Appalachian landscapes whose natural beauty Americans project onto the rundown homes of the other Americans. Urban poor work in kitchens and basements and live in physically isolated ghettos. Clothes play a role in making poor people invisible by simulating material equality. And many of the poor are either too old or too young to be seen. These factors contribute to the political invisibility of poor people. Harrington notes that past poverty was a condition of life of an entire society. For this reason, past poverty immediately concerned political leaders. By contrast, today's poor are the first minority poor in history. In all these ways, the poor are losing their links with the world. Harrington warns that "[t]he other America is becoming increasingly populated by those who do not belong to anybody or anything."[92] He asserts that this "insular poverty" requires anti-poverty programs aimed at ameliorating an "entire environment." The nation cannot hope that continued economic prosperity will positively affect the lives of the other Americans, for the very inventions and machines that have provided a higher standard of living for the rest of society have victimized them.

A viciously circular "culture of poverty" has entrapped the poor. Poverty twists the body and spirit. It destroys aspiration: "The American poor are pessimistic and defeated, and they are victimized by mental suffering to a degree unknown in suburbia." Contrary to Alger tales, poverty does not function as a way station to prosperity. It has become "a culture, an institution, a way of life." Harrington explains that the family structure of the poor differs from the rest of society. Poor people view authorities, such as the police, differently. Languages, psychologies, and worldviews distinguish the poor from more affluent citizens. Harrington maintains that "[t]here is, in a sense, a personality of poverty, a type of human being produced by the grinding, wearing life of the slums."[93]

Though he locates the causes of poverty structurally, Harrington's references to "culture" came under criticism from the left for obscuring exactly this dimension. Harrington calls attention to the disappearance of good-paying industrial jobs and long-term regional or group joblessness. He asserts that solutions require massive assaults on the institutions of pessimism and incompetence that develop in depressed areas. Only the larger society, with all its help and resources, can make it possible for poor people to help themselves. Emphasizing his structural diagnosis, Harrington gainsays the fact that many who could help do not because they mistakenly "view the effects of poverty — above all, the warping of the will and spirit that is a consequence of being poor — as choices."[94] Still, critics of Harrington and sociologist Oscar Lewis, who introduced the concept, countered that a *culture* of poverty occluded questions concerning the relation of culture to the distribution of power and resources as well as the ways in which cultures were embedded in political and institutional formations. Invoking the specter of Americanization, they also argued that a culture of poverty valued other groups on the basis of white, middle-class norms.[95] Subsequent conservative appropriations of culture as explicative of the undeservingness of the poor have revealed the "culture of poverty" to be a slippery concept. But Harrington holds fast to the view that "it takes a certain level of aspiration before one can take advantage of opportunities that are clearly offered."[96]

Harrington's book displays remarkable prescience of some of the developments of the 1960s. Predating concerns with family structure, Harrington explains that a fractured family life pervades the contemporary slum: serial monogamy. He describes gangs as products of the failure to establish community in the ghettos. He writes of a "multiplier effect" that would later be evoked by representatives of the OEO: the subcultures of the other America feed into each other so that effective action at one decisive point could engender changes at others. Indeed, Harrington calls for a "war on poverty" waged with a new mood of social idealism.[97]

In subject matter (poverty), method (elucidation of structures through personal stories), and tone (vivid and exhortative language), *The Other America* recalled the writings of the muckrakers. Moreover, the book functioned in the ways Progressive journals had envisioned for their efforts: it aroused a slumbering citizenry to take into their own hands the social problems of the day. For many readers, a belief in the fundamental justness of America remained, but the other Americans had been blocked from opportunity; they had not been treated fairly. From this perspective, *The Other America* advocated the removal of obstacles that hobbled individual ability. News stories and popular exposés also called for a renewed public spirit, drawing attention to social problems such as juvenile delinquency, which reflected for many people a broader deterioration in slum conditions.

The tenacity of poverty manifested in rising welfare costs also enabled its rediscovery. The evidence for this factor also revealed distrust and burgeoning fear of the poor, who represented reemerging threats to the social order. This time the threats came not from eastern and southern European immigrants but, especially as the decade proceeded, from black families. In July 1960, Louisiana dropped almost 6,000 families — including 22,051 children — from its public assistance rolls. Gov. Jimmie Davis cited newly passed suitable home legislation that declared a woman who gave birth to an out-of-wedlock child after receipt of welfare or who cohabited with a man without marriage to be providing an unsuitable home for her children and thus ineligible for ADC. The law affected black recipients almost exclusively — only 5 percent of the families dropped were white. Three days before John F. Kennedy's inauguration, on 17 January 1961, departing Health, Education, and Welfare secretary

Arthur Flemming issued a ruling that prohibited states from denying aid to an unsuitable home so long as a child remained in the home. He ruled that efforts should be made to improve the home. Failing that, the child should be moved elsewhere. After assuming the secretaryship, Abraham Ribicoff concurred.

The "Battle of Newburgh" occurred only six months later in June 1961. Newburgh, New York, was a town of 30,000 in the Hudson River valley. Though it relied annually on migrant labor, an unusually harsh winter and contemporaneous economic downturns produced a "welfare crisis" in spring 1961. The new city manager, Joseph McDowell Mitchell, issued a report blaming the city's fiscal difficulties on "a steady flux of outsiders principally from Southern states ... who apparently have no desire to take root and become a part of community life."[98] He implemented a stringent new policy that consisted of fiscal controls, work requirements, anti-fraud and anti-abuse assurances, and morality tests. In its most controversial aspects, the policy sought to require proof from applicants that they came to Newburgh with firm work offers in hand, deny aid to children conceived while the parent(s) received welfare, deny aid to those refusing work, and dispense aid in voucher form only. Though the courts eventually invalidated most of the regulations, Newburgh sparked a national debate regarding welfare. Barry Goldwater praised Mitchell; many liberals portrayed him as dangerous. Polls revealed that a majority of middle-class Americans endorsed hostile views of welfare. Yet polls also showed that a majority of Americans—80 percent in one case—thought that the government ought to "see to it that no one is without food and shelter."[99]

The persistence of poverty did not fuel only reactionary proposals. Progressive initiatives focused on facilitating entry of marginalized groups into an expanding economy. In 1964 the Council of Economic Advisors reported that economic growth in itself could not function as an anti-poverty program. It recommended that "[p]olicy will have to be more sharply focused on the handicaps that deny the poor fair access to the expanding incomes of a growing economy."[100] The report revealed two assumptions that underlay the early-1960's rediscovery of poverty. First, the United States could afford to abolish destitution. Second, poverty was anomalous in an affluent society, and it was fundamentally un-American. These assumptions received further support in reformers' confidence that the national economy could be managed and expanded. In a speech to 1962 graduates of Yale University, for example, President Kennedy admonished graduates to disabuse themselves of old truisms and stereo-types as they entered a new economy offering its participants boundless opportunities. Old visions hampered progress on important matters, such as the proper size of the federal government and the significance of federal budget deficits. The problem of spurring the economy to operate at full capacity—to "provide adequate profits for enterprise, adequate wages for labor, adequate utilization of plant, and opportunity for all"— could be solved, but this required not political, but technical answers— "the practical management of a modern economy."[101] The 1962 gradu-ates faced a different world than the generation that came of age during the Great Depression. Economic debates in the 1930s "took place in a dif-ferent world with different needs and tasks." Kennedy exhorted his au-dience, in a Jeffersonian spirit, to create "new words" and "new phrases" to describe the possibilities before them.[102]

A belief that poverty could and should be eliminated did not resolve contradictions in poverty discourse, however. The Public Welfare Amend-ments of 1962, which changed the name of ADC to Aid to Families with Dependent Children (AFDC), both expanded the availability of aid through a five-year extension of AFDC-UP, which enabled states to pro-vide assistance to two-parent unemployed households, and affirmed a casework approach by granting federal funding for the special training of social workers. The amendments funded up to 75 percent of state expen-ditures for rehabilitative or preventive social services for the needy. Fif-teen months after the passage of the amendments, the Kennedy admin-istration committed itself to broad anti-poverty measures.

It was Lyndon Baines Johnson, however, who declared war on poverty. His declaration displaced for a time the contradictions of poverty dis-course by highlighting inclusion as a means of alleviating poverty without undermining normative judgments about the relations among personal success, diligence, and virtue. Perceptions of LBJ and his predecessor combined with emergent social forces to shape the context of the presi-dent's declaration.[103] Americans still felt a lingering sense of sadness over the Kennedy assassination. Johnson needed to develop his own image and affect a transfer from his caretaker role to his own presidency. Many Americans regarded him as a southern conservative with a limited, re-gional perspective. Moreover, anti-poverty policy reflected LBJ's own roots and experiences with poverty. Still, the sociopolitical context in which he declared war suggested a forming but not yet formed public view that poverty presented a grave national problem.

LBJ put forth a battle plan for war on poverty in a 16 March 1964 special message to Congress. His message exuded confidence. Its opening
assumed a congratulatory tone, reminding Americans of their world
stature. LBJ depicted U.S. history as a story of progress toward prosperity for all. Americans started out "struggling for survival on the margin of
a hostile land." Though the path had not been easy, "we have established
a civilization of free men which spans an entire continent." In contradistinction to FDR's rebuke of debilitating cynicism, LBJ at no point
anticipated and attempted to answer charges of likely failure or naiveté.
His speech suggested that Americans everywhere were up to the task:
"The most enduring strength of our nation is the huge reservoir of talent,
initiative, and leadership which exists at every level of our society." LBJ
joined past success and present confidence to foretell the war's outcome.
He assured his audience that "[o]ur history has proved that each time we
broaden the base of abundance, giving more people the chance to produce and consume, we create new industry, higher production, increased
earnings and better income for all."[104]

LBJ highlighted opportunities, not guarantees. He did not call into question the principle that citizens had an obligation to be "self-supporting."
The president expressed his own unease with unqualified assistance. LBJ
insisted that the "war on poverty is not a struggle simply to support people, to make them dependent on the generosity of others. It is a struggle
to give people a chance." "Opportunity" pervaded the message in word
and policy. LBJ stated that the Economic Opportunity Act provided five
basic opportunities, introducing each as "the opportunity to."[105] He
announced an Office of Economic Opportunity to coordinate the war effort. LBJ claimed that his proposals were rooted firmly in American democratic traditions. Five years later, however, Nixon adopted a drastically
different tone in describing the anti-poverty efforts of the 1960s.

Part of the explanation for this shift lay in the trials and tribulations of
the OEO itself. In the initial stages of the war, OEO spokespersons managed to dissociate their efforts from welfare programs and, in the process,
deflect attention away from concerns about dependency and focus attention on poverty. A gap between the goals and achievements of the OEO
later emerged and widened. OEO representatives attempted to exaggerate
results and buy time, which weakened their credibility with legislators. In
addition, critics of the OEO inverted the value of the circular nature of
poverty so that it became an argument against the program. The "cycle of
poverty" slid into a debilitating culture of poverty that contravened the

effectiveness of intervention at various points in the cycle and raised questions about the temporary nature of some individuals' unemployed status. Finally, ambiguities surrounding community action proved to be contradictory rather than complementary. Opponents pointed to radical definitions of community action articulated by program participants and organizers as evidence that the OEO nurtured groups attacking the legitimacy of government itself.

The OEO could not maintain a strict separation between its activities and public assistance. It could not suspend forever the contradictions of poverty discourse. The OEO's shifting attitude toward "the welfare establishment" demonstrated the untenability of strict separations. In a 1965 speech to the National Conference on Social Welfare, Sargent Shriver, director of the OEO, chided social workers who "seem to think that working with the poor is their exclusive problem. They reject outsiders. They are wedded to professional opinions and ideas."[106] Shriver unfavorably compared this professional to the "inspired amateur" guided by intense commitment. Later that year, however, at a meeting of the American Public Welfare Association, Shriver assumed a more conciliatory stance, appealing to social workers as colleagues. The linkage of "welfare" and OEO programs ascribed negative valuations to the latter. Their linkage also meant that the perceived failures of the OEO — including falling confidence in its claims to prudent and efficient management — implicated already existing social welfare programs. Presaging a more general trend, the OEO, rather than poverty, came under scrutiny in 1967.

During the 1960s and into the early 1970s, the number of people enrolled in social welfare programs and the costs of the programs increased dramatically. Demographic forces contributed to these changes as higher percentages of elderly people in an aging population began to qualify for social insurance. Bureaucratic pressures also contributed. Less-heralded bills producing unforeseen consequences slipped through Congress. State and local officials pressed federal officials for relief; advocacy groups played an important role. The nation's ability to pay without reducing benefits to the middle class increased. AFDC in particular experienced explosive growth between 1965 and 1975. Improvements in medical care led to higher percentages of female-headed families. Mass migrations of the 1940s and 1950s left many such families in more generous northern states. These states began to implement AFDC-UP and increased income levels at which people could be eligible for AFDC. The most developed states extended welfare policies the most. Federal officials also encouraged

increased participation in social welfare programs. Under Secretary
John Gardner especially, the Department of Health, Education, and Welfare sought to maximize benefits and services.

The poor themselves began to organize and advance rights claims.
Though it represented only a tiny fraction of welfare recipients, the
National Welfare Rights Organization (NWRO) served as a prominent
spokesperson for the views of participants in public assistance programs.
Organized in 1966 by George Wiley, a black Syracuse University chem-
istry professor with experience in the civil rights movement, the NWRO
brought together various local welfare mothers' organizations. Its formation was urged by scholar/activists Frances Fox Piven and Richard
Cloward, who advocated rapid expansion of the welfare rolls so that local politicians would lobby federal officials for intervention and restructuring.[107] Much of the group's activities built on local grassroots organizing, as NWRO members remained active in their communities even
after they assumed administrative positions within the national organization. The efforts of the NWRO and similar local groups were aided by
the agencies of the OEO as local community-action programs organized
poor people with the goal of securing already recognized legal rights.

Poverty lawyers worked to change discriminatory laws and regulations
— the tools employed by local administrators to judge deservingness. The
most significant gains came in three Supreme Court decisions delivered
in the late 1960s and early 1970s.[108] *King v. Smith* (1968) struck down an
Alabama rule that effectively denied AFDC to any family if the mother
had sexual relations. The rule defined the partner as a "substitute father"
capable of maintaining the family. *Shapiro v. Thompson* (1969) held that
residency requirements violated a recipient's right to interstate travel and
thus denied equal protection of the law. *Goldberg v. Kelly* (1970) required
welfare agencies to offer recipients hearings that met "minimal due
process standards" before withholding benefits.

These various factors—governmental, community, and judiciary—
combined to prompt a large increase in the percentage of families that
applied for public assistance through the 1960s. The most telling statistic
of the decade concerned the sharp rise in the number of eligible families
who were actually assisted. Indeed, it may have been the most important
single explanation for the backlash marked so clearly in Nixon's address.
In the early 1960s, *33 percent* of eligible families participated in AFDC; in
1971, *90 percent* participated.[109]

At the same time that welfare costs and populations rose, race and poverty, which had been decoupled momentarily at the outset of the War on Poverty, reconnected. Mothers' pensions and ADC always engaged racial discourses. But in the past this engagement proceeded through purposeful silence and lack. The small proportion of blacks receiving pensions in 1931 spoke to administrative and community views of the deservingness and neediness of black women. The midcentury image of the deserving white widow did not overlook black women. Rather, it expressed the prevailing view that black poverty was not a *social* problem. The transformations of the 1960s enabled the articulation of "black poverty," but these transformations shaped it as something to be feared, not as an object of sympathy. Race continued to be an element of poverty discourse, structuring debates not in silence but in prominence.

For many people, riots in inner-city neighborhoods indelibly linked poverty programs and race. Critics charged that the inflated promises of poverty warriors led to the frustration and despair of poor black city dwellers. In the 1968 national campaigns, Republicans linked riots to the reckless use of inflated promises. Critics also charged that by using programs to quell volatile situations, the OEO provided implicit incentive for those seeking funds to instigate or threaten disturbances. David Zarefsky holds that the "riots of 1967 obliterated hopes of maintaining a distinction" between poverty and race.[110]

The civil rights movement connected racial and economic justice with greater frequency. This linkage was not new, of course. In 1963, prior to sharing his dream with the nation, Dr. Martin Luther King, Jr. reflected on the 100-year anniversary of the signing of the Emancipation Proclamation: "One hundred years later, the Negro lives on a lonely island of poverty in the midst of a vast ocean of material prosperity."[111] King advocated economic as well as racial justice. Moreover, King recalled his dream at a March for *Jobs* and Freedom. As the decade progressed, King's discourse exhibited increasingly explicit and amplified attention to economic concerns.

His last presidential address to the Southern Christian Leadership Conference (SCLC) in 1967 demonstrated this development. King began by reviewing some of the gains of the civil rights movement and SCLC. In its ten-year existence, SCLC had enabled many black people to achieve an "internal" integration: the reclamation of one's sense of self. Yet economic integration continued to elude blacks. Important activities in the past years included a program of economic development titled Operation Breadbasket. King pointed to successes in Chicago, Cleveland, and other cities in creating new jobs for blacks, developing black-controlled financial institutions, assisting black contractors, and promoting black-owned newspapers. In these various activities, Operation Breadbasket put into practice a simple principle: "If you respect my dollar, you must respect my person."[112]

King connected these accomplishments thematically in answering the question, "Where do we go from here?" His answer highlighted the interrelated goals of psychological and economic uplift. King called upon his auditors first to assert their dignity and worth. Though he acknowledged that this necessary first step had been accomplished to a considerable degree, King stressed that more could be done. Recalling Harrington's exhortation that anti-poverty programs could not overlook the psychology of the poor, King asserted that "[a]ny movement for the Negro's freedom that overlooks this necessity is only waiting to be buried.... Psychological freedom, a firm sense of self-esteem, is the most powerful weapon against the long night of physical slavery."[113]

Political and economic power stood as the next goals for organizing within the black community. King advocated the adoption of a national guaranteed income. In a revealing passage, he spoke of what he saw as the progressive trajectory of poverty discourse. Early in this century, people would have laughed at the idea of an income guarantee. They regarded economic status as a reliable measure of individual ability and talent. King explained that "in the thinking of that day, the absence of worldly goods indicated a want of industrious habits and moral fiber.... Now we realize that dislocations in the market operations of our economy and the prevalence of discrimination thrust people into idleness and bind them in constant or frequent unemployment against their will."[114] Gainsaying the preachers of the Gospel of Wealth, King asserted that even the most dynamically developing and expanding economy could not eliminate poverty; society must create full employment and/or create incomes.

King advanced an unqualified rights claim supported by an insightful historical analysis. As LBJ's declaration evidenced, however, this position collided with the beliefs of his contemporaries. King's shift from an ideal dream to its pragmatic realization, which paced larger changes in the civil rights movement, prompted a backlash from some whites. Few whites may have objected—or at least stated openly their objection—to a society that judged people by the content of their character and not by the color of their skin. Many did object, however, when the paths toward this vision included political organization and economic development, which many whites may have perceived as a threat to established material interests.

Changing expectations of women's roles in society also accounted for increasingly negative images of AFDC recipients as deviant. Several important events during the 1960s aided these changes. In 1961 President Kennedy appointed the President's Commission on the Status of Women. Uninterested in women's issues, Kennedy appointed the commission as a partial reward for women activists in the Democratic Party.[115] The commission issued a report that affirmed the significance of the nuclear family, but argued that barriers to full civic participation by women ought to be removed. It supported the 1963 Equal Pay Act, which outlawed in most cases different pay scales for men and women holding the same position, though the act did not open up traditionally male jobs to women. Betty Friedan's influential *The Feminine Mystique* was published in 1963. The book announced the "problem with no name": the conflicts women experienced as a result of the discrepancy between their desire to fulfill themselves in their own right and social attitudes that expected them to be fulfilled through service to someone else.[116]

The 1964 Civil Rights Act contributed unexpectedly to changing gender roles. On the House floor, Rep. Howard Smith of Virginia added the word "sex" to the list of classes that would be protected against employment discrimination. As an arch-segregationist, he hoped to scuttle the bill, but the addition passed. The Equal Employment Opportunity Commission subsequently found that one-third of received complaints were gender-based. In 1966, 300 women and men met at the founding conference of the National Organization for Women (NOW). Attendees declared their belief that "true partnership between the sexes demands a different concept of home and of the economic burdens of their support."[117] NOW and other groups in the emerging women's liberation movement challenged the view that women's proper place was in the home.

During the 1960s, the participation of married women with children in the labor force—the group to whom welfare mothers had long been compared—increased.[118] Between 1960 and 1970, the employment rate of married women with children under six rose from 18.6 to 30.3 percent. During the same period, the employment rate of married women with children between the ages of six and seventeen rose from 39 to 49.2 percent. Information for 1960 is unavailable, but the employment rates of separated and divorced women with children under six in 1970 were 45.4

and 63.3 percent, respectively. For separated and divorced women with children aged six to seventeen, rates were even higher—60.6 and 82.4 percent, respectively. As Joel Handler and Yeheskel Hasenfeld note, "the [increasing] respectability of working married mothers only heightened the perceived deviance and moral depravity of single mothers, especially those with children born out of wedlock, who are on welfare rather than working."[119] Meager grants have always forced many AFDC mothers to work, but the image of the worthy widow sometimes has obfuscated this implicit condition of assistance.

The 1967 passage of the Work Incentive Program (WIN) adumbrated movement toward mandated work force participation by all AFDC mothers. It also signaled shifting congressional views of welfare mothers from care-givers to paid laborers. WIN required state welfare agencies to screen all AFDC recipients aged sixteen and over for employment and to refer all suitable recipients to state departments of labor. WIN discounted a fixed sum for work expenses, the first thirty dollars of monthly earned income, and one-third of the remainder up to the maximum welfare grant in each state. It also provided for some childcare and training expenses. Through 1971, however, only 24 percent of 2.7 million assessments were deemed "appropriate for referral." Overall, only 2 percent of eligible AFDC recipients were placed in jobs.[120]

After 1967, economists began to dominate welfare policy analysis. They operated with a belief in economic rationality, assuming a world in which people responded to economic incentives. In the mid-1960s, American economists especially attempted to explain and popularize the idea of income maintenance. This strategy set aside prevention and rehabilitation and accepted, in some measure, the ineradicable nature of poverty. Economists advanced various strategies: non-means–tested children's allowances; job creation programs; and guaranteed cash incomes for the poor. The 1969 report of the Heineman Commission, a body recommended by an earlier presidential task force on poverty, urged a universal income supplement program making cash payments to all members of the population with income needs. Yet this movement away from the casework approach of Progressive and New Deal reformers did not reconcile the fundamental contradictions of poverty discourse.

In an 8 August 1969 address to the nation, Richard Nixon proposed the Family Assistance Plan (FAP). Following in the footsteps of LBJ, he began by congratulating Americans on their material prosperity. But

Nixon set a tone that was in exact opposition to his predecessor. LBJ infused his message with certainty; Nixon described a country facing a "crisis of confidence." He located the cause in Washington. Three decades of increasingly centralized power and responsibility in the capital had produced a failed welfare system that broke up homes and penalized work. The system's "effect is to draw people off payrolls and onto welfare rolls — just the opposite of what government should be doing."[121] Nixon proposed as his solution a "new federalism." He explained that the country "became great not because of what government did for the people, but because of what people did for themselves." In this passage and others, Nixon abstracted government from its citizens as a force acting upon them. In contrast, LBJ characterized government as a sublimation of citizen energy: the people acting in concert. Nixon's new federalism intimated opportunity, but he gave it a decidedly nongovernmental interpretation. He asserted that "[t]his new approach aims at helping the American people do more for themselves. It aims at getting everyone able to work off welfare rolls and onto payrolls."[122]

This speech by President Nixon may be the most cogently articulated example of the cross-purposes of public assistance in modern American public address. Reflecting perhaps the nation's contested social landscape, the cross-purposes of sustenance and deterrence appeared to consume each other during the course of the speech. Nixon stressed work in language that voiced the frustrations of middle-class America: "What America needs now is not more welfare, but more 'workfare.'"[123] Yet his proposal would have eliminated distinctions between the welfare and working poor. And Nixon called specific attention to the plight of the latter. Nixon proposed a guaranteed income, but resolutely denied that the FAP was any such thing. In his reflections on the ultimate defeat of the FAP, Daniel Patrick Moynihan, one of Nixon's chief domestic advisors, conceded its nature explicitly: *"this was a guaranteed income."*[124] Nixon, however, distinguished his proposed universal family grant of 1,600 dollars from an income guarantee. He insisted that "a guaranteed income establishes a right without any responsibilities; family assistance recognizes a need and establishes a responsibility."[125] The FAP would have added more than ten million people to federal social welfare programs and increased expenditures by 138 percent. Nixon described these funds, however, in terms familiar to every "businessman" and "workingman": "start-up costs."[126] Finally, Nixon noted that benefit levels were unequal among states. But he recalled the "Battle of Newburgh" when he described as a principal consequence migrations of poor people in search of generous benefits.

In crucial respects, the speech turned on itself, creating moments of alternation and indeterminacy. Incoherence pervaded Nixon's speech, revealing contradictions within poverty discourse that have continued through the present day. His attention to the working poor unwittingly undermined equations opposing worker/independence and nonworker/dependence. He described the FAP as recognizing for the first time that government "has no less an obligation to the working poor than to the non-working poor; and for the first time, benefits would be scaled in such a way that it always pays to work."[127] Yet the need for workers' benefits and the phrase working poor itself suggested that one could labor full-time and still be "dependent." Further, Nixon alternately depicted the "welfare system" as voracious and enfeebled. On the one hand, he held that without intervention the system would continue to grow: "What began on a small scale in the depression 30s has become a huge monster in the prosperous 60s."[128] For more than thirty years, the welfare system had consumed drive and energy and still its insatiable appetite could not be satisfied. This depiction — even if monstrous — implied life and vigor. On the other hand, Nixon introduced the present system as "cumbersome"; its programs had "outlived their time." He amplified this view later in proposing reforms of a weak system, describing it as an "antiquated, wheezing, overloaded machine."[129]

Through appeals to deterrence and sustenance, an unlikely coalition of liberals and conservatives defeated the FAP. Its passage appeared likely at first. The House of Representatives passed the FAP on 16 April by a vote of 243 to 135. The proposal died slowly in the Senate, failing to emerge from the Finance Committee. Conservatives viewed it as a threat to the work ethic. The National Chamber of Commerce, for instance, strongly opposed the bill. It called the work requirements fallacies that would "simply make *permanent* additions to the welfare rolls."[130] Liberals thought that the grant amount was too low. Sen. Eugene McCarthy introduced the Adequate Income Act of 1970. Backed by the NWRO, the act included a minimum income guarantee of $5,500 and no work requirement.

In October 1972, however, Congress passed Supplementary Security Income (SSI). SSI arose out of a failed attempt to reintroduce the FAP in the 92nd Congress. The legislation federalized assistance to the blind, the permanently and totally disabled, and the elderly who had been receiving

OAA. Several reasons have been offered for passage of SSI amidst the failure of the FAP: influential pressure groups supported SSI but were not interested in FAP; some welfare reformers thought that existing programs would ultimately prove adequate; and SSI received considerably less attention than the FAP.[131] An assistant to Sen. Abraham Ribicoff reflected that "if SSI had been on its own it never would have made it."[132] Whatever the explanation, the passage of SSI meant that of all the groups assisted in the 1935 Social Security Act, single mothers and their children were now the only ones without access to a program that offered aid as a federally administered right of citizenship. Though the status of poor children was ambivalent, the passage of SSI firmly established single mothers as "undeserving poor."

Using and Abusing History: Implications for 1980–96

The historical contradictions of poverty discourse provide advocates and policymakers with opportunities to revisit and refashion the past. Spaces of invention emerge in the fractures and fissures, the unfinished projects and aborted attempts of a history that has not bequeathed an agreed-upon legacy against which speakers must measure their statements and proposals. The history of American social welfare policy debate does not represent the progressive development toward a consensus that will reconcile the cross-purposes and divided populations of past eras. Rather, the history recounted in this chapter stands as a series of contiguous episodes that avail themselves to appropriation by speakers without a perceived sense by their audiences that an integral, coherent "history" has been distorted.

In retrenchment-era welfare reform debates, past discourses of poverty served as a storehouse of images and arguments — not as an ensemble in which each part derived its meaning in relation to a whole, but as a collection made available for selective appropriation. The citizens of Stuart-Tudor England prefigured subsequent divisions of the poor as they held out the hand of Christian duty to the impotent and scorned sturdy beggars and rogues. The preachers of the Gospel of Wealth sung the praises of the industrious poor boy, whose prominent image affirmed "traditional" values threatened by newly created wealth, while denouncing the moral depravity of the pauper. The muckrakers publicized the lives of those who suffered corruption and greed. They exposed dangerous conditions faced by assiduous immigrant men in the steel mills of Chicago and children in the textile mills of the South, who lived in subservience to the machinery of industry. Progressive Era welfare reformers celebrated the image of the worthy widow. Mothers' pension advocates wished to support the already virtuous and Americanize the potentially virtuous immigrant. New Deal reformers appropriated this image wholly, complementing it with a masculine depiction of the virtuous poor: the proud unemployed man who wanted to support his family as the state supported widows. As FDR asserted, this proud man wanted "work" not "welfare." The War on Poverty demonstrated the constancy of structural contradictions amid the episodic history of poverty discourse. Images of the poor in the 1960s mixed compassion and fear. Compassion lay in the vignettes of Harrington and the bold predictions of LBJ. Fear surfaced in the "Battle of Newburgh" and the enactment of work incentives. Mounting fear made explicit a long-silent dimension of poverty discourse: race. It also revealed the ever-present connection of welfare to the low-wage labor market. These dimensions coalesced in Nixon's FAP speech—a speech so infused with the contradictions of poverty discourse that it turned against itself.

As this assemblage of images and arguments intimates, the absence of a firmly established history of consensus in welfare reform has engendered tradition making.[133] Advocates have subjected the past to struggles over its import in which no one tradition asserts itself. In this process of constructing a history, advocates abstract moments of the past from their larger contexts, revaluing them in the present to meet different needs. For instance, public officials opposed to social welfare spending have repeated FDR's description of assistance as "a narcotic, a subtle destroyer of the human spirit."[134] Yet few have recapitulated the optimistic moments in his dialectic: that only government can administer programs that meet the needs of large groups of people, for the private sector is susceptible to waste and corruption. Invoked within a larger framework in which past contradictions tacitly structure key components of contemporary deliberations, these explicit references employ the past as an inventive, imagined resource.

This explicit and implicit presence of the past in contemporary policy debate suggests that although these episodes and images do not cohere into a progressively developing history, they do implicate critical social values of individual worth, self-sufficiency, work ethic, and family formation that motivate political constituencies and broach questions of identity formation. Perceived successes and failures of the War on Poverty, for instance, have been rallying points both for those who would extend the reach of the welfare state and those who would initiate and hasten its retrenchment. Advocating the latter, Ronald Reagan occasionally opined that "some years ago, the federal government declared war on poverty, and poverty won."[135] Though this judgment of failure betrayed a desire to return to an older policy framework, it also indicated the contemporary salience of this past episode in building public support for particular reforms. For Reagan and his conservative supporters, the War on Poverty represented an era of fundamental misdirection in federal policy, an era in which the federal government undermined lessons of "stable" family formation and hard work. In the view of these individuals, poverty won the war against it because the beneficiaries of 1960s social policy were not citizens rightly claiming benefits but earnest poor people led astray by a putatively caring government or worse — deviants receiving government subsidies to engage in pathological behavior. Some supporters of the War on Poverty retorted that it was a tremendous success.[136] The participation rate in AFDC increased during the 1960s from 33 percent to 90 percent. Community-action participants, welfare activists, poverty lawyers, and others transformed a situation in which a minority of eligible poor participated in programs designed for them to one in which the vast majority did. These people excelled in a framework of federal anti-poverty policy that in large measure consisted of income-support programs.

These opposing judgments of the War on Poverty indicate that employing the past to mobilize political constituencies may assist in a representational process of political identity formation. One's interpretation of the past and perceived relation to a constructed history partly shape one's present identity. Enacting a political identity through dissociation, Reagan suggested to his auditors that they were not the successors of 1960s reformers but reclaimers of a forsaken earlier era. The historical discourses of poverty provide advocates multifarious resources for the construction of an American welfare policy tradition and, in part, an American identity. In his 1980 presidential campaign, Reagan projected a rejuvenated American identity to a public diagnosed as suffering from a general malaise. In a period of inflation and recession, he promised "to make America great again."[137] His pledge entailed evicting the federal government from areas of daily life into which it had intruded improperly.

For welfare policy deliberations and AFDC recipients, this meant removing from the rolls those people Reagan and his supporters believed could and should support themselves

CHAPTER 3

Reducing Welfare

One week before the election, in his closing remarks of the only debate held between himself and President Carter, Ronald Reagan asked television viewers a series of questions that highlighted for many the most important issues of the 1980 presidential campaign: "Are you better off than you were four years ago? Is it easier for you to go and buy things in the stores than it was four years ago? Is there more or less unemployment in the country than there was four years ago?"[1] These questions encapsulated the everyday impact of harsh economic conditions confronting many Americans in the late 1970s and early 1980s. In 1980 unemployment hovered at 7 percent and inflation held firm at an unbearable rate of over 12 percent. The Carter administration tried unsuccessfully to abate inflation, producing only further unemployment and negative economic growth. Though Carter's overall economic accomplishments may have bettered the achievements of Reagan at the end of his first term, Carter faced the electorate with an election year economic record that invoked comparisons with Herbert Hoover in 1932.[2]

Reagan offered voters a simple explanation for the economic insecurity they felt so keenly: the federal government put the economy in its sorry state. Borrowing required to finance government spending reduced money in circulation, which meant that too much demand chased too few dollars. Government regulation and taxes increased the costs of consumer goods. This anti-government agenda resonated with the attitudes of many voters. Since 1966, the Harris poll has measured public confidence in a range of social institutions. In 1966, 42 percent of respondents expressed "a great deal of confidence" in Congress and 41 percent expressed "a great deal of confidence" in the executive branch. By 1979, the percentages of respondents expressing such confidence had dropped to 18 and 17 percent, respectively.[3] Public disenchantment with government and economic insecurity created opportunities for the Reagan campaign to build support among working-class ethnics, whom the campaign actively pursued. But these "Reagan Democrats" and other voters may have been responding less to orchestrated appeals than to the daily conditions they encountered. An election-day exit poll asking Reagan voters to select among issues that influenced their decision found that these voters chose "inflation and the economy" twice as often as any other issue. When asked to select a Reagan quality that attracted their vote, most checked "it is time for a change."[4]

Reagan's election as the 40th president of the United States represented a turning point in social welfare policy deliberations. Shortly after his inauguration, the president advocated a full-scale retrenchment of the welfare state that culminated in the 1996 repeal of AFDC. Reagan, however, did not turn policy debates singlehandedly or even principally. Instead, he functioned as an articulator of revived and revitalized discourses on the virtues of private enterprise and the vices of the state. As he argued for the ameliorative capabilities of markets free from government interference, Reagan played a role for which he was well-suited — one he had played for General Electric before his election to public office — spokesperson and symbol.[5] In policy terms too, Reagan and his supporters did not champion unforeseen proposals: the value of AFDC benefits peaked, leveled off, and had begun to decline in the years between the failure of the Family Assistance Plan and Reagan's first budget proposal.

The historical persistence of calls to reform welfare suggests that any identification of a "turning point" ought to be treated initially with skepticism. Yet FDR never lost his confidence in the abilities of government even as he denounced relief as "a narcotic, a subtle destroyer of the human spirit." Nixon saw the failures of government clearly in a system that took people "off payrolls and onto welfare rolls."[6] Still, his proposed solution would have guaranteed families a minimum income. A variation of this plan reappeared as late as 1978 when Congress debated Jimmy Carter's Program for Better Jobs and Income. As these earlier reforms suggest, Reagan and his supporters reversed policy priorities set in motion by reformers at the turn of the century. They turned policy debates by joining disparaging views of welfare with an assailment of government that sought not to reconfigure but to eliminate it. They did not claim to wish the poor well as they fended for themselves, however. The Reagan administration promised to protect the truly needy and to devise methods that would distinguish this group from various deviants. These promises entailed an appropriation and reconfiguration of past poverty discourse.

Reagan engaged valuational clusters that created a discursive context favorable to government retrenchment. He portrayed the marketplace as

a tough but compassionate testing arena, which rewarded good character and punished bad. He held that the businessman ought not to be seen
as the perpetrator of economic woe but rather its victim. In this way,
Reagan and his supporters reversed prevailing political language and returned to moralistic, individualistic interpretations of a person's socioeconomic status. They did not mimic historical poverty discourses, nor
was their discourse simply derivative of past eras. Instead, they invented
a Gospel of Wealth for the 1980s, gesturing to the New Deal in their
promise of a safety net for the truly needy.

Cuts in public assistance programs did not rely only on a favorable
context. Reagan and his supporters defended budget cuts by asserting the
non-neediness of many AFDC recipients. The budget debates were, in
large measure, debates about demographic proportions and contrasting
images of the typical AFDC recipient. Reagan and his supporters represented large numbers of recipients as cheats, shirkers, and double-dippers. Opponents countered with demographies emphasizing innocent,
vulnerable, and voiceless children whose mothers struggled to provide for
their families. While all representations may assert the synecdochical
claim that a part depicts the whole, the suggestions of widespread fraud,
abuse, and waste of Reagan's non-needy recipients were significant for
their comparatively widespread circulation within the debates. This wider
circulation may have arisen from their complementary relation to the
framing of the debates. These images of cheats, shirkers, and double-dippers circumscribed the reception of alternative depictions. At the same
time, the historical resonance of the budget-cutters' arguments facilitated
appeals to fear, anger, and suspicion. In removing the "non-needy" from
the AFDC rolls, the Reagan administration envisioned an alternative relation of government to its poor citizens.

In what follows, I first examine the economic transformations of the
1970s, which produced social anxieties susceptible to Reagan's reversals,
and the revival of conservative economic theory contemporaneous with
the 1980 national elections. I then describe the narrower context of the
political and legislative development of the 1981 Omnibus Budget Reconciliation Act (OBRA). My analysis begins with two speeches delivered
by Reagan shortly after he took office that played a critical role in framing
the ensuing budget debates. Next, I explicate the contesting demographies of the AFDC population that structured the 1981 deliberations. After
locating these images within the debates, I consider their relative reception and the ways in which their deployment invited generalization from

individual incidents. I then compare the budget-cutters' rendering of social relations to past eras to elucidate the historical resonance that bolstered the appeal of the budget-cutters' non-needy recipients. In the penultimate section of this chapter I address the relationship of government to its poor citizens implicit in these debates.

Stagflation and Supply-Side Economics

Nixon's Family Assistance Plan may have represented not only the apex of a mid-twentieth century, progressive trajectory of social welfare policy, but it also may have signaled the most opportune moment for such a proposal. The economic events of the 1970s belied optimistic assumptions of permanent economic growth, which intimated the resolution of social problems without conflict or sacrifice, and returned many Americans to an "older psychology of scarcity." Gas lines prompted by the oil embargo of 1973 provided visible, historically tinged evidence of the end of unlimited consumption of resources. Moreover, real median family income (i.e., income adjusted for inflation) stopped rising after a sustained post–World War II boom. Between 1948 and 1972, real median family income more than doubled. After 1972, it stalled and then fell. In 1980 real median family income dropped by 5.5 percent. The drop was the largest since the government began keeping records of real income in 1947.[7]

These transformations took place within an economy that underwent increasing deindustrialization during the 1970s. Once-dominant industries such as auto and steel faltered. Rising fuel prices and competition from overseas presented challenges to U.S. manufacturing sectors that raised doubts in the minds of some observers about the basic survival of these industries. George Arnold, president of the Wheeling Pittsburgh Steel Corporation, warned that "the future of the steel industry and our entire industrial base in the Ohio Valley is in jeopardy."[8] Troubles in these two major industries created economic hardship in additional, dependent manufacturing sectors. The loss of relatively high-wage occupations in steel, auto, and other heavy manufacturing industries forced many dislocated workers to accept jobs at reduced wages and benefits in service and light manufacturing industries. Harrington notes that jobs in the electronic components industry, for instance, increased by 25.6 percent between 1973 and 1980. But when "a man or a woman shifts from the primary metals industry to the electronic components industry, his or her new salary is only 61 percent of the old."[9] Deindustrialization changed the structure of poverty by decoupling it from unemployment. In previous decades, poverty rates decreased in step with unemployment rates. The labor market has never attached security guarantees to offers of employment, as people on the margins know well. But the changing nature of paid labor in the 1970s meant that many people who once thought themselves to be financially secure faced poverty for the first time.

The industrial Northeast and Midwest were especially hard hit. Acute suffering in these areas prompted a "reverse migration" as families sought brighter economic futures elsewhere. In previous decades, rural families moved to northern cities to secure factory employment. In the early 1980s, families moved to the Sun Belt to follow industry that had migrated south and southwest in search of "friendly business climates." The *New York Times,* for example, published a series about the experiences of a Michigan family that moved to Texas to start life anew. The Wahrenbrock family connected their move to their parents' journey to Detroit from Kansas and rural Ohio after World War II. Reflecting on her parents, Patricia Wahrenbrock asserted that "they took a chance, just like we're doing."[10] The series recounted how Robert Wahrenbrock traveled to Dallas ahead of his family and found employment, albeit at a wage lower than the job he held in Michigan, after only four days of searching. But brighter skies for some did not mean prosperity for all. The *New York Times* also depicted the migration of unskilled workers to the Sun Belt, who arrived only to struggle to secure minimum-wage jobs that barely kept them above the poverty line. Accounts of the experiences of unskilled workers relayed scenes of day-labor hiring halls in southern cities where groups of men lined up at 5:00 A.M. in "the smoky fluorescent glare" to receive work assignments.[11] The industries of the southern economy were not labor-intensive like the auto and steel industries of the North and did not provide mass employment for the unskilled.

Simultaneous inflation and stagnation — "stagflation" — during Carter's presidency alarmed laypersons and economists alike. Stagflation confounded widely applied Keynesian macroeconomic approaches and evidenced for conservatives the bankruptcy of liberal economic theory. Keynesians regarded unemployment rates as indicative of economic prosperity. High unemployment signaled business stagnation and low consumer demand. Low unemployment indicated business growth and high consumer demand. Keynesians held that government policies could lower unemployment by stimulating aggregate demand. Recognizing the association of low unemployment rates with rising wages and price levels, they also viewed inflation as alterable by government action to reduce aggregate demand. Keynesian economic theory and its inverse relationship of inflation and unemployment became a critical instrument of public policy in the decades after the Great Depression as government planners attempted to moderate the extremes of the market with fiscal and monetary policies that regulated aggregate demand. As Piven and Cloward note, "[i]nstead of business cycles that careened from trough to peak to trough again, relatively moderate recessions occurred every few years which increased unemployment without pushing it to staggering levels. In turn, higher unemployment rates produced lower wage and price levels."[12] The inflation-unemployment relation held until the 1970s. Then, prices began to rise despite high levels of unemployment.

Several explanations have been offered for the stagflation of the 1970s: the quadrupling of oil prices; transformations in the industrial sector; a flood of new workers entering the job market, mostly baby boomers and older women entering the labor force for the first time; high military spending during the Vietnam War; and individual and business investment practices.[13] Whether some combination of these events or, as Reagan and his supporters argued, the policies of the government itself explained the economic downturns of the 1970s, the decade saw the end of a postwar boom that threatened the economic standing of many Americans previously propelled into prosperity by this very boom. Garry Wills writes plainly that "[i]nflation elected Ronald Reagan in 1980."[14]

Inflation had an impact on everyone. For the poor, it meant the worsening of an already desperate situation. Dorothy Johnson, a mother of three, found that rising prices outstripped the meager resources provided by her part-time employment and welfare grant.[15] Even though she went without needed purchases and surreptitiously held a second job to maintain eligibility for AFDC, she still confronted an empty refrigerator at the end of each month. Food stamps did not provide much relief. After budgeting for shelter and telephone service, only ten dollars per day remained for Johnson to purchase food, clothing, and all other needs for her family of four.

Inflation also shrunk the pocketbooks of those generally unaccustomed to economic strain—suburbanites. Margaret Terranella saw the effects of inflation most keenly in her rising grocery and gas bills. She managed as a widow to stay current on her son's college tuition bills, but had to do without such luxuries as vacations. She described her future in uncertain terms: "There's no such thing as saving, no matter which way I try. You keep hoping for a better time. You survive but you don't save.... I'm at the age when I'm starting to look for security, and it's not there." The elderly felt especially vulnerable. One portrait relayed the circumstances of an elderly couple who were forced to sell their possessions to buy food. The couple thought they had enough money saved when they retired years ago. Now only a small emergency fund was left; rising costs had exhausted the rest. The woman conceded to a reporter that "we put on a front still. It's not easy. It's beginning to get worse."[16] These vignettes alluded to a national trend as welfare agencies around the country noted increased numbers of formerly middle-income people applying for public assistance. Receipt of food stamps rose nationally by more than 5 percent in the first few months of 1980. Madeline Collins, supervisor of the New Orleans food stamp program, explained that her agency processed more applications for assistance from formerly middle-income people than from other categories of applicants. She characterized these recipients as angry. She added that "[t]hey're a very demanding group too — very hostile and frustrated. They don't like to have to resort to this."[17]

These multiple faces of hardship demanded a response. Doubt characterized the national mood as citizens searched collectively for answers to the nation's economic woes. Headlines disclosed shared anxieties. *Newsweek* queried: "Is U.S. Inflation Out of Control?" A *Time* magazine article on the state of the economy asked in big, bold letters a more fundamental question: "Capitalism: Is It Working?" The article answered "of course, but ... ," and proceeded to delineate a choice confronting developing and developed nations alike between a command economy and a market economy. The article elucidated this choice with an urgency that suggested doubts about capitalism had arisen in the minds of American readers. The concluding sections of the article described a "fateful rivalry" between the forces of freedom and tyranny. *Time* stressed that "political freedom is impossible without economic freedom."[18] Uncertainty produced dystopian visions. *Newsweek* published a "doomsday scenario" of inflation that prophesied how Americans' lives might change if the United States replicated the hyperinflation of 1920s Weimar Germany. The scenario imagined hoarding goods as a means of survival, bartering as a replacement for monetary exchange, and rising interest rates of over 100 percent that increased by the hour. The scenario envisioned a dangerous society plagued by widespread looting, soaring crime rates, and disappearing social services such as police and fire protection.[19]

Although they did not measure indicators at doomsday levels, observers discerned various signs of social strife and melancholy. Public opinion polls linked economic stress to rising social antagonism. A *New York Times*/CBS News poll found that fear of unemployment appeared to harden divisive attitudes among Americans. The poll recorded a rise in racial stereotyping and resentment among job seekers of different backgrounds. John Oliver Wilson, director of economic policy research for the Bank of America and professor at the University of California-Berkeley, announced in an op-ed column the beginning of an "after affluence" era. The United States had suffered diminished economic growth potential. Attendant threats to the American dream had caused a "middle-class crisis of historic proportions." Wilson maintained that only its fundamental reformulation would enable the American dream to survive an era in which affluence no longer could be regarded as a "natural right."[20]

In his speech accepting the Republican presidential nomination, Reagan promised to renew the spirit of America. He promised to lift the country out of malaise. He noted that some politicians lamented that the "United States has had its day in the sun." They warned that "the future will be one of sacrifice and few opportunities." Reagan rejected this view categorically. He retorted that the United States drew its prosperity from an economic system of sound principles, one that had proven effective throughout the entire history of the nation. The problem facing the country was that government had transgressed its proper boundaries. Reagan pledged to "restore to the federal government the capacity to do the people's work without dominating their lives." Unfettered by an intrusive government, the economy would respond in its typical manner. The U.S. economy "for more than 200 years has helped us master a continent, create a previously undreamed-of-prosperity for our people and has fed millions of others around the globe and that [economic] system will continue to serve us in the future if our government will stop ignoring the basic values on which it was built." As this explanation intimated, Reagan contrasted the values of family, work, and neighborhood to expansive government institutions and action. Prosperity depended on these basic nongovernmental values. Reagan committed himself to fostering their renewal, to restoring, "in our time, the American spirit of voluntary service, of cooperation, of private and community initiative, a spirit that flows like a deep and mighty river through the history of our nation." In contrast, his opponent in the campaign, President Carter, merely uttered "the same tired proposals for more government tinkering, more meddling, and more control—all of which led us to this sorry state in the first place."[21] Reagan sought to bring government under control by reducing or eliminating programs that wasted taxpayer money and by lowering tax rates that produced economic stagnation.

The Reagan administration sought answers to the economic woes in a program referred to as "supply-side economics." Supply-siders countered the claims of Keynesians by focusing on productive capital rather than consumer purchasing power as the key to economic revival. They wished to gear government policies toward increasing supply and believed that demand would follow. Supply-siders contended that the decision to boost the prospects of consumers or capitalists was a crucial one because the poor tended to disrupt the relationship between supply and demand. They pointed to consumer inefficiency as an explanation for stagflation: "Prices rise because the money to buy is there, but employment does not rise because the money is not spent in productive ways."[22] Drawing on the theories of economist Arthur Laffer, supply-siders also held that federal tax policies, especially top-bracket tax rates on income and investment, discouraged economic growth. The Laffer Curve graphically depicted an obvious relationship between tax rates and government revenues and, for that reason, was essentially useless. It represented the fact that at extreme rates of taxation, such as zero or 100 percent, the government would receive no revenue. But the shape of the curve cannot be deduced from this general truism. Should one draw it as a half circle or an increasing/decreasing slope?[23] Supply-siders argued that tax rates had already surpassed a point of diminishing returns: lowered taxes would spark greater economic activity, larger pools of taxable earnings, and increased government revenue.

Supply-side policies do, in fact, cut taxes. But supply-siders believed that tax cuts engendered economic revival as a matter of faith. David Stockman, director of the Office of Management and Budget, conceded this basis in a series of interviews with journalist William Greider: "The whole thing is premised on faith, on a belief about how the world works."[24] He trusted that dramatic action by the president would signal to investors the dawning of a new era. When confronted with alternative scenarios in congressional hearings, Stockman defended this conviction. In one instance he responded to a Congressional Budget Office study that concluded that the policies of the Reagan administration would have little effect on inflation and unemployment but increase the deficit. He retorted: "Now, my problem with that is that it essentially says that this entire shift in economic policy will have no effect on the economy. And I don't believe that. I think that there is where the basic difference lies."[25] Administration officials articulated the goals of the budget proposals in terms of public feeling. For instance, in testimony to the Senate Finance Committee and the House Subcommittee on Public Assistance and Unemployment Compensation, labor secretary Raymond Donovan stated that the proposals were designed "first and foremost" to "break the inflationary psychology that pervades the economy."[26] To the House Ways and Means Committee, he justified the efficacy of the administration's policies with deeply held belief: "I would like you to judge me on my love for my country and my belief in the free enterprise system, both labor and management. I think that's the answer I could give to most all of the questions that were asked."[27]

Like the preachers of the Gospel of Wealth, supporters of the proposed budget cuts also drew on different conceptions of human nature and the benevolence of wealth. Piven and Cloward write that the Reagan proposals constituted a coherent theory of human nature and drives. According to this theory, "[t]he affluent exert themselves in response to rewards — to the incentive of increased profitability yielded by lower taxes. Working people respond only to punishment — to the economic insecurity that will result from reductions in the income support programs."[28] Yet advocates of reduced social spending believed that punishment was seldom carried out and then only as instruction, for capitalism was inherently altruistic.

This theme received extensive treatment in George Gilder's 1981 book *Wealth and Poverty,* which some reviewers called the "bible" of the Reagan administration. David Stockman bought the book in bulk to give away copies.[29] Gilder insisted that "[c]apitalism begins with giving." One would not profit from greed, avarice, or self-love. Rather, "[t]he gifts [of capitalism] will succeed only to the extent that they are altruistic and spring from an understanding of the needs of others." Gilder recalled most explicitly the didacticism of Alger and the social theory of Carnegie and others. He defended the compassion of wealth and the fairness of material inequality. And like the preachers of the Gospel of Wealth before him, Gilder questioned the character of the poor: "The only dependable route from poverty is always work, family, and faith. The first principle is that in order to move up, the poor must not only work, they must work harder than the classes above them. Every previous generation of the lower class has made such efforts. But the current poor, white even more than black, are refusing to work hard."[30] Psychologies of scarcity, stagflation, supply-side economics, and a renewed faith in a contemporary Gospel of Wealth enabled the Reagan administration's attack on welfare—a function of government putatively rife with waste, fraud, and abuse. Its attack proceeded quickly, employing a legislative tool called reconciliation.

Coordination and Speed in the Budgeting Process

In the weeks after his inauguration, President Reagan announced a series of proposed budget cuts in a host of federal programs. Just six months later, on 13 August, he signed OBRA into law. The act cut $35.2 billion from the fiscal year 1982 budget, including $1.2 billion from AFDC. According to the Department of Health and Human Services, the legislation dropped 408,000 families from the AFDC program altogether and cut the benefits of another 279,000. OBRA not only reduced funding, it altered provisions of the law affecting benefit calculations, eligibility requirements, "workfare" programs, accounting procedures, and child-support enforcement.[31] Employed AFDC recipients felt these changes most directly. OBRA established a cap on eligibility to families whose monthly income exceeded 150 percent of a state's need standard, effectively eliminating families with high work expenses.[32] It limited the earned income disregard, which amounted to thirty dollars plus one-third of a recipient's gross monthly income, to four months and lowered the calculation base from gross to net monthly income. It imposed standard deductions for work expenses at $75 and childcare expenses at $160 per month. Previously, recipients could deduct the total cost of reasonable expenses in both areas. Some of the other provisions included counting food stamps and housing subsidies as income when calculating benefits, counting a portion of the income of stepparents living with a child, denying AFDC benefits to families with a striking worker, and basing grant amounts on previous-month actual expenses rather than future-month prospective circumstances. These and other changes removed hundreds of thousands of families from the program and reduced the monetary incentive of paid labor for those who remained.[33]

OBRA's passage culminated a budget approval process characterized by a level of speed and coordination previously unknown to federal budget policy. One observer likened the actions of the White House to an "imposed discipline akin to that of a military chain of command."[34] Edwin Meese, a cabinet-level counselor to the president, served as the White House's field general, overseeing political maneuvers that sought quick decisions on spending reductions before potential antagonists could form opposing coalitions. Some spending decisions preceded appointments of high-ranking officials, who might have developed loyalties to their departments. As the administration named cabinet officers, it appointed deputies with closer ties to the White House than their secretaries. In any case, the Reagan administration expected secretaries to argue their case before the Congress and the public, rather than defend their departments' needs before the president. Appointees in the Department of Health and Human Services, for example, disavowed a view of their department as the federal staging area for the advancement of a populist-liberal, Great Society agenda.[35]

An important field general for the administration in the Congress was Sen. Pete Domenici, who became chairperson of the Budget Committee after the Republicans gained a Senate majority in the November elections. Viewing the election results as a mandate for slowed growth in the federal budget, Domenici employed a legislative tool known as reconciliation to enforce a hurried timetable for writing the fiscal year 1982 budget. He defended the Senate's accelerated schedule by insisting that "extraordinary times demand extraordinary efforts."[36]

Domenici's counterpart in the House, Rep. James Jones (D-Okla.), encountered a more difficult and ultimately nonnegotiable path for House adoption of a committee-sponsored budget proposal. Despite his reputation as a builder of compromise, the newly elected chair of the Budget Committee could not fashion agreement among the divergent political perspectives within his party and without. Jones may have faced an impossible situation, as a bipartisan coalition of conservatives buoyed by congressional perception of the popularity of the president and an anti-government public sentiment enabled passage of Reagan's budget. Electoral forces strengthened the conservatives' position. The Democratic Party suffered a decrease in its House majority in the "solid South" from 81–27 in 1977 to 69–39 in 1981. Some remaining Democrats emphasized ideology over party affiliation, forming the Conservative Democratic Forum with other party conservatives. The forum's leader, Rep. Charles Stenholm (Tex.), explained that "there is a place for conservative Democrats in the party, but we need to do more to be seen and heard."[37] On budget matters, many of these conservatives saw their interests represented in the Reagan proposals. The administration actively re-cruited House conservatives in a successful effort to overcome a nominal Democratic majority.

If administration officials and members of Congress served as field generals and soldiers in the budget-cutting campaign, then its chief strategist undoubtedly was David Stockman, director of the Office of Management and Budget (OMB). A representative from Michigan in the 96th Congress, Stockman first gained attention in the budget debates as author of a widely cited and influential post-election memo entitled "Avoiding a GOP Economic Dunkirk." Warning of potential economic disaster, Stockman exhorted that "if bold policies are not swiftly, deftly, and courageously implemented in the first six months, Washington will quickly become engulfed in political disorder commensurate with the surrounding economic disarray." He saw only one way to prevent a dis-solution of the "incipient Republican majority": an economic program so "bold, sweeping, and sustained" that it "totally dominates the Washing-ton agenda during 1981" and promises to engender a bullish economic psychology. [38] In subsequent reflection, Stockman called the "Dunkirk" memo his resume for the OMB position.[39] As director, he orchestrated the Reagan budget cuts. In early 1981, a "black book" of Stockman's pro-posed cuts became "the hottest document to leak from Capitol Hill in re-cent years." Observers referred to Stockman as the "34-year-old 'whiz kid'" of the Reagan administration.[40] Garry Wills described him as "a throwback to the Kennedy years of bustling competence, when Robert McNamara seemed a walking computer, radiating certitude."[41] Stock-man himself envisioned a fundamental shift in federal policy. He asserted to a group of interviewers that "[w]e cannot fund the Great Society. Sub-stantial parts of it will have to be heaved overboard."[42]

Still, Stockman's vision had to be enacted, and the most important "participant" in this process may not have been a field general or strate-gist but a congressional budgeting tool known as reconciliation. Recon-ciliation came into effect through the 1974 Congressional Budget and Im-poundment Control Act, which created procedures for the production of a coordinated federal budget. Prior to the 1974 act, the federal budget emerged through the aggregated individual spending decisions of con-gressional committees. Legislation in the 1920s authorized the president to submit to Congress an annual budget, but the House and Senate parceled out its legislative proposals to an appropriations committee in each house, which set dollar limits for government programs, and multiple authorizing committees, which established the legal basis for government programs.[43]

The 1974 act specified an ordered process for congressional budget making. It also created a Budget Committee in each house to coordinate policy and a Congressional Budget Office to provide staff expertise. The act required each Budget Committee by 15 April to report to the House and Senate floors a first concurrent budget resolution to be approved by 15 May. The first resolution set targets for appropriations, spending, revenues, deficits, and the federal debt. Only after its approval were committees, which continued to focus on particular components of the overall budget, allowed to bring bills to the floor. The act further mandated that by 15 September Congress adopt a second budget resolution that either affirmed or revised the targets set in the first resolution. The act permitted a reconciliation process that enjoined committees whose actions were considered inconsistent with the dollar limits of the second resolution to amend or rescind legislation. It instructed the Budget Committees to package without change the work of affected committees into a single reconciliation act. The 1974 act, however, failed to reduce federal spending. The Budget Committees initially refrained from adopting resolutions that would have forced committees to compete for limited funds, preferring instead to defer to committee requests. An effort to balance the fiscal year 1981 budget by attaching reconciliation instructions to the first resolution stalled amidst a developing recession and election-year politics.[44]

Building on the failed attempt of the previous year, supporters of the Reagan cuts employed reconciliation early in the budget process as a strategy for gaining approval of the president's budget. In late March, just two weeks after Reagan sent his proposed budget reductions to Congress, the Senate Budget Committee reported to the full body a reconciliation bill cutting $36.9 billion in fiscal year 1982 spending. On 2 April the Senate overwhelmingly approved the measure—nearly two months before adopting its first budget resolution. The House Budget Committee attached reconciliation instructions to its first budget resolution, which contained $15.8 billion in budget cuts. Many House members denounced the proposal as inadequate. On 7 May, sixty-three Democrats joined all Republicans in voting for an alternative sponsored by conservatives Delbert Latta (R-Ohio) and Phil Gramm (D-Tex.) that cut $36.6 billion from the fiscal 1982 budget. The result was reported as a vote of confidence in Reagan's economic recovery program.[45]

In the following weeks, House and Senate committees went to work carrying out the reconciliation instructions. By another overwhelming vote, the Senate on 25 June passed an omnibus reconciliation bill that reduced the fiscal 1982 budget by $38.1 billion. One day later, twenty-nine Democrats joined Republicans in a "stunning" 217–211 House vote to pass a second Gramm-Latta substitute that cut $37.3 billion in fiscal 1982 spending. Charging that its cuts were chimerical, Gramm-Latta II supporters rejected a Budget Committee omnibus reconciliation bill that would have cut fiscal 1982 spending by $37.7 billion. For some, the vote for the substitute suggested a bipartisan "coalition that can work the will of the president."[46] The House Democratic leadership reacted incredulously. The vote effectively abrogated the role of the House authorizing committees in the fiscal 1982 budget process.[47] The House and Senate approved a conference agreement at the end of July, enabling the president's August signature.

The quick action and effective coordination of the budget-cutters produced a truncated policy episode that restricted the input of advocates for the poor and enacted policy decisions that raised non-funding issues. The hurried schedule of the process shortened the witness lists of congressional committee hearings, an important public forum for advocates who may not have alternative access to legislators making policy decisions. In the view of many budget-cutters, advocates for the poor merited no deference. They treated these advocates as "just special interests, like all the others."[48] While supporters of food stamps and child nutrition turned, albeit with little success, to established anti-hunger coalitions to mobilize protest, low-income advocacy groups such as the Children's Defense Fund testified against the cuts but found themselves isolated in defending AFDC. The breadth and momentum of the Reagan proposals distracted more powerful allies of low-income programs such as organized labor. At the outset of the budget-cutting debates, AFL-CIO lobbyist Peggy Taylor conceded that "[a]s our basic programs are threatened, we will have to spend a great deal more time on those, and perhaps be more of a supplement on food stamps and so on, rather than playing a leadership role."[49] As advocates for the poor struggled for a voice in the proceedings, the speed of the process permitted little time for deliberation on the substantive policy changes enacted in putative budgeting decisions. To save money in AFDC, for example, legislators could have reduced the federal reimbursement rate by a few percentage points. Instead, OBRA altered eligibility conditions and methods for determining grants.[50]

Two February speeches by President Reagan contributed significantly to establishing a framework for subsequent congressional debate over OBRA. Much of this debate took place in committee hearings. The Public Assistance and Unemployment Compensation Subcommittee of the House Ways and Means Committee, the House authorizing committee responsible for AFDC and other public assistance programs, held hearings in mid-March, shortly after Reagan sent his package of proposed cuts to the Congress but six weeks before conservative House Democrats joined Republicans in passing Gramm-Latta I. The Senate Finance Committee, the Senate authorizing committee with jurisdiction over AFDC, considered the proposed cuts directly, hearing from witnesses in the weeks before and after the Senate Budget Committee reported reconciliation instructions on 23 March. Arguments may have seemed more pressing in the Finance hearings as the cuts appeared as a tangible prospect, but both sets of hearings, conducted before either the House or Senate acted as a body, provided participants opportunities to determine program needs amid calls for reduction and to support or oppose proposed cuts in anticipation of budget resolutions. The floor debates and additional statements advanced throughout this policy episode marked continuities that indicated important qualities of the debate, including competing demographies of the AFDC population. The varied receptions of these demographies arose partly from their comparative positioning to the argumentative nexus of the budget debates. Reagan's February speeches served as an early, frame-setting articulation of this nexus.

Shifting Frames of Reference: Reagan's Speeches of 5 and 18 February

Reagan's calls for reduced social welfare spending relied partially on a vision of social order and interpersonal relations that drew its vibrancy from a celebration of the market and a repudiation of the perceived ills of government. His proposed cuts emerged within the argumentative nexus through which this vision took shape. Situating specific proposals as part of a cogently expressed vision distinguished Reagan's AFDC demography from competing versions. This may have explained the ultimate success of his remarkable attempt to shift frames of reference for deliberation of social welfare policy. For Reagan, the crucial question was not "What can we do for the poor?" but "How can we stop the 'spiraling' costs of these social programs?"

The president's initial calls for social spending reductions and their discursive context appeared in two speeches outlining his plans for economic recovery, which he delivered in the weeks after his inauguration: one from the Oval Office on 5 February and another from the chamber of the House of Representatives on 18 February. Commentary in the days between the speeches suggested a recognition of the fundamental shifts called for by the new president. In anticipation of Reagan's 18 February address, one observer noted a perception on Capitol Hill that Reagan "had confronted Congress with a set of decisions on domestic policy that were probably of greater magnitude than any since the early New Deal period."[51] Acknowledging the contested status of Reagan's economic proposals, reports nonetheless identified in the reception of his speeches a public desire to shift course in social welfare policy. For its part, the White House disclosed that of the 1,253 people who telephoned the night of and morning after the 18 February speech, 1,073 supported Reagan.[52] Television critic Tom Shales fawned that though his good for the nation had not yet been determined, "Ronald Reagan sure is good for television." Reviewing the 18 February speech, Shales described Reagan's appearance as "resolute, bold, dynamic" in contrast to a Congress that seemed "calculated and political."[53]

The speeches previewed the tripartite call for budget, tax, and regulatory cuts that Reagan and his supporters would champion for the next six months. His speech before the Congress introduced many Americans to the idea of a social "safety net"; it was the first of many public commitments by Reagan and administration officials to preserve such a net. Both speeches divided participants in social welfare programs into the truly needy and others—cheats, shirkers, and double-dippers—a division that received substantial subsequent amplification. The speeches were a significant early articulation of the vision that dominated the ensuing budget deliberations as well as welfare policy debates for Reagan's entire presidency.

Reagan proceeded quickly in the opening portions of his 5 February speech from describing a dire economic situation, to explaining its effects on the average worker, to decrying unnecessary government regulations, to judging the government responsible for the present economic woes. In Reagan's view, the country was experiencing "the worst economic mess since the Great Depression."[54] As support, he enlisted "attention getters" from a previously requested and recently completed audit: "runaway" deficits, $80 billion in annual interest payments on the national debt, a government payroll that had increased more than fivefold in twenty years, "back-to-back" years of "double-digit" inflation, 15 percent mortgage rates, increased taxes, and high unemployment. He warned that the nation's ailing economy threatened the American dream: "[Today], fewer than 1 out of 11 families can afford to buy their first home." Yet, as intermingled references to government payrolls and taxes suggested, Reagan did not blame autonomous economic forces. His next sentence intimated the culprit: "Regulations adopted by government with the best of intentions have added 666 dollars to the cost of an automobile." In an abrupt transition, Reagan linked economic woes to government actions. Two sentences later, he made explicit the implicit series of associations that had been established: "I'm sure you're getting the idea that the audit presented to me found government policies of the last few decades responsible for our economic troubles."[55] In addition to the troubles caused by regulation, he explained, government spending produced inflation. Reagan's "language" defending this position enacted a shift in frames of reference.

"We are the victims of language." The statement implied a suspicion of language, a desire to escape its coloring, distorting effects so that one could speak his or her mind directly and authentically. Reagan's speech text manifested an unease and yet comfort within the confines of language. One discerned the actor wishing to free himself from the script. But this cry of victimization signaled a shift in political language, not its abandonment. Reagan asserted that "[w]e are the victims of language. The very word 'inflation' leads us to think of it as just high prices. Then, of course, we resent the person who puts on the price tags, forgetting that he or she is also a victim of inflation." Ostensibly speaking free of the colorations of language, Reagan revalued the perpetrator of high prices as its victim. His rearticulation also created a shared bond between shopper and shopkeeper against the agent actually responsible. A similar reversal rebuked advocates who looked to business and industry to bear the brunt of economic recovery:

> [B]usiness doesn't pay taxes. Oh, don't get the wrong idea. Business is being taxed, so much so that we're being priced out of the world market. But business must pass its costs of operations — and that includes taxes — on to the customer in the price of the product. Only people pay taxes, all the taxes. Government just uses business in a kind of sneaky way to help collect the taxes.

This explanation reified business practice—particular profit margins must be maintained against any encroachments—blocking questions of economic justice. In the process, it absolved industry of culpability in the present economic conditions. Yet Reagan added that one should not cast suspicious eyes on the employee. He stated plainly his belief in the superiority of the "American working man or woman against anyone in the world."[56] Taxes and regulations hobbled this worker and harmed the economy.

Reagan gainsaid alternative explanations for the economic woes plaguing the nation. The causes lay in government spending—not in the individual businessperson, larger abstractions such as industry, nor in the American worker. Previous administrations and politicians talked about lowering spending, but none acted seriously: "Well, you know, we can lecture our children about extravagance until we run out of voice and breath. Or we can cure their extravagance simply by reducing their allowance." Reagan insisted that genuine action would resolve the Keynesian dilemma. He promised his auditors that "[w]e don't have to choose between inflation and unemployment."[57] Reducing government spending by cutting budgets and eliminating waste and extravagance would accomplish both; reducing taxes would increase productivity.

"[L]anguage, as I said earlier, can get in the way of a clear understanding of what our program is intended to do," Reagan stated. After announcing his economic plan in broad strokes, just as he did after identifying the cause of economic woe, he called attention to the trickiness of language. His perceived sense of danger may have been even greater, for language now threatened to obscure the "actual" components of his plan. Pushing for a "real" understanding, Reagan explained that "[b]udget cuts can sound as if we're going to reduce total spending to a lower level than was spent the year before." On the contrary, he continued, "budgets will increase as our population increases." His reassurance implied that cuts in present rates of growth would wean those from government programs who ought not to be there. Once the calibration was right, growth would resume. Reagan articulated this implicit division shortly thereafter: "Our spending cuts will not be at the expense of the truly needy. We will, however, seek to eliminate benefits to those who are not really qualified by reason of need." Yet this qualification suggested that more than a calibration was in order. In this way, the non-needy were assigned ultimate responsibility for the country's economic woes. Reagan invoked them as the sole example of government waste. Even the truly needy did not escape suspicion, for Reagan singled out the poor as a group to be examined for waste and fraud. He affirmed his commitment to help those in need, but this commitment stood prominently apart from "the other legitimate responsibilities of government." Reagan spoke more abstractly as he concluded his speech. He returned to larger issues of "inflation, lower productivity, and uncontrolled government growth," opposing them to "the freedom of all men and women to excel and to create." He challenged the nation to increase its wealth "so all will have more."[58]

In his 18 February speech before Congress, Reagan amplified his distinction between the truly needy and others. As he had two weeks earlier, Reagan enlisted a series of statistics and examples to convey the weakened state of the economy. He described its impact on the average worker. Then he focused on the three ills hurting the economy: taxes, government spending, and government regulations. Consoling his auditors that the nation did not face structural problems, he located failure in "a lack of confidence and sometimes through a belief that we could fine-tune the economy." The soundness of the system enabled a four-point plan based on the internal strengths of the American economy and its people. Reagan described his plan as "aimed at reducing the growth in government spending and taxing, reforming and eliminating regulations which are unnecessary and unproductive or counterproductive, and encouraging a consistent monetary policy aimed at maintaining the value of the currency."[59] If enacted, he promised, the plan would create jobs and control inflation.

Shortly after introducing his economic plan and much earlier than in his previous speech, Reagan reiterated his division of the poor into the truly needy and others. Acknowledging the concern aroused by "exaggerated and inaccurate stories about these [budget] cuts," Reagan welcomed "this opportunity to set things straight." He asserted that the nation would continue to meet obligations of conscience. He promised that "[t]hose who, through no fault of their own, must depend on the rest of us—the poverty stricken, the disabled, the elderly, all those with true need—can rest assured that the social safety net of programs they depend on are exempt from any cuts." Eight programs fell into the safety net: social security benefits; Medicare; supplemental income for the blind, aged, and disabled; veterans' pensions; school breakfasts and lunches; nutrition for the aging; Head Start; and summer youth jobs. AFDC did not make the list, for groups of non-needy populated the program. Reagan insisted that "government will not continue to subsidize individuals or particular business interests where real need cannot be demonstrated." AFDC required "tighten[ing]." Program administrators needed to focus more intently on outside sources of income and legislators needed to implement "strong and effective work requirements."[60] These references to tightening, outside income, and work requirements adumbrated the composition of the AFDC population—cheats, double-dippers, and shirkers—that Reagan and his supporters would portray as debates continued through August.

After a brief interlude, Reagan returned to the three ills that began his speech. On waste and fraud in government, the president labeled the problem "an unrelenting national scandal, a scandal we're bound and determined to do something about." The speech assumed a more celebratory tone after this passage as Reagan launched into a paean about the strength of the American individual. He commanded that it was time to "give the American people room to do what they do best." He promised that a growing economy would create productive, not "make-work" jobs. This concluding portion revealed that Reagan's sympathies lay with the worker:

> The substance and prosperity of our nation is built by wages brought home from the factories and the mills, the farms, and the shops. They are the services provided in the 10,000 corners of America; the interest on the thrift of our people and the returns for their risk-taking. The production of America is the possession of those who build, serve, create, and produce.[61]

Though supporters and members of his administration may have been committed to supply-side economics, this statement reflected Reagan's allegiances: to the heroic individual, the risk-taker, the cowboy. Reagan's paean also exhibited a sermonic tone. The president acted as a "secular pastor" who sought to bolster the nation's confidence that its people could overcome the ills currently plaguing the economy. According to Kurt Ritter and David Henry, this pastoral voice served as a significant component of Reagan's presidential oratory. Ritter and Henry describe Reagan's frequent celebration of the citizen-hero as a strategy by which he sustained this persona.[62] The heroic individual resided in the "10,000 corners of America."

Multiple associations of equivalence and contrariety structured Reagan's two February speeches. In *The Philosophy of Literary Form,* Kenneth Burke stresses the importance of these relationships for discovering the "*fundamentals* of structure." He advises his critically inclined readers to explicate series of likeness and difference within literary works, including "development *from what through what to what.*"[63] Burke regards these chains of association and dissociation as revelatory of symbolic action: the capacity of language forms to manifest beliefs and values and also to make claims upon their readers and auditors. Reagan's two speeches began with the same associational cluster. He described economic malady, explained its impact on the average worker, shifted abruptly to a complaint about the present operations of government, and proceeded to a judgment of government responsibility for the country's economic woes. In this way, both speeches linked economic troubles to government action.

The major associational clusters in the two speeches circulated around the American people and the federal government. Reagan particularized the American people in the individual worker, to whom he pledged his unwavering confidence. Though they often have been viewed as adversaries in American popular and political culture, Reagan, through a sequence of reversals, linked this worker with the business operator and American industry itself. The president, of course, attached himself to this cluster. The second major cluster consisted of the federal government, politicians, non-needy participants in social welfare programs, and their defenders in the federal bureaucracy. Displayed as an equation, these two structural associations of Reagan and his opposition appeared as follows: American people = individual worker = business operator = American industry = Ronald Reagan ≠ federal government = non-needy (cheats, double-dippers, shirkers) = politicians = bureaucrats.

This structure abstracted government from the people, portraying it as an oppressive agent that acted upon Americans. This associational structure reified the economy, deemed it "off-limits," and yet made it compassionate. This transformation blocked questions of social justice. The truly needy, who do not appear in my equation, occupied an ambivalent position in Reagan's associational structure. To the extent that the truly needy received help out of an obligation borne from a national conscience, they could have been considered Americans who had fallen on hard times. And yet their participation in AFDC, a government program, attached this group to notorious politicians and bureaucrats. Moreover, the prominent position occupied by programs for the poor in discussions of waste and abuse threatened to conflate Reagan's most explicit dissociation—the truly needy from the non-needy—casting doubt on the neediness of even the truly needy. As Burke notes, to ask a question is to select a field of controversy and to deflect attention from others.[64] Reagan's two speeches divided the poor, made all poor people suspect, and linked government programs for the poor to the nation's economic troubles. To a considerable degree, Reagan's two speeches established the frame of reference and defined many of the terms of the policy debate that ensued over the next six months.

Contesting Demographies of the AFDC Population: Representing the Non-Needy

The competing demographies of the AFDC population emerged through the participation of multiple parties in the budget debates. In subsequent speeches and exchanges with reporters, Reagan stated throughout the debates his views of AFDC and its recipients, including experiences as governor of California that he deemed instructive for the nation. Legislators used committee hearings to support and oppose the administration proposals. Senator Moynihan may have been the most vocal opponent on the Senate Finance Committee, bemoaning the subdued opposition of much of the Washington lobbying apparatus. Witnesses such as the Children's Defense Fund and the American Federation of State, County, and Municipal Employees defended public assistance programs, but other forces trumped their appeals for children. Administration officials appeared regularly before congressional committees to advance the proposals. David Stockman sought to assure legislators of the soundness of the cuts. Cabinet secretaries such as Health and Human Services secretary Richard Schweiker testified as dutiful supporters of administration proposals that promised to reduce their influence in social policy. Floor debates provided continuous commentary on the status of the proposals, and witnessed the appearance of competing demographies at critical procedural junctures, such as Latta and Gramm's entreaties to colleagues to support their budget alternatives.

My explication of these demographies includes the views of these critical actors as well as others, whose statements suggested the widespread deployment of this imagery. I do not, however, develop the particular contexts of individual utterances. My reconstruction abstracts these statements from their specific moments of articulation to connect them analytically to larger discourses of welfare policy arising from the legislative

and political context of the budget debates. The significance of these individual statements lay in their participation in circulating demographies,
which in turn represented a significant quality of this first episode of a
policy trajectory that culminated in repeal of AFDC.

Reagan and his supporters spent little time characterizing the truly
needy. Aside from vague and passing references, proponents of the budget cuts did not offer portrayals of the circumstances, behaviors, motivations, or struggles of the people for whom the safety net would remain
intact, save a general condition of faultlessness. This lack of detail contributed to a reinvention of the power of poor people that facilitated the
dismantling purposes of the Reagan administration. In contrast, Reagan
and others offered detailed accounts of the non-needy — the cheats, shirkers, and double-dippers whom they believed populated the AFDC rolls in
large numbers. Moments of inconsistency notwithstanding, they deployed these images as forceful evidence demonstrating that the spending reductions would be painless.

In the morning after his address to Congress, Reagan invoked the image of the welfare cheat at a breakfast with newspaper and television news
editors. Responding to a question about improved efficiency in social services, Reagan recounted his experiences as governor of California. He
recalled that despite determined efforts to reduce the state budget, "all the
savings we were making, all the economies, were being eaten by welfare."
Reagan explained that denying the insatiable appetites of the welfare
cheat entailed a fight: HEW forced California to adhere to multiple rules
and regulations that frustrated its efforts to determine the number of
people participating in welfare programs. He complained that "[t]hey
only know how many checks they're sending out, and then we turn up
a woman in Chicago that's getting checks under 127 different names. And
just recently in Pasadena, California, living in a lovely big home there,
a woman was brought in and charged with collecting $300,000 in a wel-
fare scheme."[65]

Other advocates detailed less fantastic but equally maddening tales of
deceit. In deliberations on the chamber floor, Sen. Daniel Inouye relayed
a scandalous story of fraud involving AFDC work-expense deductions.
The case implicated a self-employed Hawaiian architect whose gross income totaled $36,000 annually. Inouye enumerated his itemized deduc-
tions: "the costs of leasing a car for $175 a month, the no-fault insurance
policy, business trips to neighbor islands, entertainment expenses such as
purchasing flower leis and lunches for his clients, gasoline expenses

incurred as a result of the business, and so forth."[66] After dishonestly deducting expenses faced by legitimate operators of small businesses, this ostensibly self-sufficient architect qualified for and received AFDC benefits. Policymakers repeated Inouye's anecdote. In this example and others, exposed fraud intimated widespread cheating. Other participants told of the way that food stamps, received by many AFDC participants, functioned as a "second currency" for the purchase of stereos, cars, and illegal drugs.[67]

These advocates maintained that fraud had become normal practice in social programs. Testifying before the House Subcommittee on Public Assistance and Unemployment Compensation, Health and Human Services secretary Richard Schweiker suggested that "unfortunately, an ethic has developed in our social programs that a little cheating goes a long way, and if you cheat that is OK. And I think that is what is killing us, as much as the direct obligations."[68] Schweiker claimed that the largest drain on the economy and government over the last three decades was the spiraling costs of social programs. He insisted that reining in these costs would be his top priority, which would not only expose the worst of the cheaters but announce a new ethos of honesty and integrity in social welfare policy. He described an additional measure to the Senate Finance Committee: a national recipient information system. When Sen. Max Baucus informed the secretary that a "data bank of the poor" struck him as "authoritarian" and "a little bit unbalanced," Schweiker reiterated his intention to level off the social spending curve. Besides, "the only ones that, I think, we are really going to hurt by these proposals are the people that have been abusing the system."[69]

Schweiker and others insisted that welfare cheats themselves inflicted serious injury. Articulating a frequent retort to critics of the budget cuts, Rep. John Rousselot explained that the administration "want[s] to make sure that those who are truly needy do not in effect pay for the abuses that have occurred in some of these programs."[70] A sense of personal injury pervaded many of the statements of the budget-cutters. In a vivid example of this quality of the deliberations, Rep. Edward Madigan recalled how, for nine years, he had watched the majority party "destroy savings with inflation, weaken our economy, and create the biggest regulatory mess in history." Madigan added an explicitly criminal dimension to charges of widespread fraud advanced by some of his colleagues. He scoffed that "[e]very time I hear a Democratic leader use the word 'compassion' I check to see if my wallet is still there."[71]

Parodies by politicians opposed to the cuts evidenced the prominence of welfare cheat imagery within policy-making forums and in daily life. Pete Stark, chairperson of the Subcommittee on Public Assistance and Unemployment Compensation, invited one witness back to his district during committee hearings. He asked the witness to come to Alameda County, California, to help him locate "this woman, and for some reason it is a woman, who is ahead of each one of my constituents in the check-out line at a supermarket and has bought a tremendous amount of Per-rier and chickens. Actually, they are never chickens; they are Cornish game hens stuffed with wild rice. A whole carton of these go into the trunk of … a new Cadillac." Stark admitted some frustration, but an-nounced that he had devised a plan to stop this woman and others who may have been tempted to follow her example: "I have a bill that I am about to introduce that would make it a felony for a Cadillac salesman to accept food stamps in full or partial payment for the Cadillac."[72]

The image of the double-dipper—the person receiving multiple ben-efits from different agencies—did not take shape through fantastic cases of excess and disturbing stories of fraud. Instead, the double-dipper ma-terialized in cool, restrained, analytic language that purported to offer an objective view of the economic situation of many AFDC recipients. A principal explicator of the double-dipper was David Stockman. In testi-mony before the Senate Finance Committee, Stockman held that to understand the level of benefits provided to people participating in social welfare programs, one needed to take into account an array of benefits in addition to cash assistance. When one considered other, in-kind pro-grams, the number of people living in poverty declined sharply:

> If you measure only cash income there are today, or in 1980, 18 million people below the poverty line, more than 8.6 percent of the popula-tion. If you then modify that basic measure, which is the statistic we normally see in the census statistics, to include all in-kind assistance, other than medical assistance, the poverty population drops from 8.6 percent to 5.9 percent. And then if you take it one step further and fac-tor in the in-kind medical assistance that we provide through Medic-aid and to some degree Medicare, the poverty population drops still further to 3.9 percent of the population.

Stockman held that federal welfare policies ignored this support network. As a result, they perpetuated "an undermeasurement … of the amount of support we are providing to the low-income families in this country." Undermeasurement did not mean that an adequate array of programs went unappreciated, however. Stockman asserted that present ways of thinking about poverty obfuscated an overly generous welfare apparatus. From this premise, he argued that welfare officials ought to include the cash value of in-kind benefits when determining the income of a welfare recipient. In the language of a management efficiency consultant, Stockman summarized his recommendations: "Benefit integration and cost reduction, better targeting of benefits to those who really have a strong claim on the federal government and can establish a clear need for this kind of assistance."[73]

The implication of widespread double-dipping was clear: the cuts would not affect the truly needy. Richard Rahn, vice president and chief economist for the U.S. Chamber of Commerce, stated this view plainly before the Senate Finance Committee: "We find that with most of these social programs you have tremendous duplication.... And when you are cutting back a program, it does not mean that you are eliminating people who have real needs."[74] When Senator Dole asked for Schweiker's reaction to reports that several hundred thousand families would be affected by the cuts in AFDC, the secretary deployed an arithmetic similar to Stockman's. He explained that of the 658,000 families whose benefits would be either eliminated or reduced, 375,000 would still have incomes above the poverty line if one considered the monetary value of their food stamps. Another 283,000 families would be unaffected if one considered stepparent income when determining benefit amounts and assumed eighteen-year-olds were eligible for work. Of the remaining 70,000 affected families, Schweiker noted that 20,000 would not be eligible by the proposed definition if they were new applicants. Only 50,000 families really would be affected: "But they will still be better off than some other low-income families who chose not to participate in AFDC." He added that his calculations did not take into account federally subsidized housing, which probably would have lowered the number of affected families even more. In various appearances before congressional committees, Schweiker frequently responded to questions about the severity of the cuts by referring to the prevalence of double-dipping. For instance, in defense of proposed 25 percent reductions in preventive health services, including popular child and maternal health programs, he asserted that multiple programs addressed the same need. "There is now duplication of coverage," he insisted, "That is why we are going through the roof at 300 billion dollars [in present-day social spending]."[75]

The image of the shirker—the person evading work and responsibility
—often informed the budget debates obliquely. The shirker frequently
appeared in passing, structuring discussion without becoming an explicit
object. Yet the image of the shirker enabled statements to be repeated like
mantras: the American people would not support those able to work;
paychecks ought to be more easily obtainable than welfare checks. The
shirker turned up in Latta and Gramm's entreaties to colleagues to support their budget bill. Latta asserted that the vote represented a historic
opportunity for the House to redirect the unbroken upward curve of
"runaway spending" and "bloated deficits." Despite much "weeping and
wailing" from the promulgators of uncontrolled entitlement spending,
Latta insisted that social programs should return to a "common sense
system" of generous support for the truly needy. He admonished that
"[o]h, it would be nice, it would be nice if we could do all of this, that is,
if we could afford it. It would be nice if we could afford it, but we cannot
afford it. It would be nice if we could do this for everybody, let everybody
in on the gravy train, but we cannot afford it." Co-sponsor Gramm argued that their budget proposal would upend "the wagon in which an
ever-increasing number of Americans are riding."[76]

The shirker often heralded the return of the forgotten man. Latta demanded that his colleagues justify their unbridled extravagance to the
"poor individual back in my district who goes to work everyday, making
$4, $5, $6 an hour." The waste and indolence subsidized by his taxes frus-
trated and fettered this earnest worker. Gramm explained that for each
appropriation passed by Congress, the average beneficiary received $500
while the average worker paid fifty cents. But fifty-cent payments added
up. The worker had grown tired of laboring incessantly for special-
interest beneficiaries "looking over their right shoulders, writing back
home, and saying all kinds of things about the old, the sick, the tired."[77]
In these kinds of arguments, Sumner's principle of poor relief reemerged:
to give money to one party, however needy, one must take money unjustly from another party. Gramm and Latta maintained that cost did not
permit the unwarranted generosity of their colleagues, who wanted more
people to climb into the wagon or board the gravy train.

At times, the shirker became an explicit object of discussion as frustration boiled over what some advocates perceived as a refusal of AFDC
recipients to seek paid labor. In one Public Assistance Subcommittee
hearing, Rep. Skip Bafalis asked Barbara Blum, commissioner of the New
York State Department of Social Services, what agencies should do about
such slothful yet clever recipients. He queried: "What do you do about

the person who understands unemployment compensation and understands extended benefits and understands AFDC and every other program there is, and just doesn't want to work? Now, there are those people out there." Blum conceded that "[t]here are a few." Bafalis retorted: "There are a lot more than a few." He encouraged her to investigate a rural West Virginia county in which he ran a business, but did not represent. According to Bafalis, the county had plenty of available jobs paying between nine and twelve dollars per hour but many residents loitered along main street "absolutely refusing to work." Bafalis called Stark's parody of the welfare cheat "farfetched." He countered that "the average hard-working American who pays taxes, goes into that grocery store, stands in that line and sees people are physically able to work using food stamps to feed their families, and knows that there is work in the county is irritated." He found such laziness intolerable: "In my own case, I can go out and dig ditches and clean toilets before I go on the welfare line."[78]

Supporters of the cuts argued that the welfare system often turned productive citizens into shirkers. Sen. Jesse Helms illustrated this point by introducing into the *Record* a newspaper article titled "The Welfarization of a Productive Family." The article narrated the experiences of the Chhem family, Cambodian refugees who resettled in rural North Carolina. Though the family arrived with no money and no knowledge of English, they soon adapted to their new culture and began to prosper economically, saving more than $7,000 their first year and sending monthly checks to relatives still in Cambodia. The Chhems even managed to avoid seductive government agencies. Over time, their resistance collapsed. Eventually, the federally funded, Minnesota-based Cambodian Refugee Association persuaded the Chhems to quit their jobs at the local chicken house and move north. Ross Graves, a St. Paul volunteer, explained to the reporter writing the story that such agencies often recruited refugees to increase their political influence. Graves said that the Chhems' prospects were dim given the greater than 70 percent unemployment rate among refugees: "They're going straight on welfare."[79]

A particular depiction of the shirker presaged subsequent policy episodes: the AFDC recipient as a mother who avoided the dual responsibilities of non-AFDC, working mothers. This image appeared only a few times, but it intimated the future prominence of policymakers' changing expectations of women's roles that had begun in the 1960s. Rep. Thomas Petri argued that reducing the Work Incentive Program (WIN) registration age from mothers with children under six to mothers with children under three was "several years overdue." Petri explained that current

AFDC requirements did not keep pace with trends in the paid labor market. He cited Bureau of Labor statistics reporting that 55 percent of all mothers with children between the ages of three and six participated in the paid labor force. When asked how he would respond to those who said that age three through six was an important period for a mother to be with her child, Petri referred once more to present-day economic trends. He held that "[t]he majority of mothers in America have found that it doesn't hurt their children to do that. We are simply modernizing a law to bring it into accord with modern social realities." Rep. Henson Moore echoed these sentiments as he urged fellow committee members to focus not on ideal situations but survival. He reminded them of the pressures placed upon the forgotten (wo)man: "I think it may be a little bit unusual to give people on a federal program the ability to do something that our own working taxpayers don't have the opportunity to do."[80]

Opponents of the cuts, however, responded that middle-class women chose to enter the paid labor force. They argued that AFDC recipients ought to have the same choice. Nancy Campbell of the Center for Law and Social Policy testified on behalf of a wide-ranging coalition of women's groups arguing this position: "All of the groups that we represent believe that women should have an adequate income to take care of their children when they have chosen that as their work, and should have adequate opportunity for jobs and training when they wish to work outside the home."[81]

Cheats, double-dippers, and shirkers populated the AFDC rolls, contended Reagan and his supporters. Thus, the rapid increase in government spending over the last few decades could be abated without having an impact on the truly needy. Proponents of the cuts did not always advance this argument without reservation, however. In his testimony, Secretary Schweiker oscillated between viewing the cuts as affecting no one in need and seeing the cuts as a necessary though painful remedy. When Public Assistance Subcommittee chair Stark objected to his claim that reductions would be made in administrative overhead and not services, Schweiker conceded that services may be cut. He reminded the committee that "[w]e are trying to slow that [spending] curve down.... So there are areas where it will certainly be a painful process."[82] Schweiker's admission of certain pain implied that the cuts would affect the truly needy. These moments of inconsistency may have confounded the intentions of advocates, but they did not prompt qualifications of major claims.

Reagan found the evidence for his demography of the welfare population in his experiences as governor of California. As committee hearings and floor debates over his budget proposals proceeded, Reagan repeatedly recalled his past experiences with welfare reform when questioned by reporters. One such exchange took place on 6 March 1981. Reagan insisted that "[w]e never had a single case turn up after our welfare reforms, and some 350,000 people in that one state disappeared from the welfare rolls. We never had a single case of anyone suddenly appearing and saying, 'I am destitute. I've been cut off welfare.' As a matter of fact, most of those people disappeared of their own free will." For Reagan, the evidence of an AFDC population with a high proportion of non-needy lay in the fact that recipients seldom complained when their benefits were cut or reduced. Or, perhaps, the governor of California seldom heard recipients complain. Whatever the reason, Reagan construed this silence as irrefutable proof. He surmised that "when they just disappeared as the spotlight began to be turned on, possibly out of recognition that they were now going to be caught, the rolls just shrank. And it's this theory that is behind what we are doing."[83]

The president traced the uproar over proposed cuts to bureaucrats whose programs were threatened. On 6 March, he warned reporters of "attempts by those in the bureaucracy who are involved in some of these programs to suggest that there is great distress being caused by them [the proposed cuts]." In a 28 May question-and-answer session with state and local officials, Reagan described contemporaneous protests similarly. He charged that "most of the screams of pain that we're hearing are coming from the bureaucracy and not from the supposed victims of our cuts."[84] In these and other statements, Reagan reproduced the association between the non-needy and bureaucrats that he articulated in his two speeches announcing his economic recovery plan, raising doubts about the motivations of advocates opposed to the cuts.

Contesting Demographies of the AFDC Population: Representing the Voiceless

Opponents of the budget cuts countered depictions of non-neediness by describing an AFDC population of voiceless children and struggling recipients who paid their fair share of taxes. Testifying for the AFL-CIO, Burt Seidman reminded policymakers that "the fact of the matter is that millions of the most deprived children in our country depend on these social programs." Seidman and other advocates stressed the innocence and vulnerability of children—the child did not choose the situation of his or her birth. They insisted that even if one held their parents responsible for their poverty, poor children could not and should not be assigned blame. Disclosing a personal sense of shock, Albert Russo, coordinator of social services for the American Federation of State, County, and Municipal Employees, called the proposals the most "regressive, punitive, and unjust" that he had encountered in his professional experience. He exhorted: "AFDC is a program for children.... Punish their mothers, who are struggling valiantly to remain totally off AFDC by continuing to work, and whom do we really punish? We punish the children."[85]

Sen. Daniel Patrick Moynihan emphasized the young constituency of the AFDC program repeatedly to multiple witnesses and his colleagues in the Senate chamber. In an exchange with Robert Ball, former Social Security commissioner, he reported that of a cohort of children born in 1980, 52 percent would live in a single-parent, female-headed family before the age of eighteen and 32 percent would be supported by the AFDC program at some point in their youth. He concluded that "[i]t is, next to the public school, clearly the most important public program for children the country has." Yet, if "you listened to presidents and secretaries, and so forth, it's not just this one, at least, you would think that the population of the AFDC program consisted entirely of adult males."[86]

As Moynihan's remark intimated, advocates could not sustain calls to focus on the high percentage of children in the AFDC program. Rev. Timothy McDonald encountered such resistance in testimony before the Public Assistance Subcommittee. Reverend McDonald, assistant pastor of the Ebenezer Baptist Church, declared his belief that "America is too great a nation to allow itself to disregard the cries of innocent children as they look toward us with tear-stained eyes, wet diapers, pleading for help." Rep. John Rousselot retorted that "all of these [social] programs together have been escalating faster than any other parts of the federal programs, including defense." He pressed McDonald for alternative suggestions, to which the latter replied: "I want you to recall we are talking about children; we are not talking about able-bodied folks who can work; 75 percent of all the recipients who receive AFDC across this nation are children." Rousselot interjected: "Maybe I misunderstood it, but I think when you get to the numbers in AFDC, 70 percent are children, aren't they?" McDonald: "That is what I just said." Rousselot: "So then the 30 percent supposedly are able to work, so you don't mind us asking that they be encouraged to work?"[87] McDonald's reply that most AFDC recipients desired paid labor and another witness's assertion that raising children was one of the most important occupations one could have did not alter the import of this exchange: the stigma of the non-needy shadowed AFDC despite its predominantly youthful composition.

Opponents of the budget reductions charged that the voicelessness of AFDC children enabled the cuts. These advocates contended that cynical calculations of political leverage shaped the budget plan. Marion Wright Edelman, president of the Children's Defense Fund, reported her organization's assessment to the Senate Finance Committee: "Our basic conclusion is that children who don't vote and don't lobby, who are homeless and handicapped and poor are being unfairly hurt in the current Reagan proposals." Edelman and others asserted that the proposals placed children in competition with influential and well-organized constituencies, and they deployed this argument in defense of a variety of programs. Supporters of renewed categorical status for adoption assistance repeated it uniformly. John Calhoun of the Child Welfare League acknowledged the need for efficient management of social services. Yet the administration's goals of "local control and reduction of social service funding by 25 percent collide directly with … providing a safety net for the needy and support for the American family."[88] Comparatively fewer groups testified in this manner directly on behalf of AFDC. This relative silence prompted expressions of anger and distress from AFDC's supporters. Senator Moynihan conveyed to successive witnesses his dismay over the length of the witness lists—reconciliation pressures notwithstanding—for the budget hearings. He stressed that "it is fundamentally important that no one comes up here to speak about the subject."[89] He fumed that had the topic been "commodity tax squabbles," the hearing room would have been filled to capacity.

Advocates described an AFDC population that consisted not only of children but of diligent, earnest adults who did not earn a living wage despite their best efforts. Of the various witnesses who testified before the Senate Finance Committee and the House Public Assistance Subcommittee, Christine Pratt-Marston and Angela Sosnowski were the only two AFDC recipients; both women represented the National Anti-Hunger Coalition. Pratt-Marston introduced herself to House members in her multiple roles as single parent, foster parent, and taxpayer. Pratt-Marston recounted her attempts to end receipt of AFDC and survive solely on wages received from paid employment. But like millions of poor women, she discovered that "we cannot make it. We cannot pay for day care, we do not have health services for our children, and we cannot pay the rent or feed our children. So we find ourselves going back on welfare." She called comparisons of AFDC recipients to working poor offensive, for they implied that AFDC recipients do not work. She expressed frustration at the paradox forced upon many poor women. She objected that "[w]hen I am home taking care of my four children and two foster children, I am a lazy welfare broad. And when I go across the street and take care of my neighbor's one child, I am employed." Sosnowski amplified Pratt-Marston's statement. She identified her occupation as an assistant manager of a dairy farm, which paid $400 per month. Sosnowski explained that her community of Aiken County, Minnesota, suffered from chronic unemployment, with rates of 16 to 18 percent over the last four years. Few of the available jobs paid well. Still, 66 percent of adult AFDC recipients across Minnesota worked for wages. Sosnowski suggested that "[i]f more attention is given to developing the jobs, as opposed to punishing the participants, I think that the whole system will work a lot better."[90]

Pratt-Marston's self-identification as a taxpayer resonated with the statements of other advocates. They argued that AFDC recipients already paid taxes; the administration demanded unjustly that poor people should bear the brunt of the budget cuts. Edelman stated that "children have already paid 45 cents a day, or 12 percent of their total benefits to fight inflation."[91] Unlike retirees and Supplementary Security Income (SSI) recipients, AFDC children and their mothers did not receive automatic cost-of-living increases. She explained that as a result, the value of AFDC benefits had dropped precipitously over the last four years as inflation had soared. Chairperson Stark opened the Public Assistance Subcommittee hearings in parallel fashion. The president's budget required the Ways and Means Committee to raise revenues by cutting services and programs for the poor. He observed that "[t]hese cuts in programs that serve hundreds of thousands of truly needy Americans living below the poverty level are being made, we are told, so that we can provide a 30,000 dollar tax break to families with incomes of 200,000 dollars or more."[92] Rep. Robert Garcia termed "morally indefensible" the administration's insistence that the poor suffer a "grossly disproportionate share" of its imposed burden.[93] In vivid language, Rep. Henry Gonzalez decried the budget for "launch[ing] a war against inflation which is a rich man's war and a poor man's fight."[94]

Advocates found charges of waste and abuse disingenuous. Rep. Robert Kastenmeier disclosed that his constituents wondered "why some of our most important domestic programs are targeted for extinction, while the military establishment, despite heavily documented waste and abuse, is slated to receive huge budgetary increases."[95] Despite putative conservative anathema to such policies, opponents argued, the budget proposals called for income redistribution. Rep. Augustus Hawkins charged that the administration intended to "redistribute wealth, income, and power from the great body of the people into the hands of the privileged few."[96] These statements highlighted the political powerlessness of AFDC recipients. They suggested as well a recognition of the power of negative images to stand for the whole and engage historical animosities.

Reinventing the Power of the Poor

The contesting demographies of the 1981 budget debates did not receive equal support among advocates nor circulation within deliberative forums. Reagan's collection of cheats, shirkers, and double-dippers figured prominently in the debates while images of voiceless children and struggling recipients emerged only as a reaction to the administration's discursive reversals. In some respects, images of the voiceless may have bolstered Reagan's demography as a description of the precarious position of the truly needy. These varied receptions intimated the displacing tendencies of these constellations of images when deployed in conjunction with argumentative structures. As part of a larger nexus, the images of the cheat, shirker, and double-dipper transfigured positive images of the poor constructed in terms of right or obligation, such as rights-bearing citizens or members of a shared community, into appeals for sympathy. Rights-bearers make claims upon governments. Images of non-needy recipients exemplified the budget-cutters' view of government as an evil usurper of freedom and disqualified government as a legitimate site of appeal. Positive visions of the poor linked up with the American people in a private, voluntaristic capacity. Sometimes, as in the late 1960s, competing images command equal attention, but when the boundaries and terms of policy debate have been established, images that challenge prevailing assumptions attract little support. Reagan and his supporters reinvented the power of the poor so that it overtook a sense of duty to the voiceless, subordinating this peripheral sensibility to sympathetic portrayals that did not demand continued support.

The images of cheat, shirker, and double-dipper invited and frequently elicited strong feelings of hostility, frustration, fear, and suspicion among participants. Economic transformations of the 1970s halted growth in median family income, forcing many Americans to labor longer to maintain an already achieved standard of living. The cheat and shirker stood as the antithesis of hard labor. Representative Bafalis articulated a widespread mood of hostility when he recounted the "irritation" of "working" people who stood in grocery lines with AFDC recipients.[97] Representatives Latta and Gramm invoked this emotion as they persuaded their colleagues to support the forgotten man who pulled the wagon and fueled the gravy train. Hostility grew not only from perceived indolence but cleverness as well, for Bafalis explained that many AFDC recipients knew the system well. The double-dipper invited frustration at a government that enrolled people in multiple programs to cover the same need. Secretary Schweiker expressed this feeling as he relayed to House and Senate committees the limited options available to him as a result of duplicate benefits. All three images exhibited elements of deception and disguise, which aroused suspicion and fear from those supporting the cuts. If cheaters and shirkers could feign neediness and double-dippers could stumble upon additional aid, then all AFDC recipients were suspect. This threatened to unravel distinctions of deserving and undeserving—distinctions that, at the very least, the federal government seemed unable to make. The power of the poor lay in their ability to form conspiracies even as they flouted the work ethic, to beguile public officials and the forgotten man as they concealed their "true" nature.

A comparison of the perception of AFDC with other programs facing reduction or elimination demonstrates the functioning of these images within an argumentative nexus. Representative Rousselot was not persuaded by Reverend McDonald's exhortation to look into the tear-stained eyes of the hungry children who comprised 70 percent of the AFDC population. Yet his questioning of McDonald contrasted sharply with promises he made to other witnesses, namely his pledge to work with majority members of the committee to ensure that the 1980 Adoption Assistance and Child Welfare Act did not become part of a social services block grant.[98] Like AFDC, adoption assistance aided families, but unlike AFDC it received overwhelming bipartisan support in both houses of Congress. Adoption assistance invoked a different set of images, however. It granted funds to help innocent and vulnerable children in homes not tainted by the tripartite stigma of the non-needy. Unlike AFDC families, the heroic families that sought to adopt children already "proved" their productivity. They connoted the values of work and normalcy denied to AFDC families.

The force of these images lay in their assertion that they depicted the AFDC population generally. This movement toward universality demonstrates Lentricchia's observation that representations assert an ontological claim that a part truly stands in for the whole.[99] In this way, representations obscure their political character. Reagan deployed images of nonneediness to advance authoritative interpretations of social forces that could have been explained variously. His comments cited earlier regarding attempts to curb welfare fraud as governor of California offer an illuminating example of this function of these images:

> We saw that welfare in California was reaching a point of an increase of as much as 40,000 cases a month being added to the welfare rolls. We finally turned the task force loose to come back with a plan for reforming welfare. And we had a long fight. We had two fights. We had a fight with our legislature to get some of it, because I had a hostile legislature at the time, and we had a fight with Washington, with the bureaucracy in HEW who had rules and regulations that for example — and this is still true today — that under those rules and regulations no one in the United States knows how many people are on welfare. They only know how many checks they're sending out, and then we turn up a woman in Chicago that's getting checks under 127 different names. And just recently in Pasadena, California, living in a lovely big home there, a woman was brought in and charged with collecting $300,000 in a welfare scheme.[100]

I have quoted Reagan at length to demonstrate his deployment of images. After citing a startling statistic, Reagan turned almost immediately to stories of abuse. His remarks constructed an association between an increase in welfare applicants and fantastic cases of fraud. Connecting the two was a bureaucracy that demanded states' rigid adherence to rules even as it engaged in indiscriminate check writing, which permitted frauds. Whether widespread fraud explained the monthly rise in the welfare cases was an open question, however. The short-lived prominence of rights claims in the 1960s may have empowered many eligible persons to apply for AFDC. Reagan's assembled images discounted this possible explanation and others.

The force of images of non-neediness lay as well in their invitation to audiences to engage in negative racial imagining without mentioning race explicitly. Reagan and his supporters told maddening tales of waste and fraud, but they identified the perpetrators by seemingly innocuous qualities such as geography. Yet images, as Michael Osborn observes, disclose a considerable amount of information in a relatively small space.[101] In this respect, Reagan's reference to the Chicago welfare cheat was exemplary. Identifying "a woman in Chicago that's getting checks under 127 different names," Reagan invited members of his audience to imagine this woman. They knew her as an urban resident. Given the images of the AFDC recipient that emerged in the 1960s and early 1970s, a history to which Reagan alluded in this passage, they likely saw her as a black woman. This reference engaged racial animosities that Reagan's majority-white audience may have harbored and transferred the stigma of non-neediness to this black woman, a transference that may have engendered racial suspicion even among those who bore no overt hostility. As an ontological assertion, Reagan's representation charged this black woman as typical. Scandalous stories of fraud and abuse thus possessed a strangely antiseptic quality. These stories invoked race while cleansing the budget-cutting debates of explicitly racist themes and protecting advocates against charges of racism. Such cleansing, however, did not remove the stain of negative racial stereotyping. This antiseptic quality was manifested elsewhere as Reagan justified his demography of the AFDC population by explaining that the cuts in public assistance he oversaw as governor of California prompted no outcry from former recipients. Advancing his view, he represented AFDC recipients as shadowy, scheming figures. He asserted that they "just disappeared as the spotlight began to be turned on."[102] AFDC recipients appeared as dark creatures that scurried from the light of publicity.

The "non-image" of the truly needy also aided the dismantling purposes of the Reagan administration. Non-specific images depend for their force on the exclusive or inclusive impulses operating within deliberative episodes. The "citizen" is often described in nonspecific terms when discussing purposefully inclusive programs such as social security. Though the abstract citizen in practice may inscribe particular subjects, its legitimization purports to describe a status that may be assumed by people who differ in terms of race, sex, class, and ethnicity. Once an exclusionary milieu has been established, however, the nonspecific subject may function in the opposite manner. It may facilitate the articulation of an ever-shrinking pool of recipients. Supporters of the budget cuts did not have to commit themselves unconditionally to a class of legitimate recipients, such as worthy widows or even children. The "non-image" of the truly needy suggested that under certain circumstances, denying aid to any potential recipient may be right and just. The one quality Reagan and his supporters ascribed to the truly needy—faultlessness—performed a parallel function. It permitted different and possibly conflicting notions of fault to cluster and exclude greater numbers of potential recipients. Opponents of the budget cuts tried unsuccessfully to rally around children as truly needy—an appeal with historical antecedents. The arguments of the budget-cutters also invited historical comparison, but theirs was a history that both justified government noninterference and suggested concern for the poor.

Re-collecting and Reconfiguring Historical Images of the Poor

Reagan and his supporters advocated a return to a putatively meritocratic individualism that sought to simplify the complexities of social policy exposed in the 1960s. They suppressed the ambiguities created in dialectics of agency and structure by viewing economic status as the sole indicator of individual virtue. They invented a Gospel of Wealth for the 1980s. Yet their gospel cannot be reduced to reiterations of earlier preachers' statements, for the budget-cutters' statements intimated eclectic antecedents and exhibited contemporary rearticulation and invention. Advocates opposed to the budget cuts also invoked historical poverty discourses as resources for invention. Participants' negotiation of the past becomes clearer when one draws historical parallels to the 1981 debates. To illustrate this resonance, I consider the budget-cutters' implicit and explicit claims about the nature of and relation among classes, the abilities of the state, and the capacities of the market. I then compare the attempted focus on children by those opposing the cuts to past calls to protect children.

The budget-cutters deployment of images and appeals invoked some aspects of historical poverty discourses and forestalled the appearance of others. Reagan's view of the social bond recalled the Gospel of Wealth in its emphasis on individualism and assistance as a personal act. One hundred years before Reagan, Andrew Carnegie instructed the wealthy not to wait until death to give to their communities. He called upon them to act as stewards in their lifetimes, "intrusted for a season with a great part of the increased wealth of the community, but administering it for the community far better than it could or would have done for itself." Though he presided over a large federal government, Reagan described aid for the truly needy as emerging from the national conscience, even if administered, in the last instance, by the state. Carnegie somewhat ambivalently regarded individualism as a natural process of survival of the fittest, the preservation of the race. His view of the concentration of wealth oscillated between praise and accommodation, welcoming the concentration of wealth as "highly beneficial" and yet noting that "it is a waste of time to criticize the inevitable."[103]

Reagan confidently enlisted individualism in the service of national prosperity. Reflecting the historical eclecticism of the budget-cutters' appeals, Reagan's first February address recalled not Carnegie but FDR in its confidence that the people would prevail. Facing a country beaten by depression, FDR in his first inaugural exhorted famously that "the only thing we have to fear is fear itself." The nation, he explained, confronted "no failure of substance."[104] Evoking a similar mood, Reagan asserted in his February addresses the fundamental soundness of American nongovernmental institutions.

Still, the budget-cutters did not appeal only to the aspirations of the public; they insinuated insidious divisions in pledging allegiance to the forgotten man. The forgotten man stood for Sumner as a "victim of the reformer, social speculator and philanthropist." His woes stemmed from the misguided application of sentiment to the social bond. Sumner envisioned a society based on free contract: "men come together as free and independent parties to an agreement which is of mutual advantage.... There is no sentiment in it at all."[105] By contrast, Reagan and his supporters dramatized public sentiment in promising to protect the truly needy, but the forgotten man as middle-class surrogate still found himself attacked not only by the reformer but by the poor and the bureaucrats as well. In the budget-cutters' vision, the wealthy took up the cause of the middle class, for the wealthy and middle class shared courage and moral strength.

The Reagan administration saw the state as a powerful institution, but denied it the positive attributes of previous eras. Spokespersons described the state as an overwhelming negative force, usurping personal freedom and causing economic misery. FDR rebuked government's critics. He challenged the citizenry to "provide a smashing answer for those cynical men who say a Democracy cannot be honest and efficient." FDR depicted the state as the manifestation of citizens acting in concert. He invited their vigilance not to raise doubts about government's capacities but to bolster confidence that the state functioned as the agent of the people. He held that "[n]either you nor I want criticism conceived in a purely fault-finding or partisan spirit, but I am jealous of the right of every citizen to call to the attention of his or her government examples of how the public money can be more effectively spent for the benefit of the American people."[106] Moreover, FDR identified the government as the people's security against the hazards of life. Remnants of the New Deal state remained in the proposals of the budget-cutters, but the safety net that Reagan promised to maintain appeared as a decidedly second-best option to private charity, which he extolled. Reagan celebrated the market as the tester of individual mettle and virtue. The market created national wealth. The president ascribed to the market a quality that preachers of the Gospel of Wealth may have considered silly and strange: compassion. He insisted that the market aided the needy more capably than government.

In their attempt to draw attention to children, opponents of the budget cuts drew upon a recurrent strategy in historical poverty discourses. In his welcoming remarks to the 1909 White House Conference on the Care of Dependent Children, Theodore Roosevelt identified no more important a subject than the welfare of the nation's children, "because when you take care of the children you are taking care of the nation to-morrow."[107] Describing mothers' pensions under his jurisdiction, Judge E. E. Porterfield offered the same justification. He argued that when every child is entitled to a chance in life, "society is the gainer in good citizenship."[108] A partial explanation for the success of these Progressive appeals, however, may be that questions of children's poor adult caretakers were deferred. Some Progressives, such as Mrs. G. H. Robertson, argued for the *work* of motherhood. But Progressive reformers and the New Deal architects who federalized mothers' pensions did not encounter objections such as Representative Rousselot's retort to Reverend McDonald that welfare policies should encourage the 30 percent of AFDC recipients who were adults to work. Of course, paid labor had not been neglected completely. Porterfield warned against dispensing grants that provided a lone mother full support. Still, no irrepressible stigma of non-neediness overtook his commitment to children as future citizens. In this way, FDR could simultaneously refer to relief as a narcotic and support an ADC program because he viewed its adult recipients as "non-employables." Opponents of Reagan's budget cuts might have mitigated the "contamination" of the non-needy in their invocation of a social bond of interdependence embodied in a cooperative relation between the state and its citizens. The budget-cutters' emphasis on individualism frustrated the wider circulation of this alternative vision of a social order.

Relations Between the Federal Government and the Citizenry

The contesting demographies of the AFDC population implied a distinct relationship between the federal government and its citizens, especially its poor citizens. Autonomy infused the statements of Reagan and his supporters; obligation informed the statements of those opposed to the cuts. Their appropriated images and appeals provided clues to the quality of this relationship. A more explicit use of history also touched upon the subject of quality as supporters and opponents of the budget cuts judged the successes and failures of past welfare policy. Supporters of the cuts pointed to non-needy participants as visible evidence of decades of increasingly inept management and overly generous benefits in social programs. Opponents countered that insofar as they raised some incomes, social programs succeeded in attenuating widespread poverty. Still, existing programs functioned as stopgap measures that did not attack causes of poverty. Some opponents found the bifurcated structure of social welfare itself problematic.

Divergent judgments of the successes and failures of U.S. social policy collided most directly in discussions of attempts by AFDC recipients to reenter the paid work force. The most revealing of these discussions may have been Rep. John Rousselot's questioning of Christine Pratt-Marston. After listening to her testimony, he posited his own interpretation of the difficulties confronting AFDC recipients searching for paid labor. He offered: "Now, what do you suppose the problem is in going back to work? What we are really saying, then, is that they are not able to get a job to encourage them to go back to work that is a level of pay that can compete with what they are getting [in public assistance]." Pratt-Marston retorted: "I would not say it is a matter of competing with what they are getting. I would say it is a matter of a level of pay that allows them to survive and feed their children and pay their rent."[109] The contiguity of these two opposed readings of the putatively same phenomenon disclosed the presence of contesting demographies in such disagreements. Rousselot's explanation impugned comfortable recipients (double-dippers) who did not wish to give up their sedentary lifestyles (shirkers) without gratuitous reward. His criticism implied that deceit (cheaters) enabled this unreasonable demand. Pratt-Marston appealed for understanding of the material conditions of the hard-working mother whose innocent children lived a tenuous existence.

As it happened in the larger debate, contrasting policy recommendations arose from these two perspectives. Rousselot insisted that he too wanted poor families to survive, but repeated his assertion that AFDC recipients refused to accept available work. Pratt-Marston informed him that "oftentimes they have no training." In reply, Rousselot introduced the Comprehensive Employment and Training Act (CETA), a principal federal job training program, into their conversation. He told Pratt-Marston that her explanation confirmed his suspicion that CETA had failed to achieve its objective of training poor people for permanent jobs. Pratt-Marston initially agreed, but as Rousselot pressed his case she shifted focus. She conceded that "[i]t may not meet some of the goals stated, but it has been immeasurably useful in providing food for tables and paying rent and providing medical service for families." Rousselot responded sharply: "Well, CETA was not intended to provide medical service. It was intended to retrain people for a better level job so that they would not be required or encouraged to stay." When she appealed that Congress not take away the program, he insisted that "[n]obody suggested taking it away. The proposal is to reduce the amount of money ... to make sure that the purpose of the program is really being carried out."[110] Rousselot's remarks revealed an effort to recuperate Pratt-Marston's testimony within the frame of the administration's vision; he attempted to restrict Pratt-Marston to the "original" objectives of CETA and he affirmed a commitment to the program reshaped by these objectives. His call to reduce social spending arose out of this vision, which refused alternative demographies.

Pratt-Marston's recommendations came in response to questions by subsequent subcommittee members. When asked for suggestions for helping more AFDC recipients find permanent paid work, she identified the concerns of a struggling mother forced to balance her children's interests with her personal desires for paid employment. Widely available daycare and healthcare were necessary, she explained. The low end of the pay scale needed serious restructuring: "And I am not talking about objecting to scrubbing somebody's toilet. I am talking about being paid adequately for scrubbing that toilet so that I can support my family. It is not the kind of job, it is the adequate compensation that gets to be the problem.... I cannot support, I cannot feed my children on a minimum wage job." Pratt-Marston held fast to the view that AFDC recipients desperately wished to survive, working as hard as the "forgotten man" for only a fraction of the pay. When a sympathetic and supportive Pete Stark suggested that policymakers place a ceiling on the amount of assistance, including in-kind support, a person may receive to allay public fears and counter fantastic stories of abuse, Pratt-Marston's reply recalled left reactions to the Nixon administration's Family Assistance Plan. She proposed that "[i]f you were willing to put on the cap at say $20,000, or even the median income of the United States, I think that most of us could live with that kind of a cap."[111]

The policy recommendations advanced by opponents of the budget proposals implied a cooperative relationship between the federal government and AFDC recipients struggling to support their families. Pratt-Marston's suggestions — daycare, healthcare, job training and creation, and wage equity — called on the federal government to fill the gaps between the ambitions of many AFDC recipients and their seemingly paradoxical economic circumstances. She placed impetus with the AFDC recipient, whose experiences served as the best determinant of what role the government ought to assume. Pratt-Marston and others also demanded that policymakers and others cooperate appreciatively, valuing the work that adult AFDC recipients performed as mothers. They construed the involvement of the federal government as obligatory. Advocates repeatedly reminded their opponents of the duty of those in power to aid the voiceless innocents; stories of desperation and quiet perseverance intimated compassionate motivations of poor people. Some advocates pointed to the history of AFDC as an established tradition of caring.

Appeals to compassion and history did not always sit well with the budget-cutters. Their antipathy revealed a vision of the relationship between government and citizens that prevailed in the 1981 debates. In floor debate over OBRA, Sen. John Danforth rose to object to calls for compassion from opponents of the spending reductions. Before he spoke, Senator Moynihan decried the empty galleries and twice reminded his colleagues of the vulnerability of poor children: "persons who have as little voice and as little influence as any group you could describe in our society." Sen. Edward Kennedy broached the same themes as he read a letter from a set of foster parents, "which states the arguments ... better than any prepared speech possibly could." To these emotional appeals, Danforth countered that "the question is not whether we are turning our

backs on needy children. The question rather is at what level of government will we vest the lead responsibility for caring for needy children."
He chided his colleagues for what he perceived as arrogance. He contended that "I think we have gotten ourselves in a trap of feeling that we
in Washington have a monopoly on compassion, that we in Washington
have a monopoly on providing for those who are in need."[112] His statement sustained this adamant tone as he denounced the "emotion-charged"
argument regularly made on behalf of categorical programs. Danforth
alluded to "innumerable episodes" in which the machinations of federal
officials obstructed and demoralized state officials with innovative plans
to care for the poor.

Moynihan responded by pointing to the historical significance of federal social welfare policy—but Danforth persisted. Moynihan bemoaned
the cynicism of the impending legislation, which contravened the national concern and commitment symbolized in federal programs. In reference to a social services block grant, he declared: "I return to the proposition, and no more, that there is something noble about the Social
Security Act having for a half century provided an entitlement to these
children, and something unattractive about our taking it away." With
equal fervency, Danforth asserted that "the whole question of the locus of
decision-making has in itself been a matter of basic, fundamental value in
this country, a matter of passion on the part of those who established the
kind of system we are to have, and that is the basic question." Of the national election seven months earlier, he held that the most important issue confronted by voters concerned the "role and scope" of government.
The American people cast votes to recover their sense of agency, sensing
"somehow they were losing control of what government decided."[113]

Supporters of the budget cuts envisioned a minimalist federal government that did not interfere with the operations of the market, as they
believed social programs inevitably did, and did not shackle the entrepreneurial spirit of the risk-taking individual. The most prominent articulator of this vision, of course, was the president himself. In his
speeches, Reagan depicted himself as a defender of individual freedom
against the encroaching, oppressive tendencies of public institutions. In
his 5 February address, he called for an economic policy that would "un-
leash the energy and genius of the American people, traits which have
never failed us." In his 18 February address, he celebrated the producers,
those rugged individuals who built the nation through their personal en-
terprises in the "10,000 corners of America." Reagan repeated these

themes throughout the budget debates. On 25 June, as Congress considered OBRA, he linked his vision with the founding of the nation. He urged that "we have to revive the spirit of America, the American Revolution.... You're just demanding, I think, some of the same opportunities the Founding Fathers risked their lives, property, and sacred honor for more than 200 years ago—a commitment that if you work and save more tomorrow than you did today, your reward will be higher than it was today." Reagan desired to "unlock the spirit and the energy of our people, to drive Americans to dream and dare to take greater risks for a greater good."[114] Throughout the debates, he traced economic suffering to government's usurpation of personal freedom and its shackling of the market. Reagan committed himself to ending these infringements and promised economy recovery as a result.

In transfigured form, this emphasis on autonomy entered into specific discussions of AFDC and workfare. During Finance Committee hearings, Sen. Russell Long argued for a work program that paid AFDC recipients directly for their labor, adding the proviso that "it would be more in line with the traditional American concept that you are paid for what you do, and you are not made to do something against your will."[115] Similarly, Sen. William Proxmire introduced a workfare proposal by explaining to his colleagues that "my program exempts many AFDC recipients and protects them against being exploited in terms of wages, hours, and conditions of employment."[116] Long's reference to free will and Proxmire's concern with possible exploitation suggested a shifting social milieu that ascribed to AFDC recipients a degree of autonomy, even if its sources arose from grounds other than a resurgent conservatism. In this way, their statements marked significant aspects of a political imagination that oriented the budget-cutting debates of 1981. Subsequent debates shifted significantly: hesitancy in requiring specific actions from AFDC recipients dissipated as advocates of various perspectives turned to the putatively baneful behavior of even the "truly needy."

Creating a Political Language, Articulating a Social Vision

The 1981 budget debates heralded a retrenchment era in welfare policy discourse and the beginning of the end of AFDC. Ronald Reagan and his supporters enacted a shift in the prevailing political language of the past four decades, creating a Gospel of Wealth for the 1980s. Suspicious of the coloring effects of language, Reagan's utterances nevertheless reflected an ease in language as they reversed value hierarchies—a perverse co-optation of Herbert Marcuse's insight that an alternative language, "if it is to be political, cannot possibly be 'invented': it will necessarily depend on the subverting use of traditional material."[117] This emergent political language turned culprits into victims and victims into culprits. Business suffered with the forgotten man at the hands of government, a reversal of FDR's depiction of government as the heroic protector against corrupt business practice. Remnants of the New Deal inflected this language as the president spoke of economic crises and the need to insure the populace against hardship. He conceded a role for the state as custodian of a minimal social safety net. Though the administration denied the possibility of effective government, its spokespersons exhibited the same enchantment with technical knowledge and confidence in their problem-solving ability as New Deal and Progressive reformers. The modern and self-assured managerial language of Stockman and others combined with Reagan's traditionalism; the new savior—business—promised to help its ailing dialectical other—government—learn the lessons of efficiency and frugality.

A nostalgic longing for an America long since passed accompanied this reversal of political language. Reagan offered "not only a path of entry into such an America, a relic of its reality, but a guarantee of its continued existence in our time." He represented "the past as a present."[118] Reagan disavowed community on a national level, for no institution could facilitate it. The federal government had failed, usurping then abrogating responsibilities once sustained through personal relations of deference and benevolence. As a counter-initiative, Reagan celebrated the "10,000 corners of America." He and others associated their cause with American lore and patriotic glory. Their vision charted a clear course of action: reduce the bureaucratic monster that endangered the dream. Senator Danforth's impassioned defense of local administration demonstrated the intensity of this vision as it transformed an ostensibly mundane decision into a moral imperative. In reply, Moynihan could not embody the America attacked in the drive toward reduction, he could express only his personal feeling of the unattractiveness of it all. The administration's argumentative nexus and images frustrated attempts to construct a community among strangers. Opponents' intimation of interdependence conflicted with the prevailing frame of the debates. Moreover,

equations of citizen with suffering taxpayer forestalled other possible renderings of citizenship that included economic dimensions. Correspond-
ingly, Nancy Fraser and Linda Gordon note the infrequent appearance in
U.S. political discourse of a notion of social citizenship—a form of citizenship that invokes liberal themes of rights, communitarian norms of
solidarity, and republican ideals of participation in public life.[119] The
terms of the debate constrained those opposed to the cuts, requiring
them to defend programs in isolation as the administration announced
further reductions.

The budget-cutters created their political language in accordance with
established relations of power. Despite promises to protect the truly
needy, despite claims that all branches of government would sacrifice for
the greater good, despite the axiomatic belief in the ineptitude of the public sector and the efficacy of the marketplace, the supply-siders preserved
those functions of the federal government that served the interests of
their benefactors. David Stockman admitted as much as he reflected on
the debates. He conceded that "[t]he power of these client groups turned
out to be stronger than I realized. The client groups know how to make
themselves heard. The problem is, unorganized groups can't play in this
game."[120] This vision of America articulated by Reagan and others entailed helping one's friends and spurning suspicious strangers, recalling
another historical practice of poor relief.

OBRA continued the historical pattern of removing "deserving" poor
people from the AFDC rolls. Amendments to the Social Security Act in
the years after its passage established this pattern. The extension of eligibility for social insurance programs in 1939 and 1950 meant that fewer
widows received ADC. The 1981 law removed families with paid employment—families with very low incomes. A widely cited study by the General Accounting Office (GAO) found that OBRA dropped between 40 and
60 percent of these families from the program. It reduced the benefits of
another 8 to 48 percent of families participating in the paid labor market.[121] These families suffered. Their earnings from alternative sources
did not replace lost benefits or medical care. In many cases, single mothers were forced to place their children in inferior daycare. The GAO concluded that "[a]ll of the evidence thus indicates that the average pre-
OBRA working recipient experienced a sharp decline in economic
well-being in the year following OBRA."[122] A painful irony of the law was
its dubious savings. Wisconsin, for instance, found that "it lost 84 percent
of the total OBRA-AFDC savings in the state."[123] As the testimony of

Pratt-Marston intimated, a number of formerly employed recipients returned to the program without paid employment and thus required
larger grants. The rising cost of food stamps offset savings in AFDC. And
Wisconsin's state treasury lost taxes previously paid by recipients with remunerative vocations.

The 1981 budget debates set in motion a policy trajectory that progressed from removing the non-needy from AFDC rolls to rehabilitating
the truly needy in the mid-1980s. As the decade proceeded, frustration
with AFDC continued even though the non-needy presumably had been
removed from the program as a result of the 1981 budget cuts. Promising
a restoration of social programs to safety net status, the images and
arguments of 1981 prompted legislators and advocates to turn their attention to a previously exempt subject: the truly needy. A consensus
emerged in the mid-1980s to focus on the putatively baneful behavior of
all AFDC recipients independent of need. Testimony by Robert Reischauer, senior fellow at the Brookings Institution, to the House Public
Assistance Subcommittee in 1987 exemplified the import of the reversals
carried out in 1981: "Few think welfare rolls are harboring large numbers
of cheaters or that recipients are living the good life. Similarly, most now
recognize that it may not be in the best interests of many needy recipients
simply to provide them with more cash assistance."[124] The consensus
combined services such as childcare and vocational training with mandatory work requirements. Consensus suggested that the 1981 debates
helped install a new object of deliberation. As policy initiatives shifted
from income maintenance to service provision, welfare debates shifted
focus from the alleviation of poverty to the elimination of dependency,
understood as "long-term" receipt of AFDC. Those who supported the
mid-1980s consensus acknowledged that recipients were poor, but no
longer regarded them in the non-specific image of the truly needy.

CHAPTER 4

Reorienting Welfare

In 1981 Reagan and his supporters paid little attention to the "truly needy," attributing only an unspecified condition of faultlessness to this group. In his frame-setting 5 February speech, the president asserted that taxpayers would "continue to meet our responsibility to those who, through no fault of their own, need our help."[1] The budget-cutters did not concern themselves with the behaviors, attitudes, or motivations of the "truly needy." In the mid-1980s, however, Reagan heeded the condition of AFDC recipients whose neediness he did not challenge. His portentous description of their deterioration in his 1986 State of the Union address helped renew congressional interest in welfare reform. "In the welfare culture," he asserted, "the breakdown of the family, the most basic support system, has reached crisis proportions." Citing FDR's view of relief as a narcotic, he exhorted Congress to "escape the spider's web of dependency." Ten days later, in a radio address on welfare reform, the president reiterated these themes. He reported somberly that "[i]n inner cities today, families, as we've always thought of them, are not even being formed."[2] Reagan traced the ills of dependency to the "famous War on Poverty," which in his view worsened the problems it sought to alleviate.

Though many objected to Reagan's attribution of cause, observers saw in adult AFDC recipients' decreased attachment to the paid labor force and increased incidence of unstable family formation evidence that impelled reform. Need became a necessary but not a sufficient condition for receipt of aid. A mid-1980s reform consensus emerged that focused on contracts and mutual obligation. Defenders of public assistance accepted the proposition that adults ought to work in private employment. Critics conceded the necessity of support services such as job training and placement, daycare, and transitional medical care. Both groups sought a strengthened system of child-support enforcement to compel mothers and fathers to meet their parental responsibilities. The reform consensus culminated in the 1988 Family Support Act (FSA).

Two years of congressional hearings and debate and presidential speeches and radio addresses preceded the passage of the FSA. Reagan's February remarks helped renew interest in reform, but his call for action suggested to some a lackadaisical effort. In his radio address, the president committed himself only to the appointment of two working groups— housed in relatively low-profile offices of the executive branch—charged with reporting recommendations by 1 December. Interested parties responded with ideas of their own. A group of former Reagan administration officials created a working seminar on the family and welfare policy to elevate welfare reform as a top political priority in 1987. In late November, the American Public Welfare Association proposed replacing AFDC with a state-by-state "family living standard" that reflected the cost of housing, food, transportation, and utilities. In late December, a coalition of ninety church, nutrition, child-welfare, and civil rights groups endorsed a statement of welfare reform principles that placed the primary responsibility for fighting poverty with the federal government.[3]

These varied calls for reform corresponded with a changing public mood that indicated a willingness to support certain types of reform. Between 1981 and 1986, the percentages of people supporting and opposing Reagan's cuts in social services reversed themselves. In 1981, 57 percent of respondents to a *Los Angeles Times* poll either approved or strongly approved of Reagan's cuts while 37 percent disapproved or strongly disapproved. When the same poll questioned people in 1985, it found that only 36 percent of respondents approved or strongly approved of cuts in social services while 57 percent disapproved or strongly disapproved. Addressing the issue of who bore responsibility for aiding the needy, the National Opinion Research Center (NORC) reported increasing numbers of people stating that both government and poor people had a responsibility to improve one's living standard—from 32 percent in 1983 to 45 percent in 1986. This increase appeared at the expense of responses assigning responsibility chiefly to government.[4] Like policy debate participants, NORC respondents appeared to emphasize mutual obligation.

Congressional involvement began earnestly in 1987. Committee hearings and interest-group lobbying revealed that the locus of action on welfare reform shifted in the mid-1980s. The Reagan administration remained in the periphery as figures from the legislative branch, statehouses, and advocacy groups argued most adamantly for reform. Of members of Congress, Sen. Daniel Patrick Moynihan may have contributed most significantly to securing passage of the FSA. Participants referred to the

senator's role as "the Moynihan factor," meaning the historical perspective brought to the debate by his twenty-five–year association with welfare policy as well as his ability to fashion agreement on broad concepts.[5]
After the Democrats gained eight seats in the 1986 midterm elections,
which placed the Senate under Democratic control for the first time during Reagan's presidency, Moynihan became the chairperson of the Social
Security and Family Policy Subcommittee.[6] This subcommittee assumed
principal responsibility for initiating Senate legislation on public assistance programs.

Moynihan held hearings in January, February, and March of 1987.
Conducted well in advance of the introduction of legislation, the hearings
enabled articulation of various reforms. Subsequent hearings held before
the full Finance Committee also addressed specific bills that surfaced in
each chamber. The Public Assistance and Unemployment Compensation
Subcommittee, the lead House committee, also held hearings during this
period, offering witnesses similar opportunities. Efforts in both chambers
received a considerable boost when the National Governors' Association
(NGA), at its annual meeting in Washington in late February, adopted
with only one dissenting vote a far-reaching reform proposal. The governors' plan centered on the notion of a contract that obligated recipients
and government to a program of work preparation and support.[7] Congress and the administration endorsed the broad outlines of the plan. The
NGA — chiefly through its agents Governors Bill Clinton (D-Ark.) and
Michael Castle (R-Del.) — promised intense lobbying for its proposal.

The House passed its version of welfare reform in December mainly
along party lines. House Republicans and the administration objected to
the overall cost of the bill, estimated at $7 billion over five years, and
charged that it promoted dependency by giving states incentives to raise
benefits. Meanwhile, legislative priorities in the Finance Committee delayed Senate consideration of Moynihan's proposal. To some observers,
the prospects of welfare reform appeared to dim. The governors, however,
again sought reform during their February 1988 meeting. Clinton and
Castle met separately with Sen. Lloyd Bentsen, chair of the Finance Committee, and Reagan. They urged Bentsen to advance Moynihan's bill and
appealed to Reagan to switch his support away from an alternative bill.[8]

After additional hearings, the Finance Committee adopted a bill, projected to cost $2.7 billion over five years, which the Senate approved by an
overwhelming vote of 93 to 3 in June 1988. The cost of the proposal
moved toward Senate figures as House and Senate conferees negotiated

differences between their bills. But Reagan threatened to veto any conference agreement because of a provision that would have extended AFDC
to two-parent families without mandating work. Negotiating with administration representatives, congressional conferees adopted a report
that pared down the cost of the bill to $3.34 billion and required "work-
fare" for one parent in two-parent families.[9] The conference report
passed the House by a vote of 347 to 53 and the Senate by a vote of 96 to 1.
On 13 October 1988, Reagan signed the Family Support Act.

As congressional vote totals suggest, a consensus characterized the
mid-1980s reform debates and enabled passage of the FSA — but this consensus was precarious. Most participants agreed on broad sociocultural
terms: women no longer could be exempted in policy from private employment but private employment required public support of some
mothers. Yet this abstract commitment did not indicate clear policy
initiatives, and consensus-threatening differences in policy preferences
persisted. Participants, however, did not permit consideration of divergent interests as explicit topics of debate. Preserving consensus at the expense of deliberation, many politicians and witnesses instead invoked
broad themes of reform to assert the existence of a deeply held consensus.
Participants' interests may have been irreconcilable, but suppression of
these interests obscured the nature of the consensus: the mid-1980s reform
consensus was an asserted rather than a deliberatively achieved consensus.
In this way, the consensus delimited the vision of those who advanced it,
recasting poverty as dependency and truncating human motivation as
economically driven. Moreover, consensus did not inform the debates
completely, functioning rather as a disciplinary force for those "outside" it.

In developing this argument, I first consider the social and political
context of the reform consensus, which grew from various sources. I then
recount briefly the major components of the FSA. My analysis of the reform consensus begins with its announcement. Consensus depended
critically on the circulation of the idea of a contract. Participants endorsed the use of a contract as a highly suitable means of detailing the
reciprocal obligations of the welfare recipient and the welfare agency. The
most conspicuous signee of this contract, whom I turn to next, was the
teenage mother. She stood as the detailed representation of the long-term
recipient, who emerged through the social and political context as an appropriate focus for reform. I then explicate the insistence on parental responsibility manifest in the widespread censure of the deadbeat dad and
his "criminal" neglect. I next consider the almost exclusive reliance of

participants on an economically driven model of human motivation. I then examine the bargained as opposed to deliberatively achieved quality of the reform consensus as well as its disciplinary force for those "outside" it.

The Social and Political Context of the Reform Consensus

The mid-1980s reform consensus grew from several sources: rising numbers of working mothers, increasing numbers of female-headed families and growing child poverty, circulation of prominent policy tracts, state reform experiments, and growing concerns about an "underclass." Together, these forces helped shape the framework of the policy debates regarding the FSA. Participants saw in these forces confirmation of their belief that reforms ought to address the behavioral problem of welfare dependency rather than the structural concern of poverty. Further, these forces suggested to participants an appropriate subject for reform: the long-term recipient.

Politicians had long argued that welfare reform ought to move recipients from relief rolls to payrolls, but increasing numbers of women entering the paid labor force over the past thirty years evidenced for mid-1980s reformers the appropriateness of making work a focal point of reform. Overall, adult women either working or looking for work rose from 38 percent in 1960 to nearly 60 percent in 1988. Participation levels for successive birth cohorts of women revealed markedly different patterns of employment. The labor force participation rate for women born between 1936 and 1940 declined from 46.1 to 38.9 percent as these women moved from ages twenty to twenty-four to their peak childbearing years of twenty-five to twenty-nine. The participation rate for the first of the baby boomers, born only ten years later between 1946 and 1950, remained virtually the same—changing slightly from 57.7 to 57.3 percent—as these women moved from ages twenty to twenty-four to ages twenty-five to twenty-nine. The rate for women born between 1956 and 1960 actually increased from 68.9 to 71.4 percent over these two age groupings. As more and more women remained in the paid labor force during their childbearing years, women's participation rates began to resemble those of men. Demographers report that by 1988, as Congress considered reform proposals in various stages of passage, the post–World War II dip in women's participation rates between the ages of twenty-five to fifty-four had almost disappeared. Women's labor force participation now resembled the male "inverted U" pattern, increasing in percentages as workers reached peak employment ages of thirty-five to forty-four, then decreasing as more and more workers neared retirement age.[10]

More important, paid employment (part-time or full-time) became the norm even for women with children, the group to whom adult AFDC recipients historically have been compared. In 1960, 39 percent of married women with children aged six to seventeen and 18.6 percent of married women with children under age six worked. By 1970, the percentages climbed to 49.2 percent and 30.3 percent, respectively. By 1980, they climbed higher still, to 61.7 percent and 45.1 percent. By 1987, when House and Senate committees began hearings in earnest, 70.6 percent of married women with children aged six to seventeen worked and 56.8 percent of married women with children under age six worked. Rates for separated and divorced mothers revealed similar upward trends.[11] The presence of a majority of mothers in the labor force — even those with young children — disqualified for most debate participants a view of the state as surrogate breadwinner.

If the prevalence of working mothers suggested new social norms, then a rise in female-headed families and their higher incidence of poverty signaled for participants a problem that called for reform. The number of female-headed families had risen from 11.5 percent of all families with children in 1970 to 19.4 percent in 1980. The rate of increase subsided in the 1980s, but the proportion continued to rise to 24.2 percent of all families with children in 1990.[12] Delivering the Godkin Lectures at Harvard University in 1985 on the subject of family and nation, Senator Moynihan held that this continuing change in family structure was "ineluctably associated with poverty."[13] He reported that in 1984 one out of every five children lived in poverty. Though this figure alone invited reprobation, even more scandalous was the situation that over half of all children in female-headed families — 54 percent — lived in poverty. Moynihan protested that social welfare programs had done much more to improve the lives of the elderly than children. Taking into account the impact of in-kind benefits on poverty rates, children under six were seven times more likely to be poor than the elderly, by a rate of 17.5 percent to 2.6 percent. He decried that "[i]t is fair to assume that the United States has become the first society in history in which a person is more likely to be poor if young rather than old." Moynihan praised an emergent realization

in policy circles that no government "can avoid having policies that pro-
foundly influence family relationships." Still, a choice remained about
"whether these will be purposeful, intended policies or whether they will
be residual, derivative, in a sense concealed ones."[14]

Calls for fundamental reform also appeared in policy tracts prominently received in the popular press and legislative forums. The arguments
advanced in these books paralleled the legislative debate in significant
respects. Poverty experts' policy tracts revealed significant levels of
agreement on broad themes of social relation. These tracts also revealed
the differences in interests that threatened the reform consensus. In his
suggestively titled book *Beyond Entitlement,* New York University professor Lawrence Mead disclosed the general contours of this agreement in
his preface:

> [T]he main problem with the welfare state is its *permissiveness,* not its
> size. Today poverty often arises from the functioning problems of the
> poor themselves, especially difficulties in getting through school,
> working, and keeping their families together. But the social programs
> that support the needy rarely set standards for them. Recipients sel-
> dom have to work or otherwise function *in return* for support.[15]

As this quote suggests, *Beyond Entitlement* indicated a willingness among
some conservatives to countenance federal involvement in social policy,
if only on their terms. As Michael Katz notes, Mead assumed a view of
poor people as intemperate and undisciplined, enabling his appeal for an
authoritative social policy to enforce social obligation.[16]

Two widely cited tracts that appeared in the mid-1980s were Charles
Murray's *Losing Ground* and David Ellwood's *Poor Support.*[17] These
books were representative of the policy debate in this period among
poverty researchers, revealing both substantial and adamant disagreements regarding policy initiatives and yet surprising areas of agreement
given the authors' identification in the popular and scholarly presses as
ideological opposites. Murray judged the federal government's anti-
poverty programs a complete failure. His explanation was simple and
straightforward. Poverty had been declining in the post–World War II
era until the launch of the Great Society in the mid-1960s. After this "reform period," both poverty rates and public funding to combat poverty
rose. Murray concluded that the federal government had worsened the
condition it sought to alleviate. He called for the abolition of all benefit
programs for the non-elderly poor, save unemployment insurance. Ellwood judged past reform efforts as failures because they did not address

adequately the four basic American value tenets of individualism, work, family, and community. Instead, past reforms had emphasized one value at the expense of others, entangling policy in "helping conundrums" that accompanied aid. Ellwood sought a solution that recognized the diverse experiences of the poor. For those full-time workers whose income did not place them above the poverty line, he called for an income supplement. For people without paid employment, he envisioned the replacement of "welfare" with a transitional program designed to prepare, place, and support people in the paid labor market.

Published in 1984, before the start of the FSA debates, *Losing Ground* attracted an influential constituency. *Washington Post* columnist Meg Greenfield protested that "[n]o matter what kind of government effort you may argue for these days … you are likely to be 'Charles Murrayed,' and that will be the end of the argument. The simple invocation of the book's existence will be taken as an answer to the question." Though he objected to its explanation of social pathology and prescriptions for reform, Senator Moynihan nevertheless acknowledged the influence of *Losing Ground.* He observed that "[i]nside the beltway, where conservative forces now preside (much as it may discomfort them), the thesis of *Losing Ground* prevails; certainly in the executive, and subtly elsewhere."[18]

The focus of an orchestrated public-relations campaign, *Losing Ground* received generally favorable reviews in the popular press. In 1982 the Manhattan Institute recruited Murray to write a book about the failures of social policy after its president read a Heritage Foundation pamphlet Murray had written that argued for aiding the poor by abolishing poverty programs.[19] The institute secured funding from the Scaife and Olin Foundations to support promotional activities. These activities included the distribution of more than 700 free copies of the book to academics, public officials, and journalists as well as the organization of seminars about the book. Also, the institute served as booking agent for a nation-wide speaking tour, scheduling multiple media appearances in cities visited by Murray. Though it identified exaggeration as one of his "pardonable sins," *Newsweek* retorted that Murray convincingly argued that government programs contributed to the "feminization" of poverty. *Time* responded that "no one has documented it as thoroughly as Murray does" the claim that federal programs perpetuated poverty.[20] Reviewers for periodicals such as *Fortune* and *Commentary* offered similar evaluations.[21]

Scholarly reviewers judged the book more harshly. They charged Murray with distorting the record of 1960's reform by ignoring social and economic forces affecting federal policy-making since the early 1970s.[22] Reviewers retorted that 1970's economic stagnation and inflation complicated efforts to combat poverty. Nevertheless, the poverty rate remained constant, or was slightly lower, throughout this period. They also reproached Murray for misleading readers by selectively citing evidence.[23] For instance, Lester Thurow discerned that although Murray mysteriously excluded consideration of the elderly at the outset, he nevertheless included spending on the elderly when supporting his argument that poverty and anti-poverty spending had risen contemporaneously. Robert Greenstein rejected Murray's contention that policy changes between 1960 and 1970 made nonwork and nonmarriage financially more attractive for a fictitious couple Harold and Phyllis.[24] Greenstein noted that Murray selected figures from a high-benefits state (Pennsylvania) without informing his readers; included the value of food stamps only when calculating Harold and Phyllis's welfare budget, though poor working families also were eligible; and did not mention the loss in the real value of AFDC benefits of almost 30 percent between 1970 and 1980. Reviewers further rebuked Murray for oversimplifying complex policy questions.[25] Christopher Jencks confirmed that research had found that higher AFDC benefits made single mothers more likely to maintain their own households and had increased the divorce rate—but the consequences of these actions remained open to debate. Clouding Murray's anecdote, he asked: "Are we to suppose that Phyllis is better off in the long run married to Harold if he drinks, or beats her, or molests their teenage daughter?" Regarding the book as seriously flawed, scholarly reviewers admitted its likely influence. Robert Reich warned against dismissing *Losing Ground* as rants of a conservative apologist, for it "will make up part of the new conventional wisdom about the nature of poverty."[26]

Reich and others recognized that part of the book's potential lay in its presentation. They described it as lucidly written, extensively documented, and tightly argued. Murray tells a persuasive tale of how social meddling directly increased the misery of the poor. He alternates between a persona of objective expert invoking a cult of expertise and neighborly everyman affirming "common sense." Murray devotes half of the book to statistical analysis of the adverse effects of government policies for black people in the categories of poverty, employment, wages and occupations, education, crime, and the family, promising repeatedly to help readers through the complex numbers he assembled. In the persona of the objective scientist, Murray distances himself from the racial overtones of his arguments. While the popular press views differences in economic status among blacks and whites as evidence of persistent racial discrimination, the analyst "tries to find out how much of the racial discrepancy remains after other explanatory factors are taken into account."[27]

At the same time, Murray embraces the "folk wisdom" of his general reader. He appeals to and celebrates "common sense." He holds that a popular wisdom has paralleled the "elite wisdom" that shaped social policy in the 1960s and 1970s. Such wisdom can be found in "most blue-collar bars or country club lounges in most parts of the United States. It is the inarticulate constellation of worries and suspicions that helped account for Ronald Reagan's victory in 1980." Murray concedes that this popular wisdom has contained "a good deal of mean-spirited (often racist) invective," but history has demonstrated the truth of its core premises: people respond to incentives and disincentives; people are not inherently moral or hard-working; and people must be held accountable for their actions.[28] He also creates a series of vignettes to support his claims—the aforementioned Harold and Phyllis have elicited the most response. Murray's two personas enable him to appear careful as he considers explanations for the persistence of poverty and impassioned as he reproaches the arrogance of 1960s intellectuals. His personas suggest to readers that their incredulity, anger, and frustration at public assistance programs are justified and confirmed by data. Moreover, they ought not feel responsible for economic deprivation, for its cause lies in personal behavior.

Published in 1988, *Poor Support* appeared too late to affect the specific shape of the FSA, but the book synthesized Ellwood's research on AFDC, which did circulate within policy-making circles. Its evaluation of past policy and justification of new directions reflected the themes of the reform consensus. And some reviewers viewed many of its proposals as "squarely in line with welfare-reform thinking of the 1980s."[29] Still, Ellwood's advocacy of time-limited assistance for certain recipients and other proposals prompted some reviewers, such as David Whitman in the neo-conservative journal the *Public Interest,* to praise the book for revealing the paucity of the FSA.[30] *Poor Support* did not engender the popular stir of *Losing Ground,* but it did receive a generally favorable response among scholarly reviewers. Some praised Ellwood's analysis of the complex dynamic among social, economic, and cultural factors.[31] Others lauded his treatment of troubling social problems with reason and hope rather than hand-wringing and despair.[32] Unfavorable comments typically focused on his proposed reforms, calling them unclear or unrealistic.[33] Robert Greenstein wondered if time limits did not ignore the complex lives of single mothers.[34]

Ellwood situates *Poor Support* within the ongoing reform debate. He attempts to adjudicate the competing claims of Murray and Mead and their detractors. Ellwood holds that Murray's provocative claims raise important policy questions: though Murray wrongly blames the social welfare system for poor people's woes, he rightly rebukes it for not reflecting and reinforcing the nation's most basic values. Only a fundamental reform has the potential to resolve adequately the conundrums that accompany aid: security-work, assistance-family structure, and targeting-isolation. Ellwood points to widespread agreement that when one provides money, food, or housing to the poor, one reduces "the pressure on them to work and care for themselves." Emphasizing a lack of scientific corroboration, Ellwood notes as well the widespread belief that "the welfare system may be inducing changes in the family." Further, he explains that the "more you target [a particular group for rehabilitation], the more you tend to isolate the people who receive the services from the economic and political mainstream."[35] Values also imbricate explanations of poverty: society cannot "solve" poverty until it determines a set of behavioral expectations. Ellwood argues that shared social values suggest a reorientation of welfare around a sense of mutual obligation. The history of AFDC indicates that "the further we move toward a system that makes judgments about the causes of poverty, that tries to link benefits to work, that avoids excessive targeting, the less bothersome the conundrums seem to be." In contrast, "the closer we move to time-unlimited, cash-like, income-tested assistance — that is, the closer we move to pure welfare programs — the more difficult the value dilemmas become."[36]

Attempts to induce behaviors in light of explicitly expressed values require a recognition of the diversity of poverty. Ellwood devotes the majority of his book to exploring the different circumstances confronting poor two-parent, single-parent, and "ghetto" families. These explorations lead him to the identification of vexing "problem areas." Many families remain poor even though one parent works full-time. Poor single parents invariably face a difficult choice: work full-time or be supported by welfare. Moreover, absent parents typically provide little financial support for their children. The "ghetto poor" suffer the multiple ills of a hopeless, futureless world: deprivation, isolation, joblessness, and discrimination. To address these varied situations, Ellwood recommends five reforms:

first, ensure medical protection universally; second, "make work pay" through various means such as the Earned Income Tax Credit, a higher minimum wage, or a refundable childcare tax credit; third, adopt a uniform child-support assurance system; fourth, convert welfare into a transitional system designed to provide serious yet short-term financial, educational, and social support for people experiencing temporary setbacks; fifth, provide minimum-wage jobs to those who have exhausted their transitional support.

Clearly, Ellwood advocates a very different solution than Murray, who wishes to abolish public assistance. But both authors make similar thematic appeals. Both identify their object of concern as welfare dependency rather than poverty. Ellwood, for instance, asserts that poverty cannot be explained solely by a lack of money.[37] Each author judges the present welfare system a failure, for in each case the system neglects determinant problems. Both writers highlight the long-term recipient. Murray offers a decidedly conservative inflection of the "culture of poverty" thesis. Ellwood argues for a differentiated perception of poverty and poor people. Each author views recipients as economic actors. Murray constructs elaborate vignettes to depict the calculations carried out by young prospective parents. Ellwood explicates in detail the choices forced upon the poor by the present system. Both commentators interrogate the present system against changed sociocultural expectations. Murray, for example, asks: "Why should the [welfare] mother be exempted by the system from the pressures that must affect everyone else's decision to work?"[38] Such similarities signaled broad themes of consensus in legislative forums.

These books intimated the pivotal role played by poverty experts throughout the debates over the FSA, which was not limited to authorship of policy tracts. Mead, Murray, and Ellwood testified before Congress. In addition to these wide-ranging critiques of past welfare policy, researchers produced specific evaluations of state reform efforts. After the 1981 enactment of OBRA, the Manpower Demonstration Research Corporation (MDRC) contracted with eight states to evaluate the effectiveness of work and training programs. According to the principal drafter of the Senate reform bill, MDRC's reports provided reform planners "timely" and "unambiguous" findings that "were not subject to challenge on methodological grounds."[39] MDRC's evaluations of welfare-to-work experimental projects found that a focus on "long-term" poor women rather than the most job-ready produced a greater gain for states.[40] Politicians often cited the work of poverty researchers, especially MDRC's findings.

The FSA's principal Senate drafter recalled that "[r]ight up through the final days of the House-Senate conference committee in September 1988, we were reviewing the latest MDRC findings."[41] Moynihan remarked that "[f]or the first time, we're proposing legislation based on research."[42] One observer, who served as a senior policy advisor to some members of the Ways and Means Committee, recollected that "there is no question that social science research contributed substantially to creating the policy situation in which welfare reform became possible."[43]

Two state demonstration projects unaffiliated with MDRC's study attracted the interest of policymakers pursuing reform: Massachusetts's Employment and Training Choices (ET) and California's Greater Avenues for Independence (GAIN). A voluntary program, ET encouraged participation through an array of services: education, training, childcare, and transitional child- and healthcare. Sixty-seven percent of adult recipients participated. Of these participants, 44 percent obtained jobs and 49 percent of these jobholders stayed off public assistance. Critics contended, however, that a favorable economy accounted for the program's success. When ET started in 1983, Massachusetts's unemployment rate of 3.9 percent was the lowest in the country. Moreover, the combination of a prospering economy and OBRA-induced cuts produced a 29 percent reduction in the AFDC rolls in the three years preceding the program. Critics also charged ET with "creaming": selecting only the most employable recipients.

GAIN combined mandatory work for mothers with children aged three and over with a package of services to bolster their employability. This program's success was limited, however, because California's financial troubles prompted budget reductions in GAIN shortly after enactment and much higher than expected proportions of registrants suffered basic literacy deficiencies, which shifted the program focus from jobs to compensatory education. This new emphasis was derided by critics. Gov. George Deukmejian demanded that GAIN become a "true 'workfare' program."[44] Measures of ET's success and rebukes of GAIN's educational component signaled the primacy of work for many reformers.

Charges of "creaming" and MDRC's recommendations intimated that the emergence of long-term recipients as a distinct group revealed for some academics and citizens the presence of an "underclass" in American society. Its representation in the media depicted a suspect and potentially fearsome class. In his popular 1982 book *The Underclass,* journalist Ken Auletta grouped long-term recipients with street criminals, hustlers, drunks, drifters, shopping-bag ladies, and released mental patients as denizens of the underclass.[45] His analysis of this social category focused on deviant behavior and family structure as correlates of poverty. Even more sympathetic observers employed the term. Sociologist William Julius Wilson advocated in his 1987 book *The Truly Disadvantaged* a progressive policy agenda of universal, non-means–tested reforms such as a national employment strategy, child-support assurance, family allowances, and childcare strategies. Noting the eschewal of the term "underclass" by some liberals, Wilson countered that "one cannot deny that there is a heterogeneous grouping of inner-city families and individuals whose behavior contrasts sharply with that of mainstream America." He included in the underclass "individuals who lack training and skills and either experience long-term unemployment or are not members of the labor force, individuals who are engaged in street crime and other forms of aberrant behavior, and families that experience long spells of poverty and/or welfare dependency."[46] In the view of many, the underclass was associated prominently with female-headed families. Summarizing scholarly literature on the topic, Douglas Muzzio identified black, urban, and female-headed families as frequently enumerated qualities of an underclass. According to Michael Katz, although commentators such as Wilson sought a careful definition, the use of the term "underclass" revived notions of poverty that emphasized poor people's behavior over the sources of their deprivation, deflecting attention away from structural reforms.[47] Deflection manifested in the legislative debates as a focus on welfare dependency rather than poverty, which the social and political context of the FSA legitimated. This framework facilitated deferral of significant disagreement.

The 1988 Family Support Act

A brief description of the FSA's major provisions needs to be appended to my discussion of the policy history of the FSA and its wider context before proceeding to the debates themselves. An explication of these provisions completes the narrative I have recounted thus far. The beginnings of the FSA lay in its wider context as well as early calls for reform by Reagan and others. The efforts of Moynihan, the NGA, and others constituted its development. The passage of the act marked the culmination of this welfare reform episode. The provisions of the FSA also suggested the translation into law of some of the prominent features of the mid-1980s reform debates.

Reflecting the widespread censure leveled at the "deadbeat dad" by debate participants, the first title of the FSA concerned child-support enforcement. The act required automatic withholding of child support from an absent parent's paycheck for all cases enforced by child-support agencies, regardless of whether an individual's payments were in arrears. It permitted waivers only if both parents signed an alternative agreement. Further, it instructed judges and others responsible for support orders to employ state guidelines as a "rebuttable presumption." The FSA also required states to meet federal standards for paternity establishment in out-of-wedlock births. Some of the additional child-support provisions included increasing government information available to the federal Parent Locator Service, creating a Commission on Interstate Child Support, and implementing within each state an automated system for tracking and monitoring support payments.

The FSA's second major area centered on work. It replaced existing employment, education, and training programs for AFDC recipients with the Job Opportunities and Basic Skills Training Program (JOBS). Reflecting disagreement among participants over specific measures to move recipients to paid employment, the FSA permitted each state to establish its own JOBS program. State programs had to include the following activities: basic education, including high school or its equivalency; remedial literacy education; education for people with limited proficiency in English; job-skills training; job-readiness activities; job development and placement; and support services. The FSA also required each state to offer two of the following activities: group and individual job search; on-the-job training; wage subsidization to be paid to the employer; and community work experience, or "workfare." It directed all nonexempt welfare recipients to participate in the JOBS program. Among those exempted were caregivers of children under age three or, at state option, age one. The FSA targeted potential long-term recipients, including families in which the custodial parent was under twenty-four and had not completed high school or its equivalent nor had any significant work experience in the preceding year, as well as families receiving aid for more than thirty-six of the preceding sixty months. The FSA established participation rates for the states to meet for mandated recipients, which reached 20 percent of the nonexempt caseload by 1995.

The FSA's work emphasis also required an individualized approach. States had to provide an initial assessment of an individual recipient's needs, and then consult with the recipient to develop an employability plan that explicated the services to be provided by the state and the activities to be performed by the recipient as well as an employment goal for the recipient. The FSA permitted states to enter into contracts with recipients to underscore these mutual responsibilities. It also authorized the assignment of a case manager to each participant. Any violations of the employability plan or contract invoked sanctions, namely, the loss of the adult portion of the AFDC payment in both single-parent and two-parent families. Related provisions included benefits for childcare and transportation to and from employment or program sites.

The support component of the reform consensus appeared in the transitional services provisions of the FSA. The act required states to guarantee twelve months of childcare services for families who had become ineligible for AFDC. It also made these families eligible for twelve months of transitional Medicaid coverage. States could not charge families for coverage for the first six months. For the second six months, states could charge families with incomes between 100 and 185 percent of the federal poverty line a premium that would vary with coverage, but could not exceed 3 percent of the family's gross monthly earnings. The FSA also mandated AFDC-UP — AFDC for two-parent families in which the principal wage earner was unemployed — for all fifty states. Previously, less than half of the states offered AFDC-UP. The FSA required, as the president insisted, that at least one parent in an AFDC-UP family participate for sixteen hours weekly in a work program in addition to their JOBS activities.[48]

My analysis of the debates leading to enactment of this legislation draws principally from hearings conducted in the winter and spring of 1987 by the Social Security and Family Policy Subcommittee and the Public Assistance and Unemployment Compensation Subcommittee as well as April 1988 hearings by the Finance Committee. Occasional reference is made to hearings held in spring 1987 by the House Health and Environment Subcommittee and House Education and Labor Committee. Reagan speeches delivered throughout the FSA debates are cited. House and Senate floor debates are referenced almost entirely from summer and fall 1988 when both bodies voted on their respective welfare reform bills and the conference committee report. My analysis does not attempt to reproduce these debates chronologically, but draws excerpts from disparate hearings to sketch the development of the debates thematically through key concepts and images. I consider individual statements in greater detail to explicate the functioning of the reform consensus.

Shifts in Object and Purpose

The mid-1980s reform debates exhibited a shifting conception of the object of welfare policy from poverty to welfare dependency and a concomitant conceptual shift in the purpose of such policy from maintaining recipients' incomes to providing services to combat their dependency. The persuasiveness of Ellwood's contention that poverty cannot be explained solely by a lack of money may depend on one's economic standing, but it clearly prevailed in the reform debates of the mid-1980s. If participants perceived poverty primarily as a problem of economic lack, then income transfers would have been highly effective anti-poverty mechanisms. The reform debates would have reiterated the 1981 division of AFDC recipients: cut off the non-needy and assist the truly needy. In the mid-1980s, however, assistance meant a bundle of services and a set of expectations, not money.

In his testimony before the Public Assistance Subcommittee, Douglas Besharov, a resident scholar at the American Enterprise Institute, disclosed the findings of the Working Seminar on the Family and American Welfare Policy, the group formed in 1986 by former Reagan administration officials displeased with the pace and priority of White House reforms. He reported that "[o]ur recommendations center around the problem of long-term dependency.... We called those people [persons receiving AFDC for more than ten years] the behaviorally dependent and we made a series of recommendations about how public and private institutions should respond to their needs, to help break their cycle of dependency." Military metaphors appeared frequently as participants called for attacks on dependency. Rep. Dan Lungren sounded a call-to-arms, advocating "a cultural assault on poverty that enlists government and society as a whole in an effort to root dependency out from local economies and from the minds of the poor." His reference to poverty as indicative of dependency demonstrated the perceived epiphenomenal relation of poverty to dependency throughout the debates. In this respect, Governor Castle explained to the Family Policy Subcommittee that the NGA supported a comprehensive approach because the governors believed that an array of services would best combat "the root cause of welfare dependency."[49]

If dependency was behavioral, cognitive, and prior to economic explanations of poverty, then it could be learned among generations. Testifying before the Senate, Public Assistance Subcommittee chair Harold Ford stressed the need to design programs that addressed the "core group" of AFDC recipients. He insisted that "it is that group that we need to break the cycle with. We cannot afford to see the dependency on welfare passed from one generation to another." His intimation of family inheritance resonated with the statements of someone committed to a decidedly different political philosophy, which indicated the breadth of the focus on dependency. In his 1988 State of the Union Address, President Reagan bemoaned the scarce resources of many poor families. In such sparse circumstances, "[d]ependency has become the one enduring heirloom, passed from one generation to the next, of too many fragmented families." Participants insisted that federal policies had done little to arrest this intergenerational transmission. Representing the National Association of Counties, Doris Kearns described to the Education and Labor Committee the tendency of current federal programs "to encourage long-term dependency."[50]

Not all participants concurred with the shift to dependency, however. Douglas Glasgow of the National Urban League objected specifically to the displacement of poverty. He noted that "the welfare reform debate has truncated around the axiological issue of dependency rather than the economic issue of poverty." He countered that in 1985 AFDC served only one-third of America's poor. Moreover, adults constituted only one-third of this group. Others voiced concern about the goals of a reform effort concentrated on dependency. Susan Rees shared the hope of the Coalition on Human Needs that the Public Assistance Subcommittee "will have as its overriding goal the reduction of poverty. Too often, many who are advocating welfare reform today seem to have as their central focus the reduction of the welfare rolls."[51] The focus on dependency prevailed in spite of these kinds of objections.

Though some participants objected to the focus on dependency, few defended AFDC as principally an income maintenance program. Senator Moynihan articulated the mid-1980s turn to services and expectations in his opening statement as chair of the Family Policy Subcommittee. Reminding his auditors that AFDC was primarily a children's program, he asserted that "[w]e need a wholly new system of child support which, without abandoning ultimate security, puts its first emphasis on earned income and which, without giving up on the problems of deeply dependent children, extends coverage to all needy ones." In her appearance before the committee, Dr. Mary Jo Bane persisted in her advocacy of a service orientation. In 1983 she co-authored with David Ellwood a report for the Department of Health and Human Services entitled *Dynamics of Dependence.* The report called for an array of services to enable recipients to enter the paid labor force. In her testimony, she described promising reforms in New York State, which "has shifted the focus of welfare programs from simply providing maintenance and support to the needy to giving them the tools they require for self-sufficiency." Former HEW secretary Arthur Flemming reiterated this call for changes in policy focus in his committee testimony: "Public assistance for low-income families should be reoriented toward more emphasis on job readiness and job development for those able to work and less emphasis on income maintenance."[52]

A shift to services and expectations as anti-dependency tools entailed movement away from other, previously established commitments. Prefiguring the mid-1990s debates, some participants intimated limits beyond which needy families would be denied assistance. In an exchange with Governor Clinton, Rep. Fred Grandy of the Education and Labor Committee inquired about a potential "subclass" of AFDC recipients. He cited the committee's unanimous agreement to shift from "an income assistance program to a job creation and job placement program," but wondered about these recipients who were possibly not restorable. He asked: "What are we saying about that percentage of individuals that cannot or will not be trained, whether they are behaviorally dependent and can do nothing in this kind of program? What is society's responsibility to them in your estimation?" Governor Clinton insisted on mutual obligation: "Well, if they refuse to do anything, I don't know that we have any responsibility to them." A few witnesses and elected officials objected to this "missing piece" of the reform consensus.[53] In the face of dangerously transmittable welfare dependency, however, such possibilities had to be countenanced. Dependency could be tolerated no longer. In this respect, some witnesses admitted to personal guilt in its perpetuation. Carl Williams confessed to the Senate Finance Committee the counter-productive attitudes of many program administrators. He regretted that "the philosophy of welfare for the last fifty-some odd years has been that we are a maintenance program. Our jobs as welfare administrators are dependent on other people's dependency." As the Senate considered final passage of the FSA, Moynihan asserted confidently that the act would "redefine the whole question of dependency. Receiving income support is no longer to be a permanent or even extended condition but, rather, a transition to employment and an immediate gain of parental support for children."[54]

Dependency, of course, did not appear ex nihilo in the mid-1980s. Disavowal of dependency had long been a quality of public statements regarding social welfare policy. In his 1964 message to Congress proposing a nationwide war on poverty, Lyndon Baines Johnson distinguished his anti-poverty proposals from indiscriminate assistance. He insisted that "[t]he war on poverty is not a struggle simply to support people, to make them dependent on the generosity of others."[55] Yet the different political moods of these two periods signaled some of the concerns animating mid-1980s reformers. President Johnson's message exuded optimism. He sought to expand opportunity for disadvantaged citizens and expressed confidence in the ability of government to contribute positively to this effort. Mid-1980s reformers, however, diagnosed the dependency of AFDC recipients amidst growing concerns about an emerging "underclass."

In popular discourse, not only welfare recipients but hustlers, street thugs, drug addicts, and mental patients populated the underclass. Writers such as Ken Auletta linked these figures through a singular focus on deviance. He explained that the "underclass usually operates outside the generally accepted boundaries of society. They are often set apart … by their 'deviant' or antisocial behavior, by their bad habits, not just by their poverty." Auletta's explanation illustrated how media accounts represented the underclass as a fearsome group whose pathologies were behavioral in nature. Auletta amplified these qualities in asserting an "indisputable" fact that "violence" is more common among the underclass: "Some see crime as a profitable and exciting career and would engage in it even if offered a good job. For others, hustling and behavior society considers aberrant becomes the chief means of achieving success."[56] Young unmarried women were implicated in these crimes because they birthed and raised the members of the underclass. Auletta identified the "feminization" of poverty as the social development of the past several decades most responsible for the emergence of the underclass. Journalists indicted AFDC too. In Mickey Kaus's view, which he articulated in a controversial 1986 article in the New Republic, AFDC, "as the umbilical cord through which the mainstream society sustains the isolated ghetto society, permits the expansion of this single-parent culture." For most commentators, the underclass referred primarily to an African-American population. Kaus insisted that "it is simply stupid to pretend that the culture of poverty [which he equated with the underclass] isn't largely a black culture."[57]

As a metaphor, the "underclass" heightened the potential danger of welfare dependency and exacerbated the negative standing of welfare recipients. Depicting its members as a "class," the underclass metaphor intimated that welfare recipients shared essential character traits with criminals and the mentally ill. In associating diverse figures, this metaphor attached outright criminality and insanity to AFDC recipients. Further, the "class" reference in underclass ascribed a structural stability to the behavioral deviance diagnosed by various commentators. The underclass with its behavioral pathologies now appeared as a social category, one that could be contrasted to the middle class. As a social category, the underclass demanded attention apart from socioeconomic analyses of poverty that located its root causes in such factors as unemployment or industrial transformation. Moreover, the members of the underclass appeared more threatening through their representation as a "class." A class intimated large numbers of people—larger than the separately enumerated categories of welfare recipients, mental patients, muggers, homeless people, and others. And ostensibly disparate acts such as welfare receipt and gang warfare appeared connected by some degree of class cooperation.

In this ominous environment, many mid-1980s reformers expressed nervousness and fear of what might happen should welfare dependency continue unabated. While some participants asserted consensus hopefully and approvingly as the result of progress in thinking about welfare reform, others expressed a sense of foreboding. In the view of these reformers, policymakers had no choice but to strive for consensus—or suffer potentially disastrous consequences.

Announcement of Consensus

"[W]e may just have one of those rare alignments that brings about genuine social change," Daniel Patrick Moynihan announced. In his remarks that opened Senate hearings on welfare reform, Moynihan called attention to the special quality of their enterprise. He articulated a theme that would be repeated often: a virtually unprecedented tone characterized deliberations regarding potential reform initiatives, promising widely agreeable legislation. Indeed, he likened the debates to a state of "'syzygy,' by which astronomers describe a rare alignment of the sun and the moon and the earth which cause all manner of natural wonders."[58] Though not fully perceptible, participants insisted that something significant was happening, and they meant to take full advantage of it. The degree of consensus reached by experts and public officials would have been unimaginable even five years ago, Robert Reischauer told the Public Assistance Subcommittee. He recalled that "many conservatives seemed only to be interested in scaling back government, and in saving money by throwing undeserving recipients off the rolls. Many liberals ... seemed to feel that more was always better, and that the imposition of any obligations on recipients represented an unwarranted infringement of individual freedom." He praised the maturity of the current deliberations:

> Virtually everyone has accepted the fact that government has a major responsibility to provide some form of assistance to those who are in need. Few think welfare rolls are harboring large numbers of cheaters or that recipients are living the good life. Similarly, most now recognize that it may not be in the best interests of many needy recipients simply to provide them with more cash assistance.[59]

Reischauer's summary of the mid-1980s consensus elucidated the trajectory established by the 1981 budget-cutting debates: once cheats, shirkers, and double-dippers had been "eliminated" from AFDC, continued public frustration with welfare programs found its target in the formerly exempt truly needy.

Many legislators perceived this confluence of opinion in starkly pragmatic terms, viewing the reform consensus as a reaction to growing public frustration and trepidation with increasingly acute social problems. During Education and Labor Committee hearings, Rep. Harris Fawell relayed the fear he shared with his constituents. He admitted that "we are scared, too. I mean the whole problem is terrible.... We have communities sitting by watching its own community go to hell, so to speak." Rep. Matthew Martinez, his committee colleague, emphasized deteriorating social conditions over time: "If you lived in the neighborhood that I lived in growing up, then you understand that this [the struggle against dependency] is an everyday occurrence. But the problem has become so big that now everybody is concerned with it. And they know that it is getting to the proportion where it is going to affect each and every one of us."

Moynihan highlighted to the full Finance Committee the likely losses if legislators let the moment pass. "If we lose this chance," he warned, "I think in the next century we may return to the subject, and another generation of children will be lost."[60] The prominent attention given to consensus in all of these explanations installed as presumptive the shifts in object and purpose as well as a contractual frame that oriented the debates.

Just as they announced the existence of consensus throughout the debates, most participants asserted their version of the policy shape of this concordance. The aggregate list of widely agreed upon components was both extensive and contradictory: child support; work; training; education; childcare; healthcare; transportation; employment incentives; job opportunities; job placement; state flexibility; family living standards; case management; nationwide AFDC-UP; teen pregnancy programs; Medicaid extensions; unemployment insurance; counseling; contracts; Earned Income Tax Credit expansion; mandatory/voluntary participation; and minimum benefits. The FSA contained only those provisions that corresponded with a focus on dependency and met with a service orientation. In the context of a shift away from income maintenance, for instance, an insistence on mandatory participation prevailed in the face of promises from some legislators that mandates would require minimum benefits, which were not incorporated into the FSA. Others, such as former representative Steve Corman, recognized the untenability of these demands. He suggested that legislators had little bargaining power with respect "to the mandatory work provisions … I think it is clear that in this day and age, there is going to be movement in that direction."[61]

Whatever its concrete form, the consensus presumed success in removing non-needy recipients from welfare programs. President Reagan, who instigated the 1981 drive toward reduction, called attention directly to these successes as preconditions of further reform. In a 1987 speech to conservative supporters of welfare reform, Reagan congratulated his auditors for their past achievements yet urged further action. He confided that conservative interest in welfare too frequently "has been interpreted as merely a desire to prevent waste or fraud or stop welfare abuse." Reagan insisted that though these were praiseworthy goals, "waste and fraud isn't all we conservatives have to offer on the poverty problem — not by a long shot." Citing *Losing Ground,* he explained that increases in the poverty rate had matched increases in federal expenditures to combat poverty. The federal welfare system had wreaked havoc on the poor family. Yet the reform consensus offered hope for an alternative direction.

Reagan explained that "our traditional concern with strengthening the family is directly related to this emerging national consensus."[62]

Reagan called for a "strategic assault on poverty" centered on family life. This assault depended on the suppression of an impulse to view Washington as the agent of reform. Combating poverty necessitated community involvement. It also required a changed outlook: "[I]nstead of citing at the end of each year how many people were being maintained on welfare—if the program was really correct, every year they would be saying how many people we had been able to remove from welfare and restore to a position of independence." His concluding comments bridged the impulses of 1981 and the mid-1980s. He shared his judgment that "truly ... the bulk of the people on welfare aren't just lazy bums or cheaters—they want nothing more than to be independent, free of the social workers, and out on their own once again."[63] From delinquents to needy dependents, Reagan also gestured toward conciliation and assent. And Senator Moynihan, who opposed the 1981 cuts adamantly, expressed relief: "I think the day is past when we have gone through our phase that 'government is not the answer to our problems; government is the problem.' We have heard that theory, and that, thank heavens, is past."[64] Moynihan acknowledged the limits of government, but viewed the reform consensus as an earnest attempt at positive change. Still, the reform consensus needed a vehicle to make tangible its broad contours in an image that could attain the assent of various participants. Its vehicle had to be specific enough to give shape to the feelings of mutual obligation expressed by participants yet general enough to forestall particular disagreements over policy. Toward these ends, participants invoked the notion of a contract.

Contracts and Signees

The idea of a contract between the individual recipient and the welfare agency was the centerpiece of the reform consensus. Participants invoked the idea of a contract both as a written document and as a model of social relations. As a written document, a contract functioned as a highly appropriate and effective method of defining concretely the sense of mutual obligation that characterized the mid-1980s debates. For many skeptical legislators and witnesses, it offered assurances that the changed orientation of the policy deliberations would be implemented in local welfare offices across the nation. As a model of social relations, a contract encapsulated the broad contours of the reform consensus. A contract connoted responsibility and obligation. Both manifestations emphasized this dimension. Judith Gueron, president of the highly regarded MDRC, identified the "common core" of most reform proposals as "a redefinition of the social contract, whereby welfare programs such as AFDC would be changed from a broad entitlement to benefits to a reciprocal obligation between the citizen and the state."[65]

Many viewed the contract as a means of reconnecting recipients to their communities, which entailed a modification of the demands that a recipient could place on her neighbors. According to Moynihan, "you can't just say, 'take care of me.' You have to take care of yourself because you have an obligation to society at large. You are part of the whole, as well as being an individual." Connections established through a contract were not casual or easily broken. Their "binding" quality transformed as well the demands that communities could place on recipients. In requiring high school education, for instance, Robert Reischauer explained: "So, we are saying: this is what is best for you. We know what is good for you, and please ignore the previous thirteen years of your life during which you have had bad experiences in this environment."[66] Reconnecting to one's community required a circumscription of autonomy.

The invocation of a contract signaled fundamental values held by its champions. Sen. William Armstrong viewed recipient obligations as "simple justice." He maintained that "[m]ost people fully share the view that those on welfare who are able to do so should work in return for the subsistence and support society is providing them." Senator Moynihan connected the idea of a contract fundamentally to citizenship and democracy.

> [I]t seems to me that what you are talking about ... is citizenship. You are not talking only about welfare or employment or anything. You are talking about what it means to be a citizen in this country. Governor Clinton spoke about "contract," that you owe the society something, and the society owes you something.... And that is what the whole notion of American democracy is about, that notion of "covenant." It is a powerful idea.[67]

Indications of the contract model's sway lay in the absence of alternative configurations of citizenship or social relations. Some witnesses questioned the applicability of a contract to social welfare policy, but they did not suggest noncontractual frames on which to construct policy. Objections

to the fundamental premises of the reform consensus intimated a community that belied the demands of a contract, but these perspectives were
confined to the periphery of the deliberations.

Representatives of state welfare programs utilizing written contracts
appeared before congressional committees to vouch for their efficacy.
Linda Wilcox, director of welfare employment in the Maine Department
of Human Services, shared with senators her state's case management approach. A case manager worked with each recipient throughout her
training and job placement. Individual programs proceeded in accordance with a mutually agreed-upon employability plan. Wilcox noted
that "[e]ach step the participant will take is preceded by a signed agreement specifying what the participant will do and what the case manager
will do. We have found this clear statement of the responsibilities of both
parties to be an effective mechanism for structuring the participant's
movement towards independence." State Assembly member Art Agnos
appeared before the Family Policy Subcommittee to describe the use of "a
legally binding contract between the clients and the welfare office itself"
in California's lauded GAIN program. His testimony elicited an observation from Moynihan on the progress of reform debates since 1981. Moynihan reflected that "[i]f you think of the distance that we traveled from
the stereotype of 'welfare queens' and so forth to a genuinely creative notion of how to work together without stigmatizing the recipients, while
acknowledging that if society has responsibility, so do the individuals."[68]
He praised debate participants for discussing recipient responsibility
without recourse to stereotypes. His praise proved more an expressed
hope than a description of deliberative conditions.

In some instances, discussions of mutual obligation and contracts
became a veiled attack on shirkers and cheats. Reiterating the themes of
Beyond Entitlement, Lawrence Mead insisted to the Family Policy Subcommittee that the "real" problem with employing welfare recipients was
not a lack of jobs: "The problem, rather, is that welfare itself has not generally required participation on the part of the recipients in some form of
meaningful activity." Mead held that mandatory work programs benefited recipients and governments; such programs resulted in longer work
hours and higher earnings for recipients, which in turn recouped administrative costs. But the "most important consequence is simply participation itself, simply that these programs have raised the share of the
employable recipients who have to do something in return for benefits."
Mead stressed the importance of satisfying public expectations. He

asserted that "the public is interested in that participation in and of itself. They want that. They want people involved at higher levels of effort on their own behalf."[69] Mead's testimony depicted a significant portion of welfare recipients as shirkers. He insisted that mutual obligation be mandated.

Although he gestured toward positive reform, the president charged that welfare programs harbored cheats and other ineligible persons. In a 1987 message to Congress, he noted that "many Americans who are not poor receive public assistance benefits, even as many others remain in poverty." And Phil Gramm continued to defend the "forgotten man" who pulled the social welfare wagon. He maintained that "we all know the fellow who pays for all these programs is the guy that does the work and pays the taxes and pulls the wagon in every state in the Union." Gramm insisted that Congress demand effort from those riding in the wagon; he insisted on paid work. He complained that "the plain truth is there are a lot of people in this country who have trouble holding jobs because they cannot get to work on time, because they cannot or do not want to fit into the regimentation that most persons find to be commonplace and necessary."[70] The return of the forgotten man and other disabling images of the poor revealed the persistence of arguments and images from the 1981 debates.

Not everyone supported the utilization of contracts. A few witnesses voiced concerns about the conditions under which contracts would be signed. Kevin Aslanian, executive director of the Coalition of California Welfare Rights Organizations, noted widespread discussion of "contract, client choice, and mutual decisions and all these other things." Aslanian defined a contract as the "product of a bargain between two equal parties." Yet he labeled the opinion that welfare recipients and social workers encountered one another on equal ground illusory. He argued that "[t]here is no way that a client could bargain with the all mighty social worker who holds the money in her or his hand and if the client is not obedient, then the client will not get the money to pay for the rent and for the housing and for the utilities and all this other stuff." Aslanian held that mandatory participation also prevented fair bargaining. He noted that "if the client does not comply with the provisions of the contract, they will be sanctioned. What happens to the state if they do not comply with the provisions of the contract? Nothing.... So, you see, there is enforcement for the client but no enforcement for the state. There is no equality." This kind of objection encountered a hostile reception. Moynihan responded vehemently when Aslanian appeared before the Finance Committee. He retorted: "The idea that there is an energetic bureaucracy out there that is just waiting to seize the moment to take these poor people and force them into jobs—no. No, it is just the opposite. It is just to send them their checks and leave them alone."[71] Moynihan and others believed that the utilization of contracts would reverse this destructive apathy.

The contract withstood additional criticisms. Some participants expressed alarm over the possibly baneful effects on children of grant reductions and other sanctions for breach of contract. Sanctions might exacerbate an already intolerable condition. Rep. Thomas Downey contrasted the wide discrepancies and inadequacies in AFDC grants with benefits given to people eligible for SSI. He asked James Miller, director of the Office of Management and Budget, to elucidate the reasons for such different treatment. To Miller's evasive response, Downey concluded: "So what we are simply talking about is that we are prepared to accept a standard of care for one group of our population and a significantly smaller standard of care for, in many instances, the most helpless among us." When his committee colleague Hank Brown noted that SSI recipients were neither able nor expected to work, Downey observed that children comprised two-thirds of the AFDC caseload. Brown replied: "Certainly a valid point. That point, though, does not diminish a parent's obligation to the child and to earning an income."[72] In this exchange and others, participants arguing against the application of a contractual model for social welfare encountered assertions of a need to amplify explicitly the mutual obligations of the social bond itself.

This unreflective reliance on themes of mutual obligation obscured the limits of a contract even within the assumptions of a contractual model. A signed contract between recipient and welfare agency could not guarantee the one provision necessary to reduce "dependency" on welfare programs: paid employment. Education and Labor chairperson Augustus Hawkins questioned Governor Clinton about the likelihood of available jobs in Clinton's testimony to the committee. The governor admitted flatly: "I think the contracts, it is not contemplated that the contracts will promise jobs per se." Clinton added that his state of Arkansas had been successful in placing recipients into jobs in the paid labor force "even though we have one of the highest structural unemployment rates in the United States."[73] His reply, however, deflected the implicit charge that a contract failed to fulfill the claims of its most ardent supporters.

The intended signee of the contract was the long-term recipient, represented most vividly and urgently in the image of the teenage mother.

However, just as the 1981 debates divided the welfare population into two groups—truly needy and others—so too did the mid-1980s deliberations. In this episode, participants made moral distinctions with reference to a temporal index: short-term versus long-term recipients. In this way, legislators and witnesses emphasized the heterogeneity of the AFDC population even among people in need.[74]

Participants did not regard short-term recipients as a pressing problem. Short-term recipients frequently entered the AFDC caseload as a consequence of sudden, adverse changes in familial or employment circumstances. These recipients typically possessed job skills and established work histories. They tended to exit the AFDC caseload without much assistance from welfare agencies. Short-term recipients elicited some concern because low-wage jobs enabled few short-term recipients to withstand family traumas and other personal disasters. But most participants believed that transitional services included in the proposals would address this need. In contrast, long-term recipients engaged the fears, frustrations, and hopes of most legislators and witnesses. They seemingly entered the AFDC caseload as their cohorts entered the private labor market. Long-term recipients often possessed few job skills and no work histories, and they remained in the AFDC population despite the "efforts" of social workers and welfare administrators. In Senate testimony, Public Assistance Subcommittee chairperson Harold Ford stressed the need to break the "cycle of dependency" with the "core group" of AFDC recipients. In agreement, Moynihan pointed to the tenuous position of many children in the welfare population: "Some are in a very temporary state of dependency; others are in a long-term state and in danger of themselves becoming dependent adults."[75]

The teenage mother, whom participants imagined as black, uneducated, frequently an inner-city resident, and often part of a lineage of poor women, embodied the long-term recipient. Dr. Michael Carrera informed the Family Policy Subcommittee that more than one million American teenagers became pregnant every year, and 44 percent of these pregnancies resulted in births. Carrera explained that one-half of these new mothers "have dropped out of school and have not yet reached their eighteenth birthday. More than half [of the births] are to young women who are not married.... Teen marriages, when they occur, are characterized by a huge degree of instability." The future prospects for these mothers appeared bleak. Teen mothers rarely received financial or parental support from the fathers of their children. Teen parents were more likely than older parents to experience "chronic unemployment, inadequate income, and reduced educational experiences." Teen mothers were more likely to become long-term recipients. Carrera judged that "[t]he emotional toll of these young people is staggering as is society's economic burden in sustaining these families."[76] His reference to emotional suffering adumbrated a psychological profile of teenage mothers sketched by debate participants.

Images of teenage mothers commonly represented a melancholic young woman plagued by functional incapacities. Participants described her as hopeless and forlorn. Rep. Charles Rangel asserted to the Public Assistance Subcommittee that if one discounted short-term recipients, the composition of the remaining AFDC caseload consisted of "hard-core welfare recipients, career welfare recipients, people that are without jobs, without hope, that live in misery." Similarly, Senator Rockefeller shared with the Family Policy Subcommittee his view of long-term recipients as "thoroughly discouraged, thoroughly nonverbal, thoroughly without hope." Participants saw teenage mothers as sufferers of low self-esteem. Sen. John Chafee expressed concern over states' abilities to rehabilitate this recipient: "the teenager who has no education and has no self-respect or self-confidence, has not married, has a child."[77]

The functional incapacities of these young mothers compounded their emotional woes. Rep. Harold Ford summarized the beliefs of many participants when he characterized teenage mothers as "those least able to help themselves." Rep. Barbara Kennelly dramatically illustrated their limitations. Questioning one witness who testified before the House Public Assistance Subcommittee, Kennelly cited studies that judged the average reading level of the teenage mother between ages seventeen and twenty-one as "sixth grade." Kennelly imagined a typical scenario: "So she is bringing up a child in a very low-income area, and that child has a mother who doesn't read very well so [she] is not going to read to him a lot, and there are some problems as a role model."[78] The welfare system overlooked this troubled young woman. Participants held that her emotional instabilities and functional incapacities threatened to isolate the teenage mother from mainstream society permanently.

A medical tone informed this psychological profile. Dr. Carrera, of course, offered his bleak prognosis as a physician. But other participants diagnosed serious conditions as well. They spoke frequently of impending illness. In this respect, teenage mothers occupied a precarious position.

They embodied the long-term recipient not because they had been receiving welfare for an extended period of time; these mothers were, after all, young. Rather, they embodied the long-term recipient in embryonic form. As such, they constituted an important link, one that potentially could be broken, in the intergenerational transmission of dependency. Teenage mothers formed a "high-risk" group for contracting the disease of welfare dependency. Secretary of Labor William Brock reported to the Education and Labor Committee that "young, unwed mothers who enter the welfare system when their child is less than three" were "at greatest risk" of welfare dependency. Likewise, Robert Greenstein, executive director of the Center on Budget and Policy Priorities, wondered about the efficacy of a particular reform measure for "the most high-risk group such as young mothers." Evaluations of risk frequently accompanied discussions of dependency. After Joseph Delfico of the General Accounting Office identified mothers with young children as "the greatest risk of becoming long-term recipients," Rep. Cass Ballenger made explicit in subsequent questioning the implicit medical tone of their discussion. Ballenger complained that "all the systems we have are to treat the symptoms rather than finding out the basis of the disease."[79]

Medical diagnoses sometimes conjured an illicit realm. Some participants characterized young mothers as belonging to a "hard-core" group of recipients. Representative Rangel employed this phrase when he spoke of the depressed emotional state of teenage mothers. Senator Chafee offered his diagnosis of low self-esteem in teenage mothers during Finance Committee hearings as an illustration of what he viewed as "the 'hard-core' cases." In earlier hearings before the committee, Robert Helms, assistant secretary for planning and evaluation in the Department of Health and Human Services, supported administration reforms because they "focus on the hard-core group who are benefited most by these programs."[80] The phrase "hard-core" suggested the strong resistance to remedy presented by certain types of welfare cases, but "hard-core" also intimated prurient interests. The early sexual activity of teenage mothers constituted a threat to mainstream social values and norms. Images of the teenage mother thus reverberated with underclass stereotypes even when participants did not employ the term. Psychological profiles invoked the mental patients who, as homeless people wandering city streets, populated the underclass. References to "hard-core" dependency elicited criminal undertones in teen pregnancy, bolstering linkages between welfare recipients and the muggers and gang members of the underclass. In these ways, the image of the teenage mother connected the problem of welfare dependency to the feared and suspected "underclass."

Some objected to the potentially disabling and disparaging connotations of an "underclass." When it surfaced in debates over the FSA, the phrase suggested the nondeliberative quality of the reform consensus. In testimony before the Public Assistance Subcommittee, Patrick Grace Conover of the United Church of Christ argued that the "most basic myth to overcome is that of the underclass. There are some individuals who fit the crudest stereotypes, and most of them are not receiving welfare benefits. The great majority of those in poverty, and of those receiving welfare benefits, do not fit the underclass stereotype." In subsequent questioning, Representative Kennelly challenged his objection to the phrase. She stressed that "[w]hen we use it, we often refer to the 15 percent who are the long-term welfare recipients, who are on over eight years and use 50 percent of the funds that we have in our welfare program.... It is the young mother, the single mother.... Now, is that your basic myth or is that there?" Conover retorted that the phrase implied a lack of motivation; he called instead for attention to increased opportunity. Kennelly expressed agreement, elaborating: "And yet, because of the lack of basic skills and the lack of ability or avenues to get out of this abject poverty, we are finding that we have an underclass in the United States that we never had before. A child is born and does not have the same shot that everybody else has of getting up there.... And, to me, that is an underclass, a wasted life."[81]

Though they described the present circumstances of the teenage mother as baneful, legislators and witnesses believed that significant reforms could improve her prospects. Participants turned to studies of demonstration projects as evidence of the efficacy of a shift to services and mutual obligations. Indeed, researchers argued that education, training, and work programs helped those most in need. Senator Rockefeller posed this question to MDRC President Judith Gueron directly. He asked if long-term recipients constituted a "permanent underclass" or if they could be reached through basic skills and other types of training that had not yet been pursued intensively. Gueron answered: "The consistent lesson from careful research is that programs are most effective in that they make the largest difference for people who are least likely to succeed on their own."[82] Though a sense of foreboding spurred some participants to support welfare reform, they nevertheless shared a belief, even if they sought reassurances from others, in the power of a contract to compel long-term recipients to alter their behaviors. In positioning these recipients as contract signees, participants appealed to them as rational economic actors.

Success among long-term recipients required a commitment to adequate funding. Gueron reported to the Education and Labor Committee a "threshold effect in working with very dependent welfare recipients." She instructed that "[t]his finding suggests that relatively low-cost programs may not be effective for individuals below some minimum level of employability." Participants acknowledged the hesitancy of the general public and many elected officials to fund significant reform initiatives. If financial constraints forced choices among competing policy aims, some witnesses argued, then states ought to offer intensive services for a limited group of long-term recipients. In this vein, Robert Greenstein objected to participation rates proposed by the Reagan administration. He cited state tendencies to spread resources thinly over many people. Such an approach detracted from "what ought to be our most important goal: reducing long-term welfare dependency."[83] Reducing dependency meant requiring recipients to alter their behavior.

Although a contract did not promise employment, agreement to its terms indicated that the recipient would seek a job. The extent to which the state would aid in this search, perhaps acting as an "employer of last resort," remained unresolved. The attention given to paid employment represented a dramatic shift from the 1981 debates. In 1981 only a few witnesses compared the employment rates of AFDC mothers to non-AFDC mothers. In the mid-1980s, changing social norms entered the policy debates full stride. Legislators and witnesses presented themselves as simply asking AFDC mothers to assume the same responsibilities as mothers in the paid labor force. Senator Moynihan marveled that "nothing has so transformed our possibilities in this field than the change in the perception of female employment in the last fifteen years." Rev. Thomas Harvey connected women's participation in the paid labor force not to program possibilities but to public expectations. He observed that "changing female participation in the work force, for whatever reasons, has clearly changed the view of what the public will support through public assistance."[84] Harvey and others urged that comparisons of paid employment be made with care. As Robert Greenstein explained, the majority of working mothers did not work full-time, year-round. He reported that only 29 percent of married mothers with children worked full-time, year-round.

Of the employed wives in non-welfare families who would be poor if not for her income, only one in three of these women worked an average of thirty hours or more weekly throughout the year.[85] Most debate participants, however, focused on the signals sent by work, equating its importance with the traditional caregiver role ascribed to single mothers. John Heintz, representing the American Public Welfare Association, expressed the sentiments of many in his testimony to the Public Assistance Subcommittee: "Children do not benefit in the long run from having a single parent at home full-time, if they do not also learn about self-sufficiency and the options available to them in the larger community."[86]

Compelling paid employment required resolution of dilemmas confronted by working AFDC recipients and former recipients. Many legislators argued that current policies forced AFDC mothers to choose between insuring medical care for their children and accepting paid employment. Shirley Lawson, a former AFDC recipient employed as a community outreach counselor, confirmed these arguments in her testimony to the Health and the Environment Subcommittee:

> You may ask what will happen to us if we need health care. What would I do if my daughter has another asthma attack. I would make sure I got her the medical care she needs, and in so doing, I would make a lot of bills I couldn't pay. Then I probably would have collection agencies after me and get my wages garnished. Before long, I would be back to wondering why I was working for so little pay.[87]

AFDC mothers faced another vexing decision with childcare. Describing Massachusetts's highly regarded ET program, Gov. Michael Dukakis informed the Family Policy Subcommittee that inadequate daycare often inhibited one's search for paid employment.[88] Participants believed that a signed contract would include medical and childcare provisions in its reorientation of the AFDC program.

The demand that single mothers secure paid employment signaled a vastly different historical moment from the adoption of Title IV of the 1935 Social Security Act. This fifty-year history of transformed social and cultural practices figured prominently in the statements of some participants. They argued that AFDC was outdated. The program had not kept pace with social change. It needed restructuring. Senator Moynihan referred to the history of the AFDC program most frequently. He opened the Family Policy Subcommittee hearings by explaining that ADC's designers construed it as a temporary program for widows and orphans that would "wither away" as more workers and their dependents qualified for survivors' insurance. In the years since its adoption, however, "an earthquake [has] shuddered through the American family structure." Moynihan observed that today only a minority of children could expect to live continuously with both of their parents through their eighteenth birthday. He reminded committee members and witnesses that "when AFDC began in the 1930s, it was primarily assumed that the typical beneficiary would be a West Virginia miner's widow." The program acted as the breadwinner in his absence; its designers did not anticipate the emergence of single mothers receiving public assistance for many years. More recent history informed the deliberations as well. Moynihan called attention to the turn away from income maintenance. Noting the failure of the Family Assistance Plan, he remarked: "A guaranteed income which was not high enough in 1969 can't even be talked about now."[89] He also cited the drive toward reduction initiated in 1981. The massive deficit increases that arose in the aftermath of the early-1980s budget deliberations severely circumscribed the vision of reformers.

Key concepts and images of the reform consensus enabled the changed demands, which marked the passage of a half-century, placed upon single mothers. The shift from poverty and income maintenance to welfare dependency and service provision attained tangible form in the vehicle of a contract, which served both as a model of human relations and a specific policy tool. Contracts implied signees, and concerns about long-term recipients directed participants to the teenage welfare mom as the embodiment of this figure. Her qualities also intimated the urgency and fear that motivated some participants to seek reform. The contract required work and obligated the state to support such efforts in some measure. Along these lines, work-related provisions constituted one major area of the FSA. Another area, the first title of the legislation, concerned child support. Addressing this dimension of the reform consensus, participants invoked not the poor mother but the poor father: the "deadbeat dad."

Demanding Parental Support

A second representation circulated throughout the deliberations: the absent father who did not pay child support, the "deadbeat dad." While the teenage mother informed the deliberations explicitly, the absent father did so obliquely. Participants described the teenage mother in detail, identifying her circumstances, motivation, and future prospects for economic self-sufficiency. The absent father appeared as a corollary of proposed policy reforms. His image took shape as an environmental influence that had an impact on the everyday lives of young mothers. Whatever their opinion of the transformations, participants viewed the young mother as a bearer of great social and cultural change. They attributed the phenomenon of unpaid child support to a personal abdication of duties by the absent father. The teenage mother was the object of individual attention, a set of expectations, and a bundle of services. Simple demands were placed on the absent father. Governor Castle highlighted the need to send a message to young men that "if they are going to be fathers, they basically are going to have an eighteen-year contract, with the state involved in that contract, to help support the children who are theirs. I think that anyone who believes that a child is going to be born and that we are not going to make an effort to go out and get their support … is just sadly mistaken."[90] This statement and others expressed a simple demand: support your children!

Perceived abdication of parental responsibility elicited statements of outrage and incredulity. Jim Mattox, attorney general of Texas, likened the nonpayment of child support to child abuse. He held that "[w]hen there is not proper money for food, clothing, and shelter, I believe that brings about both physical and psychological abuse of the child." Senator Moynihan decried the disregard of many absent fathers. He cited a Colorado study that reported that most absent fathers spent more on their automobiles than their children.[91] Witnesses appeared before congressional committees to recount their attempts to receive payment of court-ordered support. The Family Policy Subcommittee asked Carol Curtis to testify after she had written a letter-to-the-editor detailing her struggles to receive child support. She recounted that "[i]t took me two years and 17,000 dollars in legal fees to collect a support award for my daughter of 126 dollars per week." In Curtis's case, her ex-husband earned a "six-figure salary" yet chose "to fight his legal obligation to pay support on the grounds that he was unable to afford it."[92] Like the fantastic cases of fraud repeated throughout the 1981 budget debates, stories of irresponsible executives bolstered assumptions that fathers chose not to meet their obligations.

A few witnesses expressed concern that demands for payment stereotyped all fathers and discounted adverse economic circumstances. Dr. Douglas Glasgow, vice president of the National Urban League, objected to the primary emphasis placed on child support in most reform proposals.

"By placing first emphasis on the child support collection system and by particularly proposing immediate mandatory automatic wage withholding," he explained, "this feeds into the distorted and rather disruptive public perception that all poor fathers are assumed to be irresponsible and unwilling to support their children." Glasgow contended that such an emphasis displaced the effects of high rates of black unemployment. Still, demands persisted—even from those who voiced doubts about other directions of the consensus. Marion Wright Edelman, president of the Children's Defense Fund, acknowledged the limited job and income opportunities of many young fathers, but she insisted that this situation did not relieve them of their parental roles: "[E]ven if these young men don't have adequate jobs, they can find a way to get a few Pampers in there and spend some time at least trying to learn how to become fathers."[93]

The image of the absent father circulated throughout the debates as the shadowy, suspected, and potentially dangerous outsider. He often assumed an indeterminate form. Legislators and witnesses frequently spoke of the baneful consequences of unpaid support, but they only sketched the figure of the man held responsible for this state of affairs. Still, their statements indicated treatment of his failure to support his children as criminal. The various measures incorporated into the FSA to increase child-support payments—automatic wage withholding, mandatory award guidelines, paternity establishment, and interstate tracking systems —represented an attempt to prevent such behavior and, once it occurred, bring the offender to swift justice.

Understanding Behavior Economically

As the use of a contract and the proposed penalties for absent fathers revealed, participants relied almost exclusively on a model of human motivation as economically driven. An economic model posits a person as a "rational, calculating individual whose goal is to maximize 'utility.'" This view is widespread in social scientific policy research. As Sanford Schram explains, its major consequence is to reduce "problems of poverty and welfare dependency to the rational calculations of economically minded poor people who have been encouraged by the wrong incentives to engage in counterproductive behavioral pathologies."[94] Participants employed this strategy in judging reform proposals, paralleling the arguments

advanced in the policy tracts of Ellwood, Murray, and others. For example, Health and Human Services secretary Otis Bowen observed that
everyone agreed that reforms ought to enable families to be self-sufficient. For this to occur, "[f]amilies seeking to escape dependency must
face incentives, both positive and negative, that lead them along pathways
to success."[95]

An economic view of motives implicates a larger market orientation.
It claims that social policy and even social relations can be understood as
a marketplace. Economist Robert Kuttner explains that in its optimal
(i.e., free and unregulated) state, a market model posits a set of assumptions about competition and behavior. With respect to competition, it as-
cribes to consumers "perfect information." The model posits a "mobility
of factors": capital, labor, and consumer may enter and exit as they wish.
"Perfect competition," consisting of multiple suppliers, low barriers to
entry, and no regulation of prices, typifies exchanges between buyers and
sellers in this optimal market. Behavioral assumptions view firms as
profit-maximizers, consumers as utility-maximizers, and preferences as
reflections of consumer taste. The model also assumes the absence of significant "externalities."[96] Kuttner argues that this model may reflect and
optimize the operations of entities such as grocery stores, but he questions the suitability of the market model for issues such as healthcare.
Even if one grants the assumptions of a market model, actually existing
social welfare practices fall far short of meeting the market model's operating conditions. Reformers have criticized the narrowly prescribed
choices of welfare recipients. Whether they locate its cause in a lack of
motivation or a lack of skills, reformers often have identified behavior as
a central problem. The "market" of social welfare does not function according to the market model. The consequences of applying this model
are more serious when one considers an additional assumption.

A central assumption of the market model is the concept of "revealed
preference." "Revealed preference" asserts tautologically that one's actual
choices indicate a person's preferences. Kuttner explains that this view
presumes that "people rationally express their true preferences in their
pattern of expenditure, the occupations they pursue, how they divide
work and leisure time, choose mates, and so on." To determine if people
are living as they genuinely desire, one may consider their actions. Moreover, a market model holds that "revealed preferences" work together in
an uncoordinated fashion to optimize system performance. Kuttner

maintains that the "free-market schema hinges on the claim that revealed preferences must aggregate to a general optimum."[97]

The concept of "revealed preference" encapsulates the limits of a market model for deliberations of social welfare policy. The market model occludes the historical and social forces that delineate a field of choices for welfare recipients, sometimes limiting and directing these choices. A young single mother may "choose" not to accept a minimum-wage job so her child may continue to receive medical care. Her "revealed preference" would indicate a decision to maximize her utility by retaining services provided by public assistance that are unavailable through low-wage employment. But this mother may desire both—medical care for her child and employment for herself. Her "revealed preference" may not signal her actual preference: a job with long-range opportunities that may protect her against the vacillations of the low-wage labor market. A market model cannot even recognize this ambition. It also assumes that preferences are pre-formed and unalterable through discussion. A market model denies social dialogue to those who, in the view of many legislators, seldom speak—welfare recipients located on the margins of their communities.

Participants' reliance on a market model particularized the contract that embodied the reform consensus as a kind of employment contract. Participants' apparent interest in the young mother lay in her possible transformation from caregiver to worker. Their demand for absent fathers to meet their financial responsibilities reflected a similarly narrow concern. As a model of social relations, this contract represented a truncated view of mutual obligation, occluding potentialities recognizing networks of interdependence. The employment contract was principally a private contract between two distinct and often opposed parties. This invocation of a contract heightened the perceived disjuncture of AFDC recipients from "mainstream" society, restricting the interaction of these citizens and others through the organ of the welfare agency. The particularity of its contract revealed important assumptions inherent in the reform consensus that characterized mid-1980s welfare policy debates. Consensus also functioned within the debates as a "participant" that constrained the deliberation of others.

The Functions of Consensus in Obscuring Difference and Enforcing Reasonableness

The reform consensus functioned in two significant ways: one function engaged people "inside" the consensus, participants who indicated an association with it at some point in the deliberations, and another operated against those "outside" the consensus, participants who did not subscribe to the shifts to welfare dependency and a service orientation. For those "inside," the reform consensus functioned to obscure their differences in policy directions and conflicting interests in reform. For those "outside," the reform consensus functioned as a disciplinary force that situated their views beyond the bounds of reasonable reform.

The reform consensus did not represent a deliberatively achieved consensus, but a bargained agreement negotiated under the aegis of consensus. To be sure, the deliberations reflected social and cultural transformations that enabled the negotiations. It is important to note, however, that concessions, not consensus, produced the legislation. Liberals accepted mandatory participation in job preparation and workfare in exchange for services such as childcare and medical care as well as some restoration of the employment incentives lost in the 1981 legislation. Conservatives ceded childcare, medical care, and incentives for mandated job preparation for some recipients and workfare for at least one parent in a two-parent AFDC-UP family. Like the young, single mother to whom participants devoted a great deal of attention, legislators entered into a contract to enact the FSA.

Assertions of consensus deflected attention from this quality of the reform initiatives. Participants slighted the significance of the bargain struck. In a negotiated settlement, provisions constitute the agreement. They are not the epiphenomenal specification of a widely held agreement or consensus. Through adamant assertion of the existence of consensus, participants discounted the significance of dissension. In so doing, they failed to recognize the tenuous nature of the agreement and the potential for its fissures to split apart in the ensuing years. Participants did not see, or did not wish to see, that the provisions adumbrated contrary visions of reform.

There were some early signs of the shakiness of the agreement, of its contractual as opposed to deliberative quality. As House and Senate conferees met to resolve differences in their reform bills, Major Owens told his colleagues a story of betrayal. Owens recalled that "[a]t the start of the 100th Congress we were told that there was an emerging consensus on welfare reform and in that consensus liberals would accept more draconian working requirements and conservatives would accept improvements in the criminally low AFDC benefits offered in most states." Owens identified the crime as the unfair and unjust treatment of AFDC children: legislators had permitted their benefits to lag far behind those received by SSI children. He held that the reform consensus had retreated from redressing this inequality. As the debates proceeded, the work requirements placed on adult recipients had become increasingly "draconian" as the "promised benefit improvements have gone from meager to meaningless. The conservatives, in other words, have not yielded at all in terms of steps to increase the amount of money that children have to survive on." Owens charged legislators with abandoning these children and slandering their parents. By insisting on mandatory work programs, legislators perpetuated the "lie that the unemployed do not want to work and will not work unless they are forced to do so."[98]

As the House prepared to consider the conference report, Owens again pleaded with his colleagues to vote against the bill. With respect to the childcare provisions of the bill, he stated: "I would applaud it if it were really in this bill, in this conference report. If we really provide it, child care, I would applaud this bill." In reaching agreement, however, conferees deleted a set of requirements defining adequate childcare. He added that the bill permitted recipients to continue their education only at the discretion of individual states and it did nothing to create jobs paying a decent wage. On this last point, Owens warned against viewing the FSA as a nascent jobs bill. He predicted that "if we have this one great change in the Social Security Act over the last fifty years, everybody is going to settle down and say, 'It's been done; this is it; it's accomplished,' and to revise this monstrosity would be almost an impossibility in the next few years."[99]

Participants did not heed Owens's warning that the passage of the FSA would forestall further reforms. They committed themselves to just the opposite. Individual legislators interpreted the FSA as the beginning of a reform agenda shaped according to their own competing policy visions. They promised to struggle for the enactment of these visions through additional measures in subsequent legislative sessions. In this way, the reform consensus settled very little. For example, identifying the work requirement as the most important reform, Sen. William Armstrong promised the FSA would "establish new principles and a new atmosphere within our welfare system…. Thousands on welfare will come to know that something is expected of them in exchange for assistance." Still, Armstrong expressed disappointment that Congress did not accept Charles Murray's challenge of fundamental reform. In fact, he worried that the service provisions might make welfare too attractive and increase the caseload. He called for limits on the number of times a person could receive benefits. Armstrong saw the FSA as a first step in reinstalling the private sphere as the locus of social welfare policy. In contrast, Rep. Leon Panetta envisioned a more comprehensive set of social programs and income supplements. His policy vision consisted of program simplification, benefit improvements, expanded employment and training opportunities, and adequate daycare and medical care. Still, Panetta supported the FSA as "the framework which we can fill-in to construct true welfare reform in future years."[100] These contrary embraces of the reform "consensus" revealed its precariousness and likely rupture in subsequent years if participants attempted these alternative paths. Participants' focus on consensus neglected the significance of the concessions that such consensus produced.

Participants' neglect should not indicate that "consensus is a horizon that is never reached."[101] Rather, the mid-1980s reform debates demonstrated an assertion of consensus that outpaced its deliberative achievement. Consensus continually eluded participants, as varied proposals for further legislation implied, obscuring policy differences in the process. This does not mean that the differences in this policy episode—or any other, for that matter—would have been resolved if deliberated directly. Yet the elucidation of disagreement is itself a valuable end, perhaps more so than the impression of agreement in the midst of disagreement. At the least, the nature of the economic contractual agreement regarding the FSA might have been illuminated.

For those participants "outside" the reform consensus, its assertion excluded their statements from the regular exchange of opinions. The premises of the reform consensus signaled an enforced zone of reasonableness. On this basis, those who objected to these premises held unreasonable points of view. The exclusions perpetrated by the reform consensus did not arise primarily from the claims of its premises but from the failure of participants to subject them to deliberation. To be sure, the shift in object to a focus on welfare dependency and the shift in purpose to a bundle of services situated within a milieu of mutual obligation reflected widespread, though not unanimous, shifts in social and cultural forces. By asserting rather than deliberating these shifts, however, participants denied themselves moments of self-reflection. Supporters of the reform consensus did not account for the perspectives of their interlocutors who disagreed.[102]

Viewing nonreflective consensus as a disciplinary force may appear to challenge the very idea of consensus. My point, however, is not to gainsay consensus as inherently coercive. This path has been pursued by Jean-François Lyotard, who argues that the emergence of a postmodern condition undermines efforts to link democratic legitimacy to rationally motivated consensus. He holds that this formulation relies on a discredited narrative of human emancipation. He also contends that this view of legitimacy rests on two dubious assumptions: that it is possible for all speakers to reach agreement on universally valid metaprescriptives and that the goal of dialogue is consensus. Lyotard calls for a conception of justice not linked to consensus. Yet his renunciation of terror—the threatened or actual elimination of a player from a language game—and notion of tangible justice in a computer age—"give the public free access to the memory and data banks"—belie a commitment to metaprescriptives of open access and debate.[103] My concern, then, is to highlight the exclusions of a nonreflective consensus. Isolated moments of intervention marked these exclusions.

The most sustained intervention may have been Margaret Prescod's testimony to the Finance Committee. Prescod's name did not appear on the scheduled witness list, but she announced her presence after the statements of a group of panelists: "Senator Moynihan, I would like to, if possible, register a protest on behalf of women all across the country. We feel that this is legislation that will affect women, for the most part, and that women who are housewives, women who are on welfare. And women have not had adequate time to testify."[104] Noting her objection, Moynihan permitted Prescod to speak after scheduled witnesses had completed their testimony. Representing Black Women for Wages for Housework, Prescod was one of the last people to testify before the Finance Committee.

At the outset of her testimony, Prescod presented an alternative conception of self-sufficiency skills to the one informing preceding statements. She explained that "[w]e are a different kind of expert than you have heard from so far. We are expert in caring for people, in keeping our communities going through volunteer work.... [A]s women who work full-time in our homes, we also think that that deserves dignity as well."

In demanding that mothers seek paid employment, participants have ignored these skills, or worse, have treated them as causes of a harmful dependency. Prescod noted that "[w]e don't hear as much being discussed
that women are already working, that homemaking and child rearing is
a full-time job, that those of us in waged jobs are doing the double shift."
She reported that think tanks such as Rand estimated the value of housework at $700 billion per year. She maintained that the significance of this
unpaid labor cast doubt on the orientation of many reforms. Prescod argued that "our unwaged work helps keep this country going. We are not
dependent on the state; the state is dependent on us."[105]

Prescod offered alternative explanations for women's entry into the
paid labor force and of the purpose of AFDC. Women entered the paid labor force in large numbers during the 1970s because many families could
no longer survive without two incomes. Moreover, women wanted the
dignity that society reserved only for paid workers. Prescod explained
that despite its origins in mothers' pensions, women historically used
AFDC as insurance against total dependence on men and to escape vio-
lent family situations. AFDC was "the only money women in the United
States get in our own right for the work of homemaking and child rearing."[106] Prescod concluded her testimony by reiterating her appeal for
legislators and other participants to recognize in their reforms the contributions to society made by women outside the market economy.

Prescod's testimony challenged directly the shifts in object and purpose that enabled the reform agreement. Her statement depicted
women as self-sufficient people on whom others relied. Prescod held that
society would not function but for the unpaid labor of women. On a local scale, she described women as caregivers who sustained families and
communities. These roles demanded a wide range of skills and abilities
that received little attention in discussions of welfare reform. Recalling
some Progressive Era appeals, she represented women's receipt of welfare
as payment owed. Welfare receipt signaled independence in another
sense as well: reclamation of one's selfhood in situations of abuse. Re-
configuring the actions and abilities of the AFDC mother in this way cast
doubt on the movement away from income maintenance. Still, she envisioned a role for services. Prescod described services not as a prod or
crutch for reluctant or unskilled workers, but as partial compensation for
the inability of a market economy to produce enough jobs paying a
decent wage.

Interventions against the reform consensus appeared in the state-ments of others, including its supporters as their remarks sometimes re-vealed the limitations of the proposed reforms. An example of the latter appeared in Representative Kennelly's discussion of the relation between the welfare and working poor. She expressed hope that AFDC mothers "might belong to the working poor someday." She described the reform proposals as an effort to enable self-sufficiency: "Give a person an edu-cation and skills so if they want two jobs to support their family, then they can have them." While Kennelly inadvertently conceded a lack of decent-paying jobs, Ruth Flower of Interfaith Action for Economic Justice echoed Prescod's argument about the lack of recognition for women's un-paid work. She declared that "all of our denominations honor work as a way of participating in society. We recognize a number of different things as work, including some things that are not recognized by the labor mar-ket."[107] Flower's comments were part of a persistent though marginalized objection to the premises of the reform consensus.

Fundamental objections came mostly from spokespersons of religious organizations. They sought to reassert a structural orientation focused on poverty as the problem. Rev. Thomas Harvey of Catholic Charities ar-gued that the quality of available jobs stood as the major disincentive for AFDC recipients seeking work. Noting that one had "to be unemployed in order to get Medicaid," Harvey wondered why a recipient should "take a job that for eleven years the country has said is worth only the minimum wage." These jobs served only "the need for cheap labor." In his appear-ance before the Family Policy Subcommittee, Rev. Bryan Hehir shared the perspective of the National Conference of Catholic Bishops. The bish-ops outlined their approach to reform in a pastoral letter on the U.S. economy, *Economic Justice for All.* Hehir reported that the bishops linked welfare policy to a macroeconomic strategy of full employment. They also insisted on an unwavering public commitment to the amelio-ration of poverty. Although specific provisions might be debated on their merits, "the essential moral assertion that government has a moral re-sponsibility toward the most vulnerable in our society ... is a principle that cannot be negotiated."[108]

These objections surfaced in the sermons preached by religious lead-ers in various public forums. In an impassioned speech at the 1988 De-mocratic National Convention, Rev. Jesse Jackson heartened poor people to reject labels that devalued them as a worthless, "subclass, underclass."

He exhorted them to "never surrender." Reverend Jackson gainsaid negative character portrayals of poor people. He informed his largely privileged audience of delegates that poor people were not lazy. He saw poor
people as deeply committed to society's work ethic. Imagining lives of
hard labor and struggle, Jackson admonished his audience that "[t]hey
catch the early bus. They work every day. They raise other people's children. They work every day. They clean the streets. They work every day.
They drive vans with cabs. They work every day. They change the beds
you slept in these hotels last night.... They work every day." Jackson
called upon more privileged Americans to acknowledge and to appreci-
ate the efforts of those who "cannot speak for themselves." He urged
everyone to "keep hope alive."[109] His speech, like the testimony given by
religious leaders to congressional committees, raised questions about the
premises of the mid-1980s reform consensus.

Those "inside" the consensus respectfully dismissed the concerns of
religious spokespersons as unrestrained idealism and overly charitable
character assessment. Given the longstanding advocacy by many religious
organizations on behalf of the poor, their objections may have been expected. For participants "inside" the consensus, however, the danger of
dependency, changes in women's work patterns, and crimes of unpaid
child support required a basic restructuring of social welfare policy
through the utilization of an employment contract.

Heading Toward Repeal

As it turned out, Major Owens was right. No major reform effort surfaced in the 101st or 102nd Congresses nor in the whole of the Bush administration. Participants concluded the mid-1980s reform debates with
an impression of consensus and a belief that fundamental steps had been
taken toward relieving basic, historical problems with public assistance
programs. It was not until the Arkansas governor who lobbied so dili-
gently for the passage of the FSA became president that participants once
again debated welfare reform in earnest. For his part, President Clinton
called for a renewed commitment to the FSA in the early days of his
administration. In a speech to the NGA, he affirmed his belief in an
"emerging consensus" on welfare reform. Clinton explained that a sudden increase in the AFDC caseload and a rise in healthcare costs in the
midst of a recession, which in turn reduced funding for the education

and training provisions of the legislation, prevented the FSA from performing its tasks. Still, he believed that the "bill that is on the books will work, given the right economy and the right kind of support systems."[110] Yet only four years later, Clinton signed legislation repealing Title IV of the 1935 Social Security Act. A significant question for analysis, then, concerns the factors precipitating this reversal.

When the 1990s debates began, information regarding the successes and failures of the FSA was sketchy, but available material suggested that the FSA, as with previous efforts, had an impact on only a minority of AFDC recipients. In an analysis of data from the 1994 *Green Book,* a publication providing background materials on programs under the jurisdiction of the Ways and Means Committee, Joel Handler reported that only 10 percent of all adult AFDC recipients participated in a JOBS activity. He specified the participation of these adults as follows: 32 percent in basic education, 16 percent in skills training, 15 percent in job searches, 7 percent in job readiness, and 1 percent in on-the-job training or work supplementation. Handler noted that a recent study of the GAIN program suggested disconcerting results for basic education programs. Only 20 percent of the students completed their education within the evaluation period. Most achieved a GED rather than a diploma. Another 20 percent of the students were continuing their education as the evaluation ended. Sixty percent stopped without finishing. They stopped either because they were employed or because of health problems. Childcare affected an even smaller percentage of recipients. Handler noted that only 3 percent of the entire AFDC caseload received childcare assistance, and most families who found paid employment did not receive Transitional Child Care (TCC). As participants debated the FSA, the Congressional Budget Office projected that 280,000 children would receive TCC in 1991. Handler noted that only 46,000 were actually enrolled.[111] Finally, child-support enforcement did not create the financial windfall that some witnesses predicted, relieving states of only a small portion of their AFDC expenditures.

The FSA did not palliate public displeasure with AFDC and other social welfare programs. As the lackluster performance of its provisions compelled further amplification of competing reform visions, the precariousness of the consensus portended rupture. Still, likely disagreement notwithstanding, the trajectory of the 1980s policy episodes foretold a course of action for the 1990s. The budget-cutting debates of 1981 heralded a retrenchment era in welfare policy discourse, which began by removing the "non-needy" from the AFDC caseload. In the mid-1980s, participants acted to update AFDC by altering the behaviors of its recipients. In the 1990s, public frustration and anger with AFDC persisted, even after reformers attempted to reduce the rolls and to reorient the program. On this path, repeal appeared as the next logical step.

CHAPTER 5

Repealing Welfare

The 1988 Family Support Act passed through a compromise reached under the aegis of consensus—a compromise that intimated two very different directions for future reform. A comparison of legislation and program titles from that mid-1980s episode and the mid-1990s policy episode examined in this chapter signals the direction of reform taken. The Family Support Act announced the sense of mutual obligation that permeated the debates in its name. Families would not be maintained by government agencies, but those who displayed initiative would be supported in their attempts at self-sufficiency. The identified beneficiary—a family—emphasized as well the widely expressed belief that recipients had obligations, for the act promised to support only those individuals who committed themselves to each other as families. Deadbeat dads, for instance, did not need to apply. The Personal Responsibility and Work Opportunity Reconciliation Act (PRWORA) included in its title no reference to support nor synonyms for support. The responsibility for one's well-being lay solely with the individual. The title suggested that the act did not introduce a new array of social programs but instead dismantled federal structures and rescinded past promises in a decisive reorientation of social policy. To the extent that the PRWORA suggested any commitment to affected persons by government, such commitment consisted of efforts at creating opportunities in the private sector for jobs but no work guarantee, as in a Work Projects Administration.

The most significant policy provision of the PRWORA may have been the repeal of AFDC, the federal program that provided a federal guarantee of monetary assistance to poor families, and the attendant change this repeal engendered in the financial structure of federal-state public assistance programs. Under AFDC, the federal government matched state funding at various rates according to numbers of eligible people; entitlement spending sustained this program. The PRWORA replaced AFDC with Temporary Assistance for Needy Families (TANF) block grants that provide states a predetermined amount of funds regardless of the number of poor residing within their borders; discretionary spending supports its public assistance programs. The title of TANF also signaled reform trajectories, marking a crucial temporal transformation. Aid to Families with Dependent Children promised aid until all children in a family reached the age of maturity, when a child no longer was recognized as under the immediate care of one's parents. Temporary Assistance for Needy Families makes no such promise. The title articulates finite duration explicitly, and grants may be withdrawn before the age of maturity or dispensed to families only sporadically. It implies that families should not rely on the grants for support.

More than sixty separate House and Senate committee and subcommittee hearings encompassing three different Congresses contributed to the passage of the PRWORA. The 1992 presidential election vaulted welfare reform proposals onto the national political agenda, where they remained in varying probabilities of passage until July 1996. A subject of considerable political attention between 1993 and 1994, welfare reform nevertheless appeared at times subordinate to or contingent on passage of a national system of health insurance. At the very least, health insurance proposals attracted significant attention and exhausted some energy of the president and other reformers.[1] The resounding rebuke of health insurance proposals and the election of a new Republican majority to both houses of Congress in 1994—likely not unrelated events—returned many participants' principal social focus to welfare reform.

Prospects for agreed-upon legislation dimmed after two presidential vetoes: one in December 1995 of reforms attached to a budget reconciliation bill that sparked a temporary and unpopular "shutdown" of the federal government; the second in January 1996 as a separate reform bill. As in the mid-1980s, the NGA goaded Congress toward passage, endorsing in February 1996 bipartisan proposals to reconfigure AFDC and Medicaid. The 1996 presidential campaign complicated passage, however, as Republican candidate and Senate Majority Leader Robert Dole attached public assistance reforms to Medicare restructuring while President Clinton vowed to veto any such bill that reached his desk. After Senator Dole resigned from public office to focus on the upcoming election, his former colleagues decoupled the two policy initiatives.

The conference report of the PRWORA passed the House of Representatives on 31 July by a vote of 328 to 101. The bill passed the Senate on 1 August by a 78 to 21 vote. Only one senator running for re-election, Paul

Wellstone of Minnesota, voted against it. President Clinton signed the
PRWORA into law on 18 August 1996. According to Congressional Budget
Office estimates, the legislation reduces social welfare spending by $54.6
billion through fiscal year 2002.[2]

As the 1990s reform debates began, repeal of AFDC was by no means
certain. In fact, Clinton affirmed his commitment to the FSA in his first
speech on welfare reform as president—one of the first speeches given after his inauguration. Yet only four years later, Clinton signed a bill that
repealed Title IV of the 1935 Social Security Act. What explained this
dramatic policy reversal? Two discursive factors precipitated AFDC's
demise. First, debates during 1993 and 1994 enacted a shift in representations of the AFDC mother. The contract signee still circulated through the
deliberations of the 103rd Congress, but alongside and eventually sup-
planting this figure was the image of the recipient as a youth in need of
strict, didactic, and constant supervision. A contract, for all its problems,
implied a signee whose claims could not be accommodated through the
uncertain availability and duration of a block grant. The bargaining position of the wayward youth was considerably weaker. Second, the 1994
elections ushered in a new composition of debate participants who provided a full hearing to claims that government programs had worsened
the plight of recipients. This judgment, however, received a significantly
different inflection in the 104th Congress than it did in the 1980s. Participants advanced an all-out attack on the welfare bureaucracy not to prove
pessimistically that legislators would always blunder when deciding social
policy, but rather as part of a confident discernment of a new age. The
revolutionaries envisaged a brave new world of information capital,
which required a break from a mistake-plagued and inefficient past. Entitlements might have survived the paternalistic milieu of the young ward
—legislators could attach more conditions to the recipient of aid—but
once the bureaucracy had been discredited completely, repeal appeared
as the only sensible policy option.

In what follows, I first describe the provisions of the PRWORA. My
analysis generally assumes a chronological pattern, weaving together context and interpretation to tell the story of a three-stage movement toward
repeal. I consider 1992 hearings held by the House Select Committee on
Hunger in which witnesses testified to the limitations of the low-wage
labor market and voiced their concerns of a likely voter backlash, discern-
ing still two possible paths of reform. I then examine how the paternalistic
milieu of the debates in the 103rd Congress facilitated the displacement of

the contract signee by the young ward. Statements of Clinton and others that alternated between supporting the efforts of recipients and questioning their values and behavior played a central role in this changing representation. Next, I explicate the brave new world of the reformers who took charge of the 104th Congress. Viewing the welfare bureaucracy as an uncaring and oppressive perpetrator of a Faustian bargain with young mothers, they looked to ambitious state officials and volunteers to reclaim important roles in social welfare practice.

I then place my chronological organization on hold as I consider an image that circulated in both the 103rd and 104th Congresses, but one that stood as a crucial indicator of the extent of reformers' confidence: the immigrant. If the repeal of AFDC reflected the confidence of debate participants in a changed world of increasingly mobile capital, then the figure of the immigrant, who emerged in the mid-1990s debates without antecedents in prior episodes, represented their anxieties in the face of globalizing economic and social forces. In the penultimate section of this chapter, I examine the reappearance of an ensemble of non-needy recipients in censure of SSI for disabled children and other programs as well as the peripheral presence of the citizen-worker as a representation of AFDC recipients. I conclude this chapter by explicating the symbolic import of the turn from entitlements to block grants.

The 1996 Personal Responsibility and Work Opportunity Reconciliation Act

The most significant provision of the PRWORA may have been its repeal of the federal guarantee of monetary assistance for poor families.[3] Instead of distributing federal funds according to the number of eligible people residing in a state, the PRWORA allocated TANF block grants to individual states based on their total federal funding for AFDC, JOBS, and emergency assistance in fiscal year 1994, fiscal year 1995, or the average of fiscal years 1992–94, whichever was higher. In return, states were required to dedicate at least 75 percent of the funds they spent in fiscal year 1994 to welfare-related activities. This minimum increased to 80 percent if a state did not meet work participation rates. The PRWORA mandated that states place 50 percent of their caseloads in work-related activities by fiscal year 2002.

The PRWORA imposed time limits on the receipt of TANF grants. It mandated first that any adult who had received benefits for two years must be working or in a work program to receive any additional benefits. Second, the PRWORA prohibited distribution of TANF funds to a family in which the adult head of household or spouse had received benefits for five cumulative years, a lifetime limit that could be shortened at state option. Children in families that reached the lifetime limit could qualify for TANF funding if they met state eligibility criteria as parents. States, however, were permitted to exempt up to 20 percent of their caseload from the five-year limit.

The PRWORA permitted or mandated denial of benefits to previously eligible groups of people. It enabled states to deny benefits to children born to parents already receiving TANF funds and to deny benefits to all unwed parents under the age of eighteen. The PRWORA required unwed parents receiving TANF grants to live at home or in an adult-supervised setting and attend high school or an alternative educational or training program. It also permitted states to reduce or eliminate a family's benefits if the parent did not cooperate with paternity establishment or child-support obtainment. Controversially, the PRWORA made all legal immigrants currently residing in the United States, with only a few exceptions, ineligible for SSI and food stamps unless and until they became citizens. The PRWORA denied almost all future legal immigrants most low-income federal benefits for five years after their arrival. It also allowed states to deny Medicaid and TANF grants to most present and future legal immigrants. The act also toughened eligibility requirements for receipt of SSI for disabled children.

Reform Heats Up on the Campaign Trail and in the Hearing Room

The story of AFDC's repeal begins with social and economic conditions that frustrated implementation of the FSA as well as incidents that forecasted rupture of its precarious consensus. Recession ushered in the 1990s, shrinking state budgets and depressing the ability of the states to carry out the support provisions of the FSA. By 1992, only one-fifth of the 2.5 million adult AFDC recipients required to participate in JOBS programs actually participated. Paul Offner, an aide to Senator Moynihan and former Ohio state welfare official, explained that cash-strapped states had claimed only 60 percent of available federal matching funds.[4] Moreover, as the recession constricted state budgets, it also contributed to a sharp rise in the AFDC caseload. Throughout most of the 1980s, the number of people receiving AFDC held steady between 10.5 million and 11 million recipients. To be sure, this "stability" was a product of OBRA-induced cuts. In 1990, however, the number of AFDC recipients reached 11.46 million. Their number increased by 10 percent in 1991 to 12.6 million. A similar increase of 9 percent occurred in 1992 as the total number of recipients rose to 13.82 million. By 1993, more than 14 million people—including 9.6 million children—received AFDC.[5]

As their financial crises deepened, states responded to growing welfare rolls in the early 1990s with punitive measures designed to link benefit reductions or outright cuts to undesirable recipient behavior. Some states, such as New Jersey, passed rules that prohibited the dispersal of additional grant dollars for children born to women on welfare. Wisconsin considered this approach as part of a collection of already-passed reforms. A program dubbed "learnfare" cut grants by 15 percent for families with habitually truant students and by 45 percent for teenage mothers who did not attend school regularly. Another held the parents of teenage fathers financially responsible for their sons' unmet obligations. California governor Pete Wilson proposed a similar set of reforms, including reduced benefits for families moving to California from states with lower benefits. He also proposed an across-the-board 10 percent reduction in benefits for all AFDC families and a further 15 percent reduction for AFDC families who remained on welfare for more than six months.[6]

Echoing the sentiments of other state officials, James Lee, Wilson's deputy press secretary, defended the governor's proposals plainly. He backed the reforms as "budget-driven." Lee explained that "[w]elfare rolls are growing at double the pace of population growth, even before the recession."[7] He also stressed "personal responsibility." Wisconsin governor Tommy Thompson asserted a similarly adamant defense of his proposal to deny grants to children born to AFDC mothers. He noted that "[w]hen somebody is working and they have more children, you don't automatically get a wage increase or a salary increase, but you do under welfare."[8] State reformers displayed a desire to formulate public frustration as policy. Supporters of the FSA pointed to state actions as indications that wide-ranging congressional reforms might not be received favorably. Offner observed that the "mood in Congress is not different from the mood out in the countryside." "In that atmosphere," he cautioned, "one has to wonder whether it's a good idea to bring anything up."[9]

One incident in 1992 revealed the potential explosiveness of these issues and the historical racial subtext of reform. In response to three days of violence that erupted in Los Angeles after the acquittal of four white police officers charged with beating black motorist Rodney King, White House spokesperson Marlin Fitzwater located the cause of the riots/rebellion in 1960s social programs: "We believe that many of the root problems that have resulted in inner-city difficulties were started in the 60s and 70s and that they have failed."[10] Fitzwater held that Great Society programs ignored the relationship between community pride and jobs, income, and private property. He charged "liberal Democrats" with thwarting an ameliorative Reagan-Bush urban agenda.

Fitzwater's comments met a swift and decisive negative response. The coverage of major news media exhibited skepticism. At the press briefing, reporters asked for examples. Fitzwater remarked: "I don't have a list with me."[11] The *New York Times* and other news organizations framed the comments as tendentiously motivated. The lead story in the *New York Times* paraphrased Fitzwater's remark that "the main thrust of the White House response was political." Similarly, the *Washington Post* noted that the White House response "came as a new poll showed Bush losing his lead and locked in a virtual three-way tie" with Democratic candidate Bill Clinton and independent candidate Ross Perot. News organizations prominently reported Clinton's rebuke of the administration.[12]

Various commentators and public figures also denounced Fitzwater's remarks. In his analysis of a wide range of media channels and sources, Benjamin Page reports that 75 percent of people responding to Fitzwater's statements did so negatively; 11 percent of individuals responded ambivalently; and only 8 percent of respondents positively defended the statements.[13] Commentators commonly charged the administration with a lack of moral leadership. Cynthia Tucker wondered how the nation had reached a moment that when leadership was so desperately needed its president instead resorted to partisan politics and "loose and dangerous demagoguery that panders to racial fears." Citing a legacy of presidential leadership, Tucker explained that LBJ "rose above the narrow-mindedness of his Texas origins and did what he had to do to move his country past hate." Mary McGrory expounded a similar theme in her *Washington Post* column. She recalled that "[w]hen moral indignation was needed about racism, Johnson provided it by shouting 'we shall overcome' to Congress."[14] As these responses intimated, critics discerned a thinly veiled racism in the White House charge. David Nyhan wrote in

the *Boston Globe* that Bush's 1988 presidential run adumbrated his subsequent failings. He charged that "this too-clever-for-his-own-good
president, who shaves the racist appeal as cleverly as a meat cutter giving
you ham thin enough to read through, let the country slide into a very
dirty ditch." In the *Christian Science Monitor,* Kenneth Walker called the
White House's remarks "race-baiting unequaled in recent politics."[15]

Editorialists mocked the slogans of the Reagan-Bush era and highlighted the successes of 1960s programs. The *New York Times* scoffed that
social ills revealed in the violence in Los Angeles indicated that the
"morning in America" proclaimed by Ronald Reagan had instead been a
"mourning" for many of the nation's citizens. The *Washington Post*
pointed to a "huge increase" in income inequality and the basic poverty
rate during the 1980s as the "dark side of morning in America."[16]
Though it did not deride the discourse of the Reagan era, the *Los Angeles
Times* maintained that many social programs enacted in the Johnson era
"have contributed significantly to improving the quality of life for
scores of millions of Americans." The *New York Times* noted in a separate
editorial that War on Poverty programs reduced the poverty rate by almost one-half between the mid-1960s and early 1970s. The paper used the
occasion to argue for a "uniform welfare benefit" to relieve the financial
stress of urban areas.[17]

Some commentators defended Fitzwater and the administration, of
course. Participants in a *National Review* colloquium sharply rebuked
those who censured the White House for employing racist appeals. Lorrin Anderson derided the *New York Times* for what he perceived as con-
descending treatment of black men. According to Anderson, "[a]s the
Times sees it, that is, young black men are somewhat less human than the
rest of us—no moral capacity of their own, no ability to choose or reject
criminal behavior." Holding that "blacks have in truth been given a number of advantages for more than twenty years," Charles Murray concluded that the "present problems of the black community owe more to
black behavior than to white oppression." In a subsequent essay in *Commentary,* Murray addressed Fitzwater's remarks directly. He admitted a
clumsily advanced quality to the argument, but expressed agreement with
"Fitzwater's more ambitious thesis": "the conditions in South-Central
Los Angeles in 1992 that produced the riot *are* importantly a product of
those reforms of a quarter-century ago."[18]

Supporters and opponents linked the debate sparked by Fitzwater's
remarks to the state of operating public assistance programs, disclosing

possible reform preferences among voters and policy debate participants. Fitzwater's attribution of cause clearly invited such a connection, and a staunch opponent such as the *New York Times* used the opportunity to advocate uniform benefits. On the one hand, the swift rejection of Fitzwater's claims by most commentators signaled an unwillingness to "pass the buck" for lingering social ills. As calls for leadership suggested, auditors appeared to prefer proposed solutions over assigned blame. On the other hand, observers may have feared what they perceived as potentially ominous consequences of a failed welfare policy. The riots/rebellion may have evidenced for some the need for clear-cut reforms that explicitly sanctioned perceived pathological behavior of adult AFDC recipients.

Bill Clinton's campaign promise to "end welfare as we know it" may have addressed both of these desires as it tapped into and vocalized the frustrations of middle-class voters who felt that their tax dollars increasingly subsidized the activities of people unwilling and perhaps unable to participate fully in society. His acceptance speech to the 1992 Democratic National Convention stressed the mutual responsibility of the FSA debates while emphasizing the temporary character of a reformed welfare program. He told his auditors of a Clinton administration that would "end welfare as we know it. We will say to those on welfare: you will have and you deserve the opportunity through training and education, through childcare and medical coverage, to liberate yourself. But then when you can you must work, because welfare should be a second chance not a way of life." Clinton's speech to the delegates sounded themes that formed part of his campaign discourse from the start. He announced his candidacy in a speech at the Old State House in Little Rock, Arkansas, on 3 October 1991. Addressing public assistance programs, he promised reforms that created opportunities but insisted that welfare recipients act responsibility: "We should insist that people move off welfare rolls and onto work rolls. We should give people on welfare the skills they need to succeed, but we should demand that everybody who can work go to work and become a productive member of society."[19] Clinton repeated welfare reform slogans on the campaign trail before and after the Democratic convention, pledging to dedicate more federal money to job training and tax credits and to demand work in return.

Welfare reform thus became a key component of the agenda candidate Clinton promised to pursue if elected president. It occupied a prominent position in a 1992 campaign tract titled *Putting People First,* which Clinton and his running mate Sen. Albert Gore coauthored. "Ending welfare as we know it" served to "reward work," which constituted one plank in a five-point strategy described in the introduction for reviving the nation's economy. In a chapter called "Welfare and Work," the candidates repeated in bold print the need to "end welfare as we know it." Their plan revived some themes of the mid-1980s debates, offering to support recipients with education, training, and childcare. They increased this offer, however, since recipients would be provided medical coverage under a reformed health care system that would guarantee affordable, quality care to every American. But the demand that recipients work in return for these support services now envisioned a specific time frame. Ending welfare as we know it meant that reforms would, "[a]fter two years, *require those who can work to go to work,* either in the private sector or in community service."[20] Responsible recipient behavior now would be measured by the calendar.

Putting People First presented its readers with an economic justification for reform. Clinton and Gore situated their agenda amid an emerging global economy that placed nations in competition with one another for jobs and economic growth as they courted the businesses and industries of other nations. In this context, the capacities of a nation's people emerged as key to national prosperity. Clinton and Gore explained that "[i]n the emerging global economy, everything is mobile: capital, factories, even entire industries. The only resource that's really rooted in a nation—and the ultimate source of its wealth—is its people." The skills of the American workforce needed to be upgraded for the nation to "compete and win in the twenty-first century." They observed that "[i]n Europe and Japan our competitors' economies grew three and four times faster than ours—because their leaders decided to invest in their people and Washington did not."[21] Exigencies of globalization meant that welfare recipients could not remain outside of a nationwide effort to bolster workforce productivity. A global economy demanded the utilization of everyone. In this way, Clinton's campaign discourse introduced globalization as a debate topic. Subsequent participants shared his concerns. The new majority of the 104th Congress pressed for repeal of AFDC as part of a necessary response to global economic forces; their insistence exhibited a confidence that global forces could be tamed.

Clinton's promised welfare reforms appeared to resonate with voters. A 1993 report commissioned by a group of public policy organizations, which surveyed 1,020 registered voters and interviewed eight focus groups, found that informants rejected present welfare programs overwhelmingly in favor of work-oriented reforms. Four of five voters felt that the current welfare system did not function well while fewer than one in five voters felt that "most current recipients deserve to receive benefits." When asked to select the primary goal of welfare reform, 52 percent of voters identified moving recipients toward work, while only 28 percent of voters chose eliminating fraud and abuse and 7 percent chose saving taxpayers money. A very large majority of 95 percent of voters supported childcare and 89 percent supported healthcare for mothers who obtained paid employment. Interestingly, a smaller majority of 65 percent supported Clinton's call for a two-year limit on receipt of assistance, which dropped to 55 percent when such a limit did not specify a job assurance.[22] Though voters cheered Clinton's promise to "end welfare as we know it," some commentators speculated that candidate Clinton might "waffle" if elected president. They urged him not to retreat from his "bold" plan. Mickey Kaus hoped that a President Clinton might be overtaken by "an infusion of fear." Kaus speculated that "Clinton's anti-welfare promises may be so critical to his electoral strategy ... that he doesn't have the option of failing to deliver on them in his first term."[23]

As welfare reform helped fuel presidential campaign discourse, the third policy episode began to take shape in hearings convened during the 102nd Congress by the House Select Committee on Hunger. The committee held hearings throughout the campaign season, in the months of March, April, June, August, and October. Though a few elected officials testified, most of the witnesses represented public policy organizations and state welfare departments. Held apart from specific pending legislation, the hearings provided witnesses an opportunity to discuss the status of existing legislation and future directions for reform. Participants reiterated some themes of the campaign, but also broached larger issues not addressed by Clinton or Bush.

Witnesses called for the full implementation of the FSA and legislative patience so that its effects could be known. Sabra Burdick, former director of Maine's Bureau of Income Maintenance, protested that the "Family Support Act has been declared a failure, I'm afraid, before it is even started.... I suggest we give it a chance to work." Larry Jackson, commissioner of the Virginia Department of Social Services, acknowledged the growing chorus of reformers, noting that the very criticisms being raised presently were deliberated in passage of the FSA. Yet state agencies had only begun to implement its provisions. Moreover, states had created JOBS and other programs in spite of the debilitating effects of the recession. Jackson and other witnesses urged legislators to remain committed to the framework established in the FSA and the consensus that produced it. Jackson asserted that "[w]hat most individuals want, as reflected in surveys, on radio talk shows, in political debate, is a policy already in place. What is missing because of state fiscal constraints is the ability to serve all of the individuals who are required to participate."[24]

As they requested increased financing, witnesses reiterated themes of the FSA debates in calling for government to support low-wage workers. Rep. Tony Hall opened the hearings with the assertion that wars on poverty and trickle-down economics had yet to produce "a national social policy that assures a decent standard of living for those in need that realistically encourages and supports the efforts of low-income persons who are striving to achieve economic self-sufficiency."[25] Encouragement and support took shape through arguments for specific policy initiatives, such as Jack Litzenberg's championing of a broader program of poverty alleviation that included job creation, Head Start, an expanded Earned Income Tax Credit (EITC), and a differentiated public assistance program that included time-limited support.[26]

As Hall's reference to living standards intimated, one of the principal themes that circulated throughout this series of hearings was a concern with the treatment of low-wage workers in a market economy—namely, the inability of such an economy to provide jobs that paid a sustainable income. Manpower Demonstration Research Corporation president Judith Gueron, whose organization played an instrumental role in deliberations regarding the design of FSA provisions, argued that 1980s strategies had been successful in discouraging receipt of welfare, but they had failed to provide children with security. Still, Gueron asserted that work programs for single mothers receiving AFDC could be successful. She reported that on average such programs increased earnings from employment by 50 percent and decreased costs by 13 percent. Nevertheless, analyses indicated that women who secured paid employment in welfare-to-work programs obtained relatively low paying jobs. Gueron recommended that "[r]eforms outside the welfare system may make reform within it more effective by creating incentives that support rather than pull against our strongest values." Gary Burtless, a senior fellow at the Brookings Institution, identified insufficient wages as the principal limitation of work programs: "Even the most successful programs fail to raise earnings enough to make much difference in the living standards of typical single parent families." Burtless associated this failure with a larger, fifteen-year trend of shrinking wages for low-income workers. He argued that reducing poverty in families required coordinating work or training obligations with "sizeable income supplements to bring the incomes of some full-time, low-wage workers up to the poverty line or comfortably above it."[27]

Witnesses and legislators sensed that the election might bring a voter backlash against public assistance programs. Rod Leonard, executive director of the Community Nutrition Institute, pointed to the differences between the present recession and past recessions as a cause for concern. He noted that commentators referred to the present recession as "a white collar recession. There are hundreds of thousands of middle-level management individuals who have lost their jobs, who are never going to find that same kind of job again because our corporations are downsizing." These kinds of economic dislocations created powerful resentments — especially when experienced by people who previously envisioned a stable economic future. Leonard suggested that "one of the reasons you're going to get a backlash eventually on welfare and on food stamps is that people don't think that there are really programs designed to help people in trouble." Similarly, Gueron located a potential public backlash in the misperception that "the middle-class or lower-middle-class is suffering while the poor have a soft deal." She countered that in the last twenty years AFDC grants had fallen by 42 percent when adjusted for inflation. Still, "the public's view is that, while they're getting squeezed, AFDC is becoming a better and better deal."[28]

Participants stressed the need to educate the public about the functions of public assistance programs. Rep. Bill Emerson, ranking minority member of the committee, explained the distorting effect of lurid anecdotes. He called upon committee members to disavow "harmful rhetoric" and "set the record straight." Emerson recounted disapprovingly an item he read "over the AP wire, a statement by a legislator in my home state about how homes — homes, mind you — are being bought with food stamps. Let's face it, when the maximum Food Stamp allotment for a family of four in 1991 was 352 dollars a month, or 96 cents per person per meal, no family in America is buying a home on Food Stamps." Invoking the lingering suspicion of recipients as undeserving, Rep. Mike Synar retorted that "we do not pay people not to work in this country and we do not pay people to sit around all day watching soap operas."[29] Synar exhorted his colleagues of the need to remind constituents that the typical duration for AFDC receipt was only eighteen months.

Still, even in an unusually supportive environment, there were signs of an emergent new paternalism. Robert Rector, policy analyst for the Heritage Foundation, argued for a distinction between material poverty and behavioral poverty, which was evidenced in such "dysfunctional behaviors" as out-of-wedlock births, single parenthood, criminal activity, drug use, and lack of work ethic. Rector referred to the present welfare system as a "check in the mail" system. The present system "sends welfare recipients a check in the mail without any moral obligation." In this way, it rewarded recipients for their dysfunctional behavior. Its primary consequence was "a dramatic increase in behavioral poverty in the United States," even as material poverty had been positively affected.[30] Other witnesses reported state governments' increasing reliance on punitive measures. Sabra Burdick explained that she resigned recently as Maine's Director of Income Maintenance over an adopted policy to deny additional benefits to children born to a woman after she became eligible for AFDC.[31]

Welfare reform had once again caught the attention of policymakers and the general public in 1992. Various people proposed diverse initiatives in multiple settings to reform a system seen by many as a failure. Participants questioning the capacities of the low-wage labor market broached the inefficacy of welfare reform itself that did not focus concomitantly on macroeconomic forces structuring society generally. Clinton reiterated familiar themes in promising to "end welfare as we know it," which highlighted the actions of recipients even as it stressed support. These two approaches and others suggested that though welfare reform had become a topic of public debate, an orientation for reform had not yet taken hold. This situation changed at the beginning of 1993 as participants waited eagerly for the new president's reforms.

The Ward Displaces the Signee in a Paternalistic Milieu

Although his campaign generated enthusiasm for welfare reform, Clinton did not move swiftly as president to reform the system he promised to end. A specific proposal did not appear until eighteen months into the Clinton administration, yet a significant shift in the representation of the

AFDC recipient was enacted during the 103rd Congress. A working group on welfare reform led by Bruce Reed, deputy assistant to the president for domestic policy, David Ellwood, assistant secretary for planning and evaluation at the Department of Health and Human Services (HHS), and Mary Jo Bane, assistant secretary of Administration for Children and Families at HHS, headed the administration's efforts. The group formed and forwarded its recommendations to the president slowly. The Senate delayed confirmation of Ellwood and Bane. Moreover, the same congressional committees responsible for acting on Clinton's healthcare plan also exercised authority over welfare reform, which postponed committee action, though not hearings, on welfare. The working group announced in a July press conference that it would hold a series of public hearings in the fall and subsequently present a plan to the president. Reed asserted the group's desire to work with state and local officials in a collaborative effort. Ellwood affirmed the group's commitment to a "two years and out" time limit.[32] Still, the first session of the 103rd Congress recessed without considering an administration proposal.

Frustrated by the White House pace, congressional Democrats began to call for concrete action as the end of the session neared. In October a group of moderates known as the Mainstream Forum forwarded a letter to Clinton signed by seventy-seven legislators urging reform. In November the Progressive Caucus released a letter to the president signed by eighty-six Democrats urging a broad anti-poverty strategy and denouncing time limits as arbitrary.[33]

House Republicans unveiled their version of welfare reform on 10 November, which 160 of 175 House Republicans co-sponsored. They sought to impose a two-year time limit with stiff penalties consisting of benefit reductions and eventual elimination for recipients who refused to work. The proposal required recipients unable to secure paid employment to participate in a community-service assignment or subsidized private-sector employment. It proscribed dispersal of benefits to mothers who did not identify the father of their children. Further, the proposal prohibited states from increasing grant amounts for children born to parents on AFDC or children of mothers under the age of eighteen. Denial of welfare benefits to non-citizens financed the Republican plan.[34]

The Clinton administration announced its "long-awaited" plan on 14 June 1994. The measure highlighted a two-year time limit for receipt of aid, after which unemployed recipients would be placed in federally subsidized jobs. Clinton did not wish to finance reform by raising taxes or denying legal immigrants benefits, so his reform applied only to people born after 1971. White House officials argued that a focus on the youngest AFDC recipients would force teens to take responsibility for their lives. The plan offered them work and training through an expanded JOBS program. It also permitted states to deny grant increases for children born to AFDC recipients.[35] In the weeks that followed, legislators began to doubt the passage of any reform in the 103rd Congress, and the president never pressed for passage of his plan. Rep. Dave McCurdy, leader of the Mainstream Forum, fumed that the "president struck a chord with two-year time limits and for the life of me I don't know why he was reluctant to move on this." Democratic and Republican candidates raised welfare reform as an issue in the 1994 congressional elections. Republican pollster Frank Luntz predicted that reform "is going to be the emotional battleground on Capital Hill" in 1995.[36]

The recipient as ward emerged in committee hearings and presidential statements. The Human Resources Subcommittee of the Ways and Means Committee convened hearings most frequently, addressing a broad range of topics periodically in 1993. After the administration released its reform plan in 1994, the subcommittee held a flurry of hearings throughout July and August. Its Senate counterpart, the Social Security and Family Policy Subcommittee, convened hearings in January and February 1994 to examine state reforms. It considered the administration proposal and others in July 1994. Among other participating committees, the House Education and Labor Committee conducted hearings in fall 1994 regarding various supports for employed AFDC recipients. Clinton discussed reform as a distinct issue and in the context of other measures throughout 1993 and 1994.

Clinton's first statement on welfare reform as president intimated a crucial tension in the deliberations that marked the emergence of a new paternalism, enabling a shift in the image of the AFDC recipient from contract signee to ward in need of strict, didactic, and constant supervision. He described to the National Governors' Association his view of the relationship between the FSA and his campaign promises. Clinton acknowledged that the FSA had not been implemented fully by state governments. He explained its incompleteness as a result of explosive increases in the welfare rolls over the last four years as healthcare costs had risen dramatically while the job market had declined and economic growth had slowed. At the same time, the weakened economy had reduced government revenues necessary for implementation. Nevertheless,

Clinton asserted the continued existence of a consensus that mutual obligation ought to shape welfare policy. Moreover, he asserted his belief in the legislation: "The bill that is on the books will work, given the right economy and the right kind of support systems, but we need to do more than fully implement it; we need to do that and go beyond."[37]

Clinton's reference to "going beyond" signaled the tension that structured his reform appeals. On the one hand, he insisted that government be supportive of recipients. The president reiterated provisions of the FSA and introduced additional ones. He called for job training to be made available to recipients, as well as an assurance that they would receive healthcare and childcare if they secured private-sector employment. Clinton argued for the expansion of the EITC so that low-income workers could earn a living wage. Further, he proposed increased child-support enforcement, including the creation of a national databank and the involvement of the IRS, so that working mothers could receive money owed them. On the other hand, Clinton assumed an accusatory tone that questioned the values of AFDC recipients. Clinton's reform slogans revealed this quality of his appeals. He insisted that "welfare should be a second chance, not a way of life." He envisioned "a country that gives you a hand up, not a handout."[38] Both slogans located the need for reform not only in the availability of supports, but in the character of the recipient.

This tension reappeared regularly in Clinton's subsequent speeches and statements. In a February address before a joint session of Congress and in almost every statement on welfare reform up to the passage of an expanded EITC later that year, Clinton offered his vision of a better future for poor working families: "We will reward the work of millions of working poor Americans by realizing the principle that if you work forty hours a week and you've got a child in the house, you will no longer be in poverty." Alongside supportive statements such as this one, Clinton repeated his insistence that welfare be a second chance, not a way of life. He doubted the character of recipients in other ways. In a February speech to the U.S. Chamber of Commerce, he spoke of the need to "break the psychology of poverty and dependence on the government." At a San Diego town meeting in May, Clinton shared his interpretation of ending welfare as we know it as the imposition of strict, mandatory time limits. He explained that "everybody under my plan would be required to work [after two years].... So we would end it, welfare as we know it."[39] He articulated a variation of this theme in August, broaching the issue of multigenerational receipt of welfare and the significance of titles. He protested that "there are people on welfare whose parents were on welfare, whose grandparents were on welfare, who never have worked, and who basically stay on forever as long as they have children under a certain age, because welfare's proper name is Aid to Families with Dependent Children, AFDC, that's what it means."[40]

This tension between affirmation and accusation invoked alternative images of welfare recipients differentiated by their capacity to carry out an agreement. Clinton's wish that low-income families not be poor if they worked forty hours a week acknowledged the inability of the paid labor market to provide living-wage jobs for all its participants. This slogan presented the recipient in a positive light as someone who worked full-time to support one's family against an unresponsive economy. The demand, variously stated, that after a time people leave the welfare rolls located welfare receipt ultimately in the inability or unwillingness of the recipient to seek remunerative work. Even as time limits promised support services before anyone reached a cut-off date, they assumed that only an unambiguous "push" would end welfare receipt. One could enter into an agreement with a poor, working person sufficiently confident that its obligations would be met. A recipient whose willingness and ability had been questioned, however, required strict and constant supervision. She could not be granted the measure of autonomy implicit among contractual parties. In this imaginary field, a ward would be better served by a policy tool—namely, a block grant—that gave her supervisors greater control over the recipient's everyday activities and finances, even denying her money if deemed appropriate in the opinion of the supervisor.

Clinton's statements and the images they invoked paralleled a larger tendency of the debates. In testimony to the Human Resources Subcommittee, Jodie Levin-Epstein, senior state policy analyst for the Center for Law and Social Policy, identified funding as the fundamental problem confronting reformers, "due either to fiscal constraints or due to the lack of political will, [which] have led to serious problems with JOBS implementation in a number of states." Holding that the FSA consensus formed around a notion of "social contract," Levin-Epstein questioned government's ability "to live up to its end of the contract." In his appearance before the subcommittee, Clifford Johnson, director of programs and policy for the Children's Defense Fund, cited a lack of jobs directly, identifying it as the primary reason that parents received AFDC. Johnson asserted that the assignment of single mothers to the end of the job queue ought to surprise no one in this "anything but full employment economy." He held that "proposed time limits would do nothing to alter the fundamental mismatch between jobs and job seekers."[41]

Other participants voiced concerns about the values and abilities of recipients. Rep. Dave McCurdy sought an assurance of paid employment not in an agency/recipient contract, but a time limit. He declared to the Education and Labor Committee that "[t]he ultimate guarantee of responsibility is the time limit." Mickey Kaus explained to the Human Resources Subcommittee that the "welfare problem" should be viewed as a "problem of 'ghetto poverty' or the formation of an 'underclass.'" Kaus contended that though it might not be a sufficient cause, welfare was a necessary cause of a disabling culture. For instance, women might not have children to receive an AFDC grant, but "young women look around them and recognize, maybe unconsciously, that other women have survived through welfare. They know that welfare is going to be there." The attribution of fault implicit in this analysis was made explicit by Michael Horowitz of the Manhattan Institute. In his appearance before the subcommittee, Horowitz associated himself with Frances Perkins, whom he claimed would have restricted AFDC to "deserving mothers who, through no fault of their own, found themselves in situations where they could not support their children."[42]

Insidious divisions of the poor exacerbated doubts regarding the willingness and capacity of welfare recipients to achieve "self-sufficiency." After his initial pledge to a renewed FSA in the first few months of his administration, Clinton spoke of welfare reform in the context of a national system of health insurance. He found in the situation of low-wage workers evidence of fundamental flaws in existing patterns of coverage. He objected that "we have this incredible situation in our country where if someone on welfare leaves to take an entry-level job that doesn't have health insurance, as soon as coverage of the Family Support Act runs out, you have people making low wages paying taxes to pay for health care for people who stayed on welfare and didn't make the same decision they did."[43] The accusatory force of this illustration—repeated throughout 1994—appeared most clearly in Clinton's reference to decisions made. On the one side stood those who accepted the challenges and uncertainties of paid employment. On the other side slouched those who shrank from this challenge, preferring instead the stability of public aid. In this illustration, sympathy for the worker without health insurance derived in part from an auditor's judgment that the welfare recipient lacked motivation and was rewarded for it.

Similar divisions appeared throughout the hearings. Rep. Rick Santorum responded to calls for assured daycare by pointing to "millions of
American mothers out there who have children without guaranteed, subsidized day care slots and provide for their children. And why we should
be more concerned about welfare mothers than we should about working mothers … somehow eludes me." With respect to proposals to exempt from work programs mothers with children less than one year old,
he retorted that the most generous employer plans only gave new mothers three months of paid leave. The exemption in effect would have provided one full year of paid leave. He asked: "[H]ow is that equitable
toward the working mothers who, in fact, are paying taxes to support this
system?"[44] In large measure, Santorum's call for equity drew its force
from the unequal representations of the two groups of mothers.

As tensions and divisions undermined the signee, an emphasis on
youth specified the image of the ward. Health and Human Services secretary Donna Shalala began her testimony to the Finance Committee by
noting that three million people had been added to the AFDC rolls in the
last five years. She explained that "a central part of the problem is the
growth in the number of births to young, unmarried mothers." Calling
the trends disturbing and needing urgent action, Shalala cited a recently
completed Government Accounting Office (GAO) analysis reporting
that almost half of the women receiving AFDC were teenage mothers. In
response, Chairperson Daniel Patrick Moynihan observed that "children
having children" represented a profound social transformation tantamount to a biological change in a species. Acknowledging his own uncertainty and unease regarding this trend, Sen. Kent Conrad speculated
that "children are having children and that somehow there is a trend in
the country that children have it in their mind to have a child makes
them important, is someone who is going to love them, is somebody that
is going to look up to them."[45] Conrad implied that whatever their reasons, young girls needed guidance bolstered by strict reinforcement.
Along these lines, Rep. Olympia Snowe chided the current system for
treating children like adults by permitting them to create "separate
households under the welfare system."[46]

The paternalistic milieu of the deliberations positioned participants as
adults debating parenting techniques. Some argued that teen mothers
needed a stern lecture; they crafted policies that would "send a message"
to young mothers. Secretary Shalala described the administration's reform proposals as "sending a clear message to the next generation that

welfare as we know it is history." Children tended to act impulsively. The administration sought to instill reflection on responsibility for one's behavior by clearly expressing its displeasure: "So the support will be there on the front end. It will be temporary, transitional support and that young person will have a message that this is not a game, that it is not fun."[47] Mary Jo Bane and David Ellwood relayed the messages the administration wished to send before the Human Resources Subcommittee. The administration bill envisioned a reorientation of the local welfare office so that the young parent understood that "from the day you walk in the door, we are going to have a clear message that we want you to move from welfare to work." The proposal focused on those born after 1971 "to send the message to young people that things have changed." Bane described the teen pregnancy and child-support enforcement provisions of the proposal as crucial for constructing a system "to send a very clear message to both parents that you shouldn't have a child until you are ready and able to support it."[48]

Other participants maintained that a stern lecture was insufficient. They agreed with Rep. Marge Roukema, who told the Human Resources Subcommittee that "it is time for tough love." Rep. Tom DeLay elucidated the nature of this tough love as he outlined provisions of the Republican reform proposal. DeLay professed the same goals as the administration. He and other supporters of the proposal wished to "bring in the notion that people must be responsible for their own lives, and there are consequences to decisions that they make." Tough love meant that recipients should be forced, whether by a state agency representative or by the denial of benefits, to accept any job they could find. Representative Santorum observed that "everyone in this room had a first job." He acknowledged that "it was probably not the most 'meaningful' job that they have ever had, but it was work. And it taught them the skills necessary to go to work, get up every day, put in a good day's effort, work with other employees, work with their supervisors, and learn what it is to earn a paycheck."[49] Parents learned from experience; they knew the value of a seemingly "meaningless" job.

Though attention focused on the ward, the system did not escape blame. Representative DeLay argued that the system created incentives that discouraged "self-sufficiency." He contended that "our present welfare system offers young girls the proposition of their lifetime. It says if you just have a child, don't get married and don't work, we will give you housing, health care, food stamps, and AFDC payments." Indianapolis mayor Stephen Goldsmith sought an alternative model in the laws of the marketplace. Goldsmith posed a fundamental question to the subcommittee: "Do we want the marketplace to work or do we want the marketplace to reduce jobs?" To achieve the former, he called for the removal of barriers that welfare placed in the way of developing market-based economies. For instance, welfare interfered with employer attempts to set a wage for their workers. "In our city," he disclosed, "to break even you have to start in the wage sector at $7.50 an hour and have your mom take care of your children. And that is well above the beginning wage rate in Indianapolis, Indiana. So, in addition to the other problems about welfare, we are destroying the marketplace as well."[50] These denunciations of the welfare system adumbrated a full-scale attack launched after the 1994 congressional elections.

By the adjournment of the 103rd Congress, a ward had displaced the contract signee as the prominent image of AFDC recipients circulating in policy debates. This change by itself did not compel repeal of AFDC as an entitlement. The entitlement status of the program might have been maintained in a more authoritarian environment. Repeal appeared as the only sensible policy option after a second discursive development compounded the destabilizing effects of the first. Placed in charge of Congress by the 1994 election results, confident revolutionaries pressed for dismantling a destructive welfare bureaucracy by means of block grants.

A Brave New World and a Discredited Bureaucracy

In the 1994 congressional elections, the Republican Party gained a majority of seats in the Senate and House of Representatives, controlling the lower chamber for the first time in forty years. In the lead paragraph of its story reporting the House election results, the *Washington Post* wrote that Republican candidates "rode a crest of anti-Washington sentiment." Leaving unexamined competing explanations such as low voter turnout among core constituencies, the *New York Times* reported uncritically the Republican declaration of "political revolution." The paper added: "The depth of their victory was sounded by the fact that no sitting Republican governor, senator, or representative was defeated."[51]

The election results thrust into the political spotlight the Republican "Contract with America." On 27 September 1994, 152 Republican representatives seeking reelection and 185 GOP challengers signed a ten-point list of policy initiatives that they promised to bring to a vote in the first 100 days of a Republican-controlled House of Representatives. The document sketched a conservative economic and social welfare agenda by calling for a balanced budget amendment to the Constitution, capital gains and other tax cuts, toughened public assistance and crime laws, increased defense spending, and congressional term limits.[52] Its public assistance provisions reiterated the key points of the Republican reform proposal introduced in the 103rd Congress, vowing to cut AFDC spending, to deny AFDC grants to mothers under eighteen years old and to children born to AFDC parents, and to enact a strict two-year time limit for receipt of aid. Speaking from the steps of the Capitol, Newt Gingrich, widely perceived as chief architect of the contract and presumed Speaker of a Republican House, proclaimed triumphantly: "If the American people accept this contract, we will have begun the journey to renew American civilization. Together we can renew America. Together we can help every American fulfill their inalienable right to pursue happiness and to seek the American dream."[53]

Though Republicans insisted that a "contract" would illustrate their determination to reconstruct the federal government, critics retorted that the Republican contract was full of loopholes. *Wall Street Journal* columnist Albert Hunt asserted that a balanced budget, tax cuts, and increased defense spending "don't begin to add up." He maintained that only "smoke and mirrors" would permit Republicans to meet all three of these campaign promises. Martha Phillips, executive director of the Concord Coalition, a bipartisan anti-deficit group that supported a balanced federal budget, reacted similarly. Explaining her group's opposition, she held that "most of their things increase the deficit instead of reduce it."[54] The *New York Times* and *Washington Post* editorial boards objected that the tax cuts benefited high-income families almost exclusively. Others rebuked the contract as retreads of discredited ideas. *Chicago Tribune* columnist Steve Daley asked his readers to remember the Republican-occupied White House of the 1980s, when "they insisted we would 'grow' our way out of the deficit that eventually quadrupled."[55] Outgoing Democratic Party chairperson David Wilhelm believed that the contract "reminded people why they voted for Bill Clinton in 1992." He forecasted that voters "don't want to go back to trickle-down economics."[56]

Responding to one argument of critics, some Republicans conceded the political nature of the contract. Republican pollster Frank Luntz discounted views of the contract as a gimmick, retorting that the idea of a "contract" was the only concept that impressed voters in focus groups. "By saying 'contract,' we add a seriousness, a deliberateness, that doesn't exist without it."[57] He contended that the current mood of the electorate compelled candidates' signatures: "They have to [sign it] after what George Bush did with his tax pledge and what Bill Clinton did with his tax pledge. Voters are more than skeptical; they're absolutely hostile."[58] *Newsweek* reported that provisions entered the contract only after receiving the approval of 60 percent of surveyed voters.[59] Moderate Republicans who reservedly supported the contract articulated stances for future objections. Rep. Constance Morella voiced opposition to some contract provisions, but explained her signature as a desire not to prevent the full body from debating the measures. She signed to "let the bills come up for a vote; don't lock them up in procedure. The leadership knows full well we're not pledged to vote with them."[60]

In the weeks following the election, the victors were brash and bold. Most confident among them may have been Gingrich, who received considerable credit for the overwhelming Republican victory. Comparing Gingrich to retiring House Minority Leader Robert Michel, the *Washington Post* speculated that his stewardship would likely mark "an end to accommodating House Republican leaders who tried to work cooperatively with Democrats to pass legislation." In a speech delivered shortly after the election, Gingrich vowed to hold firm to the principles of the contract. He declared that "[w]e will cooperate with anyone, and we'll compromise with no one."[61] The election produced a group of very conservative new members, who were portrayed in the media as Gingrich acolytes and committed members of the revolution that brought them to power.

The Contract with America may not have played as central a role in the Republican electoral triumph as its champions claimed after the election. The Gallup Poll reported that only a minority of adults questioned had heard of the contract — even one month after the election. Only 24 percent of respondents polled in early October indicated an awareness of the contract. The percentage of adults aware of the contract increased to 34 percent in late November and only 37 percent in early December. Though Republican pollsters recorded a clear majority of favorable responses to the contract provisions, Gallup found that four items in the contract — capital gains tax cut, litigation rule changes, increased defense spending, and restrictions on UN command of U.S. troops — did not meet the 60 percent criterion cited in *Newsweek*. Further, Gallup determined that only toughened crime laws were supported by more than 60 percent of respondents when judged by a measure of "popular demand": the percentage of people who favored a proposal and said "it 'would matter' to them" if the 104th Congress did not vote on the proposal within its first 100 days. Tax cuts and a balanced budget amendment attracted the next highest levels of "popular demand" at 53 percent and 50 percent, respectively. A call for welfare reform followed, backed by a "popular demand" of 49 percent.[62]

Still, the contract clearly marked Republican attempts to install a national focus in local House races and signaled shifting sentiments among voters. It responded, as pollster Luntz noted, to widespread voter cynicism. Moreover, it acted as a kind of party platform that enabled Republicans to highlight the differences between themselves and a president unpopular in many regions of the country. *CQ Weekly* observed that "[p]erhaps more than at any time in the past twelve years, this year's House elections are being run as a referendum on the party in control in the White House."[63]

The 1994 elections witnessed a dramatic shift in public opinion regarding the abilities of the two major political parties and the president to reform welfare. Respondents to a spring 1994 *Los Angeles Times* poll answered by nearly a 10 percent margin — 42 percent to 33 percent — that Clinton would "do a better job of reforming the welfare system" than congressional Republicans. By October, respondents favored congressional Republicans by a 41 percent to 35 percent margin. Various polls comparing the Democratic and Republican parties on this issue reported even more striking changes. A December 1993 poll indicated that 47 percent of respondents believed that the Democratic Party would "do a better job" of reforming welfare while 36 percent believed the Republican Party would handle the task better. By October 1994, the Republican Party held a slim lead on this question of 31 percent to 28 percent. A November poll disclosed that the favorable shift toward the Republican Party had ballooned to 55 percent to 35 percent.[64]

The election of new majorities in both houses of Congress had an impact on the debates in two significant ways. First, the election results increased attention given to particular policy initiatives. Leadership endorsement of block grants and other proposals meant that they would receive greater attention during subsequent hearings. Second, the election results changed committee chairs and thus affected the composition of witness lists. Witnesses appearing before the 104th Congress represented

conservative advocacy groups more frequently than witnesses who testified during the 103rd Congress. The deliberations, however, cannot be reduced to election results—whichever party holds a majority in Congress.
As this book demonstrates, discourses do not begin or end with political
parties. AFDC may not have been repealed without a change in the majority party in the House of Representatives, but the changed portrayal of
recipients and attack on bureaucracy that enabled its repeal were the exclusive province of neither party.

   The first 100 days of the 104th Congress produced a flurry of hearings
by multiple committees on various aspects of welfare reform and a re-
ordering of policy preferences. The Ways and Means Committee held
hearings on the welfare reform provisions of the contract throughout
January. Its Human Resources Subcommittee addressed the subject in
February, as did the House Agriculture Committee, the House Economic
and Educational Committee, and others. Block grants emerged as a pri-
oritized policy initiative in the first few months after the Republican victory. Though it severely restricted aid, the Contract with America did not
call for public assistance block grants. Republican governors, however—
led by Tommy Thompson (Wisc.), John Engler (Mich.), and William
Weld (Mass.)—lobbied Republican House leaders in early December and
January for greater state control of social programs. In return, they
agreed to accept reduced federal funding.[65] The NGA did not endorse
block grants during its winter meeting, as Gov. Howard Dean (Vt.) led
Democrats in opposing the repeal of welfare entitlements. Still, House
Republicans incorporated block grants as a replacement for AFDC in the
reform bill they passed in March.

   The Finance Committee, which conducted most of the Senate hearings on welfare reform, held extensive hearings throughout March and
April. Some legislators predicted that the Senate would reject the provisions of the House bill, but Finance Committee chair Bob Packwood announced in mid-May that block grants would be included in his committee's plan as well. He cited the influence of Governors Engler and
Thompson in drafting a bill.[66] The Senate bill permitted as state options
denial of grants to mothers under the age of eighteen and for children
born to mothers receiving assistance. Expressing adamant, unbending
opposition to the repeal of entitlements and other punitive measures,
ranking Finance Committee Democrat Daniel Patrick Moynihan unveiled an alternative plan that retained the structure of the FSA as it

increased funds for education and job-training components. Moynihan represented only a small group of Democratic senators. Challenges from moderate and conservative Republican senators appeared more urgent, occupying legislators throughout the summer.

The Senate approved its plan 87 to 12 in September after moderates won concessions on childcare funds, state spending assurances, and conservative attempts to mandate denials of benefits to teen mothers. Explaining the reluctant support of many Democrats, Minority Leader Tom Daschle held that "[i]t is the best deal we are going to get under the circumstances."[67] Conferees amended the bill in a more conservative direction during negotiations. President Clinton vetoed the legislation as part of a larger budget bill on 6 December. Objecting that conferees moved too far away from the Senate version, Clinton vetoed a stand-alone bill, which passed the Senate by a slim 52 to 47 vote, on 9 January 1996.

After the second presidential veto, Rep. Clay Shaw, Jr. sought to rally his colleagues around the Senate plan. As chairperson of the Human Resources Subcommittee, Shaw played a critical role in enactment of the PRWORA. His subcommittee produced a bill quickly in the first 100 days of the 104th Congress, then conducted additional hearings throughout 1995. Shaw's efforts received a considerable boost when the NGA at its 1996 winter meeting unanimously adopted a proposal to block grant AFDC and Medicaid. The Human Resources Subcommittee and the Finance Committee held hearings in February regarding the proposal. Congressional Republicans vowed to maintain the linkage between the two block grants even as the president threatened a third veto if welfare reform legislation included a Medicaid block grant. Republicans reversed themselves in July, announcing that they would pass a separate welfare reform bill. Several factors contributed to this strategy change. On 15 May 1996, presidential candidate and Majority Leader Bob Dole, who resisted sending Clinton a reform bill he might sign, announced his intention to resign from the Senate to campaign full-time. Feeling increasingly anxious about their own re-election prospects, junior Republican House members pressed their leadership for a bill. Further, Republican governors disliked the Medicaid provisions of the combined bill approved by the Finance Committee.[68] The conference report split the Democrats' vote but passed by comfortable margins in the House (328 to 101) and Senate (78 to 21). On 31 July, the day the House passed the bill and the day before the Senate vote, Clinton announced after a morning meeting with top advisors his intention to sign the legislation.[69] With this narrative of the changed participants and priorities of the 1995–96 debates in place, I now turn to the hearings themselves.

On the second day of the 104th Congress, Speaker Gingrich appeared before the Ways and Means Committee to outline his vision of the legislative agenda for the newly inaugurated term. The Speaker situated the agenda within epochal shifts in U.S. history. He held that the country was witnessing the superseding of a second-wave industrial society, which had superseded a first-wave agricultural society, by a third-wave information age. The emerging information age promised manifold wonders, but it required sober thinking about the direction and goals of public policy. Gingrich announced proudly the installment of "Thomas," an online database of information and documents of the House of Representatives. He asserted that every proposed policy should be asked the question: "Does it accelerate our transition into a third wave information age or does it slow it down?"[70]

A rapidly developing global economy raised additional questions for policymakers. Gingrich argued that rather than "complain and whine and browbeat" about the often insidious exigencies of a global market by impugning firms that relocated jobs to reduce labor costs, legislators ought to consider changes in American law, regulation, and taxation "so that the best rational investment to create jobs on the planet is the United States of America." Successful procurement of competitive, transitory jobs necessitated cooperation with and instruction from global employers. Gingrich recommended that "we need to be advised by those who are making the decisions." He contended that this strategy exhibited clear advantages over past practices, which consisted principally of "punishing businesses until they get ready to leave and then complaining because they are not patriotic after we drive them off-shore."[71]

Adjusting to changing social and economic forces required assessment of past failures—chief among them the destructive U.S. welfare system. Gingrich insisted that the present system penalized family stability and punished those who attempted "self-sufficiency." Legislators ought to reverse course so that the poor could accompany other Americans into the information age. He proposed, as an admittedly "nutty idea," a tax credit that would enable poor Americans to buy laptop computers. Such a credit might prove to be unfeasible, but "any signal we can send to the poorest Americans that says we are going into a 21st century third wave information age and so are you, and we want to carry you with us, begins to change the game." Gingrich admitted that a global market might be tough for all Americans, but he retorted that the U.S. government ought not punish its citizens as they compete. Though the possibility of misery could not be ignored, Gingrich asserted that, "if we do it right, we can actually liberate the poor to seek prosperity while making those transitions."[72] The Speaker instructed his colleagues, however, that any changes needed to be made in the context of a balanced budget by the year 2002.

As Gingrich foresaw a brave new world with little patience for cumbersome bureaucracy, others cautioned against hasty judgments of already established welfare policy. In his opening statement at the first of a series of Finance Committee hearings, Daniel Patrick Moynihan reminded his colleagues of the magnitude of the changes wrought by the FSA. The legislation represented the first congressional attempt to redefine the AFDC program, which began as a transitional widows' pension program meant to cover beneficiaries until they qualified for social security survivors' benefits. The FSA attempted to come to terms with a new population and a new set of social circumstances—and it passed the Senate 96 to 1. Moynihan expressed puzzlement regarding "how, so early into an enterprise which we said would take time, be slow, and the results would be small but positive, why so quickly we have decided that it did not work, and we have to do something else altogether."[73] Information technologies promote speed, however. The age that bears their name cannot afford to wait for gradual results. Moreover, in the view of the new reformers, the FSA did not undo but augmented a fundamentally destructive welfare system.

Many participants saw the origin of this destructive force in an insidious offer. The system purported to offer young girls the chance of a lifetime, but for the girls as well as society it had been a Faustian bargain. The system paid youths not to form families or achieve "self-sufficiency." Representative Shaw told his Ways and Means Committee colleagues that these payments constituted a lucrative package. The system told "young people, particularly a young girl, that you can have a child, not get married, not go to work, not live by any of the other rules, and we are going to have a package for you that is worth anywhere from 12,000 dollars to 16,000 dollars a year." Shaw noted indignantly that minimum-wage labor could not match the welfare system's offer. The marketplace presented young people with the less attractive opportunity to "go to work, earn minimum wage and not quite get up to 9,000 dollars a year." Some

witnesses, such as Queens College economics professor Anne Hill, suggested that an offer of welfare must appear especially seductive to recipients whose inadequate education and few job skills foretold a future of
limited labor market opportunities.[74]

The recipient as ward had succumbed to the welfare system's lures.
Her dependency was represented dramatically in a fiery exchange that
erupted on the House floor when two members of Congress likened welfare recipients to captive animals. Speaking in front of a placard that read
"Do not feed the alligators," Rep. John Mica of Florida explained that
warnings such as this one were posted around nature preserves in his
home state for the animals' own protection. He observed that alligators
left unattended could hunt food successfully on their own, but human intervention by means of "unnatural feeding and artificial care creates dependency. When dependency sets in, these otherwise able-bodied alligators can no longer survive on their own." Humans were not alligators,
Mica admitted, but he retorted that the present system "upset the natural
order." Spurred by Mica's anecdote, Rep. Barbara Cubin of Wyoming recounted difficulties surrounding efforts to reintroduce wolves into national park areas in her state. Hoping to transition wolves from captivity
to freedom, rangers placed them in pens and fed them elk and venison
daily. Cubin referred to the project as the "wolf welfare program": the
federal government "provided everything that the wolves needed for their
existence." Their actions produced less-than-encouraging results. When
keepers attempted to release the wolves from their pens, the animals
would not leave. Cubin shared her view of the moral of the story: "Just
like any animal in the species, any mammal, when you take away their
freedom and their dignity and their ability, they cannot provide for
themselves."[75]

Some members objected adamantly to the analogies of Mica and Cubin.
Boos and hisses confronted Mica's remarks. Cubin fought to hold the
floor amid several interruptions. Several speakers insisted that their interests lay in feeding children, not alligators. Immediately after Cubin's
statement, House veteran Sam Gibbons rebuked her and Mica sharply:
"Mr. Chairman, in my 34 years here I thought I had heard it all, but we
have a millionaire from Florida comparing children to alligators and we
have a gentlewoman in red over here comparing children to wolves. That
tops it all." A few moments earlier, Rep. Barney Frank wondered where
Mica obtained his copy of the Declaration of Independence. Frank concluded that "[a]pparently in his version it says all men are created equal

to alligators and we will treat them equally." Frank denounced Mica's analogy as "dehumanizing and degrading."[76]

Images of welfare recipients as captive animals illustrated controversially their Faustian bargain with the system. In exchange for food, shelter, and some amenities, recipients had sacrificed their freedom. Animal imagery also reinforced recipients' status as wards. Captive animals depend on their keepers' generosity and care. They live their entire lives as hatchlings or cubs. Moreover, they often act on instinct. They putatively do not possess the higher-level cognitive processes that guide human action. Parties to a contract, as recipients appeared in the FSA debates, must weigh advantage and disadvantage. Contract signees must be willing to forgo present gratifications for future rewards. They must maintain commitments over time. Animal instincts ostensibly exhibit none of these abilities. Further, the particular animals mentioned in the above analogies—alligators and wolves—are often viewed as savage creatures (as opposed, say, to puppy dogs). The images evoked in these comparisons thus sustained a perception of threat and potential danger to mainstream society from welfare recipients. In this way, links established in the mid-1980s to a feared and suspect underclass persisted.

Reformers argued that the system had wrought an array of social ills—teen pregnancy, out-of-wedlock births, unemployment, welfare dependency, and poverty. Advocates attributed causation with varying degrees of intensity, but all spoke of a contributory link. For instance, Peter Ferrara stated adamantly and unequivocally that the current system "is directly contributing to the problem and actually causing poverty." In forceful though slightly less direct testimony, Michael Tanner, director of health and welfare studies for the Cato Institute, asserted that "the overwhelming amount of evidence indicates that there is a substantial link between the availability of welfare benefits and the growth of illegitimacy in America." William Bennett, a former "drug-czar" of the Reagan administration and self-appointed "virtues-czar" of the conservative resurgence, also insisted on a strong link between welfare payments and out-of-wedlock births. He argued that welfare "sustains it [out-of-wedlock childbearing] and it subsidizes it, and what you subsidize you usually get more of."[77]

Others attributed a more ambiguous yet still significant role to welfare payments. For example, Representative Nussle revealed his doubts about a direct causal relationship between cash grants and out-of-wedlock births. He conceded that "I am not convinced that there is a direct provable evidentiary correlation between welfare payments and illegitimacy, that somebody consciously decides that they are going to go out and get pregnant just because they know there is a check." Still, he pointed to common sense knowledge in defending some meaningful connection: "I think that most thinking people also would suggest that the culture that is created by welfare has also established a culture where illegitimacy is acceptable and it becomes part of the norm and part of the culture." Similarly, Linda Frye, child support office director of the California Department of Social Services, did not view AFDC payments as part of a pre-sexual–intercourse economic calculation. She acknowledged to the Finance Committee that "the motive at the moment of passion is probably not the potential AFDC check coming in the door." Yet she retorted: "[W]e have a system that makes that decision less painful for people, or puts fewer moments for thought in the path of it."[78] The statements assembled in this paragraph and the previous one in descending order of direct causation evidenced a firmly established contributory link between welfare cash payments and an array of social ills. In this way, the mid-1990s debates revealed the full-fledged hearing of mid-1980s policy tracts—chiefly Murray's—that asserted links between increased poverty and the expansion of social programs.

Other witnesses objected to the attribution of cause between welfare payments and out-of-wedlock birth rates. Rebecca Blank, economics professor at Northwestern University, explicated several factors that cast serious doubt on claims of causation. She noted that AFDC grant amounts had been falling steadily in inflation-adjusted figures since the 1960s as out-of-wedlock birth rates rose. Moreover, the rise in number of out-of-wedlock births was not limited to women who subsequently received AFDC. When compared with other Western economies, the U.S. had the highest rate of out-of-wedlock births yet provided considerably less support. Blank suggested that other factors offered a better explanation. Women's economic independence had increased at the same time that men's ability to support families had decreased. Further, the social stigma regarding out-of-wedlock parenthood had diminished.[79] Sister Mary Rose McGeady, president and CEO of Covenant House in New York City, instructed the Finance Committee that her work with youths revealed a nonmonetary explanation for out-of-wedlock pregnancy. Motivation and outlook, principally a teenager's self-assessment of his or her future prospects, played a determinative role. She explained that a "delay of gratification for greater and more moral rewards in life holds little value for teenagers who fear death by guns and whose experience leads them to an attitude of live now, for tomorrow you may be dead."[80]

Still, many participants bolstered causal claims through statements of principle and judgments of human nature. Robert Rector of the Heritage Foundation asserted the indubitable implication of social programs in the problems they sought to alleviate through their effect on individual behavior. He insisted that "the government is caught in a process in which the bottom line on welfare is that welfare insidiously creates its own clientele. The more you spend on these programs, the more you erode the work ethic, the more you promote illegitimacy, the more people in need of aid are generated." Rep. Curt Weldon identified a paradox that confronted all government efforts to ameliorate social misery. Weldon recounted that he had seen genuine need in his work as a physician, but "when you step in and you see this need and you say we have to create a program to address that need, then suddenly the need begins to grow." Rep. David Camp formulated this sentiment into a basic principle of human nature: "A most fundamental principle of human behavior accepted by almost all reasonable people is that if you reward something, you get more of it."[81]

Though participants called on the absent father to reassert himself in family life, the evils of the deadbeat dad were mitigated in some degree in comparison to the debates surrounding the FSA by the havoc wreaked by the welfare system's Faustian bargain. To be sure, many participants denounced young men as irresponsible for impregnating women in the first place, then failing to support their children. Rep. Jennifer Dunn, for instance, expressed her revulsion with and alluded to criminal conduct of "a young man who commits five pregnancy acts in order to become a member of a gang." Sen. David Pryor reported that only 3 percent of Americans were behind on their car payments while 53 percent were behind on their child-support payments. He insisted that Congress "find the way to bring them to accept responsibility."[82] To accomplish this goal, many advocates proposed significant changes in child-support enforcement mechanisms. Geraldine Jensen testified that her unsuccessful attempt to collect child support, which forced her to cycle on and off AFDC for several years, convinced her that the present system assumed nineteenth-century rates of divorce and out-of-wedlock births. The state-based system permitted no uniformity in laws. Judicial review of each case delayed support orders so that they often were unenforceable when issued. Jensen called for national laws and administrative processing.

Mitchell Adams, Massachusetts Commissioner of Revenue, called for greater uniformity in state laws. He identified access to financial information as the key to effective collection, calling new hire reporting "the single-most lucrative new tool in child support enforcement." Mitchell exhorted Congress to "send a message that paying child support is as important as paying taxes."[83]

Still, many participants believed that the system shared much of the blame for unpaid child support. Penny Young, legislative director for Concerned Women for America, explained that "[f]athers are found nowhere in the children's lives because the government has paid them not to be there." Heidi Stirrup, director of government relations for the Christian Coalition, connected the system's Faustian bargain directly to the absence of fathers in many homes. She held that for many, "welfare is more attractive than entry-level jobs. It subsidizes unwed motherhood and makes husbands quite dispensable."[84] Cynthia Ewing, senior policy analyst for the Children's Rights Council, argued that even when the system collected payments from absent fathers, it disregarded their potential contributions to healthy family life. She charged that "we have archaic practices throughout the country that treat one parent as a disposable parent except for financial purposes." Along these lines, Bill Harrington, national director of the American Fathers Coalition, suggested that the key to more effective collections might not be open access to financial information, tougher policing, or national laws, but respect of the father as an integral being. He cited a 1990 census report indicating that "[w]hen fathers see their children and have shared rights, child support is paid 90 percent on time and in full. When fathers do not see their children and have no rights, it is roughly 35 percent."[85]

Enumerating its litany of ills, reformers asserted unequivocally against all expressions of doubt that the existing welfare system was the cruelest of all. This statement of ultimate cruelty served key strategic functions at various moments in the deliberations. In the statements of some reformers, the charge of ultimate cruelty served to set the parameters of the debate. In his remarks opening the first hearing of the Human Resources Subcommittee, Representative Shaw expressed hope that the committee might work together to report a bill: "I find a consensus of what brings us together and that is the realization that the welfare program we have is the cruelest program of all because it pays people not to succeed." Reformers also invoked ultimate cruelty to locate presumption. In his testimony to the Human Resources Subcommittee, Michigan governor John Engler asserted that "for those that defend the current system the burden of proof is on them to defend the failed system…. To presume that those who want to defend the current system should be given debating points for saying those who propose change have to overcome some burden, I think that is false." Ultimate cruelty deflected charges of the same. When Secretary Shalala expressed a desire not to punish innocent children as part of the reform process, Ways and Means Committee member McCrery interrupted her with a pointed rebuke: "Madam Secretary, the current system is punishing innocent children every day. If you deny that, you are missing the point."[86]

A centralized bureaucracy—an oppressive, arrogant, and heartless bureaucracy—created this cruelest of all systems. Legislators and witnesses attacked it relentlessly, discrediting the federal government as a reasonable locus of change, except insofar as federal agencies extricated themselves from social welfare policy. Michael Horowitz, a senior fellow at the Hudson Institute, expressed glee and relief in his appearance before the Human Resources Subcommittee. He celebrated as an extraordinary phenomenon the change in committee leadership. He proclaimed that "we as a country are finally liberated from the notion that has shackled us all, and the poor most of all; that one's compassion is a function of how much more of the same solutions one supports. We are freed of that, thank goodness, and thank goodness for the poor, who have been savaged by this program." While Horowitz expressed gratitude at the new-found willingness to break with an "entitlement psychology," Rep. Michael Bilirakis revealed scorn for a bureaucracy that for a half-century had sought to increase its power over state governments. When Secretary Shalala raised concerns about devolving responsibility for medical care for poor people to the states, Bilirakis objected to what he perceived as an arrogance and lack of trust underlying her position. He reacted indignantly to the implicit suggestion that only "ivory tower" Washingtonians exhibited compassion. He asked incredulously: "[H]ow can we say that the governors don't care enough about poor people who need health care, don't have the sense of compassion?" Bilirakis accused the administration of an unwillingness to "trust in the states. Now, isn't that really what it comes down to?"[87]

Instead of meeting the needs of the poor, the bureaucracy served its patrons in the poverty industry. In his testimony to the Human Resources Subcommittee, Michigan governor John Engler impugned the motives of those supporting a continuation of entitlement status. He

charged that "there is a poverty industry in this town that has done quite
well talking about poverty for forty years." Reformers insinuated that
over the years this industry had become increasingly skillful at undermining challenges to its authority and repelling attempts to restrain its financial excesses. When Governmental Affairs Committee chair William
Roth questioned the inclusion of programs for the elderly in expansive
definitions of welfare, Robert Rector insisted on the significance of an
"aggregate figure" in light of what he called the "horror/slashing the
safety net game." He explained that this insidious shell game protected
inefficient and corrupt programs against legitimate reductions. Without
a total dollar amount, the poverty industry would continue its evasion of
genuine reform. "For over fifteen years, we have played a game where
various groups take one of those seventy-five [welfare] programs and
show that perhaps it didn't grow at base line, or it might have actually
been cut," Rector asserted, "and then they go out and issue a press release, more or less pretending that that is the welfare state, that program,
and say, look, welfare spending hasn't grown." Rev. Robert Sirico stated
the reformers' case succinctly when he contended that the "primary
threat of welfare reform, it seems, is not to the poor but to the bureaucracy that justifies its existence off welfare."[88] Reformers insisted that
growth of the welfare bureaucracy could not be abated without dismantling the bureaucracy itself. The end of entitlements to federal assistance
stood as a minimum measure for many; a termination of funding altogether appeared as an even more promising option for some.

Recovering Volunteerism and Freeing the States

Reformers located the real tragedy of the welfare bureaucracy in its displacement of volunteer and private-sector efforts. If Newt Gingrich acted
as the harbinger of a brave new world, then Marvin Olasky and Robert
Sirico assumed the roles of reclaimers of an abandoned, glorious past.
Olasky served as historian; Sirico acted as theologian. Olasky recounted
to the Human Resources Subcommittee the successes of past generations
of Americans in fighting poverty—before the intrusion of the government in the Progressive Era and beyond. Olasky, a journalism professor
at the University of Texas, told this tale in detail in his book, *The Tragedy
of American Compassion,* which contained Gingrich's endorsement on the

cover of the paperback version. The "tragedy" is that we know how to fight poverty, Olasky instructed the subcommittee, "[w]e had successful programs a century ago, successful because they embodied seven points that can be remembered in alphabetical order: affiliation, bonding, categorization, discernment, employment, freedom, and God."[89] Olasky explained that each element implied personal involvement as well as material and spiritual challenge, capabilities that bureaucracies did not possess. Volunteers, not bureaucrats, supported and staffed the tens of thousands of local, private charitable agencies and religious groups working independently in the nineteenth century to wage war on poverty.

Compassion was the greatest weapon of this volunteer army. Olasky noted that the etymology of "compassion" suggested an emphasis on "personal involvement with the needy, suffering with them, not just giving to them." He cautioned the committee against adopting uncritically the "myths of the good days." Olasky acknowledged that the old days were not always good and life was hard. Nevertheless, he characterized past efforts as "exciting" because "[v]olunteers opened their homes to deserted mothers and orphaned children. More significantly, they made moral demands on recipients of aid. They saw family, work, freedom, and faith as central to our being, not as lifestyle." Olasky contrasted this spiritual past with a hollow and apathetic present. He argued that the presence of government agencies had conditioned Americans to expect someone else to do the moral work once undertaken by a volunteer army. In this way, "[b]ad charity drives out good." He reproached supporters of the welfare state not for their extravagance but for their stinginess: "we scrimp on what many of the destitute need most—time, love, and challenge."[90] Olasky held that history offered exciting possibilities for the future—if legislators would only look back.

Reverend Sirico, president of the Acton Institute for the Study of Religion and Liberty, voiced frustration at the inability of "mainstream religious leadership" to see the "simple truth" of the virtues of voluntary charity and the ineluctable corrupting influences of government social programs. He exhorted members of the Department Operations, Nutrition, and Foreign Agriculture Subcommittee to rediscover the moral obligation to provide authentic assistance to people in need. Authenticity implied an important set of criteria, which included promoting the two-parent family as a moral norm and permitting workers to retain the fruits of their labor. Evaluated against these criteria, social welfare policy failed miserably. Fault lay in "national strategies for welfare [that] have

attempted to help the individual person in need from the most distant
and bureaucratic level—the federal government. The result has been a
system that tends to lump all the poor in one class, yet in reality poor
people are individuals with different situations, talents, resources, and
weaknesses." Sirico insisted that the federal government could never be
an effective moral teacher. He called instead for a principle of "sub-
sidiarity," which "holds that social functions that can best be accomplished by a lower order of society should not be taken over by a higher
order."[91] Sirico maintained that individuals, churches, and neighborhoods should be the resources of first resort in efforts to alleviate poverty.

Echoing Olasky, Sirico argued that federal social policy had effectively
driven out good charity with bad charity. He explained to the subcommittee that the very existence of the welfare state "lessens the incentive of
people at the local level to become involved in needed projects." Secular
agencies of the federal government attenuated the moral influence of religious mediating institutions, displacing the efficacious instruments of
individual moral rehabilitation. When interacting with the poor on a personal basis, caregivers "also encourage moral renewal. In many cases, this
is a dramatic transformation of the individual from a state of moral
weakness to strength, dependence to independence." This process required diligent, strenuous effort of the recipient, "and many will reject it
if an easier alternative is provided through government programs." In
testimony to the Human Resources Subcommittee, Sirico boldly predicted that "[i]f and when bad charity comes to an end, we can expect an
explosion of interest in helping those in need.... [W]e have forgotten just
how powerful the forces of genuine charity are in American society."[92]

Sirico rebuffed suggestions by religious leaders that terminating federal assistance to young mothers would increase abortions. He retorted
that "[f]ar from encouraging abortion, removing subsidies will discour-
age promiscuity" by clarifying the risks of pregnancy. Sirico contended
that an environment in which out-of-wedlock births imposed hardships
on young mothers ought not to be seen as wholly undesirable by policymakers. Still, a change in policy direction would reduce the incidence of
such hardship. For "if the individual circumstance is being closely mon-
itored by a secular agency or religious ministry, the individual becomes
acutely aware that sexual responsibility has a price." Sirico explained that
a personal, voluntary approach to social welfare relied on a classical, two-
dimensional view of moral tutoring: "We abstain from immoral behavior
because we fear its effects and we abstain because we love the good."[93]

Although he asserted the ineffectiveness of government social policy, Sirico argued for legislation to encourage the growth of private charity. Given his call for legislators "to shift the burden of welfare from citizens in their role as taxpayers to citizens in their role as good people with charitable hearts," Sirico contradictorily appealed for changes in the tax code to make charitable giving more financially rewarding. He cited one proposal that would permit individuals to deduct 110 percent of their charitable contributions — effectively reintroducing, by crediting an amount greater than the actual donation, government funding of social welfare programs. When a member of the Human Resources Subcommittee wondered if the eligibility criteria of charitable organizations might limit the "types" of low-income people participating in such programs, Sirico responded in a manner that belied his confidence in the power of the forces of genuine charity. He confessed that "the idea is that right now just a charitable deduction is really a net loss to the person who is contributing it." Moreover, such a bonus might be necessary to stimulate further contributions: "[I]n order to pick up a lot of the slack that would be needed to be picked up if the federal government begins moving out of these various programs, you want to give some kind of incentive for people to be even more generous."[94]

In their appearances before congressional committees, religious leaders stressed the limits of charities and nonprofits. Rev. Fred Kammer, president of Catholic Charities USA, the nation's largest private social-services network, reiterated the unavoidable obligations of public institutions. He asserted that "[w]e believe that only government has the resource capacity not to mention the final political and moral responsibility in justice to promote the general welfare." The nation recognized the limited capacities of churches and charities sixty years ago. Kammer dismissed as "sociological speculation fueled by ideological wishfulness" statements by "some think-tank theoreticians and arm-chair theologians [who] have told the Congress and the public that the churches and charities will pick up the slack when food and income supports are slashed for America's poorest families."[95] Wishful thinking of this type ignored factual experience and the scope of existing need in every community across the nation. Kammer reported to the Human Resources Subcommittee that the demand for Catholic Charities' services had increased by 700 percent in the past twelve years; he insisted that his organization and others could not meet the needs of the estimated five million people who would be affected by provisions in the Contract with America. Along these lines,

Rabbi David Saperstein, director of the Religious Action Center of Reform Judaism, emphasized that religious organizations were "filled to overflowing" with people in need of assistance. He retorted that "those who suggest that the private charity sector, above all the religious sector, can fill the void of a government withdrawal from guaranteeing assistance for the poor greatly misread the realities that we face."[96]

Sirico, however, charged that their affiliation with the state compromised the views of mainstream religious organizations. The federal government's subsidization of many private religious charities providing care for the poor severely restricted the flexibility of these charities to reach out to the greatest human need. As a result, "charities become less adaptable in difficult circumstances." In a more insidious development, the agencies themselves had become dependent on government assistance. Sirico insinuated that "[s]lowly agencies that began with the intention of serving those in need begin to look for ways in which the government can aid them in doing this, and they tend to rely less and less on charitable donations." He suggested that this turn away from private donations transformed the very nature of some religious organizations: "Eventually their role may change from servant to the poor to lobbyist for an ever-expanding welfare state. They may even find themselves dependent on the federal government for their very existence."[97] Thus, even the objections to block grants of groups typically viewed as outside the institutions of government confirmed in the opinions of some reformers the irredeemable nature of the welfare bureaucracy.

For many reformers, salvation lay in the state governments as well as the private sector. They demanded the dismantling of the welfare bureaucracy, which would free states to become "laboratories of innovation." Of the nation's governors, Michigan's John Engler advanced this position most adamantly. He appeared before congressional committees triumphantly, an example of a creative, daring, and responsible state executive whom legislators could trust with America's social welfare system. As the first witness to testify to the Human Resources Subcommittee, Engler relayed the successes of Michigan's reform efforts under way through waivers with the Department of Health and Human Services. He boasted that Michigan had reduced its AFDC rolls by 75,000 cases in the last two years alone. He argued that this success could be sustained and replicated if Congress would only "get Washington out of the way" by ending entitlements and giving block grants to states. "Conservative micromanagement is just as bad as liberal micromanagement," Engler insisted, "States must have the freedom with no strings attached to implement change."[98] He insisted that a federal "one-size-fits-all" approach had failed. States needed flexibility to meet the distinct needs of their populations.

Engler described himself as fighting "to free the power and money that has been held captive in Washington." As an alternative, he envisioned "fifty different laboratories of innovation."[99] He recommended that if Congress insisted on attaching conditions to block grant appropriations, such conditions should be formulated as benchmarks. This minimal involvement intimated the necessity of a redefined relationship between the Congress and state governments. Engler called upon legislators to adopt a new discipline in domestic policy. When confronted with appeals by interest groups for the creation of federal social programs, members could practice the new discipline by "uttering the phrase, 'I am sorry, that is the state's responsibility.'" Engler found support for his reformulation in the U.S. Constitution: "I remember this amendment called the 10th Amendment of the U.S. Constitution.... [I]t has vitality today and perhaps we are entering a period of renewal for the 10th Amendment."[100]

Other participants expressed similar confidence in the states' abilities. In subsequent testimony before the subcommittee, Wisconsin governor Tommy Thompson described a creative, ameliorative competition among governors: "Instead of having a run to the bottom, we are always trying to outdo each other to develop better programs, more efficient programs, more ways to help our people, and that is why we need the flexibility." For their part, legislators saw themselves relinquishing control to more appropriate levels of government. Some legislators, such as Rep. Richard Burr, argued that block grants should replace entitlements because state-elected officials were closer to their constituents than federal elected officials. Addressing the question of whether block grants prevented accountability, Burr responded that "I trust my Governor because the fact is that he's closer to people who can vote for him than I am up here." Rep. Tom Coburn, his Commerce Committee colleague, chastised witnesses who raised concerns about appropriating federal funds without proper oversight. He contended that the "fact is that it's their money. It's not our money." Coburn also expressed impatience with the assumption that "the only place that we can see compassion is in Washington."[101] Reformers held that if states freed from the federal bureaucracy served as innovative laboratories, then the direction for further reforms lay in increasing the responsibilities of the former and preventing the interference of the latter.

Some participants objected strongly to proposed block grants. As opponents had done in the early 1980s, opponents in the mid-1990s invoked the innocence of the child to gainsay block grant proposals as well as calls by some reformers to deny benefits to the children of mothers under eighteen years old.[102] In vivid language, Rep. Patsy Mink argued that benefit denials revealed a brutal callousness portending disastrous consequences. She exhorted that "[p]oor children should not be left to die on the streets of America because of the lack of a two-parent household." With respect to benefit denials and block grants, Sen. Carol Moseley-Braun reminded her Finance Committee colleagues that "there are nine million children out there that are not responsible for the sins of their parents and that as we fix the system we do not want to leave them worse off and suffering more than they are today."[103] Opponents worried about the limited bargaining power of children and their advocates if federal mandates regarding eligibility and funding were repealed. Jeff Crowley, representing the Consortium for Citizens with Disabilities, included children in his assessment that "[f]ull state discretion will lead to discrimination against vulnerable populations." Maine governor Howard Dean expressed similar concerns from his perspective as a state executive. He reiterated his faith that none of the fifty governors "would consciously set out a welfare policy that would harm children. But I do believe that over time things do not always work out as we planned." Dean suggested that within the context of state budget deliberations, the more expansive lobbying efforts of other organized groups might upset previously articulated priorities placed on children's programs. Considerations of power and privilege revealed that "no matter how flexible you want to make things for us, ... we are going to have tremendous financial pressure put upon us."[104]

Images of the working poor also appeared in the statements of participants opposed to block grants. Robert Fersh, president of the Food Research and Action Center, voiced the concerns of many participants when he asserted that block grants "will be inherently unresponsive to need." Fersh explained that because block grants operated with fixed funds rather than a varying amount based upon numbers of eligible people, they would be unable to meet increased need produced by economic recessions. He observed that the working poor, the very people praised by legislators, "will be the ones who could be most hard hit if there is not enough money to go around." Secretary Shalala emphasized this ironic potential outcome in her appearance before the Ways and Means Committee. She insisted that Congress not "forget about those hard-working Americans who have used these programs—food stamps, AFDC in particular—for very short periods of time when they were between jobs and all they wanted to do was make sure that they had food on the table for their children."[105]

Proponents of block grants and other changes in the system met these objections by pointing to the necessity of making some cruel calculations, reasserting the cruelty of the present system, and affirming their belief in modifying behaviors. Expressing these views, Charles Murray presented a spirited defense of the new policy directions before the Finance Committee. Murray diagnosed the problem confronting low-income communities not as a steep increase in welfare receipt but a dramatic rise in the number of out-of-wedlock births. He argued that such births would be reduced only by a radical change in the present system. Murray identified an "immutable law of welfare reform" that impelled fundamental transformation: "carrots drive out sticks." He explained that augmenting the present welfare system through the creation and expansion of job training and placement programs, for example, would only make it more attractive to prospective young parents. Reading from his recent essay in *Commentary* magazine, Murray advised senators to pursue an opposite course. He insisted that "major change in the behavior of young women and the adults in their lives will occur only when the prospect of having a child out of wedlock is, once again, so immediately, tangibly punishing that it overrides everything else, the importuning of the male, the desire for sex, the thoughtlessness of the moment, the anticipated cuddliness of the baby."[106]

Murray held that circumstances forced the Senate into "a necessarily brutal calculation trying to estimate what strategy will result in the least net suffering." He described as a false choice the suggestions of some advocates that senators should weigh a need to be tough on parents against an obligation to be compassionate toward their children. "Massive suffering among children is already among us, despite a labyrinth of programs that are supposed to prevent it, and you can double the spending on all those programs and not get rid of the suffering," Murray testified. He disclosed contempt for people who pretended that hard choices could be avoided: "Those who say we should not punish the children for the mistakes of their parents must come to grips with the fact that millions of children alive today are being punished for the mistakes of their parents beyond Congress' power to do much about it."[107]

The strategies of refutation employed by Murray appeared in statements of reformers across the deliberations. For instance, under questioning by members of the Human Resources Subcommittee, William Bennett admitted that "[w]e are bound to have unintended consequences pretty much no matter what we do." Yet he quickly reasserted the locus of presumption. He stated that "the thing that I want to emphasize is that the burden of proof has got to be on anyone who wants to say that we shouldn't experiment." Representative McCrery reasserted the cruelty of the system after David Liederman, executive director of the Child Welfare League of America, argued that ten million AFDC children ought not to be made guinea pigs for fifty state laboratories. McCrery retorted: "[T]he current program is a disaster. It is hurting kids all the time."[108] Other reformers met objections by expressing faith that the poor would change their behavior—or be forced to change. Human Resources Subcommittee chairperson Shaw admonished other participants to have confidence in recipients. He held that "[w]e have to realize that just because people are on welfare does not mean they are somewhat inferior and have to be paid just to exist, and that we should have no faith in their ability to pull out of welfare." For Michael Tanner of the Cato Institute, however, a different motivator likely would spur changes in recipient behavior: "Fear of bad things motivates us to avoid bad things and I think we have to restore that level of fear of bad consequences."[109]

The new Republican majority of the 104th Congress envisaged a brave new world, described by the new Speaker as a "third-wave information age." Engaging this new world required unlinking the heavy bonds of a confining, self-serving bureaucracy—one that had been offering youths, who in the popular imagination represent a people's future, a Faustian bargain. A policy future lay in the states, in the capable hands of visionary, energetic governors who requested only the freedom to experiment. This confident discernment of a new age and appropriate remedies together with the image of recipient as ward constituted the major themes of mid-1990s welfare policy debates. Confidence, however, was not the only response to perceived social and economic transformations. An undercurrent of anxiousness pervaded the debates, manifest in discussions of immigration and welfare policy.

The Image of the Immigrant and the Anxiousness of the Age

The image of the immigrant preceded Gingrich's triumphant proclamation of a third-wave information age, circulating in both the 103rd and 104th Congresses. Unlike the prefiguration of the ward through a trajectory sustained in the contract signee and significant policy disagreements belying the reform consensus of the mid-1980s, constituents of previous federal policy episodes did not foreshadow the immigrant's arrival. Why, then, did the immigrant, with no antecedents in the early 1980s or mid-1980s, appear throughout the mid-1990s deliberations?

Certainly, participants did not discover the immigrant between 1988 and 1992. Immigrants have figured historically in the popular imagination. The United States has characterized itself proudly as a "nation of immigrants." Michael Walzer writes that the coupling of ethnic particularity and civic commonality constitutes the distinctive doubly hyphenated quality of American citizenship, which is expressed in such identities as Irish-American, Jewish-American, and Asian-American. Walzer notes that immigrant nations such as France often have welcomed foreigners as citizens but have been suspicious of any form of ethnic pluralism. The United States has "made peace" with the particular characteristics of its immigrant groups, regarding "American nationality as an addition to rather than a replacement for ethnic consciousness. The hyphen works, when it is working, more like a plus sign."[110] The doubling in this operation arises from the mutually informing relationship, culturally and politically, of the two terms. Yet Walzer's eloquent defense of the hyphenated American too often stands as an expression of hope rather than a description of fact.

Negative images of immigrants have evidenced suspicion, fear, and contempt of previous generations of immigrants who perceived threats to established economic and political power. The immigrant has long been a favorite target of "American political demonology."[111] Noting that anti-immigrant sentiments frequently appear during periods of economic downturn, Kitty Calavita explains that nativist agitators have represented immigrants differently in alternative historical periods. Though some figures during the Gilded Age such as Andrew Carnegie valued the economic advantages of immigration, others viewed immigrants as strikebreakers. Nativists discovered in the alleged racial inferiority of the immigrant an explanation for depressed wages, labor strife, and an emerging sweatshop system. Rev. William Lawrence gainsaid government interference in the economy as abetting the newly arrived, ignorant masses, "represented by their own kind in city or state government, strongly organized by a leader who is in it for what he can get out of it, and who is ever alert with his legislative cohorts to 'strike' the great corporations." Images shifted after the turn of the century, but the threat of the immigrant in nativist discourse did not dissipate. Antagonists saw immigrants as socialists and anarchists. The *Bulletin of the National Association of Wool Manufacturers* attributed the rise of the Industrial Workers of the World to a "foreign invasion of the anarchists and socialists, criminals and outcasts from other nations." Images changed again around World War I as a program of "Americanization" took hold. It sought to instruct immigrants in the putatively universal values of middle-class reformers. Americanization, Theodore Roosevelt insisted, left "no room" for "hyphenated Americans." He likened the hyphenated quality of life celebrated by Walzer to treason.[112]

Like anti-immigrant sentiment, policy proposals denying benefits to immigrants surfaced before passage of the PRWORA. In the same 1994 election cycle that vaulted Republicans into House majority status, California, a state that contributed significantly to federal policy debates, passed an anti-immigrant ballot initiative known as Proposition 187. Although it was aimed at illegal immigrants, Proposition 187 informed discussions of restrictions to legal immigrants in federal policy debates because legal immigrants often served as surrogates for illegal immigrants. Proposition 187 prohibited illegal immigrants from attending public schools and universities and obtaining nonemergency medical care at facilities receiving public funds. It denied illegal immigrants access to many social services such as disability insurance and family planning. The measure also required schools, hospitals, and social-service agencies to report suspected illegal immigrants, including parents of native-born children, to federal and state authorities.

The campaign for Proposition 187 appealed to the fears and prejudices of voters, portraying a California under invasion. Gov. Pete Wilson's re-election campaign ran television advertisements depicting late-night pandemonium at checkpoints as immigrants ran northward across the U.S.-Mexico border. Wilson, who initially trailed his Democratic challenger by twenty points in campaign polls, cynically embraced Proposition 187 to revive his re-election prospects. When asked in a televised debate how he might enforce the exclusion of undocumented children from public schools, Wilson replied that enforcement would be unnecessary because opponents would file suit in federal court to stop its implementation.[113] His reply revealed a disingenuous embrace of this policy. Public acknowledgment of its unlikely implementation suggested a willingness among voters to favor such gestures even as proponents conceded their inefficacy.

The campaign for Proposition 187 involved groups advocating immigration reform in federal policy-making forums. One such group was the Federation for American Immigration Reform (FAIR), whose spokespersons testified before various congressional committees on the immigration-related components of the mid-1990s welfare reform debates. FAIR claimed credit for a variety of measures enacted in California such as the withholding of driver's licenses without proof of legal status and the invalidation of local sanctuary decrees. It funded and staffed pro-Proposition 187 campaigns. After its passage, FAIR executive director Dan Stein asserted that "Proposition 187's success sends the unequivocal message to the new House and Senate that the people of California and the people of our nation won't accept a few extra border guards—they want comprehensive reform."[114] Conservative support for the measure was not univocal, however. National figures and eager welfare reformers such as William Bennett and Jack Kemp opposed Proposition 187. Linda Chavez of the Manhattan Institute charged that groups such as FAIR championed the initiative as a ruse to build public support for restrictions on legal immigrants.[115]

In her analysis of Proposition 187 debates, Kitty Calavita holds that the focus on tax burdens posed by immigrants, unusual in the history of U.S. nativism, arose from the revival of anti-immigrant sentiment within the context of a resurgent conservatism that developed in the 1970s and 1980s in response to changed U.S. fortunes at the end of the post–World War II economic boom.[116] Her account—suspicion of government spending, resistance to taxes, displacement of citizen by taxpayer—recalls the themes developed in my analysis of the early-1980s budget-cutting debates. Although it may explain portrayals of immigrants in California's Proposition 187 campaign, this formulation does not explain the immigrant's sudden appearance in federal deliberations of welfare policy. The budget-cutters successfully installed an argumentative frame that allied the private sector and the American people against government, but images of immigrants did not circulate in the early-1980s debates or in the mid-1980s debates as this frame still held sway. The immigrant did not appear in the welfare reform debates until participants broached the topic of globalization—of markets, culture, and perhaps the nation-state. A concern with legal immigrants' enrollment in Supplemental Security Income (ssi) and other programs signaled anxiousness with a brave new world confidently embraced in the reformers' attack on the welfare bureaucracy.

With seemingly dizzying speed, forces of economic and political globalization have transformed or promise to transform the legitimacy and sovereignty of the modern state. In an especially lucid series of lectures, Saskia Sassen describes a process in which geographical dispersal of factories, offices, and service outlets in an integrated corporate system as well as the rise of global financial and stock markets have interconnected and transformed the economies of developed and developing nations. This process has been hastened by the "virtualization of a growing number of economic activities" through the use of new technologies.[117] As a corollary and consequent of this economic activity, some processes of governance and accountability traditionally vested in states have been ceded to supragovernmental bodies such as the World Trade Organization.

These forces of economic and political globalization present challenges to the modern state. Global markets reduce the ability of central banks to manage national economies. International agreements and structures suggest that limits may be placed on a state's authority to determine conditions of membership, regulate its national borders, or conduct itself within these borders (e.g., international human rights agreements). Yet the relation between globalization and the modern state should not be seen simply as the diminished authority of the state in a new age. As Sassen notes, states themselves have worked to ease the flow of capital, goods, and labor across national borders, and global processes materialize in national territories. Seen in the context of globalization, the immigrant may function as a site for displaced anxiety because this figure occupies a liminal space between the surreptitious movement of globalization represented by the illegal alien and the visibility of the citizen. Moreover, the immigrant may invite participants' suspicion because the immigrant straddles the contradiction between states' advocacy of globalization and their insistence on modern territorial sovereignty.

Intimating unease with larger global transformations, debate participants held that the nature of immigration to the United States had changed for the worse. Sen. James Exon bemoaned that for too many immigrants the United States had become a promised land of "fairly liberal welfare means." Sadly, "immigration is not what it once was—a chance for an opportunity in a new land, for me to move freely ahead—but in many instances, I am afraid that it has become an opportunity in a new land for welfare." Other participants suggested that foreign operatives had worsened this situation. Rep. Harold Ford traced the current "immigration problem" to "middlemen" operating in foreign countries "who have persuaded these immigrants to come into this country as legal immigrants, rather, and that they have been coached in many instances."[118]

The "immigration problem" concerned the 103rd and 104th Congresses. In 1993 testimony to the Human Resources Subcommittee, David Simcox, senior fellow at the Center for Immigration Studies, argued that direct services to immigrants cost $31 billion more than the amount immigrants paid in taxes. Further, immigrants received public assistance at a higher rate than U.S. households. Simcox recommended a change in immigration policy that exhibited "more concern for the human capital they bring while slowing somewhat the flow of the unskilled." At the same hearing, Theresa Parker, under secretary of the California Health and Welfare Agency, reawakened nineteenth-century fears of "race suicide" in her discussion of the growing problem of "citizen children of illegal immigrants." Parker explained that these "citizen children," whose numbers already exceeded the entire AFDC caseload of twenty-five states, were the fastest growing portion of California's caseload.[119]

Many participants located rising immigration costs in families' failure to support their newly arrived relatives. Susan Martin, executive director of the U.S. Commission on Immigration Reform, shared with the Finance Committee the commission's position that "the principal responsibility for assistance to immigrants rests with the immigrants themselves and their sponsors, not the U.S. taxpayer." In one of its principal recommendations, the commission held that affidavits of support signed by U.S. sponsors on admittance of an immigrant should be legally enforceable contracts. Martin explained this as the most important action the Congress could take: "If the children cannot provide support, they have to understand that there is no free lunch for their parents in this country." Martin's remarks reiterated commission chairperson Barbara Jordan's 1993 testimony to the Human Resources Subcommittee, during which Jordan advanced this recommendation and others. Some participants argued that even a legal contract would be insufficient to control costs. FAIR's Dan Stein charged that many children of elderly immigrants instructed their parents to transfer their assets, "rendering the parent eligible for SSI as soon as the deeming period expires."[120]

Stein and other reformers characterized eligibility denials to legal immigrants as an assertion of the importance of citizenship. Stein argued that immigration ought to be regarded as a first step toward citizenship. He envisioned that "to the extent we send that signal, and tell immigrants that it is important to become a citizen in order to obtain certain benefits and rights, such as voting, we will strengthen the civic fabric and once again make the immigration policy consistent with the national need and national interest."[121] When pressed by his colleagues to justify benefit denials to elderly people—including some who had been residents of the United States for twenty or thirty years—Senator Santorum conceded that denying benefits to legal immigrants "may not be the most altruistic way of encouraging citizenship, but I am not too sure that is necessarily a bad thing."[122]

If the image of the immigrant marked participant anxiety of a new age, then the turn to citizenship may have been a defense of an institution perceived as under siege. Sassen holds that economic globalization has engendered an emergent "economic citizenship." Some actors do possess an empowering "aggregation of economic rights," permitting these actors to demand accountability from governments. Sassen argues, however, that this emergent form of citizenship summons a new rights-bearer: "economic citizenship does not belong to citizens. It belongs to firms and markets, particularly the global financial markets, and it is located not in individuals, not in citizens, but in global economic actors."[123] In an era of globalization, reformers may not be willing or able to exert a territorial sovereignty that inhibits the transnational flow of labor, but reformers can require legal immigrants—highly visible representatives of foreignness—to choose a sovereign allegiance.

The legal immigrant may have functioned in the demands of some participants as a surrogate for the more dangerous and elusive illegal immigrant. The reprobation leveled at the illegal immigrant—manifest in the passage of Proposition 187—may have contaminated more sympathetic portrayals of immigrants as gentle elders. In the budget debates of 1981, pathologies associated with cheats, shirkers, and double-dippers overwhelmed participants' concern for children. Earnest budget-cutters promised witnesses their support in counteracting proposed reductions in programs such as adoption assistance but reacted coldly to appeals stressing the innocence of AFDC children. Similarly, the threat of illegal immigration generally hindered appeals highlighting the membership of many legal immigrants in voluntary associations and their status as taxpayers. Both immigrants and AFDC recipients represented to participants economic threats as drains on the public treasury. Both groups threatened social norms, albeit differently. AFDC recipients undermined the work ethic and the nuclear family. Immigrants challenged "American" cultural practices. From these different sources arose different justifications for denying benefits. Reformers insisted that the repeal of AFDC would bring poor people back to their American community. Denials of benefits to immigrants suggested demarcations of community boundaries.

The Return of the Non-Needy

The anxiousness participants directed toward immigrants and the confidence they displayed toward wards marked the major features of the mid-1990s reform debates. Still, an additional argument in the deliberations may reveal an initial strategy in conservative attacks against broadly supported social programs: interrogating the validity of all program recipients. Like Reagan and his supporters, some participants evoked a cast of non-needy recipients to illuminate abuses and inefficiencies in Supplemental Security Income for disabled children, food stamps, and the Earned Income Tax Credit. Strong parallels arose between the debates of the early 1980s and this component of the mid-1990s deliberations as distinctions emerged between the truly needy and others and as participants relayed fantastic instances of abuse.

Scandalous tales and subjective eligibility tests pervaded deliberations concerning SSI reform. In his remarks opening Human Resources Subcommittee hearings on the topic, Chairperson Shaw expressed a widely shared intention not "to diminish the benefits of anyone who has severe disabilities and is deserving of those benefits." Still, Shaw pointed to "overwhelming evidence" of SSI abuse. He charged that some parents had taken advantage of "foggy SSI guidelines" for children to receive undeserved cash benefits and medical coverage. Shaw cited a recent newspaper account of a woman collecting nine SSI checks. He disclosed that "[h]er take was 46,716 dollars in tax-free income per year." Like Shaw, Carolyn Weaver, resident scholar at the American Enterprise Institute, supported reforms that would eliminate inappropriate benefits while "finding a better way" to deliver benefits to the truly needy. She explained that under the current system, temptations to defraud the government were great: "a poor family on AFDC can double its income by getting one child on SSI and triple its income by getting two kids on SSI."[124]

Representative McCrery located the source of abuse in Individualized Functional Assessments (IFAS), which determined eligibility from an individual assessment of a "child's ability to act in an age-appropriate manner."[125] IFAS, he held, delegated too much discretion to test administrators. McCrery called instead for "objective medical criteria" as the basis for eligibility. Other participants, such as Rhoda Schulzinger, countered that IFAS took into account complexities in diagnoses of childhood disability. She reported that the Social Security Administration investigated 600 cases in the Arkansas-Louisiana Delta, where a number of stories of abuse had originated, and found no questionable IFAS. McCrery stated his disagreement with the SSA study, insisting on the immediately recognizable, common-sense inappropriateness of diagnosed disabilities. He reiterated his belief that "there is ample evidence of fraud—not necessarily fraud, but ample evidence that there are children receiving SSI who most ordinary Americans would agree do not deserve to be on SSI."[126]

Food stamps were a more embattled program and had been a target of Reagan and his supporters in the early 1980s. Nevertheless, food stamps had been supported by such stalwart conservatives as Sen. Bob Dole, Majority Leader of the 104th Congress. The attention to food stamps in the mid-1990s deliberations centered on fraud and abuse. In testimony to the House Agriculture Committee, Roger Viadero, inspector general of the Agriculture Department, described in detail examples of street and retailer trafficking in food stamps. As part of his presentation, Viadero played a videotape of six vignettes of fraud, including the exchange of food stamps for drugs. The videotape also showed street "runners" who purchased food stamps from recipients for 50 percent of their value as well as the thriving businesses of dishonest merchants engaged in food stamp trade. Viadero advocated the implementation of Electronic Benefits Transfer as an alternative to paper coupons in an effort to curtail fraud. Some legislators questioned the ability of government to stop a determined defrauder. Rep. Nick Smith recounted an exchange with a frustrated store owner in his district, who constantly witnessed "kids [who] would come in with food stamps and buy two cases of pop, dump the pop out, bring the two empty cases back in for a refund on the bottles and buy a six-pack of beer with the refund."[127]

While attacks on ssi and food stamps relied principally on images of welfare cheats, arguments for changes in the EITC evoked the other two images of Reagan's tripartite division of the non-needy: shirkers and double-dippers. As some participants remarked, reformers deployed these images against a program that Reagan had supported enthusiastically.[128] Marvin Kosters, a resident scholar at the American Enterprise Institute, held that the EITC reduced work incentives for 30 percent of all families with children: the tax credit produced its own shirkers. Kosters explained, however, that this disincentive could be reversed by lowering the income eligibility level for the EITC. He asserted that the present level "raises questions about whether we should regard the cut-off levels where the EITC is phased out as appropriately describing the working poor." Kosters's concern employed a variant of the double-dipper—the person who wrongly received benefits, though not through intentional scheming. Other participants alluded to outright fraud. Senator Roth observed incredulously that because the EITC did not consider one's assets, a multimillionaire in assets could qualify for a low-income tax credit.[129]

The "appeal to non-neediness" does not challenge the fundamental purpose of a program. The charge that the EITC cutoff was too high, for instance, did not question the good of supplementing the wages of low-income workers. Unlike a program confronting calls for repeal, a program challenged in this way is not seen as flawed in its assumptions, but rather led astray, carelessly managed, or corrupt in practice. As the failed attempt to block grant food stamps may suggest, a program that receives broad support from legislators and their constituents can withstand and may even be strengthened by such a radical "reform." Calling into question the legitimacy of all recipients, however, introduces doubt about the program. As the retrenchment-era trajectory of AFDC suggests, such doubt can increase dramatically, with corollary policy implications.

The Peripheral Presence of the Citizen-Worker

I have focused thus far on telling the story of AFDC's repeal. Still, debate participants did not advance this call monolithically. Alternative possibilities sometimes intervene in policy debate amidst influential themes and narratives. As in previous retrenchment-era episodes, this indeterminate quality of policy debate also characterized debates regarding the PRWORA. The macroeconomic and structural analyses that emerged in the 1992 hearings before the Select Committee on Hunger continued to circulate through the deliberations, pacing prominent themes while residing at the periphery. But their implicit and sometimes explicit invocation of a citizen-worker was sorely out of step with the impetus of the deliberations.

Still, some advocates continued to reference a living wage. In 1994 testimony, AFDC recipient Dorothy Amadi recounted her experience of cycling on and off welfare as familial circumstances and support structures changed. Amadi's personal experience and contact with others convinced her that millions of poor women possessed job skills and desperately wanted to work. But they confronted a situation in which "[t]here are just no jobs out there that will pay us a living wage, that will buy the child care and health care that we need."[130] Others raised doubts about the current capacities of the economy directly. In 1995 testimony, Ronald Field identified the creation of "family supporting jobs" as the most effective reform measure. He maintained, however, that "[i]t is highly questionable whether the economy is currently in the position to do so to any great extent." To claims that such jobs existed, advocates such as Denise Ripley, a member of the Philadelphia Unemployment Project, reproached legislators for their lack of understanding. She charged that "[y]ou just do not understand the realities of what so many of us have to face every day. If you did, I am sure you would not even consider these cuts. Instead of cutting my only means of survival when I am unemployed, you should be trying to find ways of helping me become employed by creating more jobs." Others questioned employer motivations. Sonia Perez, director of the Poverty Project of the National Council of La Raza, admonished legislators to examine "the role of employers who are reluctant to hire AFDC recipients or who hire workers part-time solely to avoid providing benefits."[131]

Employer-employee relations figured in the statements of other advocates as they spoke of reforms creating a reserve army of labor. Katherine McFate of the Joint Center for Political and Economic Studies predicted that lauded reforms would be successful only in placing low-wage workers in harmful competition with each other. She suspected that "[w]idespread workfare will create a subtier of laborers who are not subject to the normal rules of the labor market and are working somewhat involuntarily at less than the minimum wage." Nanine Mieklejohn, leg-islative affairs specialist for the American Federation of State, County, and Municipal Employees, concurred. She forecasted that "large-scale workfare programs will drag down other workers, as employers see that they can get free labor." Moreover, this devalued worth would eventually impugn all low-wage workers, because poor women circulated between AFDC receipt and low-wage labor. Advocates resisted these insidious di-visions. Renee Pecot, a member of the Women's Economic Agenda Pro-ject, demanded that legislators "[d]o not divide us. Poor women on wel-fare are like poor workers in the workforce."[132]

Advocates implied and asserted the dignity of all workers and their rights as citizens. The mayor of Kansas City, Missouri, Emanual Cleavor II, appeared before the Social Security and Family Policy Subcommittee to relay the successes of a job program in his city that "provides the worker with a level of dignity that is commensurate with citizenship in the United States." Meiklejohn insisted that if an AFDC recipient worked in the same capacity as a paid worker, then she should have "all of the rights and benefits of an employee."[133] Sharon Daly articulated to the Human Resources Subcommittee the conviction of the National Con-ference of Catholic Bishops that parents possessed rights in addition to their responsibilities. These rights compelled government to "promote full employment and make sure that assistance is available when parents cannot find jobs at decent wages." Sandra Corder asserted her citizen-worker status emphatically. Angered by a comparison of the benefits of a minimum-wage job versus AFDC receipt, Corder halted the entire line of questioning: "I will not settle for a minimum wage job. I have worked too hard; I have gone through too much, and too many people have taken things away from me, sitting up there making decisions about my life and my children. No, sir, no!"[134]

Rights claims went against the prevailing tendencies of the debates, however. An objection by Pat Gowens, a member of Milwaukee's Welfare Warriors, that prisoners were the only other group in the United States forced to perform community-service work signaled the positioning of welfare recipients in the debates.[135] Generally thought of as having re-linquished their rights, prisoners are in no position to make demands on society. Although their portrayal as victims of a destructive bureaucracy may have absolved recipients of the direct guilt of the convicted criminal, recipients' shifted portrayal from signee to ward rescinded their ability to adopt the stance of a rights-bearer.

From Entitlements to Block Grants: The Repeal of AFDC

A brave new world, like its technologies, must be mobile and fast. It must be capable of changing shape quickly. It must be rapidly set up and easily disassembled. Social institutions and arrangements must follow the movement of global capital. Just as corporations must be increasingly flexible, so too must government. In the victorious afterglow of the Second World War, as Western industrialized nations displayed their economic strength, British sociologist T. H. Marshall asserted confidently the emergence of the third phase in a continuous 250-year evolution of citizenship. Building on "civil" — "the rights necessary for individual freedom" — and "political" — "the right to participate in the exercise of political power" — elements of citizenship, this "social element" promised a wide-ranging social equality, from "the right to a modicum of economic welfare and security to the right to share to the full in the social heritage and to live the life of a civilised being according to the standards prevailing in the society."[136] Marshall's seminal essay, as much a counterfactual normative construct as a description of the evolution of citizenship rights, has enabled trenchant analyses of social orders. But new worlds must always be forward-looking; they must not be hindered by voices from the past. Entitlements bind governments. They assert relationships that may not be altered. They establish commitments that are nonnegotiable. Sassen contends that historicizing citizenship entails recognizing the possible erosion of some of the conditions that have supported its evolution as "hypermobile" capital searches the globe for the most profitable short-term opportunities.[137] As reformers routinely noted, block grants offer states flexibility. They may be used to fund a variety of program structures and may be withdrawn at any time. In extricating states from particular situations and individual commitments, block grants simulate the liquidity of global capital.

Early indications that the president might sign a bill repealing AFDC — and the federal guarantee of aid that it promised — appeared in the first State of the Union address he delivered before a newly triumphant, oppositional Congress. In this address, Clinton implicated public assistance programs in a far-reaching effort to rethink the scale and function of the federal government. He likened the epochal shift facing the nation to one encountered sixty years ago. At that time, FDR offered Americans a New

Deal, which heralded a new era and defined the relationship between citizens and the federal government for more than a half-century. Clinton
agreed that the New Deal "approach worked in its time. But we today, we
face a very different time and very different conditions. We are moving
from an industrial age built on gears and sweat to an information age demanding skills and learning and flexibility." Clinton asserted that governance ought to be restructured for the exigencies of the new age. Federal
agencies needed to desist from the cumbersome ways of the past:

> The old way dispensed services through large, top-down, inflexible
> bureaucracies. The New Covenant way should shift these resources
> and decision-making from bureaucrats to citizens, injecting choice
> and competition and individual responsibility into national policy.
> The old way of governing around here actually seemed to reward fail-
> ure. The New Covenant way should have built-in incentives to reward
> success. The old way was centralized here in Washington. The New
> Covenant way must take hold in the communities all across America.[138]

The 1995 State of the Union address recapitulated the argument against
bureaucracy advanced by participants in committee hearings. Delivered
in temporal proximity to Speaker Gingrich's testimony before the Ways
and Means Committee, it too called for the nation to embark on a journey into a brave new world, throwing off bureaucratic chains that may
have been appropriate for a lumbering industrial-age capital.

The president's futurism persisted in succeeding statements: he did
not object to block grants on principle but pragmatic policy grounds. In
a March speech to the National Association of Counties, Clinton repeated
his insistence on "very big changes in the way government works. We
don't need big, bureaucratic, one-size-fits-all government in Washington." One week later, he told the National League of Cities that the information age enabled government to be "far more decentralized and
flexible than we ever have been before. No one will ever again have to rely
on a distant bureaucracy to solve every problem in today's rapidly changing environment." In an April address to the Iowa state legislature, Clinton
specified two concerns with block grant proposals as written. He argued
that current proposals were unfair to states with growing numbers of eligible children and relieved states of the responsibility to disperse
matching funds presently required.[139]

If the 1995 State of the Union address rebuked the federal bureaucracy
and, by implication, the public assistance programs its agencies oversaw,
Clinton's 1996 State of the Union address repudiated the old bureaucratic

way of governance. The president proclaimed: "We know big government does not have all the answers. We know there's not a program for every problem. We know, and we have worked to give the American people a smaller, less bureaucratic government in Washington. And we have to give the American people one that lives within its means. *The era of big government is over.*"[140] Subsequent remarks regarding AFDC revealed Clinton's movement from pragmatic concern to advocacy of a block grant as opposed to an entitlement approach. In a July interview with network television news anchor Tom Brokaw, the president asserted that "get[ting] rid of the guarantee" to federal assistance would provide states with greater flexibility in moving recipients from welfare to paid employment.[141]

Calling the bill strong on work, better for children, and tough on child-support enforcement, Clinton announced his intention to sign the Personal Responsibility and Work Opportunity Reconciliation Act "first and foremost because the current system is broken."[142] Here, he advocated block grants with even greater assurance as he chided groups that opposed his decision. When asked for his reaction to some advocacy groups' claims that the legislation would harm children, Clinton responded accusingly that "there are some groups who basically have never agreed with me on this, who never agreed that we should do anything to give the states much greater flexibility on this if it meant doing away with the individual entitlement to the welfare check."[143]

Clinton's remarks on signing the PRWORA emphasized newness. He described the legislation as a change in the parameters of policy debate, a re-creation of the "nation's social bargain with the poor." He promised that "[w]e're going to make it all new again and see if we can't create a system of incentives which reinforce work and family and independence." He also appealed inchoately yet eloquently to a sense of national community and mutual interdependence. Clinton described the new start offered by the legislation as "something really good" because job creation "becomes everybody's responsibility." AFDC's repeal meant that "[w]e cannot blame the system for the jobs they [recipients] don't have anymore. If it doesn't work now, it's everybody's fault—mine, yours, and everybody else." This shared responsibility required cooperation from the business sector: "Every employer in this country that ever made a disparaging remark about the welfare system needs to think about whether he or she should now hire somebody from welfare and go to work." And shared responsibility implicated previously disaffected citizens. Clinton exhorted that "every person in America tonight who sees a report of this who has ever said a disparaging word about the welfare system should now say, 'Okay, that's gone. What is my responsibility to make it better?'"[144]

The repeal of AFDC culminated a sixteen-year attack on public assistance programs that progressed from removing recipients from caseloads to specifying demands of those remaining to rescinding the federal government's guarantees. In his February 1981 speeches launching this policy trajectory, Reagan blamed government for the nation's economic woes and lauded the market as a tester of individual character. Over the succeeding sixteen years, this relationship persisted as the market's virtues multiplied while government's culpability widened to include the misery of the poor. And yet, as he signed legislation that fulfilled a campaign promise to end welfare as we know it, Clinton appealed to the non-market ideal of community. The brave new world embraced by President Clinton, Speaker Gingrich, and other reformers, however, may be more inclined to throw off community as an unnecessary weight as it races into a more flexible, mobile, and high-speed future.

CHAPTER 6

Imagining an Inclusive Political Community

Policymakers in the retrenchment era ostensibly ended welfare as we knew it. Until its repeal in the 1996 Personal Responsibility and Work Opportunity Reconciliation Act, welfare had come to be known as the dispersal of cash grants to poor families through the Aid to Families with Dependent Children program. This was not the only form by which welfare could have been known, of course, for Americans of varied economic standing receive monetary benefits from the federal government ranging from social security retirement benefits to income tax deductions on home mortgage interest payments. "Welfare" pejoratively understood had meant AFDC and to a lesser extent food stamps and other public assistance programs. Yet in another sense, retrenchment-era legislation did not end welfare as we knew it. The block grants that replaced the federal entitlement to assistance ultimately may have the effect of transferring the perceived problems shared by federal and state governments to state and local governments administering the Temporary Assistance for Needy Families (TANF) funds. Moreover, the PRWORA did not end welfare as we knew it because the legislation did not—indeed, could not—repeal the contrary beliefs, competing values, and malevolent images that historically have plagued deliberation of welfare policy. Public suspicion toward persons imagined as cheats and shirkers and public anger with governments unable to correct their pathological behavior did not end with the repeal of AFDC. The animosities and, though less frequently articulated, aspirations that had been directed at AFDC will find new targets as poverty and dependency persist for the foreseeable future.

In this concluding chapter, I look backward to see where welfare policy debates have been and forward to envision where they might lead to ameliorate the lives of poor Americans. Looking back entails taking notice of three important themes that emerge from my analysis of retrenchment-era

debates: the historically situated character of welfare reform, the doubly disabling tendencies of representation that undermined the interests of poor
people, and the interrelationship of images and arguments during and
across policy episodes. Looking forward involves discussion of two interconnected areas: first, determining what constitutes success in welfare
reform and how this may be achieved; second, explicating the crucial role
of imagining in this process. Enacting shifts in processes of collective
imagining must go beyond debunking disabling images to craft and circulate affirming images of the poor. Debate participants may envision
affirmative images by highlighting community as an alternative to the market model of political institutions and human relationships that framed
retrenchment-era debates. Within this alternative framework, welfare
policy debate may proceed as an effort to bring about the minimum conditions necessary for all members to participate fully in community life.

Looking Back at Welfare Policy Debates

Retrenchment-era welfare policy debates engaged and enacted historical
discourses of poverty. Moments in this history assembled as a resource
for invention available for selective appropriation by debate participants.
These moments signal to observers that welfare policy debate is always
situated in the interstices of collective perceptions of the low-wage labor
market, gender roles, and race. Sometimes, participants invoked these
domains explicitly. In every instance, however, they informed the policy
deliberations.

The deterrence principle regulating the poorhouse revealed in no uncertain terms the intimate relationship between public assistance and
low-wage labor. Poor Law reformers sought to create conditions of such
misery in poorhouses that nothing but extreme necessity would motivate
recipients' entry. Though compassion for some recipients replaced disdain in the Progressive Era, work remained a central concern of policy
debate. It was precisely the nonparticipation in the labor force of abandoned and widowed mothers that legitimated their receipt of monthly
grants in the eyes of many reformers. Bemoaning hooliganism and other
social ills that they attributed to motherly neglect, reformers viewed mothers' pensions as an investment in citizenship. They regarded motherhood
itself as work deserving of remuneration. Yet Progressive reformers could

not suppress entirely a fear of pauperization. Judge E. E. Porterfield explained that pensions operating in Kansas City purposely provided only partial support to mothers to prevent "impoverishment" of family and community.

The nonparticipation of mothers in the labor force remained crucial in legitimating pensions in the 1935 Social Security Act. FDR could denounce relief as "a narcotic, a subtle destroyer of the human spirit" and support Aid to Dependent Children without contradiction: the president and others considered ADC recipients as "non-employable" persons whose spirit did not thrive in paid labor. The burgeoning women's movement of the 1960s and the rising numbers of employed married mothers thereafter unsettled the official relationship between mothers and low-wage labor. Participants no longer could appeal to the work of motherhood as an irrefutable justification for the receipt of aid. The Family Support Act codified this changed relationship as it represented the mother as the signee of an employment contract. In his opening statement for Senate hearings regarding the FSA, Daniel Patrick Moynihan noted the portentousness for social policy of this changed relation: "A program that was designed to pay mothers to stay at home with their children cannot succeed when we now observe most mothers going out to work."[1]

Closely linked to the relation of low-wage labor and public assistance, socially sanctioned gender roles informed deliberations of welfare policy. Progressive and New Deal reformers emphasized the mother as caregiver and nurturer. Attendees at the 1909 White House Conference on the Care of Dependent Children resolved that home life was the supreme product of civilization, the great molding force of mind and character. Key participants in the mothers' pension movement, such as the National Congress of Mothers, celebrated the mystical power of mother-love as an ameliorative social force. Still, these qualities of motherhood stood as achievements and not inherited abilities—only women of "worthy character" deserved pensions in the eyes of reformers.

The image of the mother as worker gained momentum from the 1960s onward. Nixon's failed Family Assistance Plan represented the first attempt to imagine the mother as worker as a focus of federal welfare policy. By the time the retrenchment era commenced in full force in 1980, participants aided by the stigma of the non-needy trumped appeals to nurturing and caregiving with appeals to work. In Public Assistance Subcommittee hearings held in 1981, Representative Rousselot responded to the exhortations of Reverend McDonald to look in the tear-stained eyes of children by interrogating that "the 30 percent [of AFDC recipients who are adults] supposedly are able to work, so you don't mind us asking that they be encouraged to work?" As the image of the adult AFDC recipient shifted from contract signee to ward in 1993–94, belief in the appropriateness of work for mothers was strong enough to sustain insidious divisions of poor people that undermined the character of all recipients. For instance, President Clinton campaigned for a national system of health insurance by disclosing fundamental flaws in existing patterns of coverage for low-wage workers. He objected that "we have this incredible situation in our country where if someone on welfare leaves to take an entry-level job that doesn't have health insurance, as soon as coverage of the Family Support Act runs out, you have people making low wages paying taxes to pay for health care for people who stayed on welfare and didn't make the same decision they did."[2]

Race often shaped welfare policy debates silently. For much of the history of mothers' pensions, race disqualified black women at the outset as potentially worthy recipients of aid. The Children's Bureau revealed in a 1931 survey of mothers' pensions that of those recipients whose race was known, only 3 percent were black. Moreover, roughly half of the black families aided resided in counties in Ohio and Pennsylvania. In a comparison of the percentage of black families in the total population of counties reporting race with the percentage of black families aided in these counties, the bureau concluded that "provision for Negro families was limited in a number of states."[3] The shifting demographics, rising caseloads, and increasing costs of the 1950s and 1960s intimated the veiled but powerful influence of race. The "worthy" white widows who left ADC for Old Age and Survivors' Insurance did so at least in part because their white husbands had been able to obtain jobs covered by social insurance — jobs frequently unavailable to blacks because of racial discrimination. The exclusions of farm and domestic workers from coverage under the Social Security Act stemmed in part from a concern among employers to protect easy access to low-paid minority laborers in the South and Southwest.[4] As blacks began to receive AFDC in greater numbers in the 1960s, race became an explicit subject of welfare policy debate. Joseph McDowell Mitchell's 1961 denunciation in the "Battle of Newburgh" of a steady flow of outsiders from principally southern states who drained the city treasury adumbrated successive appeals. Reagan's stories of "welfare queens" living fabulously through fraud helped set the framework for the retrenchment-era debates. The diffusion of racial lenses for seeing recipients was manifest in the descriptions of sympathetic observers such as William Julius Wilson of welfare recipients as denizens of an urban underclass that included street criminals and other aberrant types.[5]

Amidst convergent perceptions of low-wage labor, gender roles, and race, a fundamental tension in representation between absence and presence, between standing for something and embodying that something, shaped the collective imagining of retrenchment-era debate participants. Welfare recipients suffered doubly from representation as they were largely excluded from the debates initially, then brought into the debates subsequently through disabling images. In these ways, welfare policy debate generally proceeded within a constricted spectrum of opinion. Experts affiliated with universities, private foundations, advocacy groups, and think tanks were overrepresented among debate participants and recipients were severely underrepresented. Of the 1,099 witnesses who testified in the committee hearings examined in this book, only 42 identified themselves as former or current AFDC recipients and/or affiliates of recipient organizations. This constriction of opinion should not be understood solely as a product of the composition of witness lists: such a view would advance the reductive claim that only recipients can offer distinctive or useful perspectives on welfare policy.

Experts representing recipients themselves felt a pressure to conform to prevailing beliefs and attitudes. In some respects, limited resources created this pressure. Advocates supporting social programs and services for low-income people typically operated with limited finances, personnel, and media connections in comparison to large trade organizations and other antagonists. Low-income advocacy groups frequently found themselves in a mode of reaction, defending important programs from multiple indictments. Yet this pressure arose as well from a desire among experts not to be excluded from debate. Such desire produced a kind of self-censorship. In a telephone interview with me, one advocate who testified before congressional committees throughout the retrenchment era admitted that participants supporting services and programs for the poor had to moderate the manner in which they confronted basic assumptions and arguments in policy deliberations. She admitted that "I think that, to a certain extent, people in our community who are trying to maintain any kind of relevance to debate or to have reporters call them or to continue to have their phone calls returned have, as I said, have to adjust their way of speaking. I don't think that we've changed our positions on things, but we're likely to describe our positions differently."[6] As retrenchment-era debates demonstrated, however, describing one's position differently may constitute changing one's position.

Recipients excluded from welfare policy debates reappeared in trans-figured form. In an insightful study, Oskar Negt and Alexander Kluge explain that participants in public debate often appropriate and re-present the lived experiences of excluded persons through a process that denudes these experiences of critical impulses. Excluded persons are subjected to and objectified in public debate: subjected because they are bound by the decisions of debate participants, objectified because their lived experiences become material for reconstruction.[7] As the images that served as the basis of my narrative of AFDC's repeal revealed, recipients in re-trenchment-era debates obtained an almost hyper-visibility. During the three key episodes of the retrenchment era, images of poor people linked up with arguments to further particular policy initiatives. Across these three episodes, images of the poor functioned as a cumulative imaginary field that constrained the deliberations of successive participants.

Imagining recipients as cheats, shirkers, and double-dippers in con-trast to a group of truly needy recipients justified Reagan and the budget-cutters' insistence on reducing federal funding for AFDC and other public assistance programs. Their cuts could be enacted without harming those who genuinely required assistance. Images of assorted non-needy recipients—so long as these figures could be removed from the caseload—did not call into question the basic purpose of the AFDC program, a tactic that offered the budget-cutters some defense against charges of callousness. The budget-cutters had no quarrel with the truly needy, only with those who were abusing AFDC. At the same time, images of cheats, shirkers, and double-dippers elicited suspicion and hostility among many debate participants. For these participants, the stigma of non-neediness overtook appeals from others to support innocent and vulnerable children, who emerged as opposing images of the typical AFDC recipient. The nonspecific image of the truly needy aided the budget-cutters' agenda. This image enabled Reagan and his supporters to refrain from committing themselves to safeguard a specific type or group of recipients, such as mothers with infants or toddlers. No specific characteristic emerged as a sure indicator of need. Moreover, the ambivalent position of the truly needy, who were caught between the American people and the bureaucrats and politicians supporting welfare programs, raised concerns about their neediness and introduced doubts about the AFDC program.

Imagining recipients as contract signees permitted debate participants to locate in a specific case the notions of mutual obligation that shaped a consensus around reorienting the AFDC program. Contract signees could be expected to fulfill the obligations to which they agreed by signing. Likewise, these signees could expect similar commitments from the other parties to the contract. The image of the contract signee was specific enough to give shape to the feelings among participants that spurred reform, yet general enough to forestall disagreement over policy initiatives, which lay just under the surface of the mid-1980s reform consensus. For debate participants, the teenage mother embodied the contract signee, and she appeared quite vividly as a black, urban, uneducated young person from a lineage of dependency. This more concrete image, however, also postponed particular disagreements. Participants did not have to agree on the reasons for her dependency to identify her as an appropriate subject for reform. Whatever or whomever may have been responsible for her dependent condition, the teenage mother had to be compelled to undertake actions leading to "self-sufficiency." In this respect, the image of the deadbeat dad played a crucial role. Anger that otherwise may have been directed at the teenage mother could be focused on this figure, whom participants denounced uniformly. The deadbeat dad could not make claims upon participants; quite the contrary, they demanded unequivocally that he support his children.

Imagining recipients as young wards signaled a paternalistic turn in welfare policy debates that anticipated changing policy goals. Although it did not compel repeal, this shift in images from contract signee to ward facilitated repeal by weakening the bargaining position of the AFDC recipient. Contract signees, even if they entered into an agreement from a position of little leverage, could make demands upon the other parties to fulfill the obligations specified in the contract. In contrast, young wards depended on the judgments of their guardians regarding appropriate courses of action. Moreover, imagining recipients as young wards constituted a co-optation of the arguments of participants defending AFDC, who appealed to childhood innocence. Rather than supporting the program, however, images of innocent youths in this usage bolstered the case against AFDC. If recipients were not responsible in the sense that they were not capable of sound judgment, then the program itself appeared as the problem and repeal as the solution. In this respect, even the deadbeat dad escaped some censure as some mid-1990s reformers traced his failures partly to the system. In seeking repeal, reformers exhibited the confidence of parents convinced that they knew what was best for their children. Yet their confidence was not boundless, and its limits appeared in the image of the immigrant, which served as a site for displaced anxiety. Reformers embraced the challenges posed by globalization in seeking to scale back the federal bureaucracy, but their suspicion of the immigrant signaled at the same time a perceived threat to modern territorial sovereignty and national citizenship.

Images exerted influence in successive policy episodes of the retrench-ment era as a cumulative imaginary field that constrained choices of sub-sequent participants. As historical relationships between low-wage labor, gender roles, and race suggest, welfare policy debates in any particular episode in any era do not begin with a tabula rasa. Still, the socioeco-nomic context informing policy debates in 1980 and 1981, a time in which contrasting images of AFDC recipients circulated prominently, adum-brated varied paths of possible reform: decrease or increase of monthly grant amounts, greater uniformity in grant amounts across geographic regions, or renewed effort toward a mandatory work/minimum income program. Injecting a distinction between the truly needy and non-needy into the policy debate compelled an accounting in future policy propos-als. Participants had to address the question of whether the non-needy had been vanquished from the welfare rolls. Most reformers answered that the non-needy indeed had been vanquished, but that society had not asked enough of needy recipients. Once reformers demanded behavioral changes from long-term recipients, participants could not return to a non-specific image of the truly needy to advance welfare policy without first accounting for mandated behavioral changes. As frustration with wel-fare lingered, participants had to consider the extent to which recipients changed their ways. The emergence of the signee further delineated a field of choices for participants. Repeal could proceed only after the ward dis-placed this image.

The importance of this cumulative quality to imagining is not that any image that emerges in one episode restricts participants in a subsequent episode to a predetermined and unalterable policy trajectory. Rather, imag-ining welfare recipients as people of a certain type, if one can advance this representation prominently and avoid its relegation to the margins of pol-icy debate, compels an accounting from future participants. If participants imagine poor people through a particular portrayal, then others wishing to develop future policies must heed the images that inform existing poli-cies. In important respects, Reagan and his supporters' representation of

AFDC recipients as cheats, shirkers, and double-dippers responded to the expansionist era of the 1960s and early 1970s: providing cash assistance to needy people did not constitute a misguided policy goal as long as the recipients of this cash assistance exhibited genuine need.

An additional implication of the cumulative quality of imagining is that images circulating across policy episodes do not constrain participants equally. Rather, the constraining force of images imparts advantages to some participants and disadvantages to others. Whether disparaging, truncated, or paternalistic, retrenchment-era images of the poor presented their subjects mostly in a negative light. Participants defending the basic framework of existing public assistance programs confronted these negative images as symbolic obstacles that they, but not their opponents, had to negotiate. Throughout the retrenchment era, presumption went against these advocates in favor of those participants calling for reform. In addition, the stigma of non-needy adult recipients impaired the credibility of poor people and their advocates, casting doubt on the veracity and sincerity of their claims.

The disabling images of poor people circulating in welfare policy debates contribute to the political powerlessness of recipients inside and outside of the institutional forums of public policy debate. Recipients themselves often believe that these images accurately describe the attitudes and behaviors of the poor — that is, *other* poor people. For this reason, recipients are reluctant to ally with other recipients from whom they wish to distinguish themselves. Former AFDC recipient Nancy Peterson appeared before the Human Resources Subcommittee in 1996 not to advocate programmatic reform consisting of increased benefits and support services, but rather strict time limits and unequivocal work requirements. Speaking of reforms adopted in her home state, Peterson asserted that "the changes that Michigan has made have been positive changes. We do not need to be as soft as it has been. I am motivated. But other people are not. There needs to be a little bit of a push to motivate people to work, to get a feel of what that is like, to make them responsible."[8]

This is the sort of statement that one regular committee witness, himself a former public assistance recipient, has heard repeated again and again in his advocacy and organizing work with recipients. In a telephone interview he told me a story of his experience with the formation of a welfare advisory committee in a county of the state in which he works. County officials first went through the case list and selected one name from every 100 recipients. This advocate then participated in a meeting in which he and others went through the names and narrowed the list to an ethnically diverse group of twenty. County officials subsequently "brought them in this room and then went around and asked them why they wanted to be on the committee. They all said: 'so we can get those welfare recipients to work. So they can get off their butts.'" This incident revealed dissociation on two levels. First, it indicated that these recipients shared society's frustration with people perceived as flouting social codes of initiative and self-reliance. Second, and perhaps more subtly, this incident disclosed their aspirations. These recipients wanted to participate meaningfully in work and community; they did not require external motivations. On both levels, dissociation inhibited political organization. This interviewee cited difficulties in organizing AFDC recipients for program improvements and benefit increases. He explained that "the biggest problem with AFDC recipients is that they don't have any commitment to the program because they don't view themselves as being a lifetime recipient, contrary to popular belief. If they really believed that for the rest of their lives they are going to be on AFDC, they would be more interested." He explained that AFDC recipients viewed public assistance as a temporary support and believed that soon they would secure a job.

The failures of retrenchment-era welfare policy debates are not insuperable. The perspective-taking potential of deliberation holds out the promise that participants may come to understand and respect others of different backgrounds. To participate in deliberation is to value the perspectives of one's interlocutors. Participation in itself establishes alternative perspectives as important enough to be engaged rather than overcome by physical strength or numerical advantage. Deliberation admits a vulnerability among interlocutors, as the possibility arises that one's views may be transformed through discourse with others. Although it can be practiced more fully and inclusively, deliberation still contributes to the policy-making process. In his study of the importance of deliberation to policy-making bodies in American national government, Joseph Bessette holds that the most detailed and extensive deliberation in the Congress occurs in committees and subcommittees, and hearings play an important role in committee deliberations. Hearings also may "shape the subsequent debate in Congress by surfacing the major arguments for and against the pending measure and by clarifying the strengths and weaknesses of each position."[9]

Deliberation of welfare policy may be enhanced by building on the power of publicity of committee hearings. Hearings, as the oft-repeated phrase suggests, "puts people on record." The recording of participants' statements may prompt reflection about one's views; it may engender a search for good reasons to support one's position. In any case, hearings compel a public announcement, which attaches a position to a person and heightens accountability. Committee hearings present a record of disagreement. Either through actual attendance or by reading transcripts, observers can learn that alternative perspectives exist. Hearings make participants themselves aware of these alternative perspectives and place participants in a position of responsibility for their views amidst dissent. In telephone interviews with me, some participants disclosed a feeling that retrenchment-era welfare reform hearings—especially those concerning the PRWORA—had been perfunctory. I asked these advocates why, in situations in which legislators appeared unwilling to hear alternative viewpoints, they testified. They replied that testimony fostered accountability. One respondent held that testifying on these occasions was "a way to look the members in the eye and say 'we think you're going down the wrong road here.'" Dissent publicly stated becomes something of which legislators must take note: legislators cannot plead ignorance later. Testimony may spur further interaction and deliberation with members of Congress, media figures, and citizens generally. Testimony enters the flow of welfare policy discourse and may be taken up subsequently as a topic of discussion.

Looking Forward to Future Welfare Policy Debates

How, then, may future participants build upon this power of publicity and the perspective-taking potential of deliberation to debate welfare policy more inclusively and fully in seeking to ameliorate the lives of poor people? An answer to this question requires amplification of two interconnected areas: first, a brief discussion of appropriate measures for determining the success of policy initiatives and a brief description of initiatives that might achieve this success; second, explication of the crucial role of imagining in this process. My discussion of these two areas in this concluding section is not meant to fix future debates along a predetermined trajectory or present a programmatic agenda for reform. Rather, I conclude this book in this fashion, in the spirit evoked by Michael Harrington in 1962, to spur further debate. In the end, collective imagining is formed and reformed through social dialogue.

As the 1990s reform debates proceeded and in the years after the passage of the 1996 Personal Responsibility and Work Opportunity Reconciliation Act, AFDC/TANF caseloads decreased sharply across the nation. According to the Administration for Children and Families (ACF) of the Department of Health and Human Services, the total number of recipients decreased by 48 percent between 1993 and 1999, from an all-time high of 14.27 million recipients in 1994 to 7.33 million recipients in 1999. This drop reduced caseloads to their lowest figure since 1969. In some states, caseload reductions were even greater. The total number of recipients in Wisconsin and Wyoming, the states with the largest drops, declined an astonishing 88 and 90 percent, respectively. The smallest reductions occurred in New Mexico and Rhode Island, which still reported impressive declines of 15 and 12 percent, respectively.[10] These decreases have been a source of satisfaction for supporters of the PRWORA, even though the reductions began in 1994—two years before its passage and, perhaps not coincidentally, as the economy emerged from an early-1990s recession.[11]

The significance one should attach to these statistics is unclear, for the socioeconomic standing of former recipients has not improved appreciably. In an analysis of tracking data from seven states, the U.S. General Accounting Office reported that between 61 and 71 percent of former recipients were employed at the time of a follow-up contact, which occurred once in most cases from two to eighteen months after termination of welfare receipt.[12] Employed former recipients received an average hourly wage of $6.75. They worked an average of 35 hours weekly, and their average quarterly earnings totaled $2,910.[13] Recipients held these jobs within an economy that sustained extremely low levels of unemployment. Moreover, reports from some cities and states identified potentially alarming outcomes. Although New York City reduced its welfare caseload by 350,000 between 1994 and 1997, a state survey found that of the people who left the rolls in the city from July 1996 through March 1997, only 29 percent found full-time or part-time employment in the first several months after they terminated receipt of public assistance. In Mississippi only 35 percent of former recipients contacted through a state-sponsored survey indicated that they had obtained employment. Only 23 percent said that they were employed full-time. Many employed former recipients found low-wage jobs in the fourteen riverboat casinos along the state's western border. A review of unemployment insurance records revealed that less than 25 percent of former recipients' monthly earnings totaled more than $500 in a fifteen-month period after they left the rolls. Meanwhile, the state of Mississippi amassed more than $100 million in federal funds meant for the needy and returned unspent child-care funds to the federal government.[14]

These findings suggest that if participants intend for welfare reform to improve the lives of recipients, then determining success by the number of recipients removed from caseloads is an inappropriate measure. A better indicator may be the number of recipients who are helped to secure living wage jobs that provide financial stability and overall well being to earners and their families. This goal is complicated by the limited employment prospects of recipients and the uncertain and contested employment capacities of the low-wage labor market. Acknowledging the difficult case of New York City, Robert Lerman, Pamela Loprest, and Caroline Ratcliffe nevertheless maintain in an Urban Institute analysis that the national low-wage labor market can absorb former welfare recipients. They attribute this predicted outcome to the ability of a dynamic labor market to generate new jobs. This view has been opposed by Peter Edelman, former assistant secretary for planning and evaluation in the Department of Health and Human Services, who resigned his post because he objected to the PRWORA. Edelman counters that a "jobs gap" stands as an obstacle to any reform effort. Articulating a perspective that admits both scenarios, Nobel prize-winning economist Robert Solow speculates that an increase in the aggregate number of low-wage jobs may occur through an indirect form of job displacement. In the 1996–97 Tanner Lectures on Human Values at Princeton University, Solow explains that an influx of job applicants in the private labor market may drive down the wages of unskilled workers enough so that employers hire former recipients to replace slightly more qualified workers who perform their tasks more efficiently but have to be paid more.[15]

Available jobs are crucial for the success of present and future reforms, since studies of successful "welfare-to-work" programs indicate that they succeed when explicitly identifiable jobs are open to recipients who complete training activities. Felice Perlmutter reaches this conclusion in a study of one such program carried out by Pennsylvania Blue Shield in the late 1980s and early 1990s. The company needed to fill 500 permanent positions in medical-claims processing. Spurred by low unemployment in the Harrisburg area (the location of Pennsylvania Blue Shield's corporate offices) and bold, committed corporate leadership, Pennsylvania Blue Shield eventually trained 242 recipients for skilled technical jobs and hired 208 of these recipients as regular employees. Perlmutter observes that "the operation was driven by the fact that jobs were reserved for successful graduates of the training program. This is in sharp contrast to most job-training projects for welfare clients, which provide training but leave the quest for a job in the hands of the applicant."[16]

Reforms seeking to improve recipients' lives ought to provide jobs for people unable to secure employment in the private labor market, raise the incomes of low-wage workers, and offer accompanying benefits such as healthcare. These prescriptions do not envision a previously unseen path. Indeed, some observers have developed cogent reform agendas. In his compelling book, *When Work Disappears,* William Julius Wilson contends that any attempt to relieve the widespread joblessness of poor communities must include a federally administered program of WPA-style public jobs for people unable to find paid employment in the private sector.[17] He argues that these jobs should be available to all who desire them to avoid the stigma associated with public-service jobs in the past. Wilson also advocates further expansion of the Earned Income Tax Credit (EITC). Enacted in 1975 and expanded in 1986, 1990, and 1993, the EITC has become a significant income-transfer program. The Council of Economic Advisors notes that in 1997, the EITC lifted 4.3 million people — including 2.2 million children — out of poverty.[18] In addition to expansion of the EITC, Wilson regards universal healthcare as crucial for improving the condition of poor families, especially families headed by single mothers. On this score, the power of familial illness to undermine the employment situations of single mothers is well documented.[19] Necessary corollary programs include childcare services and subsidies, transportation services, and city-suburban cooperative programs. These programs cannot be developed in isolation; some of the failures of past reform efforts can be attributed to their unnecessary delimitation to "welfare" programs. Future reforms must be part of a broadly conceived policy agenda of education, economic, and health initiatives.

Whatever the specific forms of these initiatives, they must be informed by shifts in processes of collective imagining. In the preceding chapters, I mapped the interrelationship of images and policy arguments. Images circulate prominently in welfare policy debates to justify and evidence claims. Images help explain complex, seemingly inscrutable phenomena. Images signal portentous social and cultural trends. Images elicit sympathy, fear, compassion, and hostility. Images prompt discussion of the purposes, possibilities, and limitations of social welfare programs.

Images spur participants to action. Considering the trajectory of retrenchment-era welfare policy debates, it appears as no surprise that
researchers interviewing members of Congress to gauge their support for
various social welfare programs have concluded that "Congress members
who explain their support for public assistance with a positive portrayal
of recipient deservingness are considerably more supportive … than
those presenting negative views of deservingness."[20] Against the disabling
images of poor people that circulated throughout the retrenchment era,
enabling and empowering images must accompany—perhaps anticipate
—potentially efficacious policy initiatives.

Confronting and transforming retrenchment-era images of the poor
must go beyond debunking existing disabling representations. Debunking is an important activity, for images circulating in welfare policy debates represent recipients in ways that are partial, distorting, and often
plainly untrue.[21] For example, the image of the recipient as lazy discounts
the paid employment histories of many recipients who, because of various familial disruptions and the limits of the low-wage labor market, find
themselves cycling on and off public assistance rolls. The image of the
lustful teen engaging in careless sexual activity because she knows that the
public will support her baby ignores contrary evidence of the steady decline in value of inflation-adjusted welfare grants as out-of-wedlock birth
rates have risen. When images address aspects of recipients' lives, they often present these aspects as completely determinative of one's character;
these aspects stand for the whole person. Debunking these images and
others is the first step in engendering shifts in processes of collective
imagining. A further step entails imagining affirming representations of
recipients and other poor people. Affirmative images must be crafted and
circulated to create reasons for addressing the concerns of the poor. In establishing a population that would be served by new initiatives, affirmative images are necessary to motivate policymakers to enact potentially
efficacious reforms.

When crafting affirmative images of recipients, debate participants
should not abstain from including behavioral components. For a period
of time between the 1960s and early 1980s, sympathetic observers had
been reluctant to address recipient behavior when debating welfare policy. One could trace this hesitancy in large measure to negative reactions
among activists to reports issued during poverty's rediscovery—most notably Daniel Patrick Moynihan's 1965 report *The Negro Family: The Case
for National Action*—that considered disconcerting patterns of family

formation in African-American communities. Critics charged that a focus on family formation valued other groups through the particular framework of white, middle-class norms. The subsequent reluctance to discuss recipient behavior led to the ironic consequence of analysts disregarding the influences environmental forces exerted on individual behavior.[22] By avoiding discussion of behavior altogether, analysts left unchallenged disparaging assumptions that attributed socially disruptive behavior to the putatively nefarious motives of poor people. This strategy forestalled alternative explanations that may have drawn attention to the environment by viewing socially disruptive behavior as a response to limited opportunities such as nonexistent job prospects in some communities.[23] But addressing recipient behavior requires participants to recognize the complexity of the lives of the poor, including the difficult choices recipients confront—choices that middle- and upper-class individuals may not face. Participants ought to craft and circulate images that disclose, for example, the difficult dilemmas encountered by the single mother who "chooses" not to work because, although she desires paid employment, she worries that low-wage labor cannot secure the health of her child.

So long as it continues to guide welfare policy, the market model that oriented retrenchment-era debates complicates the process of crafting and circulating enabling images of the poor. Throughout the retrenchment era, the market stood as exemplar. Reagan extolled the virtues of the market as he condemned the vices of government. A market orientation shaped the employment contract that functioned crucially in the mid-1980s reform consensus; and 1990s reformers trusted a market ideal as they turned over federal welfare programs to the "competitive" fifty states. But the market is a misguided metaphor for political institutions and interpersonal relations. Markets seek profitability, but political institutions perform functions that by their very nature are not profitable. Markets seek short-term gain and flexibility, but political institutions confront problems that require a long-term perspective and commitment. Markets sustain a truncated view of interpersonal relations. This view manifests itself in the celebration of privatization that characterizes the current political climate. Privatization entails transferring functions that have been regarded as properly the responsibility of governments to private agents and market forces.[24] But this transference turns citizens into consumers, which threatens the prospect and potential of deliberation. Consumers need not deliberate. They may engage in introspective examination of their desires, but consumers do not initiate dialogue with others to consider collectively what ought to be social goods. Producers do not initiate deliberation. They may conduct market research as part of a development strategy, but producers assess the desirability and undesirability of goods through the aggregated purchasing decisions of independently acting consumers. No goods are imagined collectively in the processes of deliberation. A consumer orientation transfigures public interest into consumer desire and social goods into available products. In these ways, a market model undermines the legitimacy of public intervention into pressing social problems and reduces interpersonal relations to purchasing decisions.

Debate participants might begin to displace this market model by imagining "work" anew. Throughout this book, when presenting my analysis, I have not distinguished public assistance receipt from "work" but rather from "paid employment," "paid work," "low-wage labor," and other such specifications. My reference to these more specific terms rather than the general term "work" has been meant to indicate what reformers demanded of recipients when they insisted that recipients earn their way. Reformers demanded tacitly not that recipients work but that they work in a remunerative job. Indeed, not all work is recognized socially as "work." "Work" is understood in our collective imagination only as those activities valued by market forces. As a consequence, we devalue in our collective imagination many functions important to nourishing and sustaining community such as serving on citizens' advisory boards, aiding elderly parents, participating in neighborhood watch programs, and caring for children.[25] Moreover, this narrow vision of work produces perverse policy positions that, as Christine Pratt-Marston explained to the House Public Assistance Subcommittee in 1981, denounce recipients when they care for their own children and yet praise these same recipients when they care for another recipient's child as employees of a "welfare-to-work" daycare program. I am not arguing that we resurrect a women's sphere of domesticity. Quite the contrary, the nation as a whole is strengthened when women pursue opportunities and choices that historically have been restricted to men. Rather, my position is that we need to broaden our view of work to include activities devalued by market forces. We might imagine work as all those activities that contribute to the sustainment of a community whether or not women and men are paid for these activities. A specific policy implication of this redefinition may be that we should support present and former recipients — not penalize them by creating a category of substandard jobs — as they work in this broader sense.

My proposals regarding "work" suggest that a focus on community might present an affirmative alternative to the market model that oriented retrenchment-era debates. Community signifies mutual regard and concern which resist translation into calculations of profit and loss. In their individual and collective visions, a community's members look out for one another. Especially important for welfare policy is the idea of commonality signified by community, for debates in the retrenchment era and earlier eras often treated poor people as figures who did not share the values, beliefs, drives, and dreams of the middle and upper classes. My appeal to community is not meant to erase differences among its members — certainly, the varying opportunities sometimes available to people simply because of their race, sex, or class ought to concern participants — but to affirm membership in a larger collective. A focus on community may motivate debate participants to seek out common experiences and interests among all members of the American polity. Believing that a healthy public life could develop only when people recognized their mutual affection by the consequences of human actions, John Dewey held that "democracy ... is the idea of community life itself."[26]

In important respects, the 1996 repeal of AFDC signaled a retreat from community, from a national commitment to one another's well being. However much this commitment may have been diluted and even vitiated in practice, AFDC's prescription of an entitlement to assistance for all who qualified inscribed in law a collective understanding of the interdependent condition of an American political community. Repeal symbolized a disavowal of interdependence. Community now must find its place in the spaces forged by relatively autonomous global market forces. This search must proceed as the increasing economic isolation of poor Americans further jeopardizes a sense of national community. When Harrington called on his readers to rediscover the inhabitants of an other America, between one-fifth and one-quarter of all Americans lived in poverty. Though the poverty rate, especially among the elderly, has declined since 1962, income inequality has reached its highest point since 1945. Economist Richard Freeman observes that the "facts are not in dispute." From the left of the ideological spectrum to the right, "virtually all analysts agree that something has gone seriously awry with our income distribution."[27] Increasing income inequality portends, in the view of some observers, a return to invisibility for poor Americans. The disappearance of poor people from public view is seen by James Fallows as a potential consequence of "the unusual social and imaginative separation between prosperous America and those still left out."[28]

Adopting a community framework, debate participants might imagine welfare reform as an effort to secure the minimum conditions necessary for all members to participate in sustaining an inclusive political community. Debate could elucidate the specific content of these minimum conditions, and participants could design and evaluate policy initiatives with regard to their success in establishing a threshold of individual and familial well being that fosters participation in community life. One could argue, for example, that people may not be able to participate fully in community life if they are burdened by the worry that a sudden illness might precipitate financial as well as physiological traumas. One could argue that people cannot participate fully in community life if the limitations of the low-wage labor market produce adverse consequences so that a person employed full-time still cannot provide financial stability for oneself and one's family.

Some have sought to advance these arguments by claiming for welfare policy the aura of citizenship. Holding that "[n]o decent welfare policy can emerge without a vision of honorable entitlement for those who require help," Nancy Fraser and Linda Gordon propose that reformers circulate an idea of "social citizenship" that draws upon themes of rights, solidarity, and civic participation.[29] Their proposal stems from the observation that "citizen" is a uniformly honorific term in national political discourse. But as Fraser and Gordon admit, citizenship discourse raises some potential problems, for restrictive conditions of attainment and xenophobic treatment of non-citizens may perpetuate participatory exclusions. For example, Lawrence Mead argues that poor people must first become "better citizens"—principally through employment in the paid labor force—before they can stake a greater claim to public resources.[30] Xenophobic attitudes toward non-citizens surfaced in the anxiety displayed by some 1990s reformers toward the image of the immigrant.[31] Yet the promise of associating social welfare provision with ideals of citizenship lies in focusing debate participants' attention on establishing the minimum conditions necessary for participation in community life. Refocusing welfare policy debates in this manner envisions an alternative to the market model that held sway during retrenchment-era debates. Against the market model's truncated view of human relationships, a focus on community recognizes the interconnectedness of all members of the American polity.

From the rediscovery of poverty in the early 1960s to the retrenchment of federal programs for poor families in the 1980s and 1990s, seeing the poor engaged our collective imagination. To imagine anew our connections and commitments to one another, we must exercise our collective intellect and will. In *The Other America,* Michael Harrington recounts how he came to understand the necessity of exerting these two faculties. Through his research, Harrington had compiled statistics indicating that fifty million people lived in an other America: "Yet, I realized that I did not believe my own figures. The poor existed in the government reports; they were percentages and numbers in long, close columns, but they were not part of my experience. I could prove that the other America existed, but I had never been there."[32] A similar realization, which also entails collective introspection, must take hold in welfare policy debate. Disabling images of the poor may arise from misunderstanding, ignorance, and even prejudice. Studies of policy debate cannot prohibit these sources at the outset of deliberation. Debating welfare policy to ameliorate recipients' lives requires participants to imagine poor people not as delinquents, contract workers, or wards, but as similarly situated agents who may participate in an inclusive political community.

Notes

CHAPTER ONE

1. Michael Harrington, *The Other America: Poverty in the United States* (1962; reprint, with an introduction by Irving Howe, New York: Collier Books, 1994), 4.

2. Ibid., 2.

3. Elaine Scarry, "The Difficulty of Imagining Other People," in *For Love of Country: Debating the Limits of Patriotism,* ed. Martha C. Nussbaum (Boston: Beacon Press, 1996), 98.

4. Benedict Anderson, *Imagined Communities: Reflections on the Origin and Spread of Nationalism,* rev. ed. (London: Verso, 1991), 6.

5. Harrington, *Other America,* 172, 174.

6. Committee on Economic Security, *Report to the President of the Committee on Economic Security* (Washington, D.C.: Government Printing Office, 1935), 6.

7. Jane M. Hoey and Zilpha C. Franklin, "Aid to Dependent Children," *Social Work Yearbook* 5 (1939): 31, 32.

8. Robert C. Lieberman, *Shifting the Color Line: Race and the American Welfare State* (Cambridge: Harvard University Press, 1998), 136–40.

9. James T. Patterson, *America's Struggle Against Poverty 1900–1994* (Cambridge: Harvard University Press, 1994), 179.

10. For various meanings of the words "imagine," "imagining," and "imagination," including historical usages of each term, consult the second edition of the *Oxford English Dictionary.*

11. Arjun Appadurai, *Modernity at Large: Cultural Dimensions of Globalization* (Minneapolis: University of Minnesota Press, 1996), 53. Appadurai protests that he does not mean to "imply that the world is now a happier place." Rather, he subscribes to the position that "even the meanest and most hopeless of lives, the most brutal and dehumanizing of circumstances, the harshest of lived inequalities are now open to the play of the imagination" (54).

12. Nancy Fraser, "Women, Welfare, and the Politics of Need Interpretation," in *Unruly Practices: Power, Discourse, and Gender in Contemporary Social Theory* (Minneapolis: University of Minnesota Press, 1993), 149–51; Nancy Fraser and Linda Gordon, "A Genealogy of *Dependency:* Tracing a Keyword of the U.S. Welfare State," *Signs: Journal of Women in Culture and Society* 19 (1994): 309–36; Janice Peterson, "'Ending Welfare as We Know It': The Symbolic Importance of Welfare Policy in America," *Journal of Economic Issues* 2 (1997): 428–29.

13. See, e.g., Linda Gordon, *Pitied but Not Entitled: Single Mothers and the History of Welfare* (Cambridge: Harvard University Press, 1994), 5.

14. See, e.g., Kenneth J. Gergen, *An Invitation to Social Construction* (Thousand Oaks, Calif.: Sage, 1999).

15. Charles Taylor, *Modernity and the Rise of the Public Sphere,* The Tanner Lectures on Human Values, vol. 14 (Salt Lake City: University of Utah Press, 1993), 218–19.

16. Cornelius Castoriadis, *The Imaginary Institution of Society,* trans. Kathleen Blamey (Cambridge: MIT Press, 1987), 353–69.

17. Kathryn M. Olson and G. Thomas Goodnight, "Entanglements of Consumption, Cruelty, Privacy, and Fashion: The Social Controversy over Fur," *Quarterly Journal of Speech* 80 (1994): 249–52.

18. G. Thomas Goodnight, "Controversy," in *Argument in Controversy: Proceedings of the Seventh SCA/AFA Conference on Argumentation,* ed. Donn Parson (Annandale, Va.: Speech Communication Association, 1991), 1–13.

19. See, e.g., Richard Dyer, *The Matter of Images: Essays on Representations* (New York: Routledge, 1993), 1–5; Linda Hutcheon, "The Politics of Representation," *Signature: A Journal of Theory and Canadian Literature* 1 (1989): 23–44.

20. Frank Lentricchia, *Criticism and Social Change* (Chicago: University of Chicago Press, 1983), 153.

21. Raymond Williams, *Keywords: A Vocabulary of Culture and Society,* rev. ed. (New York: Oxford University Press, 1983), 267. This tension in representation between absence and presence implicates welfare policy debates in what Linda Alcoff has called "the problem of speaking for others." According to Alcoff, recognition of this problem arises from two sources. First, a growing critical awareness admits that varying experiences of social privilege accompanying a person's social location have an impact on the meaning and truth attributed by others to one's claims. Speakers cannot transcend the social contexts in which they speak to offer completely disinterested pronouncements. Second, critics and theorists have noted that certain privileged locations, besides reflecting their own biases and interests, are "discursively dangerous." That is, in some instances, when privileged persons speak on behalf of less privileged persons, even when they speak with the best of intentions, unequal relations of power and unjust social arrangements actually may be reinforced. Linda Alcoff, "The Problem of Speaking for Others," *Cultural Critique* 20 (1991): 6–7.

22. On the aesthetic and political "codes" of representation, see Jacques Derrida, "Sending: On Representation," *Social Research* 49 (1982): 298–99. See also Carol Corbin, ed., *Rhetoric in Postmodern America: Conversations with Michael Calvin McGee* (New York: Guilford Press, 1998), 53, 175–76.

23. Jürgen Habermas, *Between Facts and Norms: Contributions to a Discourse Theory of Law and Democracy,* trans. William Rehg (Cambridge: MIT Press, 1996), 361.

24. Seyla Benhabib, "Toward a Deliberative Model of Democratic Legitimacy," in *Democracy and Difference: Contesting the Boundaries of the Political,* ed. Seyla Benhabib (Princeton, N.J.: Princeton University Press, 1996), 67–94; Nancy

Fraser, "Rethinking the Public Sphere: A Contribution to the Critique of Actually Existing Democracy," in *Habermas and the Public Sphere*, ed. Craig Calhoun (Cambridge: MIT Press, 1992), 109–42; Nancy Fraser, "What's Critical about Critical Theory? The Case of Habermas and Gender," in *Unruly Practices*, 113–43; Jane Mansbridge, "Using Power/Fighting Power: The Polity," in *Democracy and Difference: Contesting the Boundaries of the Political*, ed. Seyla Benhabib (Princeton, N.J.: Princeton University Press, 1996), 46–66.

25. In a related manner, proponents of deliberative democracy discern in deliberation a universal moral respect and an egalitarian reciprocity that affirm the integrity of others. See, e.g., Seyla Benhabib, *Situating the Self: Gender, Community, and Postmodernism in Contemporary Ethics* (New York: Routledge, 1992), 29; Joshua Cohen, "Deliberation and Democratic Legitimacy," in *Deliberative Democracy: Essays on Reason and Politics*, ed. James Bohman and William Rehg (Cambridge: MIT Press, 1997), 77–78; Amy Gutman and Dennis Thompson, *Democracy and Disagreement: Why Moral Conflict Cannot Be Avoided in Politics, and What Should Be Done about It* (Cambridge: Harvard University Press, 1996), 52–94.

26. Benhabib, "Toward a Deliberative Model," 71–72.

27. Though it can be practiced more fully and inclusively, deliberation still contributes significantly to the policy-making process. Responding to a predilection among sociologists and political scientists to adopt non-deliberative analytic frameworks, Joseph Bessette counters that bargaining is limited as an explanation of public policy-making. Reviewing twenty-nine case studies of the formation and passage of domestic legislation conducted between 1945 and 1970 during the ascendancy of bargaining interpretations, he finds that only four attribute any particular significance to bargaining. In these cases, bargaining appears to account for only a small fraction of legislators' votes in committee or on the floor. Moreover, behavior attributed to bargaining may be better explained through deliberation. Bessette observes that "[t]he very existence of policy preferences — of ideas and beliefs about what government should or should not do — inclines legislators to be receptive to information and arguments." Joseph M. Bessette, *The Mild Voice of Reason: Deliberative Democracy & American National Government* (Chicago: University of Chicago Press, 1994), 99.

    A resurgence of deliberative explanations appears to be developing as notions of deliberative democracy gain adherents among political theorists, philosophers, and social scientists, however. See, for example, James Bohman, *Public Deliberation: Pluralism, Complexity, and Democracy* (Cambridge: MIT Press, 1996); Bohman and Rehg, eds., *Deliberative Democracy;* Habermas, *Between Facts and Norms*.

28. Robert A. Levine, *The Poor Ye Need Not Have with You: Lessons from the War on Poverty* (Cambridge: MIT Press, 1970), 46; James L. Sundquist, "Origins of the War on Poverty," in *On Fighting Poverty: Perspectives from Experience*, ed. James L. Sundquist (New York: Basic Books, 1969), 9.

29. John F. Kennedy, *Public Papers of the Presidents of the United States: John F. Kennedy, 1962* (Washington, D.C.: Government Printing Office, 1963), 98.

30. Ibid., 100, 101.

31. Ibid., 103.

32. House Committee on Ways and Means, *Public Welfare Amendments of 1962: Hearings on H.R. 10032*, 87th Cong., 2d sess., 1962, 165.

33. Ibid., 166.

34. Ibid., 167.

35. Michael Harrington, for example, depicted not only the plight of rural transplants but the faces of poverty in rural areas themselves. See Harrington, *Other America*, 39–60.

36. House Committee, *Public Welfare Amendments*, 350.

37. John F. Kennedy, *Public Papers of the Presidents of the United States: John F. Kennedy, 1963* (Washington, D.C.: Government Printing Office, 1964), 791–92. The influence of Kennedy's encounter with Appalachian poverty during the 1960 presidential campaign in shaping his overall perceptions of poverty has been noted by Daniel Patrick Moynihan among others. Daniel Patrick Moynihan, *Maximum Feasible Misunderstanding: Community Action in the War on Poverty* (New York: Free Press, 1969), 24–25.

38. Lyndon B. Johnson, *Public Papers of the Presidents of the United States: Lyndon B. Johnson, 1963–64*, bk. 1 (Washington, D.C.: Government Printing Office, 1965), 114.

39. Ibid., 376, 377.

40. Ibid., 757.

41. Ibid., 757, 758.

42. Throughout this book, I use the terms "participants" and "debate participants" interchangeably to refer to the people — legislators and others — who appeared in institutional forums to debate retrenchment-era welfare policy.

CHAPTER TWO

1. Quoted in Gertrude Himmelfarb, *The Idea of Poverty: England in the Early Industrial Age* (New York: Vintage Books, 1985), 151. Murray and Tocqueville employ a principal argument advanced by conservative social theorists in reaction to progressive social reforms: the perversity thesis. Albert Hirschman defines the perversity thesis as the view that "any purposive action to improve some feature of the political, social, or economic order only serves to exacerbate the condition one wishes to remedy." Albert O. Hirschman, *The Rhetoric of Reaction: Perversity, Futility, Jeopardy* (Cambridge: Harvard University Press, 1991), 7.

2. *Congressional Record*, 97th Cong., 1st sess., 1981, 127, pt. 11:14555.

3. William Graham Sumner, "The Forgotten Man," in *American Rhetorical Discourse*, ed. Ronald F. Reid, 2d ed. (Prospect Heights, Ill.: Waveland Press, 1995), 614.

4. Frances Fox Piven and Richard A. Cloward, *Regulating the Poor: The Functions of Public Welfare*, updated ed. (New York: Vintage Books, 1993), 12, 17–18.

5. William C. Carroll, *Fat King, Lean Beggar: Representations of Poverty in the Age of Shakespeare* (Ithaca, N.Y.: Cornell University Press, 1996), 4, 24–27.

6. Ibid., 39.

7. Michael B. Katz, *In the Shadow of the Poorhouse: A Social History of Welfare in America* (New York: Basic Books, 1986), 33; Piven and Cloward, *Regulating the Poor*, 35–37.

8. Katz, *Shadow of the Poorhouse*, 13–14.

9. Joel F. Handler, *The Poverty of Welfare Reform* (New Haven, Conn.: Yale University Press, 1995), 12; Katz, *Shadow of the Poorhouse*, 14.

10. Katz, *Shadow of the Poorhouse*, 12.

11. Quoted in Piven and Cloward, *Regulating the Poor*, 33–34; see also Himmelfarb, *Idea of Poverty*, 163–65.

12. John C. Cawelti, *Apostles of the Self-Made Man* (Chicago: University of Chicago Press, 1965); Gary Scharnhorst, "Dickens and Horatio Alger, Jr.," *Dickens Quarterly* 2 (1985): 50.

13. Yves Lemeunier, "Vision of Poverty and the Poor in Alger's Novels," in *All Men Are Created Equal: Ideologies, Reves et Realites,* ed. Groupe de Recherche et d'Etudes Nord Américaines (Aix-en-Provence, Fr.: Université de Provence, 1982), 121.

14. Cawelti, *Apostles,* 122.

15. Olivier Zunz, *Making America Corporate 1870–1920* (Chicago: University of Chicago Press, 1990), 13–14. As Zunz notes, these displaced merchants were not "entrepreneurial heroes who fit C. Wright Mill's notion of the risk-taking individual before the rise of corporations.... Rather, they were the inheritors of precorporate forms of local wealth and power" (19). These local merchants belonged to a wealthy elite who displayed their economic and social power through prominent positions in religious and professional organizations and local elected offices.

16. Cawelti, *Apostles,* 112.

17. Andrew Carnegie, "Wealth," in *Democracy and the Gospel of Wealth,* ed. Gail Kennedy (Boston: Heath, 1949), 2. This essay, originally titled "Wealth," was published in two installments in the June and December 1889 issues of the *North American Review.* William T. Stead, editor of the *Pall Mall Gazette,* referred to Carnegie's essay and philosophy as "The Gospel of Wealth." See Andrew Carnegie, *The Gospel of Wealth and Other Timely Essays,* ed. Edward C. Kirkland (Cambridge: Harvard University Press, 1962), 14, 29–30.

18. William Graham Sumner, "The Concentration of Wealth: Its Economic Justification," in *Democracy and the Gospel of Wealth,* 85.

19. William Lawrence, "The Relation of Wealth to Morals," in *Democracy and the Gospel of Wealth,* 69.

20. Ibid., 74.

21. Carnegie, "Wealth," 5.

22. Ibid., 8.

23. Andrew Carnegie, "The Road to Business Success," in *The American Gospel of Success: Individualism and Beyond,* ed. Moses Rischin (Chicago: Quadrangle, 1965), 93.

24. Ibid., 97.

25. Russell Conwell, "Acres of Diamonds," in *American Rhetorical Discourse,* ed. Ronald F. Reid, 2d ed. (Prospect Heights, Ill.: Waveland Press, 1995), 629.

26. Ibid., 634.

27. Quoted in Ralph Henry Gabriel, *The Course of American Thought: An Intellectual History Since 1815* (New York: Ronald, 1940), 147.

28. Ibid., 146.

29. Sumner, "Forgotten Man," 613, 614.

30. Lawrence, "Relation of Wealth," 74.

31. Mark Wahlgren Summers, *The Gilded Age or, the Hazard of New Functions* (Upper Saddle River, N.J.: Prentice Hall, 1997), 33–34, 88–89.

32. Quoted in Katz, *Shadow of the Poorhouse,* 76.

33. Richard L. Dugdale, *The Jukes: A Study in Crime, Pauperism, Disease, and Heredity* (1877; reprint, New York: Arno Press, 1970), 38.

34. Kristin Luker, *Dubious Conceptions: The Politics of Teenage Pregnancy* (Cambridge: Harvard University Press, 1996), 31–35.

35. Katz, *Shadow of the Poorhouse,* 103, 106–7.

36. Quoted in Patricia T. Rooke and R. L. Schnell, "From Binding to Boarding Out in Britain and English-Canada," *Paedagogica Historica* 24 (1984): 468.

37. Theda Skocpol, *Protecting Soldiers and Mothers: The Political Origins of Social Policy in the United States* (Cambridge: Harvard University Press, 1992), 424.

38. Mark Leff, "Consensus for Reform: The Mothers'-Pension Movement in the Progressive Era," *Social Service Review* 47 (1983): 398, 404.

39. For Roosevelt's naming of the "muckrakers," see Theodore Roosevelt, "The Man with the Muckrake," in *The Muckrakers: The Era in Journalism That Moved America to Reform — the Most Significant Magazines of 1902–1912,* ed. Arthur Weinberg and Lila Weinberg (New York: Simon and Schuster, 1961), 58–65.

40. Will Irwin, "The First Ward Ball," in *The Muckrakers,* 137.

41. Ida M. Tarbell, "The History of the Standard Oil Company: The Oil War of 1872," in *The Muckrakers,* 39.

42. Charles Edward Russell, "The Tenements of Trinity Church," in *The Muckrakers,* 311, 312.

43. Edwin Markham, "The Hoe-Man in the Making," in *The Muckrakers,* 364.

44. William Hard, "De Kid Wot Works at Night," in *The Muckrakers,* 369–84.

45. Richard Hofstadter, *The Age of Reform: From Bryan to FDR* (New York: Vintage Books, 1955), 202.

46. Ibid.

47. Samuel S. McClure, "Concerning Three Articles in this Number of *McClure's*, and a Coincidence That May Set Us Thinking," in *The Muckrakers*, 5.

48. Lincoln Steffens, "The Shame of Minneapolis," in *The Muckrakers*, 15.

49. Child-saving embraced a variety of causes. Some of its components were at odds with each other. These included the practices of the CAS, attempts to replace institutional care with foster care, and eventually the push for mothers' pensions. See Katz, *Shadow of the Poorhouse*, 114. The list of attendees of the White House conference exemplified child-savers' diverse interests. Senate, *Proceedings of the Conference on the Care of Dependent Children*, 60th Cong., 2d sess., 1909, S. Doc. 721, 20–31.

50. Senate, *Proceedings of the Conference*, 36.

51. Ibid., 9–10.

52. Quoted in Skocpol, *Protecting Soldiers and Mothers*, 431.

53. Ibid., 437.

54. Quoted in Donileen R. Loseke and Kristen Fawcett, "Appealing Appeals: Constructing Moral Worthiness, 1912–1917," *Sociological Quarterly* 36 (1995): 65.

55. See Skocpol, *Protecting Soldiers and Mothers*, 442–56.

56. Mrs. G. H. Robertson, "The State's Duty to Fatherless Children," *Child-Welfare Magazine*, January 1912, 157, 159. *Child-Welfare Magazine* published the speech subsequently. The contrast between Mrs. Robertson's subordinate identity—she is known only through her husband's initials—and the adamant, autonomous tone of her speech exemplified the tensions of this reform era and historical poverty discourses generally. *Child-Welfare Magazine* also ran editorials that supported Robertson's call for unrestricted eligibility. See, e.g., Agnes H. Downing, "A Wider Pension Move," *Child-Welfare Magazine*, October 1912, 59.

57. Skocpol, *Protecting Soldiers and Mothers*, 451.

58. Gordon, *Pitied but Not Entitled*, 44.

59. Skocpol, *Protecting Soldiers and Mothers*, 470; Gordon, *Pitied but Not Entitled*, 47.

60. Theodore Roosevelt, "Americanism," in *Americanism: Addresses by Woodrow Wilson, Franklin K. Lane, and Theodore Roosevelt* (n.p.: Veterans of Foreign Wars of the United States, n.d.), 18.

61. E. E. Porterfield, "How the Widow's Allowance Operates," *Child-Welfare Magazine*, February 1913, 209.

62. Ibid., 210.

63. Skocpol, *Protecting Soldiers and Mothers*, 464.

64. Ibid., 472.

65. Department of Labor, Children's Bureau, *Mothers' Aid, 1931* (Washington, D. C.: Government Printing Office, 1933), 17.

66. Franklin D. Roosevelt, *The Public Papers and Addresses of Franklin D. Roosevelt: The Court Disapproves*, vol. 4 (New York: Random House, 1938), 20.

67. Committee on Economic Security, *Report to the President*, 2.

68. Committee on Economic Security, *Social Security in America: The Factual Background of the Social Security Act as Summarized from Staff Reports to the Committee on Economic Security* (Washington, D.C.: Government Printing Office, 1937), 231.

69. Gordon, *Pitied but Not Entitled*, 256.

70. *Social Security Act of 1935, U.S. Statutes at Large* 49 (1935): 629.

71. Committee on Economic Security, *Report to the President*, 6.

72. Roosevelt, *Public Papers*, 20, 19.

73. Ibid., 137.

74. The novel's literary milieu involved American writers politically like none before. Lionel Trilling holds that one cannot overestimate the importance of the radical movement of the 1930s for creating an American intellectual class in size, influence, and character "as being, through all mutations of opinion, predominantly of the left." Quoted in Ralph F. Bogardus and Fred Hobson, introduction to *Literature at the Barricades: The American Writer in the 1930s* (Tuscaloosa: University of Alabama Press, 1982), 2. On the resonance of Steinbeck's novel with the emerging theoretical scene, see Sylvia Jenkins Cook, "Steinbeck, the People, and the Party," in *Literature at the Barricades*, 83.

75. Quoted in David Wyatt, introduction to *New Essays on "The Grapes of Wrath"* (New York: Cambridge University Press, 1990), 3.

76. John Steinbeck, *The Grapes of Wrath* (1939; reprint, New York: Penguin Books, 1976), 43.

77. Ibid., 31.

78. Ibid., 536.

79. Ibid., 405, 406.

80. Gordon, *Pitied but Not Entitled*, 284. Administrative machinations played an important role in this campaign. As Jerry Cates recounts in his history of the formative years of the Social Security Board, federal administrators bolstered the standing of social insurance programs in part by blocking the development of public assistance programs. Cates maintains that "[t]his occurred even though the ssb recognized that actual and potential clients would be deprived of needed help." The ssb's campaign proceeded through the uneven application of a formula that subtracted a prospective public assistance recipient's requirements from resources to determine one's need. The ssb exhaustively examined recipient resources, including indirect household income and assets, while glossing over and purposely discounting recipient requirements for a decent standard of living. This uneven application of a needs-determination formula produced low

monthly grant allowances. The SSB also halted various state efforts to increase benefits to public assistance recipients. Jerry R. Cates, *Insuring Inequality: Administrative Leadership in Social Security, 1935–54* (Ann Arbor: University of Michigan Press, 1983), 105, 104–35.

81. Gordon, *Pitied but Not Entitled,* 275. On the desires of southern congressmen to maintain racial inequalities in the SSA through purposeful exclusions and other means, see Jill Quadagno, *The Color of Welfare: How Racism Undermined the War on Poverty* (New York: Oxford University Press, 1994), 19–25.

82. Hoey and Franklin, "Aid to Dependent Children," 31, 32.

83. Quoted in Blanche D. Coll, *Safety Net: Welfare and Social Security 1929–1977* (New Brunswick, N.J.: Rutgers University Press, 1995), 127.

84. Quoted in Lisa Brush, "Worthy Widows, Welfare Cheats: The Professional Discourse on Single Mothers in the United States, 1900–1988" (Ph.D. diss., University of Wisconsin-Madison, 1993), 212. Brush notes that the shift in program focus concentrated exclusively on white women. The rehabilitative model ignored black women, "leaving them to the discriminatory mercies of local welfare administrators more interested in the labor power than the maternal qualities or mental health of these women" (209–10). On the differing approaches of social workers and social insurance administrators, see Edward D. Berkowitz, *America's Welfare State from Roosevelt to Reagan* (Baltimore, Md.: Johns Hopkins University Press, 1991), 100.

85. Coll, *Safety Net,* 170–72.

86. Ibid., 167.

87. Richard M. Nixon, *Public Papers of the Presidents of the United States: Richard M. Nixon, 1969* (Washington, D.C.: Government Printing Office, 1971), 639.

88. Patterson, *America's Struggle Against Poverty,* 99.

89. Dwight MacDonald, "Our Invisible Poor," *New Yorker,* 19 January 1963, 84, 131.

90. Irving Howe, introduction to *The Other America: Poverty in the United States,* by Michael Harrington (1962; reprint, New York: Collier Books, 1994), xi.

91. Harrington, *Other America,* 17.

92. Ibid., 3, 11.

93. Ibid., 2, 16, 122.

94. Ibid., 15–16.

95. Lewis, however, stressed these very connections among culture, power, and socioeconomic conditions. His solution to the culture of poverty was radical, militant organizing. As Katz explains, "pride, organization, and class (or racial) consciousness led swiftly away from the culture of poverty. In the United States, the great example for Lewis was the civil rights movement. In the Third World, it was revolution." Michael B. Katz, *The Undeserving Poor: From the War on Poverty to the War on Welfare* (New York: Pantheon Books, 1989), 19–20. For an explication of the arguments of Harrington and Lewis's critics, see Katz, *Undeserving Poor,* 41–43.

This charge of judging black families by white, middle-class norms was leveled at a 1965 report prepared by then assistant secretary of labor Daniel Patrick Moynihan entitled *The Negro Family: The Case for National Action*. Moynihan concluded that at "the heart of the deterioration of the fabric of Negro society is the deterioration of the Negro family." Moynihan maintained that the exclusion of black men from mainstream economic activity had engendered family breakup, trapping female-headed families in a "tangle of pathology." He proposed massive federal intervention as a response. Quoted in Lee Rainwater and William C. Yancey, eds., *The Moynihan Report and the Politics of Controversy* (Cambridge: MIT Press, 1967), 51. A full text of *The Negro Family* as well as reactions from civil rights leaders, White House officials, and social scientists are included in the Rainwater and Yancey volume.

96. Harrington, *Other America*, 153.

97. Ibid., 172, 174.

98. Quoted in Berkowitz, *America's Welfare State*, 104.

99. Quoted in Patterson, *America's Struggle Against Poverty*, 110.

100. Ibid., 112.

101. Kennedy, *Public Papers*, 475, 473. On the assumptions of poverty as solvable and un-American, see Patterson, *America's Struggle Against Poverty*, 113.

102. Kennedy, *Public Papers, 1962*, 475. In his history of the United States during the Great Depression and the Second World War, David Kennedy explains that FDR and other New Dealers "believed that they were addressing not a transient disruption in the labor markets but a long-term, perhaps permanent, deficit in the ability of the private economy to provide employment for all who sought it." For this reason, a clear economic logic complemented humanitarian considerations in FDR's support of the components of the Social Security Act. Kennedy writes: "Depression America had produced work only for so many, the president reasoned. Forcibly idling some was the price of securing a living wage for others." David M. Kennedy, *Freedom from Fear: The American People in Depression and War, 1929–1945* (New York: Oxford University Press, 1999), 249, 257.

103. David Zarefsky, *President Johnson's War on Poverty: Rhetoric and History* (Tuscaloosa: University of Alabama Press, 1986), 21–24. Zarefsky notes that LBJ's use of a war metaphor in describing his agenda enabled an objective that enlisted a previously unmotivated populace (total victory), an enemy that allowed individual and environmental explanations of poverty (cycle of poverty), and weapons that fostered productive ambiguities (community action and maximum feasible participation).

104. Johnson, *Public Papers*, 375, 378, 377.

105. Ibid., 376, 377.

106. Quoted in Zarefsky, *President Johnson's War on Poverty*, 149. Zarefsky provides a cogent discussion of the OEO's difficulties in maintaining distinctions between poverty and public assistance programs.

107. See Frances Fox Piven and Richard Cloward, *Poor People's Movements: Why They Succeed, How They Fail* (New York: Vintage Books, 1979), 264–361; Nick Kotz and Mary Lynn Kotz, *A Passion for Equality: George A. Wiley and the Movement* (New York: W. W. Norton, 1977), 222–23.

108. Katz, *Undeserving Poor*, 107.

109. Patterson, *America's Struggle Against Poverty*, 179.

110. Zarefsky, *President Johnson's War on Poverty*, 169.

111. Martin Luther King, Jr., "I Have a Dream," in *I Have a Dream: Writings and Speeches that Changed the World*, ed. James M. Washington (New York: HarperCollins, 1992), 102.

112. Martin Luther King, Jr., "The President's Address to the Tenth Anniversary Convention of the Southern Christian Leadership Conference," in *The Rhetoric of Black Power*, ed. Robert L. Scott and Wayne Brockriede (New York: HarperCollins, 1969), 151.

113. Ibid., 155.

114. Ibid., 157.

115. David Farber, *The Age of Great Dreams: America in the 1960s* (New York: Hill and Wang, 1994), 245.

116. Friedan writes: "[W]hen women do not need to live through their husbands and children, men will not fear the love and strength of women, nor need another's weakness to prove their own masculinity. They can finally see each other as they are. And this may be the next step in human evolution." Betty Friedan, *The Feminine Mystique* (New York: W. W. Norton, 1963), 377–78.

117. Quoted in Farber, *Age of Great Dreams*, 248.

118. Department of Commerce, Bureau of the Census, *Statistical Abstracts of the United States, 1988* (Washington, D. C.: Government Printing Office, 1989), 374.

119. Joel F. Handler and Yeheskel Hasenfeld, *The Moral Construction of Poverty: Welfare Reform in America* (Newbury Park, Calif.: Sage, 1991), 137.

120. Ibid., 141.

121. Nixon, *Public Papers*, 639.

122. Ibid., 638.

123. Ibid., 644.

124. Daniel Patrick Moynihan, *The Politics of a Guaranteed Income: The Nixon Administration and the Family Assistance Plan* (New York: Random House, 1973), 138.

125. Nixon, *Public Papers*, 641.

126. Ibid., 644.

127. Ibid., 640.

128. Ibid., 639.

129. Ibid., 637, 644.

130. Quoted in Moynihan, *Politics of a Guaranteed Income,* 292.

131. See Patterson, *America's Struggle Against Poverty,* 197–98.

132. Quoted in Jill Quadagno, *The Transformation of Old Age Security: Class and Politics in the American Welfare State* (Chicago: University of Chicago Press, 1988), 150.

133. See Lentricchia, *Criticism and Social Change,* 125. My reference to tradition-making broaches scholarly investigation of "collective memory," a concept that signifies the attachment by social groups of special meanings to past events. As Bruce Gronbeck notes, "[t]he collective memory is recalled, seemingly, so as to let the past guide the present, but it can do so only when the past itself is re-made." In this reconstructive process, advocates invoke the past to examine some present concern, "shaping it [the past] into a useful memory that an audience can find relevant to the present." Bruce E. Gronbeck, "The Rhetorics of the Past: History, Argument, and Collective Memory," in *Doing Rhetorical History: Concepts and Cases,* ed. Kathleen J. Turner (Tuscaloosa: University of Alabama Press, 1998), 56–57.

134. See, e.g., Ronald Reagan, *Public Papers of the Presidents of the United States: Ronald Reagan, 1986,* bk. 1 (Washington, D.C.: Government Printing Office, 1988), 128.

135. Ronald Reagan, *Public Papers of the Presidents of the United States: Ronald Reagan, 1988,* bk. 1 (Washington, D.C.: Government Printing Office, 1990), 87.

136. See, e.g., Sar A. Levitan and Robert Taggart, "The Great Society Did Succeed," *Political Science Quarterly* 91 (1976–77): 601–18.

137. Quoted in Richard S. Frank, "GOP Pulling Together for Reagan," *National Journal,* 26 July 1980, 1214.

CHAPTER THREE

1. Quoted in Elizabeth Drew, *Portrait of an Election: The 1980 Presidential Campaign* (New York: Simon and Schuster, 1981), 325.

2. Paul Krugman, *The Age of Diminished Expectations: U.S. Economic Policy in the 1990s* (Cambridge: MIT Press, 1992), 2; William C. Berman, *America's Right Turn: From Nixon to Bush* (Baltimore, Md.: Johns Hopkins University Press, 1994), 76.

   Reports in January 1980 indicated that the Consumer Price Index, a prime measure of inflation, rose 13.3 percent in 1979, the largest increase in thirty-three years. Early measures in 1980 showed no signs of improvement. Rather, inflation appeared to be worsening. The inflation rate averaged 18 percent for the first quarter of the year. In its last disclosure before the 1980 presidential election, the Bureau of Labor Statistics reported that a September rise in the inflation rate produced a compound annual rate of 12.7 percent. Steven Rattner, "'79 Prices Up 13.3 % in Biggest Increase for a Year Since '46," *New York Times,* 26 January 1980, late city edition, 1; Clyde H. Farnsworth, "Consumer Prices Up by 1% in September and 12.7% in a Year," *New York Times,* 25 October 1980, late city edition, 1.

3. Richard E. Cohen, "The Political System Attempts to Cope with Public Loss of Faith in Government," *National Journal,* 19 January 1980, 112.

4. Neal R. Peirce and Jerry Hagstrom, "The Voters Send Carter a Message: Time for a Change — to Reagan," *National Journal,* 8 November 1980, 1877. On the recruitment of "Reagan Democrats," see William J. Lanouette, "Turning Out the Vote — Reagan Seeks Larger Share of Blue-Collar Vote," *National Journal,* 11 January 1980, 1832–35.

5. Garry Wills, *Reagan's America: Innocents at Home* (New York: Doubleday, 1987), 283–84, 320–21.

6. Roosevelt, *Public Papers,* 19; Nixon, *Public Papers,* 639.

7. Katz, *Shadow of the Poorhouse,* 278; Krugman, *Age of Diminished Expectations,* 3; "Real Income Down 5.5% in 1980 in a Record Drop," *New York Times,* 21 August 1981, late city edition, A12.

8. Quoted in Agis Salpukas, "Depressed Industrial Heartland Stressing Urgent Need for Help," *New York Times,* 19 August 1980, late city edition, A1.

9. Michael Harrington, *The New American Poverty* (New York: Penguin Books, 1984), 47; see also Katz, *Shadow of the Poorhouse,* 275–77.

10. Quoted in Iver Peterson, "Michigan Family Chases American Dream in Texas," *New York Times,* 13 June 1981, late city edition, 8.

11. William K. Stevens, "Unskilled Northerners Find Sun Belt Job Climate Cooling," *New York Times,* 18 August 1981, late city edition, A1.

12. Frances Fox Piven and Richard A. Cloward, *The New Class War: Reagan's Attack on the Welfare State and Its Consequences,* rev. ed. (New York: Pantheon Books, 1985), 22–23.

13. William Greider, *The Education of David Stockman and Other Americans* (New York: Dutton, 1982), 107–8; Piven and Cloward, *New Class War,* 25.

14. Wills, *Reagan's America,* 362.

15. Matthew L. Wald, "Welfare Means Bare Cupboards as Inflation Grows," *New York Times,* 18 March 1981, late city edition, A1.

16. Quoted in Fred Ferretti, "In the Suburbs, Inflation Takes the Edge Off the Good Life," *New York Times,* 29 March 1980, late city edition, 20; quoted in Carol Pogash, "In Fact, December's Cruelest," *New York Times,* 8 August 1980, late city edition, A29.

17. Quoted in Iver Peterson, "Inflation Compelling Middle-Income People to Ask for Public Aid," *New York Times,* 20 April 1980, late city edition, sec. 1, 1.

18. Harry Anderson, Rich Thomas, Gloria Borger, Thomas M. DeFrank, Elaine Shannon, and Susan Dentzer, "Is U.S. Inflation Out of Control?," *Newsweek,* 3 March 1980, 54–55; George M. Taber, "Capitalism: Is It Working?" *Time,* 21 April 1980, 55.

19. Allan J. Mayer, "Inflation: A Doomsday Scenario," *Newsweek,* 24 March 1980, 29.

20. Adam Clymer, "Poll Links Economic Slide and Social Antagonism," *New York*

Times, 27 June 1980, late city edition, A1; John Oliver Wilson, "After the Fall," *New York Times,* 24 September 1980, late city edition, A31.

21. Ronald Reagan, "Text of Reagan's Speech Accepting the Republicans' Nomination," *New York Times,* 18 July 1980, late city edition, A8. Martin Medhurst notes that Reagan regularly asserted the values of "family," "work," and "neighborhood" as well as the values of "peace" and "freedom" before friendly audiences early in his presidency to signal to conservative supporters that he remained committed to social issues such as school prayer and anti-abortion even as economic issues appeared as his most urgent political priorities. Martin J. Medhurst, "Postponing the Social Agenda: Reagan's Strategy and Tactics," *Western Journal of Speech Communication* 48 (1984): 266–67.

22. Wills, *Reagan's America,* 364.

23. Garry Wills recounts the development of Laffer's theorem into a curve. Jude Wanniski, an editor at the *Wall Street Journal* and an enthusiastic supply-sider, had Laffer explain the unobjectionable claim that taxes can be high enough to deplete their source "to one of President Ford's aides (who must have been rather dense) by drawing an igloo shape on a napkin to explain the trajectory of tax returns." Noting the "simplistic" and "tendentious" qualities of this drawing, Wills writes: "Yet, from Jude Wanniski's unparalleled publicity campaign, built around this doodle, the mystique of supply-side economics grew." Wills, *Reagan's America,* 364.

24. Greider, *Education of David Stockman,* 8.

25. Senate Committee on Finance, *Spending Reduction Proposals, Part 1: Hearings before the Committee on Finance,* 97th Cong., 1st sess., 1981, 109.

26. Senate Committee, *Spending Reduction Proposals, Part 1,* 351; House Subcommittee on Public Assistance and Unemployment Compensation of the Committee on Ways and Means, *Administration's Proposed Savings in Unemployment Compensation, Public Assistance, and Social Services Programs: Hearings before the Subcommittee on Public Assistance and Unemployment Compensation of the Committee on Ways and Means,* 97th Cong., 1st sess., 1981, 155.

27. House Committee on Ways and Means, *Tax Aspects of the President's Economic Program: Hearings before the Committee on Ways and Means,* 97th Cong., 1st sess., 1981, 317.

28. Piven and Cloward, *New Class War,* 38–39.

29. Katz, *Undeserving Poor,* 144; Henry Allen, "George Gilder and the Capitalists' Creed," *Washington Post,* 18 February 1981, final edition, B1, B9.

30. George Gilder, *Wealth and Poverty* (New York: Basic Books, 1981), 21, 27, 68.

31. For a complete explanation of the changes, see "Welfare Benefits Cut by Reconciliation," *Congressional Quarterly Almanac* 37 (1981): 473–75; Harrison Donnelly, "Working Mothers' Benefits Cut in New AFDC Provisions in Reconciliation Measure," *CQ Weekly,* 15 August 1981, 1493–94.

32. Each state devised a need standard to calculate AFDC eligibility: a monthly income that met minimal needs for food, clothing, and shelter. Families with no income or income below a state's need standard could enroll. States also determined a payment standard; family grant amounts were based on the difference between this second standard and net monthly income (i.e., income after allowable disregards). In 1980 only New York had a need standard that exceeded the poverty line. No state's payment standard equaled its need standard. In the median state, benefits totaled one-half of the poverty line. And grant amounts varied widely among states. Maximum benefits ranged from $120 per month for a family of four in Mississippi to $563 per month for the same size family in California. Tom Joe and Cheryl Rogers, *By the Few for the Few: The Reagan Welfare Legacy* (Lexington, Mass.: Lexington Books, 1985), 25–27.

33. See Robert Moffitt and Douglas A. Wolf, "The Effect of the 1981 Omnibus Budget Reconciliation Act on Welfare Recipients and Work Incentives," *Social Service Review* 61 (1987): 247–60; Deborah K. Zinn and Rosemary C. Sarri, "Turning Back the Clock on Public Welfare," *Signs: Journal of Women in Culture and Society* 10 (1984): 355–70.

34. Dick Kirschten, "Reagan: 'No More Business as Usual,'" *National Journal,* 21 February 1981, 300.

35. "Carefully Orchestrated Campaign Unfolds," *CQ Weekly,* 21 February 1981, 333; Linda E. Demkovich, "HHS Department: It's Humphrey's No More," *National Journal,* 25 April 1981, 713.

36. Quoted in Gail Gregg, "Reagan Plan Clears 1st Hurdle as Senate Backs Cuts," *CQ Weekly,* 21 March 1981, 502.

37. Quoted in Richard E. Cohen, "In the Conservative Politics of the '80s, the South Is Rising Once Again," *National Journal,* 28 February 1981, 353.

38. Quoted in Greider, *Education of David Stockman,* 148, 150.

39. David A. Stockman, *The Triumph of Politics: How the Reagan Revolution Failed* (New York: Harper and Row, 1986), 73.

40. Timothy Clark, "Want to Know Where the Ax Will Fall? Read David Stockman's Big 'Black Book,'" *National Journal,* 14 February 1981, 274; Gail Gregg and Dale Tate, "Reagan Economic Officials Put Differences Behind Them," *CQ Weekly,* 7 February 1981, 259.

41. Wills, *Reagan's America,* 366–67.

42. David A. Stockman, "Stockman on the Budget Outlook — 'We Cannot Fund the Great Society,'" *National Journal,* 19 September 1981, 1665.

43. Thomas J. Arrandale, "Control of the Purse Strings," in *Budgeting for America: The Politics and Process of Federal Spending,* ed. Martha V. Gottron (Washington, D.C.: Congressional Quarterly, 1982), 29–44.

44. Thomas J. Arrandale, "Experiment in Budgeting," in *Budgeting for America,* 62; Thomas J. Arrandale, "Struggle for Spending Control," in *Budgeting for America,*

57–59; Robert W. Hartman, "Congress and Budget-Making," *Political Science Quarterly* 97 (1982): 387–88.

45. Dale Tate, "House Provides President a Victory on the 1982 Budget," *CQ Weekly,* 9 May 1981, 783.

46. Dale Tate and Andy Plattner, "House Ratifies Savings Plan in Stunning Reagan Victory," *CQ Weekly,* 27 June 1981, 1128.

47. Joe and Rogers, *By the Few for the Few,* 55.

48. Bill Keller, "Special Treatment No Longer Given Advocates for the Poor," *CQ Weekly,* 18 April 1981, 659.

49. Ibid., 662.

50. Joe and Rogers, *By the Few for the Few,* 34.

51. Hedrick Smith, "A Bold and Risky Venture: Party's Political Future May Depend on Results," *New York Times,* 19 February 1981, late city edition, A1.

52. Steven R. Weisman, "Optimism on Budget," *New York Times,* 20 February 1981, late city edition, A1; Bill Peterson, "For Nation, 'It's Time to Switch Lanes,'" *Washington Post,* 20 February 1981, A1.

53. Tom Shales, "The Economic Speech: Sugarcoating a Bitter Pill," *Washington Post,* 19 February 1981, final edition, D1.

54. Ronald Reagan, *Public Papers of the Presidents of the United States: Ronald Reagan, 1981* (Washington, D.C.: Government Printing Office, 1982), 79.

55. Ibid., 80.

56. Ibid., 80, 81.

57. Ibid., 81.

58. Ibid., 82, 83.

59. Ibid., 109.

60. Ibid., 109, 110, 111. Despite Reagan's initial statement, his safety net assumed several forms and successively shrank as many of these eight programs were cut. Also, there never appeared to be agreement within the Reagan administration regarding the specific programs that constituted the safety net. See David Zarefsky, Carol Miller-Tutzauer, and Frank Tutzauer, "Reagan's Safety Net for the Truly Needy: The Rhetorical Uses of Definition," *Central States Speech Journal* 35 (1984): 355–70.

61. Reagan, *Public Papers, 1981,* 112, 114.

62. Other strategies noted by Ritter and Henry, which also appear in varying degrees in his 5 and 18 February speeches, include praise of the inherent virtue of the American people, appeal to a self-reliant spirit at the base of American values, and invocation of a higher spiritual authority. Kurt Ritter and David Henry, *Ronald Reagan: The Great Communicator* (Westport, Conn.: Greenwood Press, 1992), 66–73.

63. Kenneth Burke, *The Philosophy of Literary Form: Studies in Symbolic Action,* 3d ed. (Berkeley: University of California Press, 1973), 74, 71.

64. Ibid., 67.

65. Reagan, *Public Papers, 1981,* 135. The welfare cheat figured prominently and recurrently in Reagan's political imagination. Campaigning for the presidency in 1976, he repeatedly cited the case of the "Chicago welfare queen." At many campaign appearances, he enraged audiences with the story of a woman in Chicago who "has 80 names, 30 addresses, 12 Social Security cards and is collecting veterans' benefits on four nonexisting deceased husbands. And she's collecting Social Security on her cards. She's got Medicaid, getting food stamps and she is collecting welfare under each of her names. Her tax-free cash income alone is over $150,000." "'Welfare Queen' Becomes Issue in Reagan Campaign," *New York Times,* 15 February 1976, late city edition, sec. 1, 51. See also Michael Weiler, "The Reagan Attack on Welfare," in *Reagan and Public Discourse in America,* ed. Michael Weiler and W. Barnett Pearce (Tuscaloosa: University of Alabama Press, 1992), 232; Amos Kiewe and Davis W. Houck, *A Shining City on a Hill: Ronald Reagan's Economic Rhetoric, 1951–1989* (New York: Praeger, 1991), 79. For a chronology of important Reagan campaign speeches as well as other significant speeches he delivered between 1928 and 1991, see Ritter and Henry, *Ronald Reagan.*

66. *Congressional Record,* 97th Cong., 1st sess., 1981, 127, pt. 3:3755.

67. See, for example, the comments of Sen. Paula Hawkins, *Congressional Record,* 97th Cong., 1st sess., 1981, 127, pt. 7:8457.

68. House Subcommittee, *Administration's Proposed Savings,* 24.

69. Senate Committee, *Spending Reduction Proposals, Part 1,* 45.

70. House Subcommittee, *Administration's Proposed Savings,* 49.

71. *Congressional Record,* 97th Cong., 1st sess., 1981, 127, pt. 11:14058.

72. House Subcommittee, *Administration's Proposed Savings,* 74.

73. Senate Committee, *Spending Reduction Proposals, Part 1,* 102, 105. Portrayals of double-dippers were subject to parody, however. Rep. Thomas Downey quipped that David Stockman appeared to have found a method to end poverty: "If you thought the war on poverty was effective, wait until you see what Mr. Stockman can do by defining it." *Congressional Record,* 97th Cong., 1st sess., 1981, 127, pt. 11:14353.

   Stockman did not sustain the self-assurance he exhibited in his congressional testimony at all times. He confessed to William Greider: "None of us really understands what's going on with all these numbers. You've got so many different budgets out and so many different baselines and such complexity now in the interactive parts of the budget between policy action and the economic environment and all the mysteries of the budget. People are getting from A to B and it's not clear how they are getting there." Greider, *Education of David Stockman,* 33.

74. Senate Committee, *Spending Reduction Proposals, Part 1,* 389.

75. Ibid., 84, 54.

76. *Congressional Record,* 97th Cong., 1st sess., 1981, 127, pt. 11:14556, 14558.

77. Ibid., 14555, 14558.

78. House Subcommittee, *Administration's Proposed Savings*, 79, 80.

79. *Congressional Record*, 97th Cong., 1st sess., 1981, 127, pt. 2:2267.

80. House Subcommittee, *Administration's Proposed Savings*, 182, 183.

81. Ibid., 329.

82. Ibid., 19.

83. Reagan, *Public Papers, 1981*, 208. See also Reagan's comments on 19 February and 28 May. Reagan, *Public Papers, 1981*, 135–36, 466–67.

84. Ibid., 208, 468.

85. House Subcommittee, *Administration's Proposed Savings*, 200, 262.

86. Senate Committee on Finance, *Spending Reduction Proposals, Part 2: Hearings before the Committee on Finance*, 97th Cong., 1st sess., 1981, 43–44. Efforts to feature innocent children sometimes broached the bifurcated American welfare structure of public assistance and social insurance programs and their attendant positioning of participants as clients and citizens respectively. During his questioning of Robert Ball, Senator Moynihan asked: "[H]ow come the AFDC was made a state sharing program and the retirement system was not?" Ball did not elucidate the motivations of the architects of the 1935 Social Security Act, but he did note the different status of social security and AFDC recipients:

> [AFDC] goes to the poorest of the poor. It is very, very largely for women who have small children.... Social insurance is contributory, is based on past earnings, and is not, by any means, just for low-income people, but is the base on which everybody builds protection.... So, you have a different kind of support for social security. The AFDC program doesn't have a broad constituency; it isn't based to the same degree on a sense of right, and I deplore that. (43)

Some advocates, such as Burt Seidman, argued for maintaining this distinction among programs despite their objections to proposed reductions.

87. House Subcommittee, *Administration's Proposed Savings*, 312, 320, 321.

88. Senate Committee, *Spending Reduction Proposals, Part 1*, 216, 245.

89. Senate Committee, *Spending Reduction Proposals, Part 2*, 44.

90. House Subcommittee, *Administration's Proposed Savings*, 84, 86.

91. Senate Committee, *Spending Reduction Proposals, Part 1*, 217.

92. House Subcommittee, *Administration's Proposed Savings*, 3.

93. *Congressional Record*, 97th Cong., 1st sess., 1981, 127, pt. 3:4064–65.

94. *Congressional Record*, 97th Cong., 1st sess., 1981, 127, pt. 5:6437.

95. *Congressional Record*, 97th Cong., 1st sess., 1981, 127, pt. 6:7500.

96. *Congressional Record*, 97th Cong., 1st sess., 1981, 127, pt. 11:14672.

97. See, e.g., Steven V. Roberts, "Food Stamps Program: How It Grew and How Reagan Wants to Cut It Back," *New York Times*, 4 April 1981, late city edition, sec. 1, 11.

98. See, e.g., House Subcommittee, *Administration's Proposed Savings,* 310.

99. Lentricchia, *Criticism and Social Change,* 153.

100. Reagan, *Public Papers, 1981,* 135.

101. Michael Osborn, "Rhetorical Depiction," in *Form, Genre, and the Study of Political Discourse,* ed. Herbert W. Simons and Aram A. Aghazarian (Columbia: University of South Carolina Press, 1986), 79. Osborn introduces rhetorical depiction as a discursive process. He quotes George Campbell's characterization of significant metaphor to describe depiction as "an allegory in miniature," and Osborn explains that "[r]hetorical depiction typically does not arise from any single technique or moment in discourse. More often it is a controlled gestalt, a cumulative impact." Ibid., 80. Still, Osborn notes that rhetorical depiction occurs in verbal and visual media, and he cites novels, speeches, films, and television programs as examples.

102. Reagan, *Public Papers, 1981,* 208.

103. Carnegie, "Wealth," 8, 1.

104. Franklin D. Roosevelt, "First Inaugural Address," in *American Rhetorical Discourse,* ed. Ronald F. Reid, 2d ed. (Prospect Heights, Ill.: Waveland Press, 1995), 720.

105. Sumner, "Forgotten Man," 608, 613.

106. Roosevelt, *Public Papers,* 137, 138.

107. Senate, *Proceedings of the Conference,* 35.

108. Porterfield, "Widow's Allowance," 209.

109. House Subcommittee, *Administration's Proposed Savings,* 95.

110. Ibid., 95, 96.

111. Ibid., 98, 99.

112. *Congressional Record,* 97th Cong., 1st sess., 1981, 127, pt. 10:13315, 13316, 13318.

113. Ibid., 13319.

114. Reagan, *Public Papers, 1981,* 82–83, 114, 568.

115. Senate Committee, *Spending Reduction Proposals, Part 1,* 40.

116. *Congressional Record,* 97th Cong., 1st sess., 1981, 127, pt. 4:4446.

117. Herbert Marcuse, *Counterrevolution and Revolt* (Boston: Beacon Press, 1972), 80.

118. Wills, *Reagan's America,* 375.

119. Nancy Fraser and Linda Gordon, "Contract Versus Charity: Why Is There No Social Citizenship in the United States?," *Socialist Review* 22, no. 3 (1992): 46–47.

120. Greider, *Education of David Stockman,* 60.

121. General Accounting Office, *An Evaluation of the 1981 AFDC Changes: Initial Analyses,* Washington, D.C., 2 April 1984, 4.

122. Robert Hutchens, "The Effects of the Omnibus Budget Reconciliation Act of 1981 on AFDC Recipients: A Review of the Studies," discussion paper 764–84, Institute for Research on Poverty, University of Wisconsin-Madison, 1984, 51.

123. Joe and Rogers, *By the Few for the Few,* 97.

124. House Subcommittee on Public Assistance and Unemployment Compensation of the Committee on Ways and Means, *Welfare Reform: Hearings before the Subcommittee on Public Assistance and Unemployment Compensation of the Committee on Ways and Means,* 100th Cong., 1st sess., 1987, 557.

CHAPTER FOUR

1. Reagan, *Public Papers, 1981,* 82.

2. Reagan, *Public Papers, 1986,* bk. 1:128, 214.

3. Dick Kirschten, "Low-Profile Reagan Welfare Study Prompts Ex-Aides to Do Their Own," *National Journal,* 17 May 1986, 1208; "Groups Urge U.S. to Ease Poverty," *New York Times,* 23 December 1986, late edition, B5.

4. Robert Y. Shapiro, Kelly D. Patterson, Judith Russell, and John T. Young, "The Polls: Public Assistance," *Public Opinion Quarterly* 51 (1987): 124–26.

5. Julie Rovner, "Daniel Patrick Moynihan: Making Welfare Work," *CQ Weekly,* 21 March 1987, 503–7.

6. Paul Taylor, "Democrats Wrest Control of Senate from GOP," *Washington Post,* 5 November 1986, final edition, A1.

7. Neal R. Peirce, "Governors' Breakthrough on Welfare Reform," *National Journal,* 14 March 1987, 637; Julie Rovner, "Governors Jump-Start Welfare Reform Drive," *CQ Weekly,* 28 February 1987, 376–78.

8. Patrick L. Knudsen, "After Long, Bruising Battle, House Approves Welfare Reform Bill," *CQ Weekly,* 19 December 1987, 3157–65; Julie Rovner, "Governors Press Reagan, Bentsen on Welfare," *CQ Weekly,* 27 February 1988, 512–13.

9. Julie Rovner, "Congress Clears Overhaul of Welfare System," *CQ Weekly,* 1 October 1988, 2699–701.

10. Department of Labor, Bureau of Labor Statistics, *Working Women: A Chartbook* (Washington, D.C.: Government Printing Office, 1991), 4, 6; Susan E. Shank, "Women and the Labor Market: The Link Grows Stronger," *Monthly Labor Review,* March 1988, 4.

11. Census Bureau, *Statistical Abstracts of the United States, 1988,* 374.

12. Department of Commerce, Bureau of the Census, *Household and Family Characteristics: March 1990 and 1989* (Washington, D.C: Government Printing Office, 1990), 7; see also Brush, "Worthy Widows," 356–57.

13. Daniel Patrick Moynihan, *Family and Nation* (New York: Harcourt Brace Jovanovich, 1987), 111.

14. Ibid., 112, 117.

15. Lawrence Mead, *Beyond Entitlement: The Social Obligations of Citizenship* (New York: Free Press, 1986), ix.

16. Katz, *Undeserving Poor,* 157–59.

17. Charles Murray, *Losing Ground: American Social Policy, 1950–1980,* 10th anniversary ed. (New York: Basic Books, 1994); David T. Ellwood, *Poor Support: Poverty in the American Family* (New York: Basic Books, 1988).

18. Greenfield quoted in Chuck Lane, "The Manhattan Project," *New Republic,* 25 March 1985, 15; Moynihan, *Family and Nation,* 124.

19. Lane, "Manhattan Project," 14–15; see also S. M. Miller, "Faith, Hope, and Charity — the Public Relations of Poverty," review of *Losing Ground,* by Charles Murray, *Contemporary Sociology* 14 (1985): 684–87.

20. Robert J. Samuelson, "Escaping the Poverty Trap," *Newsweek,* 10 September 1984, 60; Charles P. Alexander, "Broadsides from the Supply Side," *Time,* 5 November 1984, 58.

21. Herbert Stein, "A Poverty Paradox," review of *Losing Ground,* by Charles Murray, *Fortune,* 21 January 1985, 169, 172; Brigitte Berger, "Government and the Poor," review of *Losing Ground,* by Charles Murray, *Commentary,* January 1985, 66–70; see also Edward J. Harpham and Richard K. Scotch, "Rethinking the War on Poverty: The Ideology of Social Welfare Reform," *Western Political Quarterly* 41 (1988): 193–207.

22. Sar A. Levitan, review of *Losing Ground,* by Charles Murray, *Society* 22 (1985): 82–83; John L. Rury, "The New Moral Darwinism," review of *Losing Ground,* by Charles Murray, *Urban Education* 21 (1986): 316–24; Hugh Wilson, review of *Losing Ground,* by Charles Murray, *Science & Society* 49 (1985): 501–4.

23. Victor Fuchs, review of *Losing Ground,* by Charles Murray, *Population and Development Review* 11 (1985): 768–70; Douglas Muzzio, review of *Losing Ground,* by Charles Murray, *American Political Science Review* 79 (1985): 1198–99.

24. Lester C. Thurow, "Of Grasshoppers and Ants," review of *Losing Ground,* by Charles Murray, *Harvard Business Review* (July-August 1985): 44–45; Robert Greenstein, "Losing Faith in *Losing Ground,*" review of *Losing Ground,* by Charles Murray, *New Republic,* 25 March 1985, 12–13.

25. Alvin Boskoff, review of *Losing Ground,* by Charles Murray, *Annals of the American Academy of Political and Social Science,* no. 481 (1985): 194–95; S. E. Clarke, A. N. Kirby, and R. F. McNown, "*Losing Ground* — or Losing Credibility? An Examination of a Recent Policy Debate in the United States," review of *Losing Ground,* by Charles Murray, *Environment and Planning A* 19 (1987): 1015–25.

26. Christopher Jencks, "How Poor Are the Poor?" review of *Losing Ground,* by Charles Murray, *New York Review of Books,* 9 May 1985, 45; Robert B. Reich, "Prescriptions from the Right," review of *Losing Ground,* by Charles Murray, *Dissent* (spring 1985): 238.

27. Murray, *Losing Ground,* 54.

28. Ibid., 146.

29. Robert Moffitt, review of *Poor Support,* by David Ellwood, *American Journal of Sociology* 85 (1990): 1328. See also Edward J. Blakely, "Villains and Victims: Poverty and Public Policy," review of *Poor Support,* by David Ellwood, *APA Journal* (spring 1992): 248–52; Sheldon Danziger, review of *Poor Support,* by David Ellwood, *Journal of Economic Literature* 27 (1989): 1212–14.

30. David Whitman, "The Return of the New Dealers," review of *Poor Support,* by David Ellwood, *Public Interest* 94 (1989): 107–9.

31. Charles J. Barrilleaux, review of *Poor Support,* by David Ellwood, *American Political Science Review* 83 (1989): 634–35; John A. Hall, review of *Poor Support,* by David Ellwood, *Social Science Quarterly* 70 (1989): 538–39.

32. George T. Haskett, review of *Poor Support,* by David Ellwood, *Social Casework: The Journal of Contemporary Social Work* 70, no. 1 (1989): 57–61.

33. Howard E. Freeman, "Dwarf Steps for the Poor," review of *Poor Support,* by David Ellwood, *Contemporary Sociology* 17 (1988): 805–7; Robert Hutchens, review of *Poor Support,* by David Ellwood, *Industrial and Labor Relations Review* 43 (1990): 486–87.

34. Robert Greenstein, "New Thinking About Poverty," review of *Poor Support,* by David Ellwood, *Dissent* (spring 1989): 271.

35. Ellwood, *Poor Support,* 19, 20, 23.

36. Ibid., 43.

37. Ibid., 6, 43.

38. Murray, *Losing Ground,* 231.

39. Erica B. Baum, "When the Witch Doctors Agree: The Family Support Act and Social Science Research," *Journal of Policy Analysis and Management* 10 (1991): 609. See also Stacey J. Oliker, "Does Welfare Work? Evaluation Research and Welfare Policy," *Social Problems* 41 (1994): 195–213.

40. Catherine S. Chilman, "Welfare Reform or Revision? The Family Support Act of 1988," *Social Service Review* 66 (1992): 353. See also Mark Rom, "The Family Support Act of 1988: Federalism, Developmental Policy, and Welfare Reform," *Publius* 19 (1989): 59; Peter L. Szanton, "The Remarkable 'Quango': Knowledge, Politics, and Welfare Reform," *Journal of Policy Analysis and Management* 10 (1991): 590–602.

41. Baum, "When the Witch Doctors Agree," 608.

42. Quoted in Julie Kosterlitz, "Transforming Theories into Legislation That'll Fly," *National Journal,* 27 February 1988, 543.

43. Ron Haskins, "Congress Writes a Law: Research and Welfare Reform," *Journal of Policy Analysis and Management* 10 (1991): 628. William Epstein argues that the influence of social-science research in welfare policy may not be illuminating. He charges that evaluation research, which was represented prominently in MDRC's studies of state reform initiatives, typically "ends up as advocate and spokesperson, an agent for the reigning orthodoxy." William M. Epstein, *Welfare*

in America: How Social Science Fails the Poor (Madison: University of Wisconsin Press, 1997), 179.

44. Handler, *Poverty of Welfare Reform,* 64–67.

45. Ken Auletta, *The Underclass* (New York: Random House, 1982), xvi. For a cogent explication of the emergence of the phrase, see Herbert J. Gans, *The War Against the Poor: The Underclass and Antipoverty Policy* (New York: Basic Books, 1995), 27–53. Gans explains that media usage of the term, as measured by its appearance in a sample of major newspapers and newsmagazines, peaked between 1985 and 1990.

46. William Julius Wilson, *The Truly Disadvantaged: The Inner City, the Underclass, and Public Policy* (Chicago: University of Chicago Press, 1987), 7, 8. Wilson announced in his 1990 presidential address to the American Sociological Association that he had decided to replace the term "underclass" with "ghetto poor" in his work. Wilson explained that his decision arose from a concern that debates over the appropriateness of the term "underclass" distracted media and scholarly attention from important research issues regarding urban poverty. William Julius Wilson, "Studying Inner-City Social Dislocations: The Challenge of Public Agenda Research," *American Sociological Review* 56 (1991): 6.

47. Douglas Muzzio, "The Urban Basement Revisited," *Urban Affairs Quarterly* 25 (1989): 354–55; Katz, *Undeserving Poor,* 234. See also Sanford F. Schram, *Words of Welfare: The Poverty of Social Science and the Social Science of Poverty* (Minneapolis: University of Minnesota Press, 1995), 15–16.

48. For a complete and detailed description of the provisions of the Family Support Act as well as its progress through Congress, see "After Years of Debate, Welfare Reform Clears," *Congressional Quarterly Almanac* 34 (1988): 349–64.

49. House Subcommittee, *Welfare Reform,* 548; *Congressional Record,* 100th Cong., 1st sess., 1987, 133, pt. 6:7764; Senate Subcommittee on Social Security and Family Policy of the Committee on Finance, *Welfare: Reform or Replacement? (Child Support Enforcement): Hearings before the Subcommittee on Social Security and Family Policy of the Committee on Finance,* 100th Cong., 1st sess., 1987, 183.

50. Senate Subcommittee, *Child Support Enforcement,* 65; Reagan, *Public Papers, 1988,* bk. 1:87; House Committee on Education and Labor, *Hearings on Welfare Reform: H.R. 30, Fair Work Opportunities Act of 1987 and H.R. 1720, Family Welfare Reform Act of 1987,* 100th Cong., 1st sess., 1987, 42.

51. House Committee, *Hearings on Welfare Reform,* 80; House Subcommittee, *Welfare Reform,* 281.

52. Senate Subcommittee, *Child Support Enforcement,* 43, 86, 157.

53. For Clinton's testimony, see House Committee, *Hearings on Welfare Reform,* 341. For objections to his position, see, e.g., House Subcommittee, *Welfare Reform,* 436.

54. Senate Committee on Finance, *Welfare Reform, Part 3: Hearing before the Committee on Finance,* 100th Cong., 2d sess., 1988, 38; *Congressional Record,* 100th Cong., 2d sess., 1988, 134, pt. 18:26578.

55. Johnson, *Public Papers,* 376.

56. Auletta, *Underclass,* 28, 47. Fearsome portrayals were not restricted to media accounts. For instance, in the introduction to a Brookings Institution publication, albeit one published after the 1988 Family Support Act, political scientist Paul E. Peterson wrote that the "under" in "underclass" connoted "the lowly, passive, and submissive, yet at the same time the disreputable, dangerous, disruptive, dark, evil, and even hellish." Peterson supported use of the term because it offered an explanation for the paradox of poverty in "an otherwise affluent society that seems to have made strenuous efforts to eradicate this problem." Paul E. Peterson, "The Urban Underclass and the Poverty Paradox," in *The Urban Underclass,* ed. Christopher Jencks and Paul E. Peterson (Washington, D.C.: Brookings Institution, 1991), 3, 4.

    Although they did so less enthusiastically, others supported usage of the term. For example, Richard Nathan, professor of public and international affairs at Princeton University, concluded that underclass "is an accurate and functional term and that we should use it in diagnosing and prescribing for American social problems in the current period." Nathan advanced one reason as "purely practical": "The word has caught on." Yet he also saw functional value in the term. He explained that "[t]he word *underclass* reflects a real and new condition in the society with which we must come to terms." Richard P. Nathan, "Will the Underclass Always Be with Us?" *Society* (March/April 1987): 57. A more narrowly circumscribed usage appears in William Kornblum, "Who Is the Underclass?" *Dissent* (spring 1991): 211. For an argument against scholarly usage, see Herbert J. Gans, *People, Plans, and Policies: Essays on Poverty, Racism, and Other National Urban Problems* (New York: Columbia University Press, 1991), 328–43.

57. Mickey Kaus, "The Work Ethic State," *New Republic,* 7 July 1986, 24, 22. Kaus's disapproval of the underclass and, in his view, its sustaining institutions intensified in his subsequent book *The End of Equality,* which appeared in the 1992 presidential election year. In this book, he charged that the underclass "most obviously sets in motion the vicious circle in which the degradation of public life in cities encourages the flight to the suburbs." The underclass "destroys the possibility of a sufficiently capacious civic sphere." For this reason, Kaus denounced the underclass as "a class whose values are so inimical to America's potential universal culture that its negation, and transformation, will allow those universal values to flower." Mickey Kaus, *The End of Equality* (New York: Basic Books, 1992), 104, 105. In *The End of Equality,* Kaus further developed his proposals, first expressed in the 1986 *New Republic* article, for transforming the welfare state into the "work ethic state."

58. Senate Subcommittee, *Child Support Enforcement,* 41, 46.

59. House Subcommittee, *Welfare Reform,* 557.

60. House Committee, *Hearings on Welfare Reform,* 339; Senate Committee, *Welfare Reform, Part 3,* 32.

61. On the demand for minimum benefits, see, e.g., House Committee, *Hearings on Welfare Reform,* 125. For Corman's testimony, see ibid., 76.

62. Ronald Reagan, *Public Papers of the Presidents of the United States: Ronald Reagan, 1987*, bk. 1 (Washington, D.C.: Government Printing Office, 1989), 116, 117.

63. Ibid., 118. Reagan did not dispense entirely with imputations of wrong-doing and images of undeservingness. He continued to tell stories of welfare cheats. In a 1986 interview with editors and broadcasters, for instance, Reagan recounted his experiences as governor of California. He stated that "we found that thousands of people who'd gotten the order to report for work never showed up, and we stopped their welfare checks. And we never had a single complaint. And the only thing I can conclude is that some people were collecting under more than one name, and when they had to show up in person, they couldn't do it." Reagan, *Public Papers, 1986*, bk. 1:189.

64. Senate Subcommittee, *Child Support Enforcement*, 279.

65. Senate Subcommittee on Social Security and Family Policy of the Committee on Finance, *Welfare: Reform or Replacement? (Work and Welfare): Hearing before the Subcommittee on Social Security and Family Policy of the Committee on Finance*, 100th Cong., 1st sess., 1987, 163.

66. Senate Subcommittee, *Child Support Enforcement*, 74; House Subcommittee, *Welfare Reform*, 573.

67. *Congressional Record*, 100th Cong., 2d sess., 1988, 134, pt. 18:26583; Senate Committee on Finance, *Welfare Reform, Part 1: Hearing before the Committee on Finance*, 100th Cong., 1st sess., 1987, 33.

68. Senate Committee on Finance, *Welfare Reform, Part 2: Hearings before the Committee on Finance*, 100th Cong., 1st sess., 1987, 56; Senate Subcommittee, *Work and Welfare*, 88.

69. Senate Subcommittee, *Work and Welfare*, 211.

70. Reagan, *Public Papers, 1987*, bk. 1:182; *Congressional Record*, 100th Cong., 2d sess., 1988, 134, pt. 11:14915.

71. House Subcommittee, *Welfare Reform*, 448; Senate Committee, *Welfare Reform, Part 2*, 39.

72. House Subcommittee on Public Assistance and Unemployment Compensation of the Committee on Ways and Means, *Family Welfare Reform Act: Hearings before the Subcommittee on Public Assistance and Unemployment Compensation of the Committee on Ways and Means*, 100th Cong., 1st sess., 1987, 263, 264.

73. House Committee, *Hearings on Welfare Reform*, 332. Detailing a history of unachieved goals, William Epstein offers a decidedly skeptical evaluation of welfare-to-work programs. He holds that these programs wrongly assume that an adequate number of jobs exist to employ program trainees. Or, in the absence of such jobs, these programs falsely assume "the presence of a sufficiently fluid market place that shares employment fairly among qualified applicants so that deprivation is not concentrated among particular individuals or groups." Epstein, *Welfare in America*, 142.

74. On the heterogeneity of the AFDC population, see, e.g., Senate Subcommittee, *Child Support Enforcement*, 242, 296.

75. Ibid., 66.

76. Senate Subcommittee on Social Security and Family Policy of the Committee on Finance, *Welfare Reform Hearings in New York City: Hearings before the Subcommittee on Social Security and Family Policy of the Committee on Finance*, 100th Cong., 1st sess., 1987, 42.

77. House Subcommittee, *Welfare Reform*, 107; Senate Subcommittee, *Work and Welfare*, 170; Senate Committee, *Welfare Reform, Part 2*, 83.

78. Senate Subcommittee, *Child Support Enforcement*, 63; House Subcommittee, *Welfare Reform*, 538.

79. House Committee, *Hearing on Welfare Reform*, 344; Senate Committee, *Welfare Reform, Part 3*, 52; House Committee, *Hearings on Welfare Reform*, 213.

80. Senate Committee, *Welfare Reform, Part 2*, 83; Senate Committee, *Welfare Reform, Part 1*, 101.

81. House Subcommittee, *Welfare Reform*, 508, 538–39.

82. Senate Subcommittee, *Work and Welfare*, 169.

83. House Committee, *Hearings on Welfare Reform*, 170; Senate Committee, *Welfare Reform, Part 3*, 53.

84. Senate Subcommittee, *Child Support Enforcement*, 87; House Subcommittee, *Welfare Reform*, 427.

85. House Subcommittee, *Welfare Reform*, 265. In a 1986 paper prepared for the Institute for Research on Poverty, David Ellwood confirmed this information. He noted that women heading households worked more than wives with children of similar ages. Moreover, working more than 1,500 hours annually remained the exception rather than the rule. Using figures between 1977 and 1981, Ellwood reported that only 23 percent of wives with children under six worked 1,500 hours or more annually. A greater percentage of female heads of households worked 1,500 hours or more — 37 percent — but they remained a minority. When he compared hours worked by female heads of households to hours worked by wives whose families would be poor if not for their income, Ellwood found that poor female heads worked more than poor wives. Twenty-four percent of poor wives with children under six worked 1,500 hours or more compared to 39 percent of poor female heads. David T. Ellwood, "Working Off of Welfare: Prospects and Policies for Self-Sufficiency of Women Heading Families," discussion paper 803–86, Institute for Research on Poverty, University of Wisconsin-Madison, 1986, 7–10.

86. House Subcommittee, *Welfare Reform*, 13.

87. House Subcommittee on Health and the Environment of the Committee on Energy and Commerce, *Medicaid Issues in Family Welfare and Nursing Home Reform: Hearings before the Subcommittee on Health and the Environment of the*

Committee on Energy and Commerce, 100th Cong., 1st sess., 1987, 17. See also, e.g., Senate Subcommittee, *Child Support Enforcement,* 75.

88. Senate Subcommittee on Social Security and Family Policy of the Committee on Finance, *Welfare: Reform or Replacement? (Child Support Enforcement II): Hearing before the Subcommittee on Social Security and Family Policy of the Committee on Finance,* 100th Cong., 1st sess., 1987, 93.

89. Senate Subcommittee, *Child Support Enforcement,* 43; Senate Subcommittee, *Child Support Enforcement II,* 207.

90. Senate Committee, *Welfare Reform, Part 2,* 27.

91. For Mattox's testimony, see Senate, *Welfare Reform, Part 3,* 8. For Moynihan's comments, see ibid., 55–56.

92. Senate Subcommittee, *Child Support Enforcement II,* 241.

93. Senate Committee, *Welfare Reform, Part 2,* 71; Senate Subcommittee, *Child Support Enforcement II,* 202.

94. Robert Kuttner, *Everything for Sale: The Virtues and Limits of Markets* (New York: Alfred A. Knopf, 1997), 41; Schram, *Words of Welfare,* 6.

95. Senate Committee, *Welfare Reform, Part 1,* 64.

96. Kuttner, *Everything for Sale,* 16–17.

97. Ibid., 41, 44.

98. *Congressional Record,* 100th Cong., 2d sess., 1988, 134, pt. 13:18073, 18075.

99. *Congressional Record,* 100th Cong., 2d sess., 1988, 134, pt. 18:26804, 26805.

100. Ibid., 26585; *Congressional Record,* 100th Cong., 2d sess., 1988, 134, pt. 19:27185.

101. Jean-François Lyotard, *The Postmodern Condition: A Report on Knowledge,* trans. Geoff Bennington and Brian Massumi (Minneapolis: University of Minnesota Press, 1984), 61.

102. There is a strand of rhetorical theory that opposes every consensus with another consensus. Barry Brummett argues that "one *can never* disprove one consensus without invoking meanings generated by some *other* consensus." Some have objected that this consensus theory provides little space for dissent. Brummett replies: "[O]ne has a wide variety of groups with which one *could* identify. People are *persuaded* to rally with one consensus or another. Although one often *does* agree with the majority of those in one's consensual groups, nobody argues that one *should.*" Brummett's usage invokes consensus as a kind of shorthand for the social construction of reality. This expansive view may not elucidate the significance of consensus in the reform debates and other controversies. Barry Brummett, "On to Rhetorical Relativism," *Quarterly Journal of Speech* 68 (1982): 427, 428. For objections to this theory of consensus, see, e.g., Earl Croasmun, "Realism and the Rhetoric of Assent," in *Argumentation Theory and the Rhetoric of Assent,* ed. David Cratis Williams and Michael David Hazen (Tuscaloosa: University of Alabama Press, 1990), 35–37.

103. Lyotard, *Postmodern Condition,* 67.

104. Senate Committee, *Welfare Reform, Part 3,* 44.

105. Ibid., 64, 65.

106. Ibid., 66.

107. House Subcommittee, *Welfare Reform,* 466, 495.

108. Ibid., 463; Senate Subcommittee, *Child Support Enforcement,* 274. Michael Katz praises *Economic Justice for All* as "the most comprehensive, articulate, and humane recent dissection of the ways in which America's economy generates poverty." Katz, *Undeserving Poor,* 180. See National Conference of Catholic Bishops, *Economic Justice for All: Pastoral Letter on Catholic Social Teaching and the U.S. Economy,* 10th anniversary ed. (Washington, D.C.: United States Catholic Conference, 1997).

109. Jesse Jackson, "Common Ground and Common Sense," *Vital Speeches of the Day,* 15 August 1988, 653, 652.

110. William J. Clinton, *Public Papers of the Presidents of the United States: William J. Clinton, 1993,* bk. 1 (Washington, D.C.: Government Printing Office, 1994), 33.

111. Handler, *Poverty of Welfare Reform,* 76–81. Handler noted the gaps in national reporting on the efficacy of JOBS programs: "no information on whether participation has led to changes in employment, in average entry wages, in retention rates, in benefits, in gains from education, or even in the effectiveness of the use of sanctions." Ibid., 80.

CHAPTER FIVE

1. On the preemptive quality of healthcare debates, see Daniel Patrick Moynihan, *Miles to Go: A Personal History of Social Policy* (Cambridge: Harvard University Press, 1996), 29.

2. Jeffrey L. Katz, "Welfare Overhaul Law," *CQ Weekly,* 21 September 1996, 2696.

3. For an extensive summary of the PRWORA's provisions from the House committee responsible for many of the major elements of U.S. social welfare policy, see House Committee on Ways and Means, *Summary of Welfare Reforms Made by Public Law 104–193 the Personal Responsibility and Work Opportunity Reconciliation Act and Associated Legislation,* 104th Cong., 2d sess., 1996, Committee Print 15. For a thorough, non-governmental explication of its provisions, see Mark Greenberg and Steve Savner, "A Detailed Summary of Key Provisions of the Temporary Assistance for Needy Families Block Grant of H.R. 3734," Center for Law and Social Policy, Washington, D.C., 1996. As Handler and Hasenfeld note, the implications of this repeal are far-reaching: "Presumably, states are free to determine which families receive assistance, how much, and under what circumstances; if a state runs out of funds, applicants can be placed on waiting lists or rejected." Joel F. Handler and Yeheskel Hasenfeld, *We the Poor People: Work, Poverty, Welfare* (New Haven, Conn.: Yale University Press, 1997), 6. Jencks observes that the legislation, by withdrawing open-ended federal matching funds, increases the cost of state altruism from between twenty to fifty cents for

every dollar allocated to a full dollar payment. Christopher Jencks, "The Hidden Paradox of Welfare Reform," *American Prospect* (May-June 1997): 34. For a succinct, cogent elucidation focused on the block grant and work provisions of the PRWORA, see Rebecca Blank, "The 1996 Welfare Reform," *Journal of Economic Perspectives* 11 (1997): 169–77. Blank identifies four key future research areas implicated by the legislation: women's employability, job availability, effects of increased parental work on child well-being, and effects of block grants on state fiscal situations and spending patterns. For an explication and critique of the work provisions of the PRWORA as a distraction from a policy focus on the health and nurturing of children, see Morton S. Baratz and Sammis B. White, "Childfare: A New Direction for Welfare Reform," *Urban Studies* 33 (1996): 1935–44.

4. Julie Kosterlitz, "Reworking Welfare," *National Journal*, 26 September 1992, 2190.

5. Jeffrey L. Katz, "Clinton Plans Major Shift in Lives of Poor People," *CQ Weekly*, 22 January 1994, 121.

6. Kitty Dumas, "States Bypassing Congress in Reforming Welfare," *CQ Weekly*, 11 April 1992, 951; Julie Kosterlitz, "Behavior Modification," *National Journal*, 2 February 1992, 272–73.

7. Quoted in Kosterlitz, "Behavior Modification," 273.

8. Quoted in John Aloysius Farrell, "Welfare Battlefield; Bush Stakes Out Issue by Attacking 'Cycle of Dependency,'" *Boston Globe,* 19 April 1992, city edition, national/foreign sec., 1.

9. Quoted in Dumas, "States Bypassing Congress," 951.

10. Quoted in Ann Devroy, "White House Blames Liberal Programs for Unrest; 'Great Society' Initiatives Started in 1960s Are at Root of Many Problems, Fitzwater Says," *Washington Post*, 5 May 1992, late edition, A8. For a detailed description of the incident, which was videotaped by a witness and broadcast on national television within hours of its occurrence, as well as the debate it sparked regarding police use of excessive force toward African Americans, see Alex Prud'Homme, "Police Brutality!" *Time,* 25 March 1991, 16–19.

11. Quoted in Michael Wines, "White House Links Riots to Welfare," *New York Times,* 5 May 1992, late edition, A1.

12. Wines, "White House Links Riots," A1; Devroy, "White House Blames Liberal Programs," A8. For an example of coverage of Clinton's response, see Dan Balz, "Clinton Rips White House Response; Social Programs Not at Fault, He Says," *Washington Post*, 6 May 1992, final edition, A9.

13. Benjamin I. Page, *Who Deliberates? Mass Media in Modern Democracy* (Chicago: University of Chicago Press, 1996), 59.

14. Cynthia Tucker, "Bush Plays Partisan Politics," *Atlanta Journal and Constitution,* 6 May 1992, A15; Mary McGrory, "Bush's No-Show on Los Angeles," *Washington Post,* 5 May 1992, final edition, A2.

15. David Nyhan, "Reconstructing a Multiracial Community; Politicking Amid the Rubble," *Boston Globe,* 7 May 1992, city edition, op-ed sec., 15; Kenneth R. Walker, "'I Got the Breaks'—Federal Aid Can Help," *Christian Science Monitor,* 18 May 1992, 18.

16. "Fight for Mr. Bush's Mind," *New York Times,* 5 May 1992, late edition, A30; "White House Responds," *Washington Post,* 5 May 1992, final edition, A24.

17. "Playing Politics with a Tragedy; Bush Aide Lays Blame for Riots on Liberal Social Programs of the 60s and 70s," *Los Angeles Times,* 6 May 1992, Washington edition, B8; "War Against the Poor," *New York Times,* 6 May 1992, late edition, A28.

18. Lorrin Anderson, "Guilt and Gasoline," *National Review,* 8 June 1992, 35; Charles Murray, "Causes, Root Causes, and Cures," *National Review,* 8 June 1992, 32; Charles Murray, "The Legacy of the 60s," *Commentary* (July 1992): 23.

19. William J. Clinton, "We Offer Our People a New Choice Based on Old Values," *Washington Post,* 17 July 1992, final edition, A26; William J. Clinton, "Announcement Speech: Gov. Bill Clinton," appendix to *Putting People First: How We Can All Change America,* by Bill Clinton and Al Gore (New York: Times Books, 1992), 194.

20. Clinton and Gore, *Putting People First,* 165.

21. Ibid., 6.

22. Geoffrey Garin, Guy Molyneux, and Linda Divall, "Public Attitudes Toward Welfare Reform," *Social Policy* (winter 1994): 46–47.

23. Mickey Kaus, "Welfare Waffle: What's That Plan Again, Bill?" *New Republic,* 12 October 1992, 10. For further concerns about potential waffling, see David Whitman, "His Unconvincing Welfare Promises," *U.S. News and World Report,* 20 April 1992, 42.

24. House Select Committee on Hunger, *State and Local Perspectives on Welfare Reform: Rhetoric, Reality, and Opportunities: Hearing Before the Select Committee on Hunger,* 102d Cong., 2d sess., 1992, 7, 10.

25. House Select Committee on Hunger, *Beyond Public Assistance: Where Do We Go from Here?: Hearing before the Select Committee on Hunger,* 102d Cong., 2d sess., 1992, 1.

26. House Select Committee on Hunger, *Rethinking Poverty Policy: Hearing before the Select Committee on Hunger,* 102d Cong., 2d sess., 1992, 15–16.

27. House Select Committee, *Beyond Public Assistance,* 10, 14, 15.

28. Ibid., 21, 21–22.

29. House Select Committee on Hunger, *Federal Policy Perspectives on Welfare Reform: Rhetoric, Reality, and Opportunities: Hearing before the Select Committee on Hunger,* 102d Cong., 2d sess., 1992, 3; House Select Committee, *Beyond Public Assistance,* 3.

30. House Select Committee, *Federal Policy Perspectives,* 7.

31. On Burdick's resignation, see Kevin Sack, "The New, Volatile Politics of Welfare," *New York Times*, 15 March 1992, late edition, sec. 1, 24.

32. Jeffrey L. Katz, "Clinton's Welfare Reform Plan to Be Out in Fall, Aides Say," *CQ Weekly*, 10 July 1993, 1813.

33. Jeffrey L. Katz, "Welfare Overhaul Forces Ready to Start Without Clinton," *CQ Weekly*, 2 April 1994, 800–3.

34. Jeffrey L. Katz, "GOP's Two-Year Welfare Limit Sends Message to Clinton," *CQ Weekly*, 13 November 1993, 3131.

35. Jeffrey L. Katz, "Long-Awaited Welfare Proposal Would Make Gradual Changes," *CQ Weekly*, 18 June 1994, 1622–24.

36. Quoted in Jeffrey L. Katz, "Welfare Issue Finds Home on the Campaign Trail," *CQ Weekly*, 15 October 1994, 2957, 2958.

37. Clinton, *Public Papers, 1993*, bk. 1:33.

38. Ibid., 33, 35.

39. Ibid., 117, 192, 683.

40. Clinton, *Public Papers, 1993*, bk. 2:1420.

41. House Subcommittee on Human Resources of the Committee on Ways and Means, *Trends in Spending and Caseloads for AFDC and Related Programs: Hearing before the Subcommittee on Human Resources of the Committee on Ways and Means*, 103d Cong., 1st sess., 1993, 89; House Subcommittee on Human Resources of the Committee on Ways and Means, *Welfare Reform Proposals, Including H.R. 4605, the Work and Responsibility Act of 1994, Part 2: Hearings before the Subcommittee on Human Resources of the Committee on Ways and Means*, 103d Cong., 2d sess., 1994, 1159–60.

42. House Committee on Education and Labor, *Hearing on H.R. 4605, Work and Responsibility Act of 1994: Hearing before the Committee on Education and Labor*, 103d Cong., 2d sess., 1994, 115; House Subcommittee, *Work and Responsibility Act of 1994, Part 2*, 1107, 1145.

43. William J. Clinton, *Public Papers of the Presidents of the United States: William J. Clinton, 1994*, bk. 1 (Washington, D.C.: Government Printing Office, 1995), 156.

44. House Subcommittee on Human Resources of the Committee on Ways and Means, *Welfare Reform Proposals, Including H.R. 4605, the Work and Responsibility Act of 1994, Part 1: Hearings before the Subcommittee on Human Resources of the Committee on Ways and Means*, 103d Cong., 2d sess., 1994, 350, 357.

45. Senate Committee on Finance, *Work and Responsibility Act of 1994: Hearing before the Committee on Finance*, 103d Cong., 2d sess., 1994, 7, 18–19.

46. House Subcommittee, *Work and Responsibility Act of 1994, Part 1*, 525.

47. Senate Committee, *Work and Responsibility Act*, 11, 20.

48. House Subcommittee, *Work and Responsibility Act of 1994, Part 1*, 137, 328, 385. In their testimony, Bane and Ellwood advanced arguments presented in their co-authored book *Welfare Realities*, which was published in 1994. In *Welfare*

Realties, Bane and Ellwood support a shift in the culture of welfare administration from what they view as the "eligibility-compliance culture" of the 1970s and 1980s, prevalent before passage of the Family Support Act, to a "culture of self-sufficiency." They propose a number of strategies for promoting self-sufficiency among welfare recipients. Mary Jo Bane and David T. Ellwood, *Welfare Realities: From Rhetoric to Reform* (Cambridge: Harvard University Press, 1994), 19–27, 124–62.

49. Ibid., 525, 459, 465. Some policy analysts have embraced paternalism explicitly as a promising orientation for welfare reform. Lawrence Mead regards the paternalist character of 1990s reforms as a positive trend in welfare policy. Reiterating themes expressed in *Beyond Entitlement,* Mead compares paternalist policies favorably to traditional policies because they reject a philosophy of entitlement and demand instead that recipients satisfy particular behavioral requirements. Mead holds that potentially efficacious paternalism must exhibit two important qualities. First, such paternalism must be "directive." It "must tell the people obligated what they are supposed to do." Second, paternalism must judge recipient interests without hesitation. In this way, "[s]ociety claims the right to tell its dependents how to live, at least in some respects." Lawrence M. Mead, "The Rise of Paternalism," in *The New Paternalism: Supervisory Approaches to Poverty,* ed. Lawrence M. Mead (Washington, D.C.: Brookings Institution Press, 1997), 4.

50. House Committee, *Hearing on H.R. 4605,* 142; Senate Subcommittee on Social Security and Family Policy of the Committee on Finance, *Welfare Reform: Hearings before the Subcommittee on Social Security and Family Policy of the Committee on Finance,* 103d Cong., 2d sess., 1994, 93–94.

51. Kenneth J. Cooper and Eric Pianin, "GOP Rides Wave to Position of Power; Party Wins Needed Seats, Takes Charge for 1st Time in 40 Years," *Washington Post,* 9 November 1994, final edition, A21; Adam Clymer, "GOP Celebrates Its Sweep to Power; Clinton Vows to Find Common Ground," *New York Times,* 10 November 1994, late edition, A1.

52. Kenneth J. Cooper, "GOP Offers a 'Contract' to Revive Reagan Years," *Washington Post,* 28 September 1994, late edition, A1; "Republicans' Initial Promise: 100-Day Debate on 'Contract,'" *CQ Weekly,* 12 November 1994, 3216–19.

53. Quoted in David E. Rosenbaum, "Republicans Offer Voters a Deal for Takeover of House," *New York Times,* 28 September 1994, late edition, A16.

54. Albert Hunt, "The Republicans Shoot an Air Ball," *Wall Street Journal,* 22 September 1994, eastern edition, A11; Phillips quoted in George Hager, "Can GOP Count on Its Own to Back Its Ambitious Plan?" *CQ Weekly,* 1 October 1994, 2766.

55. "GOP's Deceptive Contract," *New York Times,* 28 September 1994, late edition, A20; "New Republican Plan," *Washington Post,* 28 September 1994, final edition, A22; Steve Daley, "GOP's Latest Financial Plan Recalls Those Debt-Ridden Days of the 1980s," *Chicago Tribune,* 25 September 1994, lake final edition, sec. 4, 4.

56. Quoted in Jonathan Alter, "Bracing for the Big One," *Newsweek,* 10 October 1994, 28.

57. Quoted in Paul Gigot, "GOP Actually Tries to Stand for Something," *Wall Street Journal,* 9 September 1994, eastern edition, A14.

58. Quoted in Ceci Connolly, "GOP Accentuates the Positive; Hopefuls to Sign Contract," *CQ Weekly,* 24 September 1994, 2712.

59. Alter, "Bracing for the Big One," 28.

60. Quoted in Jeff Shear, "The Santa Clauses," *National Journal,* 22 October 1994, 2452.

61. Cooper and Pianin, "GOP Rides Wave," A21; quoted in Kenneth J. Cooper, "Gingrich: 'Cooperation, Yes. Compromise, No,'" *Washington Post,* 12 November 1994, final edition, A1.

62. Lydia Saad, "'Contract with America' Still Little Known, but Goals Have Widespread Appeal," *Gallup Poll Monthly* (December 1994): 8; David W. Moore, Lydia Saad, Leslie McAneny, and Frank Newport, "Contract with America," *Gallup Poll Monthly* (November 1994): 22.

63. Dave Kaplan, "This Year, Republicans Gamble That All Politics Is Local," *CQ Weekly,* 22 October 1994, 3008. See also Juliana Gruenwald, "Shallow Tactics or Deep Issues: Fathoming the GOP 'Contract,'" *CQ Weekly,* 19 November 1994, 3361–62.

64. R. Kent Weaver, Robert Y. Shapiro, and Lawrence R. Jacobs, "The Polls—Trends: Welfare," *Public Opinion Quarterly* 59 (1995): 623–24.

65. Charles Noble, *Welfare as We Knew It: A Political History of the American Welfare State* (New York: Oxford University Press, 1997), 127–28; Gary Bryner, *Politics and Public Morality: The Great American Welfare Reform Debate* (New York: W. W. Norton, 1998), 108.

66. Jeffrey L. Katz, "Governors Group Sidelined in Welfare Debate," *CQ Weekly,* 20 May 1995, 1423–25.

67. Quoted in Jeffrey L. Katz, "Senate Overhaul Plan Provides Road Map for Compromise," *CQ Weekly,* 23 September 1995, 2908.

68. Jeffrey L. Katz, "GOP's New Welfare Strategy Has Democrats Reassessing," *CQ Weekly,* 13 July 1996, 1969–70.

69. Discussions within the administration leading up to Clinton's announcement produced sharp disagreements among cabinet officers and other presidential advisors. Labor Secretary Robert Reich recounted a meeting on the day of the announcement during which most of the cabinet officers asserted firm views against signing, while most of the political advisors advanced their strong support. Those opposed to the bill stressed its potential to harm children. When queried by the president, Reich maintained that "signing this bill would violate everything we stood for." Robert B. Reich, *Locked in the Cabinet* (New York: Alfred A. Knopf, 1997), 321. Presidential advisor George Stephanopoulos characterized the atmosphere in the meeting room on that day as "consciously statesmanlike, as if we were gathered for a council of war." George Stephanopoulos, *All Too Human: A Political Education* (Boston: Little, Brown, 1999), 420.

Though not present at the 31 July meeting, political strategist Dick Morris
warned Clinton in the days leading up to the announcement that a veto would
prove costly for his re-election. Morris recounted: "I told him flatly that a welfare veto would cost him the election." Dick Morris, *Behind the Oval Office:
Winning the Presidency in the Nineties* (New York: Random House, 1997), 300.
During the meeting, Stephanopoulos rejected this forecast. He retorted that a
veto may cause a "quick five- or six-point drop" in Clinton's polling numbers,
but "it would never cost us the race." Stephanopoulos, *All Too Human,* 421.

70. House Committee on Ways and Means, *Contract with America — Overview: Hear-
    ings before the Committee on Ways and Means,* 104th Cong., 1st sess., 1995, 12.

71. Ibid., 13.

72. Ibid., 14.

73. Senate Committee on Finance, *States' Perspective on Welfare Reform: Hearing be-
    fore the Committee on Finance,* 104th Cong., 1st sess., 1995, 2.

74. House Committee, *Contract with America — Overview,* 20; Senate Committee on
    Agriculture, Nutrition, and Forestry, *Federal Nutrition Programs: Hearing before
    the Committee on Agriculture, Nutrition, and Forestry,* 104th Cong., 1st sess., 1995,
    63.

75. *Congressional Record,* 104th Cong., 1st sess., 1995, 141, pt. 7:9194, 9200.

76. Ibid., 9200, 9198. Ruth Sidel echoes Frank's denunciation of the alligator analogy
    as "dehumanizing and degrading" in her discussion of the incident. Ruth Sidel,
    Keeping Women and Children Last: America's War on the Poor (New York: Pen-
    guin Books, 1996), 7–8.

77. House Subcommittee on Human Resources of the Committee on Ways and
    Means, *Contract with America — Welfare Reform, Part 2: Hearing before the Sub-
    committee on Human Resources of the Committee on Ways and Means,* 104th
    Cong., 1st sess., 1995, 852; Senate Committee on Finance, *Broad Policy Goals of
    Welfare Reform: Hearing before the Committee on Finance,* 104th Cong., 1st sess.,
    1995, 5; House Subcommittee on Human Resources of the Committee on Ways
    and Means, *Contract with America — Welfare Reform, Part 1: Hearing before the
    Subcommittee on Human Resources of the Committee on Ways and Means,* 104th
    Cong., 1st sess., 1995, 157.

78. House Subcommittee, *Contract with America — Welfare Reform, Part 2,* 869; Sen-
    ate Committee on Finance, *Child Support Enforcement: Hearing before the
    Committee on Finance,* 104th Cong., 1st sess., 1995, 38.

79. House Subcommittee, *Contract with America — Welfare Reform, Part 1,* 196–97.
    For a widely cited study of the relations between AFDC payments and family
    structure, see David T. Ellwood and Mary Jo Bane, "The Impact of AFDC on
    Family Structure and Living Arrangements," *Research in Labor Economics* 7
    (1985): 137–207. For an extensive summary of recent economics literature on
    welfare benefits' "effects on labor supply," see Robert Moffitt, "Incentive Effects
    of the U.S. Welfare System: A Review," *Journal of Economic Literature* 30
    (1992): 1–61.

Other scholars also have rejected the idea of a "welfare trap." For example, reviewing data on the duration of "welfare participation" among recipients, Peter Gottschalk, Sara McLanahan, and Gary Sandefur conclude that a view of welfare as "a trap from which there is no escape is clearly inconsistent with the facts." Peter Gottschalk, Sara McLanahan, and Gary D. Sandefur, "The Dynamics and Intergenerational Transmission of Poverty and Welfare Participation," in *Confronting Poverty: Prescriptions for Change,* ed. Sheldon H. Danziger, Gary D. Sandefur, and Daniel H. Weinberg (Cambridge: Harvard University Press, 1994), 97. Christopher Jencks approaches the notion of a "welfare trap" by redirecting attention to the shortcomings of the low-wage labor market: "The essence of the 'welfare trap' is not that welfare warps women's personalities or makes them pathologically dependent, though that may occasionally happen. The essence of the trap is that, although welfare pays badly, low-wage jobs pay even worse." Christopher Jencks, *Rethinking Social Policy: Race, Poverty, and the Underclass* (New York: HarperCollins, 1993), 225.

80. Senate Committee on Finance, *Welfare Reform — Views of Interested Organizations: Hearing before the Committee on Finance,* 104th Cong., 1st sess., 1995, 10. Kristin Luker notes that the birth patterns of poor and affluent women in the U.S. have bifurcated, paralleling the new bifurcated economy in which good jobs get better and bad jobs get worse. Luker explains that poor women, who have fewer educational and career opportunities available to them, have continued the traditional American pattern of early childbearing while affluent women now tend to wait until they are well established in the labor force before having a child. Luker, *Dubious Conceptions,* 105, 170.

81. Senate Committee on Governmental Affairs, *Reinventing Government: Hearings before the Committee on Governmental Affairs,* 104th Cong., 1st sess., 1995, 71; House Committee on Economic and Educational Opportunities, *Hearing on the Contract with America: Nutrition, the Local Perspective: Hearing before the Committee on Economic and Educational Opportunities,* 104th Cong., 1st sess., 1995, 119; House Subcommittee, *Contract with America — Welfare Reform, Part 1,* 134.

82. House Subcommittee, *Contract with America — Welfare Reform, Part 1,* 540; Senate Committee, *States' Perspective,* 37

83. House Subcommittee on Human Resources of the Committee on Ways and Means, *Child Support Enforcement Provisions Included in the Personal Responsibility Act as Part of the CWA: Hearing before the Subcommittee on Human Resources of the Committee on Ways and Means,* 104th Cong., 1st sess., 1995, 186, 97.

84. House Subcommittee, *Contract with America — Welfare Reform, Part 2,* 823; House Subcommittee on Human Resources of the Committee on Ways and Means, *Causes of Poverty, with a Focus on Out-of-Wedlock Births: Hearing before the Subcommittee on Human Resources of the Committee on Ways and Means,* 104th Cong., 2d sess., 1996, 96.

85. House Subcommittee, *Child Support Enforcement Provisions,* 195; Senate Committee, *Child Support Enforcement,* 7.

86. House Subcommittee, *Contract with America — Welfare Reform, Part 1*, 6, 24; House Committee, *Contract with America — Overview*, 97.

87. House Subcommittee, *Contract with America — Welfare Reform, Part 1*, 80; House Committee on Commerce, *The Unanimous Bipartisan National Governors Association Agreement on Medicaid: Hearings before the Committee on Commerce*, 104th Cong., 2d sess., 1996, 100.

88. House Subcommittee, *Contract with America — Welfare Reform, Part 1*, 34; Senate Committee, *Reinventing Government*, 71; House Subcommittee, *Contract with America — Welfare Reform, Part 1*, 239.

89. House Subcommittee, *Contract with America — Welfare Reform, Part 1*, 89. Olasky exaggerates considerably the successes of nineteenth-century social policy, and he ignores many of its most notorious practices, such as eugenics and family break-up. Michael Katz elucidates cogently the limitations of private charity as an often inadequate and inappropriate response to poverty. In the introduction to his highly regarded *In the Shadow of the Poorhouse*, Katz identifies as one of the most important themes in his historical survey the unequivocal lesson that "[v]oluntarism never was and never will be an adequate answer to the problem of dependence." Katz, *Shadow of the Poorhouse*, xiii. For Olasky's version of nineteenth-century social policy, see Marvin Olasky, *The Tragedy of American Compassion* (Washington, D.C.: Regnery Gateway, 1992). For other, less celebratory descriptions of nineteenth-century poverty practices, see, e.g., Anthony Brundage, *The Making of the New Poor Law: The Politics of Inquiry, Enactment, and Implementation, 1832–1839* (New Brunswick, N.J.: Rutgers University Press, 1978); Derek Fraser, ed., *The New Poor Law in the Nineteenth Century* (New York: St. Martin's Press, 1976).

90. House Subcommittee, *Contract with America — Welfare Reform, Part 1*, 89, 90.

91. House Subcommittee on Department Operations, Nutrition, and Foreign Agriculture of the Committee on Agriculture, *Reforming the Present Welfare System: Hearing before the Subcommittee on Department Operations, Nutrition, and Foreign Agriculture of the Committee on Agriculture*, 104th Cong., 1st sess., 1995, 546, 547. For an introduction to the Christian Right, see Clyde Wilcox, *Onward Christian Soldiers? The Religious Right in American Politics* (Boulder, Colo.: Westview Press, 1996).

92. House Subcommittee, *Reforming the Present Welfare System*, 547; House Subcommittee, *Contract with America — Welfare Reform, Part 1*, 210.

93. House Subcommittee, *Contract with America — Welfare Reform, Part 1*, 210–11.

94. House Subcommittee, *Reforming the Present Welfare System*, 548, 567.

95. Ibid., 556.

96. House Subcommittee, *Contract with America — Welfare Reform, Part 1*, 764, 736.

97. Ibid., 548. Lester Salaman argues that strict separations of private charity and public services ignore actually existing welfare practice that operates through an elaborate network of partnerships linking government and the nonprofit sector. He notes that "[s]o extensive are these arrangements, in fact, that in a number

of human service fields — such as health and social services — nonprofit organizations actually deliver a larger share of the services government finances than do government agencies themselves." Lester M. Salaman, *Partners in Public Service: Government-Nonprofit Relations in the Modern Welfare State* (Baltimore, Md.: Johns Hopkins University Press, 1995), 34.

98. House Subcommittee, *Contract with America — Welfare Reform, Part 1*, 11. In response to Engler's claims, some committee members objected that much of the caseload "reduction" in Michigan had been achieved by shifting AFDC recipients to Supplement Security Income, thus shifting costs from a program funded jointly by state and federal governments to one funded exclusively by the federal government.

99. House Subcommittee, *Contract with America — Welfare Reform, Part 1*, 12, 24.

100. Ibid., 42, 44.

101. House Subcommittee on Human Resources of the Committee on Ways and Means, *The National Governors' Association Welfare Reform Proposal: Hearing before the Subcommittee on Human Resources of the Committee on Ways and Means*, 104th Cong., 2d sess., 1996, 34; House Committee, *Unanimous Bipartisan*, 150.

102. On the efficacy of such proposals, Kristin Moore, executive director and director of research for Child Trends, responded emphatically that denying welfare benefits to teen parents and their children "will have little effect on the sexual behavior of adolescent girls, in part because their pregnancies are unintended, in part because cutting benefits has no effect on the incentives faced by their male partners, and in part because the research literature so clearly identifies other factors as the underlying causes of early sexual initiation and pregnancy." Moore identified economic and educational opportunity as strong predictors of early childbearing. Senate Committee on Finance, *Teen Parents and Welfare Reform: Hearing before the Committee on Finance*, 104th Cong., 1st sess., 1995, 10.

103. House Subcommittee, *Contract with America — Welfare Reform, Part 1*, 661; Senate Finance Committee, *Welfare Reform Wrap-Up: Hearing before the Committee on Finance*, 104th Cong., 1st sess., 1995, 52.

104. House Committee, *Unanimous Bipartisan*, 202; Senate Committee, *States' Perspective*, 21.

105. House Subcommittee, *Contract with America — Welfare Reform, Part 2*, 960; House Committee, *Contract with America — Overview*, 114.

106. Senate Committee, *Welfare Reform Wrap-Up*, 29, 43.

107. Ibid., 31.

108. House Subcommittee, *Contract with America — Welfare Reform, Part 1*, 171; House Subcommittee, *Contract with America — Welfare Reform, Part 2*, 866.

109. House Subcommittee on Human Resources of the Committee on Ways and Means, *Welfare Reform Success Stories: Hearing before the Subcommittee on Human Resources of the Committee on Ways and Means*, 104th Cong., 1st sess., 1995, 53; Senate Committee, *Broad Policy Goals*, 44.

110. Michael Walzer, *What It Means to Be an American: Essays on the American Experience* (New York: Marsilio, 1996), 45. See also John Higham, *Send to These Me: Jews and Other Immigrants in Urban America* (New York: Atheneum, 1975).

111. Michael Paul Rogin, *"Ronald Reagan," the Movie and Other Episodes in Political Demonology* (Berkeley: University of California Press, 1987), 273–74. For a classic analysis of the perception of threat and its consequent xenophobic portrayal of immigrants, see Richard Hofstadter, *The Paranoid Style in American Politics and Other Essays* (New York: Alfred A. Knopf, 1965), 54–60. Hofstadter considers hostility toward immigrants as part of a larger study of the "paranoid style" in U.S. politics. He describes the "paranoid style" as a "way of seeing the world and expressing oneself" in which "the feeling of persecution is central, and it is indeed systematized in grandiose theories of conspiracy." In contrast to the clinical paranoiac, however, who "sees the hostile and conspiratorial world in which he feels himself to be living as directed specifically *against him,*" the spokesperson of the paranoid style "finds it directed against a nation, a culture, a way of life whose fate affects not himself alone but millions of others." Hofstadter, *Paranoid Style,* 4. For a cogent summary and trenchant critique of this area of historiographical scholarship, see Rogin, *"Ronald Reagan,"* 272–81.

112. Lawrence, "Relation of Wealth," 74; *Bulletin* quoted in Kitty Calavita, "The New Politics of Immigration: 'Balanced-Budget Conservatism' and the Symbolism of Proposition 187," *Social Problems* 43 (1996): 287; Roosevelt, "Americanism," 16, 18.

113. Michael Peter Smith and Bernadette Tarallo, "Proposition 187: Global Trend or Local Narrative? Explaining Anti-Immigration Politics in California, Arizona, and Texas," *International Journal of Urban and Regional Research* 19 (1995): 666.

114. Quoted in Jean Stefancic and Richard Delgado, *No Mercy: How Conservative Think Tanks and Foundations Have Changed America's Social Agenda* (Philadelphia: Temple University Press, 1996), 21.

115. Ibid., 30.

116. Calavita, "New Politics of Immigration," 285.

117. Saskia Sassen, *Losing Control? Sovereignty in an Age of Economic Globalization* (New York: Columbia University Press, 1996), 21. Frances Fox Piven and Richard Cloward argue that globalization, as an explanation of contemporary economic developments, "has become a political force, helping to create the institutional realities it purportedly merely describes." They maintain that "globalization is as much political strategy as economic imperative." Piven and Cloward contend that this strategy has negative consequences for less powerful political actors, for it constrains workers who wish to negotiate with corporations and reduces voter influence over national governments. Frances Fox Piven and Richard A. Cloward, *The Breaking of the American Social Compact* (New York: New Press, 1997), 3.

118. Senate Committee on the Budget, *Concurrent Resolution on the Budget for Fiscal Year 1996: Hearings before the Committee on the Budget,* 104th Cong., 1st sess., 1995, 141; House Subcommittee, *Contract with America—Welfare Reform, Part 1,* 475.

119. House Subcommittee on Human Resources of the Committee on Ways and Means, *Impact of Immigration on Welfare Programs: Hearing before the Subcommittee on Human Resources of the Committee on Ways and Means*, 103d Cong., 1st sess., 1993, 84, 30. Other participants countered claims of negative net expenditures for immigrants. For instance, Michael Fix of the Urban Institute highlighted for the subcommittee important "myths and new realities" underlying the convergence of welfare and immigration policy. Fix explained that, "contrary to popular belief, the great majority of immigrants in the United States are here with the nation's expressed consent." Fix explicated several flaws in studies of the costs of immigration: understated tax collections, overstated expenditures, uncounted revenues from immigrant-owned businesses, uncounted immigrant consumer spending, and silence on the net tax use of immigrants *and* natives. House Subcommittee, *Impact of Immigration*, 67–68.

120. Senate Committee on Finance, *Growth of the Supplemental Security Income Program: Hearing before the Committee on Finance*, 104th Cong., 1st sess., 1995, 5, 20; House Subcommittee, *Impact of Immigration*, 917; Senate Committee, *Growth of the Supplemental*, 11.

121. Senate Committee, *Growth of the Supplemental*, 12. Opponents claimed that this position ignored the unattainability of citizenship for some elderly legal immigrants. Diana Aviv, director of the Washington Office of the Council of Jewish Federations, explained to the Human Resources Subcommittee in 1993 that for "more than 60 percent of these legal older immigrants, naturalization is all but impossible since they are unable to master English sufficiently well at their age to pass the exam for citizenship." House Subcommittee, *Impact of Immigration*, 1043.

122. Senate Committee, *Welfare Reform Wrap-Up*, 21.

123. Sassen, *Losing Control?*, 38.

124. House Subcommittee, *Contract with America — Welfare Reform, Part I*, 359–60, 438.

125. Ibid., 364.

126. House Subcommittee, *Contract with America — Welfare Reform, Part 2*, 1071.

127. House Committee on Agriculture, *Enforcement of the Food Stamp Program: Hearing before the Committee on Agriculture*, 104th Cong., 1st sess., 1995, 19, 70.

128. For these observations, see, e.g., House Subcommittee on Oversight and Subcommittee on Human Resources of the Committee on Ways and Means, *Earned Income Tax Credit: Hearing before the Subcommittee on Oversight and the Subcommittee on Human Resources of the Committee on Ways and Means*, 104th Cong., 1st sess., 1995, 15, 104.

129. Senate Committee on Governmental Affairs, *Earned Income Tax Credit: Hearings before the Committee on Governmental Affairs*, 104th Cong., 1st sess., 1995, 116, 26.

130. House Subcommittee on Human Resources and Intergovernmental Relations of the Committee on Government Operations, *Ending Welfare as We Know It: Progress or Paralysis? Hearing before the Subcommittee on Human Resources and*

Intergovernmental Relations of the Committee on Governmental Operations, 103d Cong., 2d sess., 1994, 13

131. House Subcommittee, *Contract with America—Welfare Reform, Part 2,* 1004, 1090, 1101.

132. House Subcommittee, *Contract with America—Welfare Reform, Part 2,* 1091, 992; House Subcommittee, *Ending Welfare,* 55.

133. Senate Subcommittee, *Welfare Reform,* 91; House Subcommittee, *Contract with America—Welfare Reform, Part 2,* 1045.

134. House Subcommittee, *National Governors' Association,* 90; House Subcommittee, *Contract with America—Welfare Reform, Part 2,* 1225.

135. House Subcommittee, *Ending Welfare,* 52.

136. T. H. Marshall and Tom Bottomore, *Citizenship and Social Class* (London: Pluto Press, 1992), 8. For a contemporary analysis employing Marshall's terms, see Fraser and Gordon, "Contract Versus Charity," 45–67.

137. Sassen, *Losing Control?,* 37–38.

138. William J. Clinton, *Public Papers of the Presidents of the United States: William J. Clinton, 1995,* bk. 1 (Washington, D.C.: Government Printing Office, 1996), 76, 77.

139. Ibid., 314, 336, 603.

140. William J. Clinton, *Public Papers of the Presidents of the United States: William J. Clinton, 1996,* bk. 1 (Washington, D.C.: Government Printing Office, 1997), 79. Emphasis added.

141. Clinton, *Public Papers, 1996,* bk. 2:1121.

142. Ibid., 1234. In this way, Clinton articulated the reasoning of other initially hesitant supporters. During House floor debates, Rep. Barbara Kennelly explained to her colleagues that "we have to decide if this legislation as a whole represents an improvement over the status quo." Kennelly answered in the affirmative. During Senate floor debates, Sen. Ron Wyden admitted frankly that he "detested" a few provisions in the bill. Still, he countered that it offered Congress an opportunity "to remake this system that doesn't work." *Congressional Record,* 104th Cong., 2d sess., 1996, 142, pt. 15:20717, 20898.

143. Clinton, *Public Papers, 1996,* bk. 2:1236.

144. Ibid., 1326, 1327. Others also regarded the legislation as a new start—but of something very different. Senator Moynihan argued that a more accurate description of the bill would be welfare repeal, not reform. He denounced the legislation as "the first step in dismantling the social contract that has been in place in the United States since at least the 1930s. Do not doubt that Social Security itself ... will be next." *Congressional Record,* 104th Cong., 2d sess., 1996, 142, pt. 15:20901.

CHAPTER SIX

1. Senate Subcommittee, *Child Support Enforcement*, 7.

2. House Subcommittee, *Administration's Proposed Savings*, 321; Clinton, *Public Papers, 1994*, bk. 1:156.

3. Children's Bureau, *Mothers' Aid*, 13.

4. Gordon, *Pitied but Not Entitled*, 275; Quadagno, *Color of Welfare*, 19–25.

5. Racial lenses have been widened in part by visual depictions through mass media channels. In a revealing analysis of pictures of poor people that appeared in the national newsweeklies *Time, Newsweek,* and *U.S. News and World Report* between 1950 and 1992, Martin Gilens reaches two troubling, but not unexpected, conclusions. First, black people were overrepresented among the poor. They appeared in 53.4 percent of the pictures though their proportion among the poor during this period was 29.3 percent. Second, as the negative tone of the coverage of poverty increased, so too did the percentage of blacks pictured, and as the negative tone of the coverage decreased, so too did the percentage of blacks among pictures of the poor. So, for example, in the years 1972–73, as expansionist-era concerns about rising welfare costs and caseloads swelled in the aftermath of the failed FAP, the percentage of blacks pictured topped 70 percent. As the economic downturn of the mid-1970s took hold and a focus on unemployment increasingly occupied magazine articles, however, the percentage of blacks pictured dropped to 49 percent. Martin Gilens, *Why Americans Hate Welfare: Race, Media, and the Politics of Antipoverty Policy* (Chicago: University of Chicago Press, 1999), 114, 122–25.

6. This interviewee and two others whom I quote in this chapter appear anonymously to avoid hindering any ongoing or future advocacy efforts. This quote and the quotes of the other two witnesses are taken from transcripts of telephone discussions, which the interviewees permitted me to record.

7. Oskar Negt and Alexander Kluge, *Public Sphere and Experience: Toward an Analysis of the Bourgeois and Proletarian Public Sphere,* trans. Peter Labanyi, Jamie Owen Daniel, and Assenka Oksiloff (Minneapolis: University of Minnesota Press, 1993), 12–18.

8. House Subcommittee, *Welfare Reform Success Stories*, 58.

9. Bessette, *Mild Voice of Reason*, 157.

10. Although the total number of recipients increased from 14.11 million in 1993 to 14.27 million in 1994, the ACF considered changes in state and aggregate caseloads between 1993 and 1999. Department of Health and Human Services, Administration for Children and Families, *Temporary Assistance for Needy Families (TANF) Program: Second Annual Report to Congress* (Washington, D.C.: Government Printing Office, 1999), 20–22.

11. The Council of Economic Advisors (CEA) assessed the caseload reductions by examining various contributory factors before and after the 1996 passage of the PRWORA. It maintained that in the period 1993–96, a strong labor market was

the most important factor in explaining the caseload reductions. The CEA held that in the period 1996–98, the TANF block grant became the most significant contributory factor, accounting for one-third of the caseload reductions. An increase in the minimum wage also contributed in an important way to decreases in that period. The CEA noted that studies have associated a 50-cent increase in the minimum wage with a 4 to 6 percent decline in welfare participation. Council of Economic Advisors, *The Effects of Welfare Policy and the Economic Expansion on Welfare Caseloads: An Update,* Washington, D.C., 3 August 1999, 9–10.

12. These figures, however, excluded families who returned to the rolls after leaving welfare briefly, raising employment rates artificially. Only three states reported the percentages of recipients who returned to the rolls during the follow-up period, which ranged from 19 to 30 percent. General Accounting Office, *Welfare Reform: Information on Former Recipients' Status,* GAO/HEHS-99–48, Washington, D.C., April 1999, 3, 16.

13. General Accounting Office, *Welfare Reform,* 18. For additional analyses, which report similar findings, see Maria Cancian, Robert Haveman, Daniel R. Meyer, and Barbara Wolfe, "Before and After TANF: The Economic Well-Being of Women Leaving Welfare," Special Report 77, Institute for Research on Poverty, University of Wisconsin-Madison, 2000; Pamela Loprest, "How Families that Left Welfare Are Doing: A National Picture," Assessing the New Federalism, Series B, No. B-1, Urban Institute, Washington, D.C., 1999; Sharon Parrott, "Welfare Recipients Who Find Jobs: What Do We Know About Their Employment and Earnings?" Center on Budget and Policy Priorities, Washington, D.C., 1998.

14. Raymond Hernandez, "Most Dropped from Welfare Don't Get Jobs," *New York Times,* 23 March 1998, national edition, A1; Clare Nolan, "Mississippi Poor Leave Welfare, but for What?" *Stateline.org,* 18 April 2000,
http://www.stateline.org/story.cfm?storyid=73226 (20 April 2000).

15. Robert I. Lerman, Pamela Loprest, and Caroline Ratcliffe, "How Well Can Urban Labor Markets Absorb Welfare Recipients?" Assessing the New Federalism, Series A, No. A-33, Urban Institute, Washington, D.C., 1999; Peter Edelman, "The Worst Thing Bill Clinton Has Done," *Atlantic Monthly* (March 1997): 43–58; Robert M. Solow, *Work and Welfare,* ed. Amy Gutman (Princeton, N.J.: Princeton University Press, 1998).

16. Felice Davidson Perlmutter, *From Welfare to Work: Corporate Initiatives and Welfare Reform* (New York: Oxford University Press, 1997), 110.

17. William Julius Wilson, *When Work Disappears: The World of the New Urban Poor* (New York: Vintage Books, 1996), 207–35. Joel Handler and Yeheskel Hasenfeld have outlined a similarly compelling agenda for reform. See Handler and Hasenfeld, *We the Poor People.*

18. Council of Economic Advisors, *Good News for Low-Income Families: Expansions in the Earned Income Tax Credit and the Minimum Wage,* Washington, D.C., December 1998, 4.

19. Recipients encounter circumstances in their everyday lives that may undo regular job attendance. Events that can be handled without disruption by other employees, such as breakdowns in childcare or transportation or the illness of family members, quickly turn into crises for low-wage workers, especially single parents. See, e.g., Handler and Hasenfeld, *We the Poor People*, 98.

20. Fay Lomax Cook and Edith J. Barrett, *Support for the American Welfare State: The Views of Congress and the Public* (New York: Columbia University Press, 1992), 113.

21. For two illuminating examples of debunking, see Evelyn Z. Brodkin, "The Making of an Enemy: How Welfare Policies Construct the Poor," *Law and Social Inquiry* 18 (1993): 647–70; "Dethroning the Welfare Queen: The Rhetoric of Reform," *Harvard Law Review* 107 (1994): 2013–30.

22. Wilson, *When Work Disappears*, 173–74.

23. Along these lines, Lucie White chides defenders of public assistance programs for remaining silent for too long on the "failure" of some women to exit welfare. This silence leaves unanswered the question of how one ought to understand the experiences of these recipients and cedes to "moralists the uncontested power to interpret poor women's lives." Lucie E. White, "No Exit: Rethinking 'Welfare Dependency' from a Different Ground," *Georgetown Law Journal* 81 (1993): 1970.

24. See Harvey Feigenbaum, Jeffrey Henig, and Chris Hamnett, *Shrinking the State: The Political Underpinnings of Privatization* (New York: Cambridge University Press, 1998); Joel F. Handler, *Down from Bureaucracy: The Ambiguity of Privatization and Empowerment* (Princeton, N.J.: Princeton University Press, 1996).

25. Lawrence Mead, for instance, contends that whatever one's view of the appropriate size and role of governing institutions in contemporary American society, "it is absolutely clear that employment is essential to being a functioning citizen. Only adults with a work connection have moral standing to demand either more government or less." Lawrence M. Mead, *The New Politics of Poverty: The Nonworking Poor in America* (New York: Basic Books, 1992), 13.

26. John Dewey, *The Public and Its Problems* (1927; reprint, Athens, Ohio: Swallow Press, 1954), 148.

27. Richard B. Freeman, *The New Inequality: Creating Solutions for Poor America*, ed. Joshua Cohen and Joel Rogers (Boston: Beacon Press, 1999), 3. See also Robert D. Plotnick, Eugene Smolensky, Eirik Evenhouse, and Siabohan Reilly, "The Twentieth Century Record of Inequality and Poverty in the United States," working paper 98–1, Center for Studies in Demography and Ecology, University of Washington, Seattle, 1998; William Julius Wilson, *The Bridge Over the Racial Divide: Rising Inequality and Coalition Politics* (Berkeley: University of California Press, 1999).

28. James Fallows, "The Invisible Poor," *New York Times Magazine*, 19 March 2000, 72. Fallows's article recalls in its title Dwight MacDonald's 1963 *New Yorker* review of *The Other America*, which was titled "Our Invisible Poor." The change

in first words in the titles from the possessive pronoun "our" to the indefinite article "the" may signal a larger change in social moods.

29. Fraser and Gordon, "Contract Versus Charity," 47.

30. Lawrence M. Mead, "Citizenship and Social Policy: T. H. Marshall and Poverty," *Social Philosophy and Policy* 14, no. 2 (1997): 220–21.

31. Discussing criteria of membership and participation in a political community, Michael Walzer articulates a principle of justice that may forestall potential mistreatment of immigrants by citizens: "the processes of self-determination through which a democratic state shapes its internal life, must be open, and equally open, to all those men and women who live within its territory, work in the local economy, and are subject to the local law." For Walzer, this principle implies that all persons admitted initially as immigrants must be given the opportunity, subject to constraints of time and qualification, to be admitted subsequently as naturalized citizens. When this process of full admission is closed after initial entry, "the political community collapses into a world of members and strangers, with no political boundaries between the two, where the strangers are subjects of the members." Walzer holds that tyranny determines the character of this sort of state. Michael Walzer, *Spheres of Justice: A Defense of Pluralism and Equality* (New York: Basic Books, 1983), 60, 61.

32. Harrington, *The Other America*, 3.

Bibliography

"After Years of Debate, Welfare Reform Clears." *Congressional Quarterly Almanac* 34 (1988): 349–64.

Alexander, Charles P. "Broadsides from the Supply Side." *Time,* 5 November 1984, 58.

Allen, Henry. "George Gilder and the Capitalists' Creed." *Washington Post,* 18 February 1981, final edition, B1, B9.

Alter, Jonathan. "Bracing for the Big One." *Newsweek,* 10 October 1994, 27–28.

Anderson, Benedict. *Imagined Communities: Reflections on the Origin and Spread of Nationalism.* Rev. ed. London: Verso, 1991.

Anderson, Harry, Rich Thomas, Gloria Borger, Thomas M. DeFrank, Elaine Shannon, and Susan Dentzer. "Is U.S. Inflation Out of Control?" *Newsweek,* 3 March 1980, 54–59.

Anderson, Lorrin. "Guilt and Gasoline." *National Review,* 8 June 1992, 35–37.

Appadurai, Arjun. *Modernity at Large: Cultural Dimensions of Globalization.* Minneapolis: University of Minnesota Press, 1996.

Arrandale, Thomas J. "Control of the Purse Strings." In *Budgeting for America: The Politics and Process of Federal Spending,* edited by Martha V. Gottron, 29–44. Washington, D.C.: Congressional Quarterly, 1982.

———. "Experiment in Budgeting." In *Budgeting for America: The Politics and Process of Federal Spending,* edited by Martha V. Gottron, 61–72. Washington, D.C.: Congressional Quarterly, 1982.

———. "Struggle for Spending Control." In *Budgeting for America: The Politics and Process of Federal Spending,* edited by Martha V. Gottron, 45–59. Washington, D.C.: Congressional Quarterly, 1982.

Auletta, Ken. *The Underclass.* New York: Random House, 1982.

Balz, Dan. "Clinton Rips White House Response; Social Programs Not at Fault, He Says." *Washington Post,* 6 May 1992, final edition, A9.

Bane, Mary Jo, and David T. Ellwood. *The Dynamics of Dependence: The Routes to Self-Sufficiency.* Cambridge, Mass.: Urban Systems Research and Engineering, 1983.

———. *Welfare Realities: From Rhetoric to Reform.* Cambridge: Harvard University Press, 1994.

Baratz, Morton S., and Sammis B. White. "Childfare: A New Direction for Welfare Reform." *Urban Studies* 33 (1996): 1935–44.

Barrilleaux, Charles J. Review of *Poor Support,* by David Ellwood. *American Political Science Review* 83 (1989): 634–35.

Baum, Erica B. "When the Witch Doctors Agree: The Family Support Act and Social Science Research." *Journal of Policy Analysis and Management* 10 (1991): 603–15.

Benhabib, Seyla. *Situating the Self: Gender, Community, and Postmodernism in Contemporary Ethics.* New York: Routledge, 1992.

———. "Toward a Deliberative Model of Democratic Legitimacy." In *Democracy and Difference: Contesting the Boundaries of the Political,* edited by Seyla Benhabib, 67–94. Princeton, N.J.: Princeton University Press, 1996.

Berger, Brigette. Review of *Losing Ground,* by Charles Murray. *Commentary* (January 1985): 66–70.

Berkowitz, Edward D. *America's Welfare State from Roosevelt to Reagan.* Baltimore, Md.: Johns Hopkins University Press, 1991.

Berman, William C. *America's Right Turn: From Nixon to Bush.* Baltimore, Md.: Johns Hopkins University Press, 1994.

Bessette, Joseph M. *The Mild Voice of Reason: Deliberative Democracy and American National Government.* Chicago: University of Chicago Press, 1994.

Blakely, Edward J. "Villains and Victims: Poverty and Public Policy." *APA Journal* (spring 1992): 248–52.

Blank, Rebecca. "The 1996 Welfare Reform." *Journal of Economic Perspectives* 11 (1997): 169–77.

Bogardus, Ralph F., and Fred Hobson. Introduction to *Literature at the Barricades: The American Writer in the 1930s,* edited by Ralph F. Bogardus and Fred Hobson, 1–9. Tuscaloosa: University of Alabama Press, 1982.

Bohman, James. *Public Deliberation: Pluralism, Complexity, Democracy.* Cambridge: MIT Press, 1996.

Bohman, James, and William Rehg, eds. *Deliberative Democracy: Essays on Reason and Politics.* Cambridge: MIT Press, 1997.

Boskoff, Alvin. Review of *Losing Ground,* by Charles Murray. *Annals of the American Academy of Political and Social Science,* no. 481 (1985): 194–95.

Brodkin, Evelyn Z. "The Making of an Enemy: How Welfare Policies Construct the Poor." *Law and Social Inquiry* 18 (1993): 647–70.

Brummett, Barry. "On to Rhetorical Relativism." *Quarterly Journal of Speech* 68 (1982): 425–30.

Brundage, Anthony. *The Making of the New Poor Law: The Politics of Inquiry, Enactment, and Implementation, 1832–1839.* New Brunswick, N.J.: Rutgers University Press, 1978.

Brush, Lisa. "Worthy Widows, Welfare Cheats: The Professional Discourse on Single Mothers in the United States, 1900–1988." Ph.D. diss., University of Wisconsin-Madison, 1993.

Bryner, Gary. *Politics and Public Morality: The Great American Welfare Reform Debate.* New York: W. W. Norton, 1998.

Burke, Kenneth. *The Philosophy of Literary Form: Studies in Symbolic Action.* 3d ed. Berkeley: University of California Press, 1973.

Calavita, Kitty. "The New Politics of Immigration: 'Balanced-Budget Conservatism' and the Symbolism of Proposition 187." *Social Problems* 43 (1996): 284–305.

Cancian, Maria, Robert Haveman, Daniel R. Meyer, and Barbara Wolfe. "Before and After TANF: The Economic Well-Being of Women Leaving Welfare." Special Report 77, Institute for Research on Poverty, University of Wisconsin-Madison, 2000.

"Carefully Orchestrated Campaign Unfolds." *CQ Weekly,* 21 February 1981, 333.

Carnegie, Andrew. *The Gospel of Wealth and Other Timely Essays.* Edited by Edward C. Kirkland. Cambridge: Harvard University Press, 1962.

———. "The Road to Business Success." In *The American Gospel of Success: Individualism and Beyond,* edited by Moses Rischin, 91–97. Chicago: Quadrangle, 1965.

———. "Wealth." In *Democracy and the Gospel of Wealth,* edited by Gail Kennedy, 1–8. Boston: Heath, 1949.

Carroll, William C. *Fat King, Lean Beggar: Representations of Poverty in the Age of Shakespeare.* Ithaca, N.Y.: Cornell University Press, 1996.

Castoriadis, Cornelius. *The Imaginary Institution of Society.* Translated by Kathleen Blamey. Cambridge: MIT Press, 1987.

Cates, Jerry R. *Insuring Inequality: Administrative Leadership in Social Security, 1935–54.* Ann Arbor: University of Michigan Press, 1983.

Cawelti, John G. *Apostles of the Self-Made Man.* Chicago: University of Chicago Press, 1965.

Chilman, Catherine S. "Welfare Reform or Revision? The Family Support Act of 1988." *Social Service Review* 66 (1992): 349–77.

Clark, Timothy. "Want to Know Where the Ax Will Fall? Read Dave Stockman's Big 'Black Book.'" *National Journal,* 14 February 1981, 274–81.

Clarke, S. E., A. N. Kirby, and R. F. McNown. "*Losing Ground* — or Losing Credibility? An Examination of a Recent Policy Debate in the United States." Review of *Losing Ground,* by Charles Murray. *Environment and Planning* A19 (1987): 1015–25.

Clinton, William J. "Announcement Speech: Gov. Bill Clinton." Appendix to *Putting People First: How We Can All Change America,* by Bill Clinton and Al Gore. New York: Times Books, 1992.

———. *Public Papers of the Presidents of the United States: William J. Clinton, 1993.* 2 vols. Washington, D.C.: Government Printing Office, 1994.

———. *Public Papers of the Presidents of the United States: William J. Clinton, 1994.* 2 vols. Washington, D.C.: Government Printing Office, 1995.

———. *Public Papers of the Presidents of the United States: William J. Clinton, 1995.* 2 vols. Washington, D.C.: Government Printing Office, 1996.

———. *Public Papers of the Presidents of the United States: William J. Clinton, 1996.* 2 vols. Washington, D.C.: Government Printing Office, 1997.

———. "We Offer Our People a New Choice Based on Old Values." *Washington Post,* 17 July 1992, final edition, A26.

Clinton, Bill, and Al Gore. *Putting People First: How We Can All Change America.* New York: Times Books, 1992.

Clymer, Adam. "GOP Celebrates Its Sweep to Power; Clinton Vows to Find Common Ground." *New York Times,* 10 November 1994, late edition, A1, B5.

———. "Poll Links Economic Slide and Social Antagonism." *New York Times,* 27 June 1980, late city edition, A1, D11.

Cohen, Joshua. "Deliberation and Democratic Legitimacy." In *Deliberative Democracy: Essays on Reason and Politics,* edited by James Bohman and William Rehg, 67–91. Cambridge: MIT Press, 1997.

Cohen, Richard E. "In the Conservative Politics of the '80s, the South Is Rising Once Again." *National Journal,* 28 February 1981, 350–54.

———. "The Political System Attempts to Cope with Public Loss of Faith in Government." *National Journal,* 19 January 1980, 110–16.

Coll, Blanche D. *Safety Net: Welfare and Social Security 1929–1977.* New Brunswick, N.J.: Rutgers University Press, 1995.

Congressional Record. 97th Cong., 1st sess., 1981. Vol. 127, pts. 2–7, 10–11.

Congressional Record. 100th Cong., 1st sess., 1987. Vol. 133, pt. 6.

Congressional Record. 100th Cong., 2d sess., 1988. Vol. 134, pts. 11, 13, 18–19.

Congressional Record. 104th Cong., 1st sess., 1995. Vol. 141, pt. 7.

Congressional Record. 104th Cong., 2d sess., 1996. Vol. 142, pt. 15.

Connolly, Ceci. "GOP Accentuates the Positive; Hopefuls to Sign Compact." *CQ Weekly,* 24 September 1994, 2711–12.

Conwell, Russell. "Acres of Diamonds." In *American Rhetorical Discourse,* edited by Ronald F. Reid, 621–34. 2d ed. Prospect Heights, Ill.: Waveland Press, 1995.

Cook, Fay Lomax, and Edith J. Barrett. *Support for the American Welfare State: The Views of Congress and the Public.* New York: Columbia University Press, 1992.

Cook, Sylvia Jenkins. "Steinbeck, the People, and the Party." In *Literature at the Barricades: The American Writer in the 1930s,* edited by Ralph F. Bogardus and Fred Hobson, 82–95. Tuscaloosa: University of Alabama Press, 1982.

Cooper, Kenneth J. "Gingrich: 'Cooperation, Yes. Compromise, No.'" *Washington Post,* 12 November 1994, final edition, A1, A10.

———. "GOP Offers a 'Contract' to Revive Reagan Years." *Washington Post,* 28 September 1994, final edition, A1, A4.

Cooper, Kenneth J., and Eric Pianin. "GOP Rides Wave to Position of Power; Party Wins Needed Seats, Takes Charge for 1st Time in 40 Years." *Washington Post,* 9 November 1994, final edition, A21, A25.

Corbin, Carol, ed. *Rhetoric in Postmodern America: Conversations with Michael Calvin McGee.* New York: Guilford Press, 1998.

Council of Economic Advisors. *The Effects of Welfare Policy and the Economic Expansion on Welfare Caseloads: An Update.* Washington, D.C., 3 August 1999.

———. *Good News for Low-Income Families: Expansions in the Earned Income Tax Credit and the Minimum Wage.* Washington, D.C., December 1998.

Croasmun, Earl. "Realism and the Rhetoric of Assent." In *Argumentation Theory and the Rhetoric of Assent,* edited by David Cratis Williams and Michael David Hazen, 33–49. Tuscaloosa: University of Alabama Press, 1990.

Daley, Steve. "GOP's Latest Financial Plan Recalls Those Debt-Ridden Days of the 1980s." *Chicago Tribune,* 25 September 1994, lake final edition, sec. 4, 4.

Danziger, Sheldon. Review of *Poor Support,* by David Ellwood. *Journal of Economic Literature* 27 (1989): 1212–14.

Demkovich, Linda E. "HHS Department: It's Humphrey's No More." *National Journal,* 25 April 1981, 713–14.

Derrida, Jacques. "Sending: On Representation." *Social Research* 49 (1982): 294–326.

"Dethroning the Welfare Queen: The Rhetoric of Reform." *Harvard Law Review* 107 (1994): 2013–30.

Devroy, Ann. "White House Blames Liberal Programs for Unrest; 'Great Society' Initiatives Started in 1960s Are at Root of Many Problems, Fitzwater Says." *Washington Post,* 5 May 1992, final edition, A8.

Dewey, John. *The Public and Its Problems.* 1927. Reprint, Athens, Ohio: Swallow Press, 1954.

Donnelly, Harrison. "Working Mothers' Benefits Cut in New AFDC Provisions in Reconciliation Measure." *CQ Weekly,* 15 August 1981, 1493–94.

Downing, Agnes H. "A Wider Pension Move." *Child-Welfare Magazine,* October 1912, 59.

Drew, Elizabeth. *Portrait of an Election: The 1980 Presidential Campaign.* New York: Simon and Schuster, 1981.

Dugdale, Richard L. *The Jukes: A Study in Crime, Pauperism, Disease, and Heredity.* 1877. Reprint, New York: Arno Press, 1970.

Dumas, Kitty. "States Bypassing Congress in Reforming Welfare." *CQ Weekly,* 11 April 1992, 950–53.

Dyer, Richard. *The Matter of Images: Essays on Representation.* New York: Routledge, 1993.

Edelman, Peter. "The Worst Thing Bill Clinton Has Done." *Atlantic Monthly,* March 1997, 43–58.

Ellwood, David T. *Poor Support: Poverty in the American Family.* New York: Basic Books, 1988.

———. "Working Off of Welfare: Prospects and Policies for Self-Sufficiency of Women Heading Families." Discussion paper, 803–86 Institute for Research on Poverty, University of Wisconsin-Madison, 1986.

Ellwood, David T., and Mary Jo Bane. "The Impact of AFDC on Family Structure and Living Arrangements." *Research in Labor Economics* 7 (1985): 137–207.

Epstein, William M. *Welfare in America: How Social Science Fails the Poor*. Madison: University of Wisconsin Press, 1997.

Fallows, James. "The Invisible Poor." *New York Times Magazine*, 19 March 2000, 68–78, 95, 111–12.

Farber, David. *The Age of Great Dreams: America in the 1960s*. New York: Hill and Wang, 1994.

Farnsworth, Clyde H. "Consumer Prices Up by 1% in September and 12.7% in a Year." *New York Times*, 25 October 1980, late city edition, 1, 15.

Farrell, John Aloysius. "Welfare Battlefield; Bush Stakes Out Issue by Attacking 'Cycle of Dependency.'" *Boston Globe*, 19 April 1992, city edition, national/foreign sec., 1.

Feigenbaum, Harvey, Jeffrey Henig, and Chris Hamnett. *Shrinking the State: The Political Underpinnings of Privatization*. New York: Cambridge University Press, 1999.

Ferretti, Fred. "In the Suburbs, Inflation Takes the Edge Off the Good Life." *New York Times*, 29 March 1980, late city edition, 20.

"Fight for Mr. Bush's Mind." *New York Times*, 5 May 1992, late edition, 30.

Frank, Richard S. "GOP Pulling Together for Reagan." *National Journal*, 26 July 1980, 1212–14.

Fraser, Derek, ed. *The New Poor Law in the Nineteenth Century*. New York: St. Martin's Press, 1976.

Fraser, Nancy. "Rethinking the Public Sphere: A Contribution to the Critique of Actually Existing Democracy." In *Habermas and the Public Sphere*, edited by Craig Calhoun, 109–42. Cambridge: MIT Press, 1992.

——. "What's Critical About Critical Theory? The Case of Habermas and Gender." In *Unruly Practices: Power, Discourse, and Gender in Contemporary Social Theory*. Minneapolis: University of Minnesota Press, 1993.

——. "Women, Welfare, and the Politics of Need Interpretation." In *Unruly Practices: Power, Discourse, and Gender in Contemporary Social Theory*. Minneapolis: University of Minnesota Press, 1993.

Fraser, Nancy, and Linda Gordon. "Contract Versus Charity: Why Is There No Social Citizenship in the United States?" *Socialist Review* 22, no. 3 (1992): 45–67.

——. "A Genealogy of *Dependency*: Tracing a Keyword of the U.S. Welfare State." *Signs: Journal of Women in Culture and Society* 19 (1994): 309–36.

Freeman, Howard E. "Dwarf Steps for the Poor." Review of *Poor Support*, by David Ellwood. *Contemporary Sociology* 17 (1988): 805–7.

Freeman, Richard B. *The New Inequality: Creating Solutions for Poor America*, edited by Joshua Cohen and Joel Rogers. Boston: Beacon Press, 1999.

Friedan, Betty. *The Feminine Mystique*. New York: W. W. Norton, 1963.

Fuchs, Victor. Review of *Losing Ground*, by Charles Murray. *Population and Development Review* 11 (1985): 768–70.

Gabriel, Ralph Henry. *The Course of American Democratic Thought: An Intellectual History Since 1815*. New York: Ronald Press, 1940.

Gans, Herbert J. *People, Plans, and Policies: Essays on Poverty, Racism, and Other National Urban Problems.* New York: Columbia University Press, 1991.

——. *The War Against the Poor: The Underclass and Antipoverty Policy.* New York: Basic Books, 1995.

Garin, Geoffrey, Guy Molyneux, and Linda Divall. "Public Attitudes Toward Welfare Reform." *Social Policy* (winter 1994): 44–49.

Gergen, Kenneth J. *An Invitation to Social Construction.* Thousand Oaks, Calif.: Sage, 1999.

Gigot, Paul. "GOP Actually Tries to Stand for Something." *Wall Street Journal,* 9 September 1994, eastern edition, A14.

Gilder, George. *Wealth and Poverty.* New York: Basic Books, 1981.

Gilens, Martin. *Why Americans Hate Welfare: Race, Media, and the Politics of Antipoverty Policy.* Chicago: University of Chicago Press, 1999.

Goodnight, G. Thomas. "Controversy." In *Argument in Controversy: Proceedings of the Seventh SCA/AFA Conference on Argumentation,* edited by Donn W. Parson, 1–13. Annandale, Va.: Speech Communication Association, 1991.

"GOP's Deceptive Contract." *New York Times,* 28 September 1994, late edition, A20.

Gordon, Linda. *Pitied but Not Entitled: Single Mothers and the History of Welfare.* Cambridge: Harvard University Press, 1994.

Gottschalk, Peter, Sara McLanahan, and Gary D. Sandefur. "The Dynamics and Intergenerational Transmission of Poverty and Welfare Participation." In *Confronting Poverty: Prescriptions for Change,* edited by Sheldon H. Danziger, Gary D. Sandefur, and Daniel H. Weinberg, 85–108. Cambridge: Harvard University Press, 1994.

Greenberg, Mark, and Steve Savner. "A Detailed Summary of Key Provisions of the Temporary Assistance for Needy Families Block Grant of H.R. 3734." Center for Law and Social Policy, Washington, D.C., 1996.

Greenstein, Robert. "Losing Faith in *Losing Ground.*" Review of *Losing Ground,* by Charles Murray. *New Republic,* 25 March 1985, 12–17.

——. "New Thinking About Poverty." Review of *Poor Support,* by David Ellwood. *Dissent* (spring 1989): 271–74.

Gregg, Gail. "Reagan Plan Clears 1st Hurdle as Senate Backs Cuts." *CQ Weekly,* 21 March 1981, 499–502.

Gregg, Gail, and Dale Tate. "Reagan Economic Officials Put Differences Behind Them." *CQ Weekly,* 7 February 1981, 259–61.

Greider, William. *The Education of David Stockman and Other Americans.* New York: Dutton, 1982.

Gronbeck, Bruce E. "The Rhetorics of the Past: History, Argument, and Collective Memory." In *Doing Rhetorical History: Concepts and Cases,* edited by Kathleen J. Turner, 47–60. Tuscaloosa: University of Alabama Press, 1998.

"Groups Urge U. S. to Ease Poverty." *New York Times,* 23 December 1986, late edition, B5.

Gruenwald, Juliana. "Shallow Tactics or Deep Issues: Fathoming the GOP 'Contract.'" *CQ Weekly,* 19 November 1994, 3361–62.

Gutman, Amy, and Dennis Thompson. *Democracy and Disagreement: Why Moral Conflict Cannot Be Avoided in Politics, and What Should Be Done About It.* Cambridge: Harvard University Press, 1996.

Habermas, Jürgen. *Between Facts and Norms: Contributions to a Discourse Theory of Law and Democracy.* Translated by William Rehg. Cambridge: MIT Press, 1996.

Hager, George. "Can GOP Count on Its Own to Back Its Ambitious Plan?" *CQ Weekly,* 1 October 1994, 2765–66.

Hall, John A. Review of *Poor Support,* by David Ellwood. *Social Science Quarterly* 70 (1989): 538–39.

Handler, Joel F. *Down from Bureaucracy: The Ambiguity of Privatization and Empowerment.* Princeton, N.J.: Princeton University Press, 1996.

——— . *The Poverty of Welfare Reform.* New Haven, Conn.: Yale University Press, 1995.

Handler, Joel F., and Yeheskel Hasenfeld. *The Moral Construction of Poverty: Welfare Reform in America.* Newbury Park, Calif.: Sage, 1991.

——— . *We the Poor People: Work, Poverty, Welfare.* New Haven, Conn.: Yale University Press, 1997.

Hard, William. "De Kid Wot Works at Night." In *The Muckrakers: The Era in Journalism That Moved America to Reform — The Most Significant Magazines of 1902–1912,* edited by Arthur Weinberg and Lila Weinberg, 369–84. New York: Simon and Schuster, 1961.

Harpman, Edward J., and Richard K. Scotch. "Rethinking the War on Poverty: The Ideology of Social Welfare Reform." *Western Political Quarterly* 41 (1988): 193–207.

Harrington, Michael. *The New American Poverty.* New York: Penguin Books, 1984.

——— . *The Other America: Poverty in the United States.* 1962. Reprint, with an introduction by Irving Howe. New York: Collier Books, 1993.

Hartman, Robert W. "Congress and Budget-Making." *Political Science Quarterly* 97 (1982): 381–402.

Haskett, George T. Review of *Poor Support,* by David Ellwood. *Social Casework* 70, no. 1 (1989): 57–61.

Haskins, Ron. "Congress Writes a Law: Research and Welfare Reform." *Journal of Policy Analysis and Management* 10 (1991): 616–32.

Hernandez, Raymond. "Most Dropped From Welfare Don't Get Jobs." *New York Times,* 23 March 1998, national edition, A1, A16.

Higham, John. *Send These to Me: Jews and Other Immigrants in Urban America.* New York: Atheneum, 1975.

Himmelfarb, Gertrude. *The Idea of Poverty: England in the Early Industrial Age.* New York: Vintage Books, 1985.

Hirschman, Albert O. *The Rhetoric of Reaction: Perversity, Futility, Jeopardy.* Cambridge: Harvard University Press, 1991.

Hoey, Jane M., and Zilpha C. Franklin. "Aid to Dependent Children." *Social Work Yearbook* 5 (1939): 28–35.

Hofstadter, Richard. *The Age of Reform: From Bryan to FDR.* New York: Vintage Books, 1955.

———. *The Paranoid Style in American Politics and Other Essays.* New York: Alfred A. Knopf, 1965.

Howe, Irving. Introduction to *The Other America: Poverty in the United States,* by Michael Harrington. 1962. Reprint, New York: Collier Books, 1993.

Hunt, Albert. "The Republicans Shoot an Air Ball." *Wall Street Journal,* 22 September 1994, eastern edition, A11.

Hutchens, Robert. "The Effects of the Omnibus Budget Reconciliation Act of 1981 on AFDC Recipients: A Review of the Studies." Discussion paper 764–84, Institute for Research on Poverty, University of Wisconsin-Madison, 1984.

———. Review of *Poor Support,* by David Ellwood. *Industrial and Labor Relations Review* 43 (1990): 486–87.

Hutcheon, Linda. "The Politics of Representation." *Signature: A Journal of Theory and Canadian Literature* 1 (1989): 23–44.

Irwin, Will. "The First Ward Ball." In *The Muckrakers: The Era in Journalism That Moved America to Reform — The Most Significant Magazines of 1902–1912,* edited by Arthur Weinberg and Lila Weinberg, 139–45. New York: Simon and Schuster, 1961.

Jackson, Jesse. "Common Ground and Common Sense." *Vital Speeches of the Day,* 15 August 1988, 649–53.

Jencks, Christopher. "The Hidden Paradox of Welfare Reform." *American Prospect,* May-June 1997, 33–40.

———. "How Poor Are the Poor?" *New York Review of Books,* 9 May 1985, 41–49.

———. *Rethinking Social Policy: Race, Poverty, and the Underclass.* New York: Harper-Collins, 1993.

Joe, Tom, and Cheryl Rogers. *By the Few for the Few: The Reagan Welfare Legacy.* Lexington, Mass.: Lexington Books, 1985.

Johnson, Lyndon B. *Public Papers of the Presidents of the United States: Lyndon B. Johnson, 1963–64.* Washington, D.C.: Government Printing Office, 1965.

Kaplan, Dave. "This Year, Republicans Gamble That All Politics Is Local." *CQ Weekly,* 22 October 1994, 3005–8.

Katz, Jeffrey L. "Clinton Plans Major Shift in Lives of Poor People." *CQ Weekly,* 22 January 1994, 117–22.

———. "Clinton's Welfare Reform Plan to Be Out in Fall, Aides Say." *CQ Weekly,* 10 July 1993, 1813.

———. "GOP's New Welfare Strategy Has Democrats Reassessing." *CQ Weekly,* 13 July 1996, 1969–70.

———. "GOP's Two-Year Welfare Limit Sends Message to Clinton." *CQ Weekly,* 13 November 1993, 3131.

———. "Governors Group Sidelined in Welfare Debate." *CQ Weekly,* 20 May 1995, 1423–25.

———. "Long-Awaited Welfare Proposal Would Make Gradual Changes." *CQ Weekly,* 18 June 1994, 1622–24.

———. "Senate Overhaul Plan Provides Road Map for Compromise." *CQ Weekly,* 23 September 1995, 2908–11.

———. "Welfare Issue Finds Home on the Campaign Trail." *CQ Weekly,* 15 October 1994, 2956–58.

———. "Welfare Overhaul Forces Ready to Start Without Clinton." *CQ Weekly,* 2 April 1994, 800–3.

———. "Welfare Overhaul Law." *CQ Weekly,* 21 September 1996, 2696–705.

Katz, Michael B. *In the Shadow of the Poorhouse: A Social History of Welfare in America.* New York: Basic Books, 1986.

———. *The Undeserving Poor: From the War on Poverty to the War on Welfare.* New York: Pantheon Books, 1989.

Kaus, Mickey. *The End of Equality.* New York: Basic Books, 1992.

———. "Welfare Waffle: What's That Plan Again, Bill?" *New Republic,* 12 October 1992, 10–12.

———. "The Work Ethic State." *New Republic,* 7 July 1986, 22–33.

Keller, Bill. "Special Treatment No Longer Given Advocates for the Poor." *CQ Weekly,* 18 April 1981, 659–64.

Kennedy, David M. *Freedom from Fear: The American People in Depression and War, 1929–1945.* New York: Oxford University Press, 1999.

Kennedy, John F. *Public Papers of the Presidents of the United States: John F. Kennedy, 1962.* Washington, D.C.: Government Printing Office, 1963.

———. *Public Papers of the Presidents of the United States: John F. Kennedy, 1963.* Washington, D.C.: Government Printing Office, 1964.

Kiewe, Amos, and Davis W. Houck. *A Shining City on a Hill: Ronald Reagan's Economic Rhetoric, 1951–1989.* New York: Praeger, 1991.

King, Martin Luther. "I Have a Dream." In *I Have a Dream: Writings and Speeches That Changed the World.* Edited by James M. Washington. New York: HarperCollins, 1992.

———. "The President's Address to the Tenth Anniversary Convention of the Southern Christian Leadership Conference." In *The Rhetoric of Black Power,* edited by Robert L. Scott and Wayne Brockriede, 146–65. New York: Harper and Row, 1969.

Kirschten, Dick. "Low-Profile Reagan Welfare Study Prompts Ex-Aides to Do Their Own." *National Journal,* 17 May 1986, 1208–9.

———. "Reagan: 'No More Business as Usual.'" *National Journal,* 21 February 1981, 300–3.

Knudsen, Patrick L. "After Long, Bruising Battle, House Approves Welfare Bill." *CQ Weekly,* 19 December 1987, 3157–65.

Kornblum, William. "Who Is the Underclass?" *Dissent* (spring 1991): 202–11.

Kosterlitz, Julie. "Behavior Modification." *National Journal,* 2 February 1992, 271–75.

———. "Reworking Welfare." *National Journal,* 26 September 1992, 2189–92.

———. "Transforming Theories into Legislation That'll Fly." *National Journal,* 27 February 1988, 543.

Kotz, Nick, and Mary Lynn Kotz. *A Passion for Equality: George A. Wiley and the Movement.* New York: W. W. Norton, 1977.

Krugman, Paul. *The Age of Diminished Expectations: U.S. Economic Policy in the 1990s.* Cambridge: MIT Press, 1992.

Kuttner, Robert. *Everything for Sale: The Virtues and Limits of Markets.* New York: Alfred A. Knopf, 1997.

Lane, Chuck. "The Manhattan Project." *New Republic,* 25 March 1985, 14–15.

Lanouette, William J. "Turning Out the Vote — Reagan Seeks Larger Share of Blue-Collar Vote." *National Journal,* 11 January 1980, 1832–35.

Lawrence, William. "The Relation of Wealth to Morals." In *Democracy and the Gospel of Wealth,* edited by Gail Kennedy, 68–76. Boston: Heath, 1949.

Leff, Mark. "Consensus for Reform: The Mothers'-Pension Movement in the Progressive Era." *Social Service Review* 47 (1973): 397–417.

Lemeunier, Yves. "Vision of Poverty and the Poor in Alger's Novels." In *All Men Are Created Equal: Ideologies, Reves et Realites,* edited by Groupe de Recherche et d'Etudes Nord Américaines, 121–36. Aix-en-Provence, Fr.: Université de Provence, 1982.

Lentricchia, Frank. *Criticism and Social Change.* Chicago: University of Chicago Press, 1983.

Lerman, Robert I., Pamela Loprest, and Caroline Ratcliffe. "How Well Can Urban Labor Markets Absorb Welfare Recipients?" Assessing the New Federalism, Series A, No. A-33. Urban Institute, Washington, D.C., 1999.

Levine, Robert A. *The Poor Ye Need Not Have with You: Lessons from the War on Poverty.* Cambridge: MIT Press, 1970.

Levitan, Sar A. Review of *Losing Ground,* by Charles Murray. *Society* 22 (1985): 82–83.

Levitan, Sar A., and Robert Taggart. "The Great Society Did Succeed." *Political Science Quarterly* 91 (1976–77): 601–18.

Lieberman, Robert C. *Shifting the Color Line: Race and the American Welfare State.* Cambridge: Harvard University Press, 1998.

Loprest, Pamela. "How Families that Left Welfare Are Doing: A National Picture." Assessing the New Federalism, Series B, No. B-1. Urban Institute, Washington, D.C., 1999.

Loseke, Donileen R., and Kirsten Fawcett. "Appealing Appeals: Constructing Moral Worthiness, 1912–1917." *Sociological Quarterly* 36 (1995): 61–78.

Luker, Kristin. *Dubious Conceptions: The Politics of Teenage Pregnancy.* Cambridge: Harvard University Press, 1996.

Lyotard, Jean-François. *The Postmodern Condition: A Report on Knowledge.* Translated by Geoff Bennington and Brian Massumi. Minneapolis: University of Minnesota Press, 1984.

Macdonald, Dwight. "Our Invisible Poor." *New Yorker,* 19 January 1963, 82–132.

Mansbridge, Jane. "Using Power/Fighting Power: The Polity." In *Democracy and Difference: Contesting the Boundaries of the Political.* Edited by Seyla Benhabib, 67–94. Princeton, N.J.: Princeton University Press, 1996.

Marcuse, Herbert. *Counterrevolution and Revolt.* Boston: Beacon Press, 1972.

Markham, Edwin. "The Hoe-Man in the Making." In *The Muckrakers: The Era in Journalism That Moved America to Reform — The Most Significant Magazines of 1902–1912,* edited by Arthur Weinberg and Lila Weinberg, 361–68. New York: Simon and Schuster, 1961.

Marshall, T. H., and Tom Bottomore. *Citizenship and Social Class.* London: Pluto Press, 1992.

Mayer, Allan J. "Inflation: A Doomsday Scenario." *Newsweek,* 24 March 1980, 29.

McClure, Samuel S. "Concerning Three Articles in This Number of *McClure's,* and a Coincidence That May Set Us Thinking." In *The Muckrakers: The Era in Journalism That Moved America to Reform — The Most Significant Magazines of 1902–1912,* edited by Arthur Weinberg and Lila Weinberg, 4–5. New York: Simon and Schuster, 1961.

McGrory, Mary. "Bush's No-Show on Los Angeles." *Washington Post,* 5 May 1992, final edition, A2.

Mead, Lawrence M. *Beyond Entitlement: The Social Obligations of Citizenship.* New York: Free Press, 1986.

———. "Citizenship and Social Policy: T. H. Marshall and Poverty." *Social Philosophy and Policy* 14, no. 2 (1997): 197–230.

———. *The New Politics of Poverty: The Nonworking Poor in America.* New York: Basic Books, 1992.

———. "The Rise of Paternalism." In *The New Paternalism: Supervisory Approaches to Poverty,* edited by Lawrence M. Mead, 1–38. Washington, D.C.: Brookings Institution Press, 1997.

Medhurst, Martin J. "Postponing the Social Agenda: Reagan's Strategy and Tactics." *Western Journal of Speech Communication* 48 (1984): 262–76.

Miller, S. M. "Faith, Hope, and Charity—the Public Relations of Poverty." Review of *Losing Ground,* by Charles Murray. *Contemporary Sociology* 14 (1985): 684–87.

Moffitt, Robert. "Incentive Effects of the U.S. Welfare System: A Review." *Journal of Economic Literature* 30 (1992): 1–61.

———. Review of *Poor Support,* by David Ellwood. *American Journal of Sociology* 85 (1990): 1327–29.

Moffitt, Robert, and Douglas A. Wolf. "The Effect of the 1981 Omnibus Budget Reconciliation Act on Welfare Recipients and Work Incentives." *Social Service Review* 61 (1987): 247–60.

Moore, David W., Lydia Saad, Leslie McAneny, and Frank Newport. "Contract with America." *Gallup Poll Monthly,* November 1994, 19–34.

Morris, Dick. *Behind the Oval Office: Winning the Presidency in the Nineties.* New York: Random House, 1997.

Moynihan, Daniel Patrick. *Family and Nation.* New York: Harcourt Brace Jovanovich, 1987.

———. *Maximum Feasible Misunderstanding.* New York: Free Press, 1969.

———. *Miles to Go: A Personal History of Social Policy.* Cambridge: Harvard University Press, 1996.

———. *The Politics of a Guaranteed Income: The Nixon Administration and the Family Assistance Plan.* New York: Random House, 1973.

Murray, Charles. "Causes, Root Causes, and Cures." *National Review,* 8 June 1992, 30–32.

———. "The Legacy of the 60s." *Commentary,* July 1992, 23–30.

———. *Losing Ground: American Social Policy, 1950–1980.* 10th anniversary ed. New York: Basic Books, 1994.

Muzzio, Douglas. Review of *Losing Ground,* by Charles Murray. *American Political Science Review* 79 (1985): 1198–99.

———. "The Urban Basement Revisited." *Urban Affairs Quarterly* 25 (1989): 352–65.

Nathan, Richard P. "Will the Underclass Always Be with Us?" *Society,* March/April 1987, 57–62.

National Conference of Catholic Bishops. *Economic Justice for All: Pastoral Letter on Catholic Social Teaching and the U.S. Economy.* 10th anniversary ed. Washington, D.C.: United States Catholic Conference, 1997.

Negt, Oskar, and Alexander Kluge. *Public Sphere and Experience: Toward an Analysis of the Bourgeois and Proletarian Public Sphere.* Translated by Peter Labanyi, Jamie Owen Daniel, and Assenka Oksiloff. Minneapolis: University of Minnesota Press, 1993.

"New Republican Plan." *Washington Post,* 28 September 1994, final edition, A22.

Nixon, Richard. *Public Papers of the Presidents of the United States: Richard M. Nixon, 1969.* Washington, D.C.: Government Printing Office, 1971.

Noble, Charles. *Welfare as We Knew It: A Political History of the American Welfare State.* New York: Oxford University Press, 1997.

Nolan, Clare. "Mississippi Poor Leave Welfare, but for What?" *Stateline.org,* 18 April 2000. http://www.stateline.org/story.cfm?storyid=73226 (20 April 2000).

Nyhan, David. "Reconstructing a Multiracial Community; Politicking Amid the Rubble." *Boston Globe,* 7 May 1992, city edition, op-ed sec., 15.

Olasky, Marvin. *The Tragedy of American Compassion.* Washington, D.C.: Regnery Gateway, 1992.

Oliker, Stacey J. "Does Welfare Work? Evaluation Research and Welfare Policy." *Social Problems* 41 (1994): 195–213.

Olson, Kathryn M., and G. Thomas Goodnight. "Entanglements of Consumption, Cruelty, Privacy, and Fashion: The Social Controversy over Fur." *Quarterly Journal of Speech* 80 (1994): 249–76.

Osborn, Michael. "Rhetorical Depiction." In *Form, Genre, and the Study of Political Discourse,* edited by Herbert W. Simons and Aram A. Aghazarian, 79–107. Columbia: University of South Carolina Press, 1986.

Page, Benjamin I. *Who Deliberates? Mass Media in Modern Democracy.* Chicago: University of Chicago Press, 1996.

Parrott, Sharon. "Welfare Recipients Who Find Jobs: What Do We Know About Their Employment and Earnings?" Center on Budget and Policy Priorities, Washington, D.C., 1998

Patterson, James T. *America's Struggle Against Poverty 1900–1994.* Cambridge: Harvard University Press, 1994.

Peirce, Neal R. "Governors' Breakthrough on Welfare Reform." *National Journal,* 14 March 1987, 637.

Peirce, Neal R., and Jerry Hagstrom. "The Voters Send Carter a Message: Time for a Change—to Reagan." *National Journal,* 8 November 1980, 1876–78.

Perlmutter, Felice Davidson. *From Welfare to Work: Corporate Initiatives and Welfare Reform.* New York: Oxford University Press, 1997.

Peterson, Bill. "For Nation, 'It's Time to Switch Lanes.'" *Washington Post,* 20 February 1981, final edition, A1, A3.

Peterson, Iver. "Inflation Compelling Middle-Income People to Ask for Public Aid." *New York Times,* 20 April 1980, late city edition, sec. 1, 1, 22.

———. "Michigan Family Chases American Dream in Texas." *New York Times,* 13 June 1981, late city edition, 8.

Peterson, Janice. "'Ending Welfare as We Know It': The Symbolic Importance of Welfare Policy in America." *Journal of Economic Issues* 31 (1997): 425–31.

Peterson, Paul E. "The Urban Underclass and the Poverty Paradox." In *The Urban Underclass,* edited by Christopher Jencks and Paul E. Peterson, 3–27. Washington, D.C.: Brookings Institution Press, 1991.

Piven, Frances Fox, and Richard A. Cloward. *The Breaking of the American Social Compact.* New York: New Press, 1997.

——. *The New Class War: Reagan's Attack on the Welfare State and Its Consequences.* Rev. ed. New York: Pantheon Books, 1985.

——. *Poor People's Movements: Why They Succeed, How They Fail.* New York: Vintage Books, 1979.

——. *Regulating the Poor: The Functions of Public Welfare.* Updated ed. New York: Vintage Books, 1993.

"Playing Politics with a Tragedy; Bush Aide Lays Blame for Riots on Liberal Social Programs of 60s and 70s." *Los Angeles Times,* 6 May 1992, Washington edition, A10.

Plotnick, Robert D., Eugene Smolensky, Eirik Evenhouse, and Siabohan Reilly. "The Twentieth Century Record of Inequality and Poverty in the United States," Working paper 98–1, Center for Studies in Demography and Ecology, University of Washington, Seattle, 1998.

Pogash, Carol. "In Fact, December's Cruelest." *New York Times,* 8 August 1980, late city edition, A29.

Porterfield, E. E. "How the Widow's Allowance Operates." *Child-Welfare Magazine,* February 1913, 208–10.

Prud'Homme, Alex. "Police Brutality!" *Time,* 25 March 1991, 16–19.

"Putting Motherhood on the State Payroll." *Child-Welfare Magazine,* July 1913, 418–20.

Quadagno, Jill. *The Color of Welfare: How Racism Undermined the War on Poverty.* New York: Oxford University Press, 1994.

——. *The Transformation of Old Age Security: Class and Politics in the American Welfare State.* Chicago: University of Chicago Press, 1988.

Rainwater, Lee, and William C. Yancey, eds. *The Moynihan Report and the Politics of Controversy.* Cambridge: MIT Press, 1967.

Rattner, Steven. "'79 Prices Up 13.3% in Biggest Increase for a Year Since '46." *New York Times,* 26 January 1980, late city edition, 1, 36.

Reagan, Ronald. *Public Papers of the Presidents of the United States: Ronald Reagan, 1981.* Washington, D.C.: Government Printing Office, 1982.

——. *Public Papers of the Presidents of the United States: Ronald Reagan, 1986.* 2 vols. Washington, D.C.: Government Printing Office, 1988.

——. *Public Papers of the Presidents of the United States: Ronald Reagan, 1987.* 2 vols. Washington, D.C.: Government Printing Office, 1989.

——. *Public Papers of the Presidents of the United States: Ronald Reagan, 1988.* 2 vols. Washington, D.C.: Government Printing Office, 1990.

——. "Text of Reagan's Speech Accepting the Republicans' Nomination." *New York Times,* 18 July 1980, late city edition, A8.

"Real Income Down 5.5% in 1980 in a Record Drop." *New York Times,* 21 August 1981, late city edition, A12.

Reich, Robert B. *Locked in the Cabinet.* New York: Alfred A. Knopf, 1997.

——. "Prescriptions from the Right." Review of *Losing Ground,* by Charles Murray. *Dissent* (spring 1985): 237–40.

"Republicans' Initial Promise: 100-Day Debate on 'Contract.'" *CQ Weekly,* 12 November 1994, 3216–19.

Ritter, Kurt, and David Henry. *Ronald Reagan: The Great Communicator.* Westport, Conn.: Greenwood Press, 1992.

Roberts, Steven V. "Food Stamps Program: How It Grew and How Reagan Wants to Cut It Back." *New York Times,* 4 April 1981, late city edition, sec. 1, 11.

Robertson, Mrs. G. H. "The State's Duty to Fatherless Children." *Child-Welfare Magazine,* January 1912, 156–60.

Rogin, Michael Paul. *"Ronald Reagan," the Movie and Other Episodes in Political Demonology.* Berkeley: University of California Press, 1987.

Rom, Mark. "The Family Support Act of 1988: Federalism, Developmental Policy, and Welfare Reform." *Publius* 19 (1989): 57–73.

Rooke, Patricia T., and R. L. Schnell. "From Binding to Boarding Out in Britain and English-Canada: A Transformation in Childhood Sentiment and Practice." *Paedagogica Historica* 24 (1984): 461–91.

Roosevelt, Franklin D. "First Inaugural Address." In *American Rhetorical Discourse,* edited by Ronald F. Reid, 720–23. 2d ed. Prospect Heights, Ill.: Waveland Press, 1995.

——. *The Public Papers and Addresses of Franklin D. Roosevelt: The Court Disapproves, 1935.* Vol. 4. New York: Random House, 1938.

Roosevelt, Theodore. "Americanism." In *Americanism: Addresses by Woodrow Wilson, Franklin K. Lane, and Theodore Roosevelt.* N.p.: Veterans of Foreign Wars of the United States, n.d.

——. "The Man with the Muckrake." In *The Muckrakers: The Era in Journalism That Moved America to Reform — The Most Significant Magazines of 1902–1912,* edited by Arthur Weinberg and Lila Weinberg, 58–65. New York: Simon and Schuster, 1961.

Rosenbaum, David E. "Republicans Offer Voters a Deal for Takeover of House." *New York Times,* 28 September 1994, late edition, A16.

Rovner, Julie. "Congress Clears Overhaul of Welfare System." *CQ Weekly,* 1 October 1988, 2699–701.

——. "Daniel Patrick Moynihan: Making Welfare Work." *CQ Weekly,* 21 March 1987, 503–7.

——. "Governors Jump-Start Welfare Reform Drive." *CQ Weekly,* 28 February 1987, 376–78.

——. "Governors Press Reagan, Bentsen on Welfare." *CQ Weekly,* 27 February 1988, 512–13.

Rury, John L. "The New Moral Darwinism." Review of *Losing Ground,* by Charles Murray. *Urban Education* 21 (1986): 316–24.

Russell, Charles Edward. "The Tenements of Trinity Church." In *The Muckrakers: The Era in Journalism That Moved America to Reform — The Most Significant Magazines of 1902–1912,* edited by Arthur Weinberg and Lila Weinberg, 311–19. New York: Simon and Schuster, 1961.

Saad, Lydia. "'Contract with America' Still Little Known, but Goals Have Widespread Appeal." *Gallup Poll Monthly,* December 1994, 7–9.

Sack, Kevin. "The New, Volatile Politics of Welfare." *New York Times,* 15 March 1992, late edition, sec. 1, 24.

Salaman, Lester M. *Partners in Public Service: Government-Nonprofit Relations in the Modern Welfare State.* Baltimore, Md.: Johns Hopkins University Press, 1995.

Salpukas, Agis. "Depressed Industrial Heartland Stressing Urgent Need for Help." *New York Times,* 19 August 1980, late city edition, A1, D9.

Samuelson, Robert J. "Escaping the Poverty Trap." *Newsweek,* 10 September 1984, 60.

Sassen, Saskia. *Losing Control? Sovereignty in an Age of Economic Globalization.* New York: Columbia University Press, 1996.

Scarry, Elaine. "The Difficulty of Imagining Other People." In *For Love of Country: Debating the Limits of Patriotism,* edited by Martha C. Nussbaum, 98–110. Boston: Beacon Press, 1996.

Scharnhorst, Gary. "Dickens and Horatio Alger, Jr." *Dickens Quarterly* 2 (1985): 50–53.

Schram, Sanford E. *Words of Welfare: The Poverty of Social Science and the Social Science of Poverty.* Minneapolis: University of Minnesota Press, 1995.

Shales, Tom. "The Economic Speech: Sugarcoating a Bitter Pill." *Washington Post,* 19 February 1981, final edition, D1, D6.

Shank, Susan E. "Women and the Labor Market: The Link Grows Stronger." *Monthly Labor Review,* March 1988, 3–8.

Shapiro, Robert, Kelly D. Patterson, Judith Russell, and John T. Young. "The Polls: Public Assistance." *Public Opinion Quarterly* 51 (1987): 120–30.

Shear, Jeff. "The Santa Clauses." *National Journal,* 22 October 1994, 2451–53.

Sidel, Ruth. *Keeping Women and Children Last: America's War on the Poor.* New York: Penguin Books, 1996.

Skocpol, Theda. *Protecting Soldiers and Mothers: The Political Origins of Social Policy in the United States.* Cambridge: Harvard University Press, 1992.

Smith, Hedrick. "A Bold and Risky Venture: Party's Political Future May Depend on Results." *New York Times,* 19 February 1981, late city edition, A1, B7.

Smith, Michael Peter, and Bernadette Tarallo. "Proposition 187: Global Trend or Local Narrative? Explaining Anti-Immigrant Politics in California, Arizona, and Texas." *International Journal of Urban and Regional Research* 19 (1995): 664–76.

Solow, Robert M. *Work and Welfare.* Edited by Amy Gutman. Princeton, N.J.: Princeton University Press, 1998.

Stefancic, Jean, and Richard Delgado. *No Mercy: How Conservative Think Tanks and Foundations Changed America's Social Agenda.* Philadelphia: Temple University Press, 1996.

Steffens, Lincoln. "The Shame of Minneapolis." In *The Muckrakers: The Era in Journalism That Moved America to Reform — The Most Significant Magazines of 1902–1912,* edited by Arthur Weinberg and Lila Weinberg, 6–21. New York: Simon and Schuster, 1961.

Stein, Herbert. "A Poverty Paradox." *Fortune,* 21 January 1985, 169, 172.

Steinbeck, John. *The Grapes of Wrath.* 1939. Reprint, New York: Penguin Books, 1976.

Stephanopoulos, George. *All Too Human: A Political Education.* Boston: Little, Brown, 1999.

Stevens, William K. "Unskilled Northerners Find Sun Belt Job Climate Cooling." *New York Times,* 18 August 1981, late city edition, A1, B11.

Stockman, David A. "Stockman on the Budget Outlook — 'We Cannot Fund the Great Society.'" *National Journal,* 19 September 1981, 1665–67.

———. *The Triumph of Politics: How the Reagan Revolution Failed.* New York: Harper and Row, 1986.

Summers, Mark Wahlgren. *The Gilded Age or, the Hazard of New Functions.* Upper Saddle River, N.J.: Prentice Hall, 1997.

Sumner, William Graham. "The Concentration of Wealth: Its Economic Justification." In *Democracy and the Gospel of Wealth,* edited by Gail Kennedy, 81–85. Boston: Heath, 1949.

———. "The Forgotten Man." In *American Rhetorical Discourse,* edited by Ronald F. Reid, 606–20. 2d ed. Prospect Heights, Ill.: Waveland Press, 1995.

Sundquist, James L. *On Fighting Poverty: Perspectives from Experience.* New York: Basic Books, 1969.

Szanton, Peter L. "The Remarkable 'Quango': Knowledge, Politics, and Welfare Reform." *Journal of Policy Analysis and Management* 10 (1991): 590–602.

Tabor, George. "Capitalism: Is It Working?" *Time,* 21 April 1980, 40–55.

Tarbell, Ida M. "The History of the Standard Oil Company: The Oil War of 1872." In *The Muckrakers: The Era in Journalism That Moved America to Reform — The Most Significant Magazines of 1902–1912,* edited by Arthur Weinberg and Lila Weinberg, 22–39. New York: Simon and Schuster, 1961.

Tate, Dale. "House Provides President a Victory on the 1982 Budget." *CQ Weekly,* 9 May 1981, 783–85.

Tate, Greg, and Andy Plattner. "House Ratifies Savings Plan in Stunning Reagan Victory." *CQ Weekly,* 27 June 1981, 1127–29.

Taylor, Charles. *Modernity and the Rise of the Public Sphere.* Tanner Lectures on Human Values, vol. 14. Salt Lake City: University of Utah Press, 1993.

Taylor, Paul. "Democrats Wrest Control of Senate from GOP." *Washington Post,* 5 November 1986, final edition, A1, A36.

Thurow, Lester C. "Of Grasshoppers and Ants." Review of *Losing Ground,* by Charles Murray. *Harvard Business Review,* July-August 1985, 44–45, 48.

Tucker, Cynthia. "Bush Plays Partisan Politics." *Atlanta Journal and Constitution,* 6 May 1992, A15.

U.S. Committee on Economic Security. *Report to the President of the Committee on Economic Security.* Washington, D.C.: Government Printing Office, 1935.

——. *Social Security in America: The Factual Background of the Social Security Act as Summarized from Staff Reports to the Committee on Economic Security.* Washington, D.C.: Government Printing Office, 1937.

U.S. Department of Commerce. Census Bureau. *Household and Family Characteristics: March 1990 and 1989.* Washington, D.C., 1990.

——. Census Bureau. *Statistical Abstract of the United States, 1988.* Washington, D.C.: Government Printing Office, 1989.

U.S. Department of Health and Human Services. Administration for Children and Families. *Temporary Assistance for Needy Families (TANF) Program: Second Annual Report to Congress.* Washington, D.C.: Government Printing Office, 1999.

U.S. Department of Labor. Bureau of Labor Statistics. *Working Women: A Chartbook.* Washington, D.C., 1991.

——. Children's Bureau. *Mothers' Aid, 1931.* Washington, D.C.: Government Printing Office, 1933.

U.S. General Accounting Office. *An Evaluation of the 1981 AFDC Changes: Initial Analyses.* Washington, D.C., 2 April 1984.

——. *Welfare Reform: Information on Former Recipients' Status.* GAO/HEH-99–48. Washington, D.C., April 1999.

U.S. House Committee on Agriculture. *Enforcement of the Food Stamp Program: Hearing before the Committee on Agriculture.* 104th Cong., 1st sess., 1995.

U.S. House Committee on Commerce. *The Unanimous Bipartisan National Governors Association Agreement on Medicaid: Hearings before the Committee on Commerce.* 104th Cong., 2d sess., 1996.

U.S. House Committee on Economic and Educational Opportunities. *Hearing on the Contract with America: Nutrition, the Local Perspective: Hearing before the Committee on Economic and Educational Opportunities.* 104th Cong., 1st sess., 1995.

U.S. House Committee on Education and Labor. *Hearing on H.R. 4605, Work and Responsibility Act of 1994: Hearing before the Committee on Education and Labor.* 103d Cong., 2d sess., 1994.

——. *Hearings on Welfare Reform: H.R. 30, Fair Work Opportunities Act of 1987 and H.R. 1720, Family Welfare Reform Act of 1987: Hearings before the Committee on Education and Labor.* 100th Cong., 1st sess., 1987.

U.S. House Committee on Ways and Means. *Contract with America—Overview: Hearings before the Committee on Ways and Means.* 104th Cong., 1st sess., 1995.

——— . *Public Welfare Amendments of 1962: Hearings on H.R. 10032*. 87th Cong., 2d sess., 1962.

——— . *Summary of Welfare Reforms Made by Public Law 104–193 the Personal Responsibility and Work Opportunity Reconciliation Act and Associated Legislation.* 104th Cong., 2d sess., 1996. Committee Print 15.

——— . *Tax Aspects of the President's Economic Program: Hearings before the Committee on Ways and Means.* 97th Cong., 1st sess., 1981.

U.S. House Select Committee on Hunger. *Beyond Public Assistance: Where Do We Go from Here?: Hearing before the Select Committee on Hunger.* 102d Cong., 2d sess., 1992.

——— . *Federal Policy Perspectives on Welfare Reform: Rhetoric, Reality, and Opportunities: Hearing before the Select Committee on Hunger.* 102d Cong., 2d sess., 1992.

——— . *Rethinking Poverty Policy: Hearing before the Select Committee on Hunger.* 102d Cong., 2d sess., 1992.

——— . *State and Local Perspectives on Welfare Reform: Rhetoric, Reality, and Opportunities: Hearing Before the Select Committee on Hunger.* 102d Cong., 2d sess., 1992.

U.S. House Subcommittee on Department Operations, Nutrition, and Foreign Agriculture of the Committee on Agriculture. *Reforming the Present Welfare System: Hearing before the Subcommittee on Department Operations, Nutrition, and Foreign Agriculture of the Committee on Agriculture.* 104th Cong., 1st sess., 1995.

U.S. House Subcommittee on Health and the Environment of the Committee on Energy and Commerce. *Medicaid Issues in Family Welfare and Nursing Home Reform: Hearings before the Subcommittee on Health and the Environment of the Committee on Energy and Commerce.* 100th Cong., 1st sess., 1987.

U.S. House Subcommittee on Human Resources of the Committee on Ways and Means. *Causes of Poverty, with a Focus on Out-of-Wedlock Births: Hearing before the Subcommittee on Human Resources of the Committee on Ways and Means.* 104th Cong., 2d sess., 1996.

——— . *Child Support Enforcement Provisions Included in the Personal Responsibility Act as Part of the CWA: Hearing before the Subcommittee on Human Resources of the Committee on Ways and Means.* 104th Cong., 1st sess., 1995.

——— . *Contract with America—Welfare Reform, Part 1: Hearing before the Subcommittee on Human Resources of the Committee on Ways and Means.* 104th Cong., 1st sess., 1995.

——— . *Contract with America—Welfare Reform, Part 2: Hearing before the Subcommittee on Human Resources of the Committee on Ways and Means.* 104th Cong., 1st sess., 1995.

——— . *Impact of Immigration on Welfare Programs: Hearing before the Subcommittee on Human Resources of the Committee on Ways and Means.* 103d Cong., 1st sess., 1993.

———. *The National Governors' Association Welfare Reform Proposal: Hearing before the Subcommittee on Human Resources of the Committee on Ways and Means.* 104th Cong., 2d sess., 1996.

———. *Trends in Spending and Caseloads for AFDC and Related Programs: Hearing before the Subcommittee on Human Resources of the Committee on Ways and Means.* 103d Cong., 1st sess., 1993.

———. *Welfare Reform Proposals, Including H.R. 4605, the Work and Responsibility Act of 1994, Part 1: Hearings before the Subcommittee on Human Resources of the Committee on Ways and Means.* 103d Cong., 2d sess., 1994.

———. *Welfare Reform Proposals, Including H.R. 4605, the Work and Responsibility Act of 1994, Part 2: Hearings before the Subcommittee on Human Resources of the Committee on Ways and Means.* 103d Cong., 2d sess., 1994.

———. *Welfare Reform Success Stories: Hearing before the Subcommittee on Human Resources of the Committee on Ways and Means.* 104th Cong., 1st sess., 1995.

U.S. House Subcommittee on Human Resources and Intergovernmental Relations of the Committee on Government Operations. *Ending Welfare as We Know It: Progress or Paralysis? Hearing before the Subcommittee on Human Resources and Intergovernmental Relations of the Committee on Governmental Operations.* 103d Cong., 2d sess., 1994.

U.S. House Subcommittee on Oversight and the Subcommittee on Human Resources of the Committee on Ways and Means. *Earned Income Tax Credit: Hearing before the Subcommittee on Oversight and the Subcommittee on Human Resources of the Committee on Ways and Means.* 104th Cong., 1st sess., 1995.

U.S. House Subcommittee on Public Assistance and Unemployment Compensation of the Committee on Ways and Means. *Administration's Proposed Savings in Unemployment Compensation, Public Assistance, and Social Services Programs: Hearings before the Subcommittee on Public Assistance and Unemployment Compensation of the Committee on Ways and Means.* 97th Cong., 1st sess., 1981.

———. *Family Welfare Reform Act: Hearings before the Subcommittee on Public Assistance and Unemployment Compensation of the Committee on Ways and Means.* 100th Cong., 1st sess., 1987.

———. *Welfare Reform: Hearings before the Subcommittee on Public Assistance and Unemployment Compensation of the Committee on Ways and Means.* 100th Cong., 1st sess., 1987.

U.S. Senate. *Proceedings of the Conference on the Care of Dependent Children.* 60th Cong., 2d sess., 1909. S. Doc. 721.

U.S. Senate Committee on Agriculture, Nutrition, and Forestry. *Federal Nutrition Programs: Hearing before the Committee on Agriculture, Nutrition, and Forestry.* 104th Cong., 1st sess., 1995.

U.S. Senate Committee on the Budget. *Concurrent Resolution on the Budget for Fiscal Year 1996: Hearings before the Committee on the Budget.* 104th Cong., 1st sess., 1995.

U.S. Senate Committee on Finance. *Broad Policy Goals of Welfare Reform: Hearing before the Committee on Finance.* 104th Cong., 1st sess., 1995.

———. *Child Support Enforcement: Hearing before the Committee on Finance.* 104th Cong., 1st sess., 1995.

———. *Growth of the Supplemental Security Income Program: Hearing before the Committee on Finance.* 104th Cong., 1st sess., 1995.

———. *Spending Reduction Proposals, Part 1: Hearings before the Committee on Finance.* 97th Cong., 1st sess., 1981.

———. *Spending Reduction Proposals, Part 2: Hearings before the Committee on Finance.* 97th Cong., 1st sess., 1981.

———. *States' Perspective on Welfare Reform: Hearing before the Committee on Finance.* 104th Cong., 1st sess., 1995.

———. *Teen Parents and Welfare Reform: Hearing before the Committee on Finance.* 104th Cong., 1st sess., 1995.

———. *Welfare Reform, Part 1: Hearing before the Committee on Finance.* 100th Cong., 1st sess., 1987.

———. *Welfare Reform, Part 2: Hearings before the Committee on Finance.* 100th Cong., 1st sess., 1987.

———. *Welfare Reform, Part 3: Hearing before the Committee on Finance.* 100th Cong., 2d sess., 1988.

———. *Welfare Reform — Views of Interested Organizations: Hearing before the Committee on Finance.* 104th Cong., 1st sess., 1995.

———. *Welfare Reform Wrap-Up: Hearing before the Committee on Finance.* 104th Cong., 1st sess., 1995.

———. *Work and Responsibility Act of 1994: Hearing before the Committee on Finance.* 103d Cong., 2d sess., 1994.

U.S. Senate Committee on Governmental Affairs. *Earned Income Tax Credit: Hearings before the Committee on Governmental Affairs.* 104th Cong., 1st sess., 1995.

———. *Reinventing Government: Hearings before the Committee on Governmental Affairs.* 104th Cong., 1st sess., 1995.

U.S. Senate Subcommittee on Social Security and Family Policy of the Committee on Finance. *Welfare Reform: Hearings before the Subcommittee on Social Security and Family Policy of the Committee on Finance.* 103d Cong., 2d sess., 1994.

———. *Welfare Reform Hearings in New York City: Hearings before the Subcommittee on Social Security and Family Policy of the Committee on Finance.* 100th Cong., 1st sess., 1987.

———. *Welfare: Reform or Replacement? (Child Support Enforcement): Hearings before the Subcommittee on Social Security and Family Policy of the Committee on Finance.* 100th Cong., 1st sess., 1987.

——— . *Welfare: Reform or Replacement? (Child Support Enforcement II): Hearing before the Subcommittee on Social Security and Family Policy of the Committee on Finance.* 100th Cong., 1st sess., 1987.

——— . *Welfare: Reform or Replacement? (Work and Welfare): Hearing before the Sub-committee on Social Security and Family Policy of the Committee on Finance.* 100th Cong., 1st sess., 1987.

Wald, Matthew L. "Welfare Means Bare Cupboards as Inflation Grows." *New York Times,* 18 March 1981, late city edition, A1, B11.

Walker, Kenneth R. "'I Got the Breaks'—Federal Aid Can Help." *Christian Science Monitor,* 18 May 1992, 18.

Walzer, Michael. *Spheres of Justice: A Defense of Pluralism and Equality.* New York: Basic Books, 1983.

——— . *What It Means to Be an American.* New York: Marsilio, 1996.

"War Against the Poor." *New York Times,* 6 May 1992, late edition, A28.

Weaver, R. Kent, Robert Y. Shapiro, and Lawrence R. Jacobs. "The Polls — Trends: Welfare." *Public Opinion Quarterly* 59 (1995): 606–27.

Weiler, Michael. "The Reagan Attack on Welfare." In *Reagan and Public Discourse in America,* edited by Michael Weiler and W. Barnett Pearce, 227–50. Tuscaloosa: University of Alabama Press, 1992.

Weisman, Steven R. "Optimism on Budget." *New York Times,* 20 February 1981, late city edition, A1, A10.

"Welfare Benefits Cut by Reconciliation." *Congressional Quarterly Almanac* 37 (1981): 473–75.

"'Welfare Queen' Becomes Issue in Reagan Campaign." *New York Times,* 15 February 1976, late city edition, sec. 1, 51.

"White House Responds." *Washington Post,* 5 May 1992, final edition, A24.

White, Lucie E. "No Exit: Rethinking 'Welfare Dependency' from a Different Ground." *Georgetown Law Journal* 81 (1993): 1961–2002.

Whitman, David. "His Unconvincing Welfare Promises." *U.S. News and World Report,* 20 April 1992, 42.

——— . "The Return of the New Dealers." Review of *Poor Support,* by David Ellwood. *Public Interest* 94 (1989): 107–13.

Williams, Raymond. *Keywords: A Vocabulary of Culture and Society.* Rev. ed. New York: Oxford University Press, 1983.

Wilcox, Clyde. *Onward Christian Soldiers? The Religious Right in American Politics.* Boulder, Colo.: Westview Press, 1996.

Wills, Garry. *Reagan's America: Innocents at Home.* New York: Doubleday, 1987.

Wilson, Hugh. Review of *Losing Ground,* by Charles Murray. *Science & Society* 49 (1985): 501–4.

Wilson, John Oliver. "After the Fall." *New York Times,* 24 September 1980, late city edition, A31.

Wilson, William Julius. *The Bridge over the Racial Divide: Rising Inequality and Coalition Politics.* Berkeley: University of California Press, 1999.

———. "Studying Inner-City Social Dislocations: The Challenge of Public Agenda Research." *American Sociological Review* 56 (1991): 1–14.

———. *The Truly Disadvantaged: The Inner City, the Underclass, and Public Policy.* Chicago: University of Chicago Press, 1987.

———. *When Work Disappears: The World of the New Urban Poor.* New York: Vintage Books, 1996.

Wines, Michael. "White House Links Riots to Welfare." *New York Times,* 5 May 1992, late edition, A1, A26.

Wyatt, David. Introduction to *New Essays on "The Grapes of Wrath,"* edited by David Wyatt, 1–26. New York: Cambridge University Press, 1990.

Zarefsky, David. *President Johnson's War on Poverty: Rhetoric and History.* Tuscaloosa: University of Alabama Press, 1986.

Zarefsky, David, Carol Miller-Tutzauer, and Frank Tutzauer. "Reagan's Safety Net for the Truly Needy: The Rhetorical Uses of Definition." *Central States Speech Journal* 35 (1984): 113–19.

Zinn, Deborah K., and Rosemary C. Sarri. "Turning Back the Clock on Public Welfare." *Signs: Journal of Women in Culture and Society* 10 (1984): 355–70.

Zunz, Olivier. *Making America Corporate 1870–1920.* Chicago: University of Chicago Press, 1990.

Index